THE EXCELLENT DOCTOR BLACKWELL

THE EXCELLENT
DOCTOR
BLACKWELL

The Life of the First Woman Physician

JULIA BOYD

SUTTON PUBLISHING

BP45

First published in the United Kingdom in 2005 by
Sutton Publishing Limited · Phoenix Mill
Thrupp · Stroud · Gloucestershire · GL5 2BU

British Library Cataloguing in Publication Data
A catalogue record for this book is available from the British Library.

ISBN 0-7509-4140-5

Typeset in Sabon 11/14.5 pt
Typesetting and origination by
Sutton Publishing Limited.
Printed and bound in England by
J.H. Haynes & Co. Ltd, Sparkford.

8/4/06

For
my family

Contents

List of Plates

Acknowledgements

I owe much to many. Piers Brendon, Mark Goldie, Patrick Higgins, Jane Schultz and Wendy Thomas, having encouraged me to set off on this project, gave me constant support until its completion. Eric Luft, Curator of Historical Collections at the Health Sciences Library of SUNY Upstate Medical University, Syracuse, and Carol Clausen of the History of Medicine Division, National Library of Medicine in Washington DC never tired of pointing me in the right direction or providing me with elusive research material. Magdelen Goffin entrusted me with both the Comtesse de Noailles' correspondence and her own friendship while Christopher Gotto deployed his extraordinary ability to track down obscure documents. Deirdre and David Stam were the most generous of hosts in America, providing me with many valuable introductions, and Robert Boyd the most generous of mentors, especially on medical matters.

My warmest possible thanks also go to the following for their help and support in various ways: Giles Agnew, Sylvia Allen, Nicholas Baring, Anne Bennett, Beryl Chesterton, Brian Clarke, Jane Entrican, Carol Fraser, Margaret Heath, Pam Hirsch, Sally Holloway, Mary Jacobus, Linda Kelly, Mary Kendall, Geoffrey Kernan, Richard Keynes, Philippe Loüet, Neil McIntyre, Sally McMullen, Tom Mansell, Vanessa Mitchell, Laura Morris, Michael Ockenden, Sandra Parsons, Lucinda Shaw Stewart, Antonia Till, Maria Tippett, Lisa White and Dalena Wright.

Very special thanks go to members of the Blackwell family: Jennifer Loewenstein, Nancy Nitchie, Anne E. Sarin and Emily H. Rose.

I wish to thank Her Majesty The Queen for permission to make use of material in The Royal Archives.

In pursuit of Elizabeth Blackwell I have contacted dozens of librarians and archivists at various institutions, all of whom have given me generous assistance. I would especially like to thank: Dawn Adiletta of the Harriet Beecher Stowe Centre, Hartford, Connecticut; K.H. Atkins of Dudley Libraries, Staffordshire; Jacalyn Blume, Jane Knowles and Ellen Shea of the Schlesinger Library at the Radcliffe Institute, Harvard University; Caroline Dalton of New College, Oxford; Caroline Dunne of the General Medical Council, London; Samantha Farhall and Marion

Rea of the St Bartholomew's Hospital Archives, London; Jan Grenci of the Library of Congress, Washington DC; Amy Hague of the Sophia Smith Collection, Smith College, Northampton, Massachusetts; David Hall of Cambridge University Library; Charlotte Hegyi of Hobart and Smith Colleges, Geneva, New York; Jill Kelsey of The Royal Archives, Windsor; Caroline Melish-Duroselle, formerly of the New York Academy of Medicine Library; Netta Mullin of the Henderson Historical Society, Kentucky; Victoria North of the Royal Free Hospital Archives, London; Frances O'Donnell of the Andover-Harvard Theological Library; Karen Osburn of the Geneva Historical Society, Geneva, New York; Susan S. Palmer of the Kroch Library, Cornell University, New York; Kate Perry of Girton College, Cambridge; Aimée Primeaux of the Massachusetts Historical Society, Boston.

I would also like to thank the staff of the Bristol Record Office; the British Library; Cambridge University Library; South Carolina Historical Society, Charleston; the Rare Books and Manuscript Library, Columbia University, New York; the Florence Nightingale Museum, London; the Metropolitan Archives, London; the Pack Memorial Library, Asheville, North Carolina; the Wellcome Library and the Women's Library, London Metropolitan University. Allen Packwood, the outstanding Director of the Churchill Archives Centre, and his staff have given me invaluable professional and logistical support as well as punctuating my microfilm reading with much-needed coffee. I owe a great debt to my agent, Andrew Lownie, and to Jaqueline Mitchell of Sutton Publishing for her expert hand on the editorial tiller.

My biggest thanks of all go to Nancy Sahli. I would probably never have started this book (and would certainly not have finished it) without her Ph.D thesis as my beacon. Her exemplary research greatly simplified my task. I am also deeply grateful to her for many valuable comments on my typescript, though clearly all errors are mine alone.

I also want to thank my husband for his critical but loving eye, my daughters for their patient listening and my dear friends Rosemary Saunders and Jenny Temple for keeping us all going through thick and thin.

Lastly, though not an academic, I cannot imagine writing a book in more perfect surroundings than Churchill College, Cambridge.

THE BLACKWELL FAMILY TREE

Samuel Blackwell (1790–1838) m. (1815) Hannah Lane (1792–1870)

Anna
(1816–1900)

Marian
(1818–97)

Elizabeth
(1821–1910)
adopted Catherine
(Kitty) Barry
(1847–1936)

Samuel Charles
(1823–1901)
m. (1856)
Antoinette Louisa Brown
(1825–1921)

Henry Browne
(1825–1909)
m. (1855)
Lucy Stone Blackwell
(1818–93)

Emily
(1826–1910)

(Sarah) Ellen
(1828–1901)

(John) Howard
(1831–66)

George Washington
(1832–1912)
m. (1875)
Emma Stone
Lawrence
(1851–1920)

Howard Lane
Blackwell
(1876–1972)
Anna Belden
(1883–1975)

Florence
(1856–1937)

Edith
(1860–1906)

Grace
(1863–1941)

Agnes
(1866–1940)

Ethel
(1869–1947)

Alice Stone Blackwell
(1857–1950)

Introduction

Young ladies all of every clime,
Especially of Britain,
Who wholly occupy your time
In novels and in knitting,
Whose highest skill is but to play,
Sing, dance, or French to clack well,
Reflect on the example, pray,
Of excellent Miss Blackwell.[1]

This was *Punch*'s response to an event that took place on 23 January 1849 at an obscure medical college in Geneva, upstate New York. On that day, Elizabeth Blackwell graduated on exactly the same basis as the male students, marking women's formal entry into modern professional medicine. Elizabeth's achievement – no small one for a young, immigrant Englishwoman with neither money nor connections – provoked a reaction ranging from utter outrage to amused condescension. Shy and slightly built, she was an unlikely trailblazer but, by placing the letters MD after her name, she had launched a movement that proved unstoppable.

Not that success followed quickly. On the contrary, years of hardship, struggle and disappointment lay ahead. But despite this, the musical, literary, complex Elizabeth Blackwell – committed Abolitionist yet fierce critic of women's rights activists – never wavered in her determination to see fully qualified female physicians established on each side of the Atlantic. Yet, paradoxically, although she herself set up in private practice both in New York (1851) and briefly in London (1869), doctoring *per se* was never her prime motive. Rather it was her vision of women doctors – armed with the high moral instincts of their sex – seeking to heal not just the physically infirm but, more importantly, the morally sick society in which they lived.

While widely known and written about in America as its first woman doctor, and as the founder of the first hospital (in New York) to be staffed by women physicians, Elizabeth's role in Britain, where she was born and spent more than half her life, has been overlooked. Yet in 1859 she became the first woman to be included on the British Medical Register. That same year, through public lectures and persistent lobbying, she laid the groundwork for the first generation of British woman doctors – directly inspiring Elizabeth Garrett Anderson to become Britain's first qualified female physician in 1865. Furthermore, after successfully launching a women's medical college in New York, with her sister Dr Emily Blackwell, Elizabeth returned permanently to Britain in 1869 where she continued to work energetically for the women's medical movement and for wider social reform until her death in 1910.

Her reputation in the United Kingdom has inevitably been eclipsed by that of her exact contemporary and lifelong sparring partner Florence Nightingale and by that of Dr Elizabeth Garrett Anderson. But in her own time, both in America and England, Elizabeth's achievements were widely recognised. Not just because she was the first qualified woman doctor in modern times but also for her tireless efforts to raise the standard of women's medical education. Today, however, while her influence is obvious, her story is virtually unknown.

And it is a story that is by no means confined to medicine. Elizabeth was involved with many of the great events and issues of her century. It was not only her medical achievements that caused George Eliot to write in 1859, 'you are one of the women I would love from all the rest in the world to know personally'.[2] Harriet Beecher Stowe (a close neighbour in Cincinnati) and Charles Kingsley knew her well, admiring the courage that took her on epic journeys across the United States and prompted her active involvement in anti-slavery and the Civil War. Abraham Lincoln and Alphonse de Lamartine, both of whom she met, and Horace Greeley, whom she knew well, were left in no doubt that this diminutive, softly spoken doctor with the glass eye was not a figure to be dismissed lightly.

What inspired Elizabeth to choose this unconventional path? Did she have a genuine medical vocation or was she an early feminist, intent on challenging the male monopoly of the professions? While the reply to the first question is emphatically no, the answer to the second is more complicated. By her own admission, Elizabeth was not an instinctive doctor; nor was she naturally drawn to science. But she was deeply concerned with the future of the human race and convinced that the world would never become a better place until women took a more prominent part in its affairs. Medicine seemed to her an excellent place for them to start. On a more prosaic plane, she also needed to earn a living – no easy matter in a society that expected middle-class women to stay within their domestic sphere unless forced by spinsterhood to teach.

Yet, perversely, Elizabeth refused to align herself with the women's rights movement. This decision seems all the more curious when it is remembered that its first significant public meeting took place at Seneca Falls in June 1848 – just a few miles from her medical college and only six months before she graduated. But Elizabeth was very much her own woman and, unlike many activists, did not hold men responsible for her sex's subservient status. Rather, she blamed women themselves for not aiming higher – 'not feeling the soul too large for the body'.[3] In any case, as she declared firmly, she had received too much kindness from men to sympathise with any 'anti-man movement'.[4]

Elizabeth's determination to stand aloof from the early women's movement at the very moment when she was attempting such a daring female 'first' was entirely typical of her courageous if contrary approach to life. She was fearless in the face of physical and emotional hardship, and the dignified, resolute manner in which she qualified as a doctor – despite every conceivable obstacle – was a genuine inspiration to those waiting more timidly in the wings. Yet her subsequent message to her sex was distinctly mixed and often surprisingly conservative. The ambiguities that emerged in her own career reflect many of the dilemmas that marked her century: religion and science; motherhood and emancipation; disease and morality; poverty and the perfect society – the list is a long one.

It was intelligence, courage and often sheer obstinacy that enabled Elizabeth to achieve her ambitions. The effort to finance her studies, gain her medical degree, launch the first hospital to be staffed by women and found a successful female medical college, required mental and physical resources that were by any standards extraordinary.

But Elizabeth came from an extraordinary family. United in their urge to make the world a better place, nearly all her eight siblings and assorted Blackwell relations made their mark. The close bond Elizabeth enjoyed with her family did not mean that relations with them were always easy. Far from it. Indeed, as her niece, Alice Stone Blackwell, noted, 'It is odd that the Blackwells, while really attached to each other, should find it so hard to live together . . .'.[5]

Nevertheless, with their widowed mother in tow, the brothers and sisters moved continuously in and out of each other's lives, sharing houses, holidays, children and endless financial crises. One issue that divided them was their commitment to America. Five of them remained in their new country, four returned to Europe. Letters flowed back and forth across the Atlantic for over half a century, providing a rich account of the family's fluctuating fortunes, their passionate engagement with the great social and political issues of the day and their friendships with some of the most eminent figures of the century.

After much internal debate, and still uncertain whether she was making the right decision, Elizabeth finally returned to her native land in 1869 where she embarked on a long and varied career in social reform. Her difficulty in deciding whether she was British or American was typical of her tendency to face two ways at once – a characteristic she acknowledged when she admitted to her close friend, the English feminist Barbara Bodichon, that she was 'too conservative for the Reformers, too progressive for the Conservatives'.[6]

It was an accurate self-assessment. Such contradictory strands were already present in her childhood when the conservative Old Testament preaching, to which she was continuously exposed, made as deep an impression on her as did her father's passion for social reform. His ambiguous position as both anti-slavery protagonist and sugar refiner (whose income depended entirely on a slave product) was echoed in Elizabeth's own efforts to reconcile divine law with the great medical discoveries of her century.

But if in the end Elizabeth chose God over science, she was by no means incapable of a fresh look at society. In her sixties, though unmarried, she championed the cause of female sexuality, maintaining that contrary to popular perception women were every bit as physically passionate as men. And if this was the case, she argued, there could be no excuse for not applying the same moral code to both sexes.

Both reactionary and modern, Elizabeth was truly a creature of her time. Certainly she was not alone in her attempts to reconcile religious authority with the liberating, but disturbing, advance of science in her lifetime. Though better placed than many to observe the fruits of scientific method, Elizabeth was, in the last resort, unable to sacrifice her vision of a moral universe in which good was rewarded by health and vigour and evil punished by sickness and sterility. In such a universe there was no place for vaccination, vivisection or bacteriology. Elizabeth died in the twentieth century but her medical philosophy sprang from a simpler past.

She would have liked to be remembered as a social prophet who had helped guide humanity towards that elusive perfect society. But her inability to compromise her ideals gave them little chance of converging with the real world. Yet it was this same determination never to concede a principle that made her such an effective pioneer. Her absolute refusal to accept second best for women doctors, whether in terms of education or practice, was an inspiring example and legacy.

Elizabeth may have resisted formal feminism but her whole career was a robust response to men, who, like a distinguished editor of the *Boston Medical and Surgical Journal*, wondered who needed women doctors in an age of 'too much bad piano playing and too little good cooking and sewing'.[7] She fully justifies her place alongside those other remarkable women of the mid-nineteenth century whose lives fundamentally changed the status of their sex. With no private income, no influential friends and no comfortable home to cushion her, Elizabeth launched herself on an improbable career hundreds of miles from her family in the midst of an alien society powered by slavery. The fact that by the time she died women were permanently established in professional medicine – on both sides of the Atlantic – was its own reward.

ONE

Bristol Beginnings

To find the source of Elizabeth Blackwell's determined and contradictory character, it is to her family and their early experiences in an expanding America with its harsh, competitive spirit that one must first look. Samuel Blackwell and Hannah Lane met as fellow Sunday school teachers in a Congregationalist chapel in Bristol and were married on 27 September 1815 – three months after the Battle of Waterloo. Domestically they were deeply happy, but Blackwell's professional life revolved around a painful moral dilemma. Although passionately opposed to slavery, he was also a successful sugar refiner whose livelihood depended entirely on a raw material produced by slaves working under the peculiarly horrific conditions of the Caribbean plantations. This tension between principle and prosperity haunted him all his life and was to have a profound effect on the lives of his remarkable brood of children.

Sugar refining was a certainly a curious choice of career for a man as active in abolitionist politics as Blackwell. But, coming from a long line of small-time traders, he was ambitious to move up in the world and quickly recognised that the sugar business offered him opportunities unimagined by his forebears. It was also a socially prestigious trade. A number of the city's sugar refiners had risen to be mayor or sheriff while others had become partners in leading banks. Furthermore, many of them, like Blackwell, were dissenters who formed a close-knit, mutually supportive society. For an upwardly mobile young man the sugar refiners' club was undoubtedly a good one.

Blackwell and his attractive young wife, Hannah, were pious but not dour. Their puritan principles were leavened with good food, servants, music, humour and holidays so that their household was for the most part a cheerful and liberal one despite Blackwell's difficult parents and demanding siblings. Their first child, Anna, was born in 1816; a second daughter, Marian, arrived in 1818; and Elizabeth, 'the whitest little round bundle of a child to be found anywhere',[1] followed in 1821. Her birth was flanked by the death of two infant brothers, both named Samuel Charles. This melancholy fact contributed to Elizabeth's lasting sense of being the odd one out, since her eight surviving siblings fell naturally into pairs. A third, but this time healthy, Samuel Charles was born in 1823, followed by Henry two years later. Two more sisters, Emily and Ellen, arrived in 1826 and 1828. Howard was born in 1831 and the youngest, George Washington, in 1832, a few weeks after the family had emigrated to America.

The Blackwell grandparents were a constant and gloomy presence in the children's lives. Anna, the eldest, and the only one of them to record their Bristol years (albeit at times fancifully) referred to her grandfather as 'excessively bitter with radical tendencies . . . an utter tyrant' and her grandmother as 'silent and downtrodden with not an atom of a mind'. Hannah first suffered her father-in-law's idiosyncrasy when she returned from her honeymoon to find that in their absence he had been to their home and nailed up all the cupboards, condemning them as 'slut holes'.

At least the grandparents did not share the Blackwells' house – the aunts did. Samuel had four spinster sisters all living under his roof. The children considered Barbara to be the most unpleasant of them, if the most intelligent. As they grew older, they understood that her bad temper was partly caused by the sheer frustration of having a good brain but no education, since old Blackwell had refused to send any of his daughters to school. Their favourite aunt, Mary, nearly married a prosperous sugar refiner but they quarrelled over baptismal rites (he was for immersion, she for sprinkling) and the match was broken off. The nondescript Ann was little trouble to the children but Lucy incurred their wrath by forcing them into clothes which she had made herself, even though: 'She knew no more of dressmaking than of Greek. The miserably ugly things we were made to wear, from a mistaken notion that dressing us badly would keep us free from vanity and love of finery, were a constant source of annoyance and *mauvaise honte* to us through our childhood.'

Blackwell also had two brothers. The elder, John, was a linen draper in Worcester who successfully went into partnership in Nottingham with the inventor of a net- and lace-making machine. His two sons, Samuel and Kenyon, anxious to seize the opportunities offered by the Industrial Revolution, later persuaded him to invest his profits in an ironworks near Dudley (close to Birmingham) that, in the middle years of the century, greatly influenced the family fortunes. Blackwell employed his younger brother, James, in his own business, and together they distilled late into the night, experimenting with crooked, long-necked bottles, pans, tubes (and, to the disgust of the children, bullocks' blood) in search of a palatable sugar that could be economically produced from beets with the hope of thus rendering slave labour redundant.

The Blackwell children much preferred their mother's side of the family but were probably ignorant of the scandal surrounding their maternal grandfather, Henry Lane. He was a gifted jeweller and watchmaker whose talents led him into temptation that almost proved fatal. Convicted in 1800 of forging £5 notes, he was condemned to death, and eight-year-old Hannah was fitted for a black dress in anticipation of her father's hanging. Reprieved at the last minute, Lane was sent (with his female accomplice) as a convict to Australia.

After a six-month voyage via Rio, he arrived in Sydney in 1802 where he was immediately set to work repairing the town clock and for the rest of his life earned a government salary as the Superintendent of Clocks. He avoided incarceration, owned a flourishing jewellery business and after seven years received a conditional pardon, eventually becoming a juror and leaseholder. But he was never allowed to return to England. He died in November 1815, unaware of his daughter's marriage to Samuel Blackwell six weeks earlier.[2]

Lane's transportation meant that his wife was left alone in Bristol to support their four children, which she accomplished by opening a millinery shop. After her mother's death Hannah went to live with an uncle and aunt whose eight sons had all 'died of convulsions in teething'.[3] When finally a daughter was born, her survival was attributed to 'the application of slices of the root of the white peony, bound on to the soles of the feet like a plaster or poultice, the moment the dreaded convulsions came on'.

The Blackwell children were particularly fond of Uncle and Aunt Browne. Warm-hearted and generous, they were also admired by Anna for their elegance – a quality she found deplorably lacking in her Blackwell relations. 'Uncle Browne' was an affluent jeweller who unwisely invested his substantial capital in setting up a bank. When it failed he lost everything. Such swift reversals of fortune were a recurrent feature in the Blackwell family history – financial stability remaining frustratingly elusive for most of them throughout their lives.

Hannah, although profoundly religious, did not entirely fit the puritan mould. She loved to dance and had an unashamedly secular attachment to the many lavish presents given to her by Uncle and Aunt Browne. She enjoyed life and liked to see others do the same. A kind, vivacious woman, she ran her large household efficiently and managed her awkward in-laws with tact. In contrast to her strong-minded daughters, she was untroubled by male supremacy and happy to fulfil the traditional role of wife and mother. In doing so she achieved great contentment within her marriage. Anna recalled her 'making the superlative custards we always had when there was a dinner party; stirring the mixture in a broad shallow brass preserving kettle, with a dozen new marbles (that we had been charged to buy for the purpose at the great toy shop in Barton) to keep it from sticking'. It was not from Hannah that her daughters inherited their radical instincts.

By the time Elizabeth was born, the family were living in a medieval gabled house on a street known as Counterslip, adjoining Blackwell's sugarhouse and backing on to the River Frome. Half a century later, Anna remembered the roaring coal fires, fuelled by cheap coal from Swansea delivered directly to the sugarhouse wharf, the beer which everybody drank like water, the thump of the watchman's cudgel on the pavement and, not least, the fear of crossing Bristol Bridge on market days: 'The streets at either end were crammed with cattle, and with drovers in white smocks . . . the agonies of terror I underwent at being conveyed under the heads of the beasts, among the lowing and shouting and swearing and quarrelling are something I have never forgotten.'

In 1824, when Elizabeth was three, the family moved to 1 Wilson Street, near Portman Square. Blackwell's business must have been thriving since it was a good address and the house expensively furnished with chintz hangings and solid rosewood furniture. Of more interest to the children was the large garden filled with fruit trees, shrubs and abundant raspberry bushes. Fresh air and long walks were part of the daily routine. Occasionally the entire family – aunts, uncles cousins and a couple of nursemaids to carry the little ones, would embark on a major expedition to one of the local beauty spots, such as Hotwells or Clifton Downs.

A description of one such excursion, to Cook's Folly, where they stood looking down from the top of the steep hill to the River Avon below, provides a snapshot of the family enjoying a memorable moment:

The weather was lovely and we had a splendid golden sunset; and we watched with immense delight and interest a grand 'West (or East) Indiaman' that was coming up the river with the tide; a mountain of snowy canvas, with a regiment of troops on board, come home from their long foreign service. The children all got up on the battlement round the top of the tower; the elders stood behind them; Uncle Browne made everybody get out their pocket handkerchiefs and fly the same as the noble ship came up with the soldiers massed on the deck. We were all greatly excited with the splendour of the scene and shouted 'Hurrah!' and 'welcome home!' at the top of our voices (inaudible on board); the troops stood stock still as though they did not see us; but just as the ship passed under the tower, every cap was lifted and waved as though by a single arm, and a ringing shout, thrice repeated, sent up a 'Hurrah!' that rang in our ears long afterwards. The whole lot of us, old and young, went off into a fit of enthusiasm that nearly took us off our feet and threatened to send us headlong into the woods that went down to the river. Didn't we fly the handkerchiefs and shout our answering 'Hurrahs!' with impassioned vigour.

Each summer the family spent a few weeks at the seaside. A large coach was reserved well in advance to carry them, the servants and their large quantities of luggage the few miles to Weston-super-Mare: 'Aunt and Uncle Browne arrived in their handsome yellow chariot and pair, packed with fruit, vegetables, poultry, and various delicacies, the elders went on delightful excursions to neighbouring points; to Hutton and Looking, to Brean Down, to the Cheddar Cliffs and grottoes. Uncle Charley [Hannah's brother] as usual was the life of all that went on. Cousins Elizabeth and Sam Lowell alternately flirted and quarrelled. Uncle Browne was always adjusting a telescope on the battlemented wall and we were always on tiptoe to look through it. The sands were splendid, the shrimps ditto; the shells plentiful and pretty. '

Despite such happy memories, the two eldest children, Anna and Marian, looked back on their Bristol childhood with little pleasure and, in Anna's case, even bitterness. Although they enjoyed a more liberal and comfortable childhood than many of their contemporaries, they found the Nonconformist circles in which they moved dull and restrictive: 'We were so stupidly brought up, so absurdly held in, and so constantly put out of the way when people came to the house that we were extremely shy of strangers.' Elizabeth, nearly five years younger than Anna, remembered her childhood with greater warmth. A calm, fair-haired child, of pale complexion, she was considered reclusive by the rest of the family. They soon recognised, however, that behind her diffident façade there lurked a strong character and iron will. She was always particularly close to her father who, because she was so much quieter than the rest of his brood, nicknamed her 'little shy'.

Blackwell enjoyed any excuse to write verse for the children, responding to a request to take their telescope on the roof with a typical piece of doggerel:

> Anna, Bessy and Polly
> Your request is mere folly,
> The leads are too high for those who can't fly.
> If I let you go there I suppose your next prayer
> Will be for a hop, to the chimney top!
> So I charge you three misses, not to show your phizes
> On parapet wall, or chimney tall,
> But to keep on earth, the place of your birth.
> 'Even so,' says Papa
> 'Amen,' says Mama
> 'Be it so,' says Aunt Bar[4]

But despite such light touches, Blackwell, along with many of the adults who inhabited the children's lives, could be oppressively devout. They were seldom allowed to enjoy any simple pleasure without being reminded to 'ascribe their youthful comfort and advantage to their merciful and generous God'. And on the rare occasions they were allowed to attend a party, it was invariably cut short by the minister who, after a few words of pious admonition, would tell all the children to get down on their knees and pray.

The Congregationalist chapel in Bridge Street was at the heart of the family's spiritual and social life. Samuel and Hannah Blackwell were intensely antagonistic to the established Church, and even more opposed to Roman Catholicism. 'Rags of popery' was a phrase drummed into the children from an early age. On a visit to Ireland Blackwell noted in his diary: 'Three quarters of the population of Cork are Roman Catholic and the remainder, though nominally Protestant, are as ignorant of spiritual things as the darkest Catholic.'[5] The Blackwell children were not brought up ecumenically.

The Blackwell family pew was the handsomest in the chapel, lined with green baize and fastened with brass nails. 'Papa always sat next to the door; then Mamma; then the row of children according to size, the little one being next to her. Whoever was the governess for the time being sat at the farther end. There were seats for the servants in another pew.' Grandfather Blackwell also had a personal pew which was placed directly in front of the pulpit. He regarded the black robes worn by the Reverend Mr John Leifchild (the flamboyant minister at Bridge Street Chapel) as unscriptural, a relic of the 'Scarlet Woman' and an imitation of 'church doings':

> As Mr Leifchild, a large, portly distingué-looking man used to emerge from the vestry in a sweeping black gown, with snowy band, his whole person and bearing being that of one well able to magnify his office, and ascended the pulpit stairs with the air of an Ambassador, Grandpa would follow every movement with a sort of gloating hatred, throw himself back in his corner of his pew, settling himself for a resolute stare of a couple of hours, one gray stockinged leg crossed square over the other and his hand on his knee, his great coat usually buttoned up and his head sinking into his collar. His presence was a perpetual torture to Mr Leifchild.

Whatever misgivings the children had about the number of prayer meetings and services they were forced to attend, they relished Anniversary Week. This took place every May, when all the religious, missionary and other dissenting societies held their annual conference. Blackwell was Secretary to the proceedings and his children listened with proud delight to the rapturous applause that greeted his report. A number of the 'jolly divines' were always quartered with the Blackwell family – some of them very agreeable but many very odd. The Reverend Unwin was especially memorable for being only a head taller than his green silk umbrella with its ivory handle.

> There was a grand dinner party one day in the evening when some of the guests had gone, the remaining ones settled in for gossip and stories and Mr Unwin and Mr Leifchild poured out anecdote after anecdote, story after story until the laughter was almost too much. I see Papa writhing on his chair as though sitting on fire, Mama laughing till the tears ran down her cheeks, Mr Unwin falling from his seat and eddying with laughter as he rolled on the floor, Mr Leifchild piling up the agony of fun til he started from his seat and rushed up and down the room, Aunt Mary splitting and speechless; all present nearly choking with the drollery of the narratives. And presently, as it grew late, everybody calming down, the servants called in, a Bible brought from the

back parlour, and prayers gone through with, after which the visitors went home and we all went to bed.

On one point of principle Congregationalists were very clear – education was a high priority. Nonconformist children were barred from attending Church of England schools, but Blackwell determinedly gave his offspring – the girls as well as the boys – a good academic grounding. The children were mostly taught at home by a series of tutors and governesses including one unfortunate Moravian lady: 'She looked like a flower and always wore snow boots . . . Mama desperately wanted her to be our governess; Mr Howells desperately wanted to marry her. But Moravians always marry by lot; basing the custom on the proverb of Solomon, "the lot is cast into the Cap but the disposing of it is of the Lord's." So at the annual lot drawing she drew a missionary, married him and went with him to some Cannibal Island (I think New Zealand) and, with her husband, was cooked and eaten a few days after getting there, to the great regret of all who had known her.'

Anna and Marian were sent briefly to a boarding school but the experiment was a failure. 'The teaching was an illusion, we were half starved and the scholars were a vulgar and corrupt lot.' The highly strung Anna rapidly contrived to have herself removed so that Elizabeth, who was only five years old, was sent in her place in order not to waste the fees which had already been paid. She never referred to this cataclysmic event in her young life but with her natural self-control and strong inner resources was already better equipped to deal with the situation than her more emotional older sisters.

The children's education was uneven but taken very seriously and they were never short of books. The proceeds of a gold watch-case Marian found on the sands of Weston ('The jealous excitement that seized on Bessy and me to think that Marian should have had such a wonderful incident, and we nothing, was deep and intense') were invested in building up their own library, which became the envy of their friends: 'How we used to pore over those stories of an evening; Father Clement, Miss Edgeworth's stories, Mrs Sherwood's, Mrs Barbauld's and quantities whose very names are now forgotten, that we read over and over again, with unfailing delight.'

Novels were another matter. In dissenting circles they were regarded with deep suspicion and considered highly unsuitable for impressionable minds. The first such stories the Blackwell girls read illicitly were smuggled in by one of their nursemaids, who managed to procure several Walter Scott novels from a circulating library. Inevitably they were caught and there was 'a dreadful scene when our beloved novels were seized and carried off to Papa'. It says much for Blackwell's liberal instincts that after reading the books himself and appreciating their quality, he allowed the girls to keep them with his blessing.

One of Mrs Sherwood's stories, intended to emphasise a wife's 'duty' to obey her husband, produced an indignant outburst from Anna: 'I gave the assembled family my views on the monstrosity and nonsense of the supposed "duty" and repudiated St Paul and his sayings on the subject, with so much anger that I got myself into disgrace thereby and was ordered off to bed as a punishment for my outbreak of rebellion against the assumption of marital authority.'

Anna's youthful revolt against male authority matured into a strong conviction, shared with her four sisters, that few marriages were likely to be worth the loss of personal freedom. Although their parents' union was obviously happy, the children were also faced with some striking examples of adult misery. In a rare outburst their grandmother warned against male flattery which lasted only until after the wedding, when 'the poor girl found out what a dreadful master marriage had given her, what a slave she was and what a world of care and labour and worry she had got into . . . those were wise who did not marry and that if she were to do it again, most certainly she would not marry Grandpapa'.

A maternal uncle provided another sharp object lesson in the hazards of matrimony. His wife had a private income, but when they separated he was entitled by law to claim it as his own. 'He never dreamed, nor did anybody else, of its being a mean or unjust thing in a husband to live on his wife's money and leave her but a pittance of her property. In the eyes of the law, and in the conviction of society, the man was regarded as the owner both of his wife and of everything belonging to her.' The Blackwell girls were thus confronted within their immediate family circle by examples of both happy and unhappy marriages but it was the latter that made the more lasting impact, influencing them all to pursue the uncertain path of the Victorian single woman.

* * *

Then, in about 1828, when Elizabeth was seven, her father's refinery burned down: 'I can see the whole household, children, servants, Mama, Aunts, all huddled against the railings at the top of Bridge St Back, a slip of a street above the river, leading down to Bristol Bridge, feeling the heat of the railings and watching the great feathers of flame, and the volumes of sparks, rushing up into the sky.' It was a calamitous but not entirely unexpected event. Fires were such a common occurrence in the sugar refining business that few insurance companies were prepared to underwrite the buildings. With no hope of compensation, Blackwell's financial loss was serious and his situation not improved by a general malaise in the Bristol sugar trade resulting from increased competition from London and Liverpool.

After the fire Blackwell rented new premises in Nelson Street and, in order to save money, moved his family into the house attached to them. As it was situated in the heart of the most built-up part of the city, a country cottage was rented in Olveston, 9 miles to the north-east of Bristol overlooking the River Avon. The family spent much of their time at this rural idyll, Blackwell commuting daily to Bristol in his yellow gig drawn by Bessie, the little grey pony he named after Elizabeth.

In addition to his problems caused by the fire, Blackwell had to cope with a disaster even more damaging. He had placed his younger brother, James, in charge of their interests in Dublin, not realising he was mentally unstable. By the time James's illness became apparent the business had been severely undermined and had run up enormous debts.

Despite his business anxieties, Blackwell's appetite for religion and politics was undiminished. A convinced liberal, his political enthusiasms were eagerly taken up by his three eldest daughters: 'We were all Whigs, and stood up for Oliver Cromwell, William and Mary, and the French Revolution, knowing precious little about these people and events, but believing them to have been for the popular benefit.' The girls were zealous Abolitionists and, without perhaps understanding the irony of their gesture, insisted on giving up sugar in protest against slavery.

The whole family became involved in the excitement of the 1830 elections. They enthusiastically wore Liberal ribbons and went to watch the Chairing of John Bright, the victorious Liberal candidate. Totally committed to the Reform Bill, the children proudly put up a poster over the parlour mantelpiece that called on all patriots for 'A long pull! And a strong pull!! And a pull altogether!!!' The eventual passing of the Bill was cause for great national celebration, and the Nelson Street house so splendidly lit and decked out in flowers that it was reported in the local newspapers.

Politics were stimulating but they could also be alarming. This the three girls discovered when they witnessed the Bristol riots of 1831 as their father drove them in the yellow gig through the city to a drawing lesson: 'We girls were horribly frightened. I remember the strange appearance of the streets, entirely deserted, shops and shutters shut, nobody visible.' Having locked his daughters in the house, Blackwell joined those attempting to quell the violence and save the Cathedral from burning down.

The riots may have contributed to Blackwell's decision to emigrate but the most pressing reason was his financial situation. Since the failure of two prominent sugar importers Blackwell was in even more difficulty, having lost some £70,000. His mother, whom he had loved dearly, was dead and his disagreeable father ever more demanding. Against this bleak background, America shone out as the land of liberty and political promise and – most importantly – as a country where Congregationalism flourished.

A further inducement came from his friend, H.C. Howells (once enamoured of the Moravian governess), who had been living for some months in the United States and wrote enthusiastic letters to Blackwell urging him to follow his example. It was a tribute to Blackwell's integrity and standing in the community that, on hearing of his intention to emigrate, a number of leading businessmen in Bristol formally offered him a low-interest loan for as long as he wished. But Blackwell had made up his mind, and neither the generosity of his friends nor the doubts of his family could deter him.

The stoical Elizabeth was eleven when the family left Bristol. In her autobiography she concedes only that 'a great change of social surroundings took place'.[6] But for Anna (writing half a century later) it was difficult 'to comprehend how so monstrous a piece of folly as this uprooting could ever have been planned and perpetrated by a sensible man'. Certainly the prosperous and relatively secure life the Blackwell family had enjoyed was over for good. Anna spent the rest of her life lamenting the loss of wealth and status that she believed her father could have regained had he remained in England. Instead, 'by his impetuous actions he plunged his numerous young family into the world of loss, ruin, anxiety, and misery which shortened his own life and . . . so nearly destroyed the peace and usefulness of ours, harassed as we have all been by finding ourselves left to battle with the world without money, connexions, or any of the aids, the lack of which makes life little else but a wearing and waiting struggle'.

In the summer of 1832 the family bade a sad farewell to their Olveston cottage. They climbed a nearby hill to look one last time over the fertile valley of the Severn and across the Bristol Channel to the distant Welsh hills. Many years later Henry, who was seven at the time, recalled the moment: 'It was a lovely sunset and we all knew, as we watched the dying colors in the sky, that it was the last time we should ever see that glorious view. As the shadows began to creep over the landscape a sensation of inexpressible sadness came over me and I felt for the first time that sense of homesickness which is the most sorrowful that ever oppresses the human soul. The idea that we were going to leave our native land forever came over me, and I felt that I was about to enter a new and strange world of which I knew nothing.'[7]

In early August the Nelson Street house was dismantled. The best things were sold and the rest crated up for transportation to New York. The children with their governess and two servants stayed in furnished lodgings near the dock where the *Cosmo* lay waiting to take them to America. Their relations were devastated, particularly Uncle Browne, by then a widower, who gave each of the children a golden guinea as a parting gift.

The boarding party was a big one. Blackwell and his pregnant wife were accompanied by their eight children, the governess, two servants and two of the aunts (a third followed later). Unlike most of their fellow passengers, the Blackwell party did not travel steerage, but their cabins were hardly luxurious. Anna, quartered with half a dozen other emigrants, was unhappy to discover that the leaking iron pillar running through the centre of the cabin was the drain leading from the 'pagoda' on deck to the sea. Although the ship had a cow on board, it soon died, leaving the passengers with only brackish water to drink. Food consisted almost exclusively of salt beef, pork and crackers but at least hot arrowroot jelly and brandy provided some relief from nausea. This was much needed by Elizabeth who suffered acutely from seasickness all her life. Nine-year-old Samuel found diversion by falling in love but for the rest of the family it was a long and tedious voyage lasting nearly eight weeks. After the driving fog and great green waves of the Newfoundland Banks, they all felt profound relief at their first glimpse of Long Island.

TWO

New Yorker

Most early nineteenth-century accounts of entering New York City harbour agree that it was an unforgettable experience. Any qualms experienced by the emigrants on board the *Cosmo* were temporarily forgotten as they admired the loveliness of the scene around them. The significance of the moment was not lost on Blackwell: 'Truly thrilling are the emotions with which an English Emigrant approaches these shores. . . . The fact that the Land before him *is* America – and . . . all his hopes and fears are about to be brought to the test . . . wonderfully affects him. Upward of two hundred emigrants crowded the sides and shrouds of our Vessel at the welcome sound of "Land" but amidst them all scarcely a word was uttered – the fixed and eager eye and the gushing tear, told their feelings better than words.'[1]

Such hopes and fears were the common experience of all emigrants arriving for the first time in America, whatever their motivation or social caste. The persecuted and plainly poor gambled on finding a better life free from political and religious tyranny, while others who like Blackwell, were idealists and relatively affluent, expected to see their dreams of a democratic society at last fully realised. Religion also drew Blackwell to America. The Congregationalist church was in complete sympathy with the values of the Founding Fathers, firmly believing that God had ordained the New World in order to set an example to the discredited old one.

But, apart from his political and religious idealism, Blackwell, in company with most other middle-class Englishmen emigrating to America in the 1830s, simply wanted to succeed in business. In contrast to the economic decline he had witnessed in Bristol, New York was booming, with a population of around 220,000 of which some 20 per cent were foreign born. The harbour, so much admired for its beauty, also gave New York a practical advantage over its rivals in the fierce competition for transatlantic trade while the opening of the Erie Canal in 1825 provided unparalleled communications with the interior. At a more local level, transport improved dramatically when the first railroad on Manhattan (with horse-drawn cars) began operating a few weeks after the *Cosmo*'s arrival. Life in New York City during the early 1830s was unquestionably on the move, and Blackwell had every reason to believe that with effort, imagination and divine guidance he could make a success of his bold initiative.

As it was already dark when the *Cosmo* docked in the East River, the passengers were unable to disembark. But having survived for so long on ship's biscuits the thought of real food was too hard to resist, and Blackwell took seven-year-old Henry ashore to buy bread. When, the next day, the family was finally able to quit the ship they were surprised to see so few people on the streets. The reason was soon apparent. New York was recovering from its first outbreak of the Asiatic cholera that in a few weeks killed some 3,500 people. The epidemic had one positive result. It forced the administration, struggling to keep pace with the city's rapid growth, to cease relying on scavenging pigs to clean the streets. The fire and police departments were almost as rudimentary as the sanitation but at least the city was well lit, and Broadway – its most spacious and elegant street – even boasted gaslight.

Whatever reservations the family may have had about their new surroundings they learned to keep to themselves. The Americans were intensely proud of their young country and wished to hear only favourable opinions from overseas visitors – often extracted from them even before they reached the shore: 'Don't you think this a wonderful country? Don't you allow that we deserve great credit for what we are doing? Do we not resemble the Old Country much more than you expected? Had you any idea of finding us so advanced? Is not our Canal the finest work in the world? Don't you admit we are becoming a great nation? What do you think of us upon the whole?'[2]

Fanny Trollope's candid, sometimes cruel but often wickedly funny account of her three years in the United States, *Domestic Manners of the Americans*,[3] was published within a few months of the Blackwells' arrival in New York and did little to diminish anti-English sentiment – rife since the 1812 war. If the family were to prosper in their new country, they soon realised that it was essential to be keenly aware of American sensitivities.

Despite its rapid expansion New York was little more than a large town in comparison with its European counterparts. Washington Square lay close to its northern boundary at 14th Street while the most fashionable quarter lay around the Battery on the southern tip of the Island. The rest of Manhattan was still largely rural. Blackwell rented a house in Thompson

Street (running south from Washington Square) and employed a fellow passenger from the *Cosmo*, a bricklayer named Dennis Harris, to move in the family's furniture. Harris, a stern and humourless lay Methodist preacher, had impressed his new employer by his tireless efforts to convert the godless on the voyage. He quickly graduated from removal man to foreman in the first of Blackwell's New York sugarhouses.

Thompson Street was a good residential area and the Blackwell family had some impressive neighbours, among them John Jacob Astor.[4] In 1832 Walt Whitman (two years older than Elizabeth) watched the enormously wealthy Astor: 'swathed in rich furs, with a great ermine cap on his head . . . carried, down the steps of his high front stoop . . . then lifted and tuck'd in a gorgeous sleigh.'[5] Within a few weeks, George Washington Blackwell was born – a perfect symbol of his parents' commitment to their new country. His nurse amused the children with her blunt American ways while the landlord excited their imagination with tales of rattlesnakes. The unpleasant drinking water, drawn from a pump at the street corner, was little better than filtered sewage, but tomatoes, peppers and pumpkin pie provided more attractive novelties. A sleigh ride along Broadway (without the benefit of John Astor's furs) introduced them to the ferocity of the American winter.

As might be expected of a young republic seeking, theoretically at least, to establish equal opportunities for its citizens, education was a high priority. The older Blackwell children were rapidly enrolled in a local school (where they were given a much better education than they could have expected at the time in England) while the younger ones remained at home under the tutelage of Miss Major. A vital part of the settling in process was the family's affiliation to a nearby church presided over by the Reverend Samuel Cox. The Blackwell children thought him a pompous and arrogant man but he was notable as one of the founders of the recently opened New York University.

While the domestic scene began to take pleasant shape, funds were still worryingly low and Blackwell's most urgent need was to set up in profitable business. A few weeks after their arrival, he received a letter from one of his erstwhile colleagues in Bristol, Sam Guppy, who had leased the Nelson Street refinery, bought all the fixtures and fittings and even the much-loved yellow gig. Guppy believed in the superiority of the vacuum pan technology with which Blackwell was fully familiar but which was as yet unknown in America. It was no doubt for this reason that Gower

Guppy & Company were prepared to enter into a partnership with Blackwell – the firm supplying the capital and Blackwell the expertise. It was clear from the outset that the investment was a cautious one since Guppy wrote to his new partner: 'I am much afraid you will find your means very inadequate . . . perhaps you can earn your expenses in a small grocery trade?'[6]. Ignoring this suggestion, Blackwell subsequently ran not only the Congress sugarhouse for Gower Guppy & Co., but also maintained his own business in Washington Street where he continued to employ Dennis Harris as his foreman.

Initially business went well and the family prospered. In 1835 they moved to Long Island, close to Flushing, into a pleasant old frame house with a large garden full of fruit and bordered by cherry trees. It was an extensive property with a barn and carriage house, surrounded by fields of clover. But near this idyllic scene lay a stagnant marsh and within a few weeks Blackwell fell seriously ill with malaria, from which he never fully recovered. Despite this setback, it was a happy period for them all. While they were living on Long Island Hannah's feckless brother, Uncle Charles, on half pay from the army, came to stay with them. He fell in love with the governess, Eliza Major, and married her. The marriage was, however, bigamous since his first wife was still very much alive. Given Samuel and Hannah's strict religious views, it is remarkable that they were prepared to countenance such a union. But with his imitations of animal noises, frog dances and endless riddles ('Why is St Luke's mother like a Turkish rider? Because she is a mammyluke')[7] he was responsible for bringing a good deal of innocent fun into the children's lives.

Anna, now nineteen, took Eliza's place teaching the youngest children, while Elizabeth and the older ones commuted daily to school in the city. They travelled into New York via Brooklyn past a thin scattering of houses and open fields where they noted the hundreds of numbered stakes marking lots up for sale for which, however, there was as yet no demand. From Brooklyn they took a short ferry ride across to Manhattan. Later, when the family lived in Jersey City, ferries became a vital and exciting part of the children's daily routine. Elizabeth, who was always deeply responsive to her natural surroundings, loved the ever-changing harbour scene.

During the six years the family spent in New York, anti-slavery politics dominated their social life and spare time. The Anti-Slavery Society of New York was founded in October 1833, exactly one year after they arrived in America, and from the beginning they were at the centre of its activities.

Blackwell was appalled by the inhumanity of the Cuban planters from whom he bought his raw sugar. In preference to using their own labourers, they argued that it was more profitable to buy slaves, work them to death and then replace them with fresh imports from Africa. He was also deeply disappointed with the tolerant views on slavery held by his fellow New York businessmen. 'Were it not for one dark and damning spot, the eye of the Philanthropist would rest upon this land with almost unmixed gratification.'[8]

Elizabeth, who attended many anti-slavery meetings, described one held in Broadway Hall on 11 March 1836 in the diary that she had begun ten days earlier, soon after her fifteenth birthday. Many luminaries of the movement were present, among them William Lloyd Garrison, Judge John Jay, Theodore Weld and Gerrit Smith, who 'has the finest countenance I ever saw'. Smith was a passionate reformer and philanthropist involved in such diverse issues as Sunday observance, vegetarianism, temperance, the national dress reform association, women's suffrage, prison reform and the abolition of capital punishment. He had joined the anti-slavery crusade relatively late but was to become one of the best-known Abolitionists in America and a powerful role model for Elizabeth.

Two years earlier in 1834, the English Abolitionist George Thompson had arrived in New York. An eloquent and passionate speaker, he enraged the local pro-slavery lobby. They obviously did not care for his message but the fact that he was English made him even more intolerable. The Blackwell family were among those at a church meeting listening to Thompson when the church was invaded: 'amid the crash of falling glass and the howls of the mob, the frightened audience dispersed, Thompson escaping in the midst of the tumult.'[9]

Little more than a year later the family were again in the front line. Their pastor, the self-important Samuel Cox, had been recently converted to the anti-slavery cause and preached a sermon in which he reminded his congregation that Jesus Christ was of Semite not Caucasian race. Two pro-slavery newspapers subsequently printed provocative editorials asserting Cox had said that Christ was not a white man. A rumour then swiftly circulated alleging that Cox had called Christ 'a nigger', with predictable results. A lynch mob attacked and gutted both Cox's house and that of his physician brother, forcing them to flee for their lives. They escaped to Blackwell's house on Long Island, remaining in hiding there for ten days. After this incident the deeply shaken minister preached less controversially, but his brother was made of sterner stuff. He spent his exile pistol shooting behind the barn, leaving the Blackwell's carriage full of bullet holes, and boasted that he would sell his life dearly should the mob pursue him.[10]

The younger Blackwell children, equally enthusiastic in support of the cause, were mobilised by their elders to help in every way possible. It fell to Henry to write the mottoes for the sugar kisses that his sisters sold on their stall at the Abolitionist fair:

> Hurrah for the banner of Stars!
> Hurrah for the banner of Stripes!
> Get up you black niggers all covered with scars
> Hurrah for the banner of stripes![11]

William Lloyd Garrison was among the first Americans to demand the immediate and complete emancipation of slaves, and for the next thirty years devoted himself to achieving that end. Imprisoned for libel, dragged through the streets of Boston with a rope round his neck by a furious mob, founder and editor of the *Liberator* (to which Blackwell was a regular contributor) and utterly unprepared to compromise his views in any way, he fired Elizabeth's reforming instincts to the very core. After one anti-slavery fair she recorded how 'to our great joy Mr Garrison came home and slept at our house . . . coming over in the boat he quoted poetry very sweetly'.

Anti-slavery events added excitement and focus to Elizabeth's teenage years – a time that in many other respects she found dull and frustrating. She deeply admired the celebrated Abolitionists who frequented her home but was characteristically blunt about their human failings. Of Theodore Weld she wrote in her diary: 'He appeared exceedingly pleasant but his gentlemanly appearance would be greatly increased by the regular use of a toothbrush.' The anti-slavery dramas she witnessed transmitted a powerful message that served to reinforce her whole Nonconformist upbringing. In short, holding fast to deeply felt principles could be an acutely uncomfortable experience. This knowledge clearly stimulated rather than frightened her and, although she never had to face a lynching mob, she was, for the rest of her life, constantly placing herself in situations that rigorously tested her commitment to her beliefs.

At the beginning of 1836 the family moved house yet again, this time to Jersey City. The change was driven by their need to find a healthier place to live – away from malarial swamps. Jersey City was a relatively cheap but pleasant suburb and, with a steamboat leaving for Manhattan every ten minutes, provided an ideal base for them. A good ferry service was essential since Blackwell had his sugarhouses to attend to each day and the children their school. Instead of the open fields of Long Island, they now looked out over the Hudson River and across New York Bay to the burgeoning city – a view that was a constant delight to them all.

Elizabeth enjoyed school and admired her teachers but was quite clear about her future academic plans: 'I should like to go to school for one year more, for then I should be able to pursue my studies by myself in a proper manner and I should most likely get a premium.' Whatever social insecurities Elizabeth may have suffered as a child, she did not lack confidence in her mental ability. The combination of a fine intelligence with strongly held views generated a quality then considered dangerously unfeminine – ambition. As yet unfocused, it was already clear that any goals cherished by Elizabeth were unlikely to be satisfied with the production of the worsted mats and wax fruit she laboured over to sell at Abolitionist fairs. 'How I do long for some end to act for, some end to be obtained in this life, for God has given us talents to be used in earthly pursuits, and to go on everyday in just the same jogtrot manner without any object is very wearisome.'

To judge by the amount of reading Elizabeth accomplished during her teens, she was certainly motivated and disciplined enough to study without supervision. On her sixteenth birthday she noted in her diary that she had finished reading the Bible from beginning to end. Within a few months she had started it all over again. But her books were by no means limited to religious works. Madame de Stael's *Corinne* moved her profoundly: 'so talented, noble and generous but such love as hers is complete idolatry and quite unfit for one mortal to entertain towards another'. She much admired Maria Edgeworth's *Belinda*, and a new edition of Cowper brought home by her father was a particular treat. She was less sure about Francis Bacon, who 'does not seem to hold the ladies in very high esteem', but *The Bride of Lammermuir* excited a particularly passionate reaction: 'Lucy Ashton's weakness is quite provoking, I think if I had been her I should have knocked down my father, overturned my mother, and fled over my elder brother into my lover's arms!!!'

This last sentence, written with such feeling, reflected the frustration Elizabeth increasingly felt towards her own family. There was fierce rivalry between herself and Anna – generally considered the brilliant and beautiful one of the family. Anna's quicksilver temperament, wit and idiosyncrasy clearly grated on Elizabeth from an early age, and the tension between them was a constant feature of their long lives. But the sisters did share one strong bond – they both longed to return to England. It was therefore with considerable sorrow that, after yet another bitter quarrel, Elizabeth faced up to reality: 'Anna and I are not yet reconciled. I am afraid our prospect of living together in England would be rather uncomfortable if put into execution.'

She had an easier relationship with the less quixotic Marian who, with her frequent attacks of dyspepsia, was not as energetic and ambitious as her sisters. But on occasions even she could criticise Elizabeth's behaviour: 'Marian seemed particularly displeased with me and said I behaved in the same manner to every gentleman, that Dr Cox thought I had taken a great dislike to him.' Elizabeth's response was typically spirited and unbowed: 'To all this I could only reply that I wished they would point out the faults of which I was guilty and that until they did so, I should most certainly behave in the same manner as I considered it perfectly proper.' Despite this, Elizabeth was all too conscious of her shyness and, in her diary at least, prepared to admit that it was a problem. In an attempt to confront her gaucheness she took some dancing lessons but they appear to have achieved little: 'Went to a party, I was the only one who did not dance except a deaf lady.' Although, as a teenager, Elizabeth's singular qualities often won admiration, many people clearly found her lack of charm disconcerting. As a result she frequently felt hurt and rejected but was unprepared to adjust her conduct simply in order to win affection.

Social occasions gave Elizabeth little pleasure but she did derive deep joy from nature and intellectual stimulus from religion: 'This morning was so exceedingly lovely that Aunt, Harry, Anna and I had a steam before breakfast . . . not a cloud to be seen and the most refreshing breeze. Oh such a morning does one good it makes you feel so lively and cheerful as if you could jump up to the skies through an over abundance of animal spirits.' She loved to walk in the countryside, covering distances of up to 20 miles a day, often in the company of her brothers – Sam, gentle and devout, and the ebullient Henry who by his own admission was a wild youth. Religion also occupied much of her spare time and was one of the few ways open to her of stretching her mind. She went to a variety of different New York churches and listened to many of the great preachers of the day including the revivalist Charles Grandison Finney. Occasionally church attendance offered inducements other than an enlivening sermon: 'Went to the Tabernacle today. I resolved to act with a little more dignity and not be so taken with the appearance of a young gentleman there, I accordingly regarded him with the most stoical indifference, thought of Bacon and Newton, determined that the outside is a worthless casket, that the mind's the standard of the man, lofty imaginations, spiritual essence, bright beams of genius etc.'

Although Elizabeth was brought up to despise the established Church, at the age of sixteen she began to flirt with Episcopalianism. At the same time she kept an open mind over other creeds and listened closely to the many different sermons she heard, later analysing them in her diary. For one so ready to question the status quo it is not surprising that she was sceptical of phrenology, or the 'bumpy science', as she disparagingly called it. Her suspicions were unfashionable, as most people in her circle were swept up in the general enthusiasm for phrenology, believing unquestioningly in its claims.

This pseudo-science, founded by Joseph Gall (1758–1828), was an attempt to establish by external examination the physical location of the brain's various perceptions. Gall and his followers were convinced that the contours of the skull corresponded to some thirty-five-odd separate faculties, each responsible for a different function. While neurology later demonstrated this localisation to be true of the brain, phrenology was concerned only with the skull and therefore produced results that were little better than fortune telling. However, its alleged scientific basis gave it a respectability that appealed to a wide public. People flocked to be phrenologised – among them the entire Blackwell clan.

Despite her scepticism, Elizabeth was secretly pleased with the report on her bumps when they were analysed on 28 January 1836. However bogus the theory, the reading of her character was remarkably accurate. Indeed, a cynic might suspect that the phrenologist already had an excellent knowledge of his subject:

Distinguished for independence and decision of character – Her will very strong – high minded and a great regard for her own opinion not disposed to trifle nor will she be trifled with . . . slow to anger and slow to forget an insult – great uniformity of feeling and thought. Can fix her mind with great intensiveness and connectedness – her attachment is strong and constant . . . frank and direct in remarks, when excited rather impudent . . . caution not being large but veneration modest – incredulous and slow to believe . . . strong imagination – when interested very enthusiastic but takes much to excite – her head very large . . . strength of feeling and good judgement . . . others do not know how much mind she has . . . not very quick to commit to memory but never forgets when acquired . . . always investigating principles wishes to know why and wherefore . . . very large talent to invent and construct, always perfects what she begins and is more original than imitative.[12]

The phrenology expedition was led by Mr Gower, a director of the firm with which Blackwell was in partnership, who had been sent to New York to protect his company's interests. He spent much of his spare time with the family and was regarded with great affection by the children. The personal friendship was strong but the partnership with Gower Guppy & Co. was not. The length of time it took letters to cross the Atlantic led to misunderstandings and suspicion on both sides and in the autumn of 1836 the arrangement came to a disastrous end when the Congress Street refinery was badly damaged by fire. Ironically it had survived the great conflagration of 1835 that had swept through Manhattan, destroying some 700 buildings, but only a few months later succumbed to flames despite Blackwell's best efforts. The English directors considered the cost of rebuilding the sugarhouse too high and decided to terminate their agreement with Blackwell. On 9 February 1837 Gower left for England: 'We watched the ship sail through the Narrows under full sail and I believe not a few of us wished we were on our way to the same beloved land.'

A few weeks after Gower's departure Blackwell sold his Washington street sugarhouse to Dennis Harris and, with the capital thus raised, determined to turn his full attention to his old obsession – the manufacture of beet sugar. Not that he discussed any of his schemes with his family – even his wife. 'Papa condescended to inform Mamma yesterday, that he had sold his Washington sugar house concern to Mr Harris and some other person, what his plans for the future are we do not know.' Elizabeth's fears had been aroused earlier: 'I hope Papa is not taking up his Michigan beet idea again but his talking so much about beets and bringing home these French books for us to translate is rather suspicious.'

In fact Blackwell's thoughts had been turning westward for some months. In a letter to his nephew, Kenyon, he unburdened himself: 'I have been in the Congress Refinery . . . literally tied down like a galley slave. I have begun to escape from my cage but hitherto in vain. Could I follow my inclinations I should scale the Alleghenies, float on the Ohio and

Mississippi – roam over the prairies, and dive into the mighty forest of the West.' He added that he had bought 320 acres in Michigan.[13]

While Blackwell dreamt of a new life in the West, his children still hoped to return to England. On hearing of King William's death, Elizabeth wrote: 'I instantly felt carried back to England & all my national feelings awoke in an instant. How ardently I hope our young queen may prove worthy & capable of governing our flourishing kingdoms, & may be an honour to our sex, the glory and pride of our nation.' The girls all wore black ribbons and Aunt Eliza a mourning bonnet to mark their respect for the King. Even their father, once so enamoured of republicanism, to his children's astonishment and pleasure wore black crepe in his hat. Surprisingly, their mother, who had been the least eager to emigrate, strongly disapproved of this display of nationalism and lectured them all on their lack of regard for America.

Business difficulties were not the only reasons that drove Blackwell to seek a new direction in his life. He had also become deeply disillusioned with American politics: 'From politics I keep aloof – all parties appear to me to be much the same – that is, utterly worthless – and the everlasting turmoil and blackguardesness of the actors utterly disgusts me. If there were nothing in America better than its politics I should soon cut the concern. The spirit of Slavery blackens and curses everything here morally and politically and I fear will work like a canker until perfect rottenness will be the end and ruin of these States.'[14]

In a letter to his old Bristol preaching friend Mr Howells, then living in Pittsburgh, Blackwell vividly expressed his bitterness at the betrayal of the American democratic dream, citing Thompson and other English Abolitionists who 'have presumptuously taken the American Declaration of Independence as an honest and authentic manual of American principles instead of treating it as it really is viz one of the barest frauds ever patented upon the confidence and credulity of Mankind'.[15] His anger was not just directed at slavery; he was equally incensed at the treatment of the Indian tribes. With dissenting fervour he wondered 'that the overthrow of Sodom and the Cities of the plain is not repeated upon a much more extensive and awful scale. Indeed I think I do see the elements of blackness and death gathering in the Horizon'.[16]

The strain of years of inner conflict between moral conviction and professional obligation had taken its toll on Blackwell. The realisation that he could no longer work with slavery sympathisers combined with his financial difficulties and natural restlessness to convince him that he must set out once more in search of a better life. Just as a few years earlier he had looked to New York as the solution to all his problems, now, in a burst of the old optimism, he was equally confident that a golden future awaited them all in the West.

But before Blackwell could execute his plans, his affairs sank to a new low. Apart from his own business worries, the country was suffering a severe economic crisis as a result of President Andrew Jackson's policies. Speculation had been rife for several years and the ensuing inflation led to a massive rise in the cost of living. By February 1837 food prices were so high that desperate New Yorkers began looting warehouses. The crash came in March when news reached Manhattan that three cotton mills had failed in New Orleans for two and half million dollars. By 15 April there were 168 failures in New York and, in May, a two-day run on the banks that happened to coincide with the annual anti-slavery fair. 'Affairs being in such a state, it was not to be expected that we should take much it being also such an unfavourable evening that our richest customers did not come.'

A number of businessmen who owed Blackwell money were ruined in the 1837 Panic, dealing yet another blow to any chance he had of retrieving something from the wreckage of his affairs. His family soon felt the effects. In an effort to economise, Hannah and her three elder daughters took turns to do the cooking, much to Elizabeth's distaste: 'This is my day for seeing to the meals, consequently I have not had much time for other things, I do really hate the employment, and look with real dread to my week for we have agreed to take it by weeks.' A few days later, she recorded that there was no money to buy candles and they had to go to bed in the dark. When the servant was dismissed, Elizabeth wrote sadly in her diary, 'how very miserable it is to be without a servant'.

In order to supplement the family income, serious thought was given to employment for the older girls. Anna decided to teach music and accepted a job with a family living in Vermont. The farewells at the dockside were emotional – at least for some members of the family: 'At parting Anna was unable to keep the floodgates fastened and Mamma ditto but unfeeling me refused to let out a single drop. We watched the boat out of sight and returned home with a feeling of melancholy at the first separation of our family.'

At the end of August 1837 Elizabeth was at last made privy to her parents' plans, which (fortunately for her) only partly materialised. Her father would travel west and find a suitable place to grow beets, taking Sam and Henry with him. Her mother and the four youngest children were to live in a cheap boarding house while Elizabeth and Marian would find jobs as governesses. It was a bleak prospect, especially since Elizabeth had already discovered how much she disliked teaching, having had experience with her younger siblings. The grim knowledge that she was to become a governess made her presence at Columbia College commencement an especially bitter-sweet occasion. She was so absorbed by what she heard that she stood under a clock for six hours without hearing it strike: 'How I long to go to college, the Speck oration called up a multitude of thoughts & the melancholy reflection that the enchanting paths of literature were not for me to walk in.'

During the autumn of 1837, Blackwell travelled constantly to Philadelphia to negotiate with the Quakers, who had long been trying to find an alternative to cane sugar and who were entirely sympathetic to his plans. With their backing, he decided to make an exploratory journey in order to establish exactly where to launch his beet sugar experiment, and set off on 24 January 1838. His letters to Hannah reflect his excitement and pleasure in his mission despite the freezing temperatures and discomforts of stagecoach travel. His route took him by railroad from Philadelphia through Lancaster, Harrisburg to Chambersburg, thence by coach to Bedford, across the mountains to Greensburg and on to Pittsburgh. From Pittsburgh he travelled by steamboat down the Ohio to Cincinnati where a relative of Hannah's, Sam Browne, was ready to receive him and act as his local agent.

Whatever Blackwell's failings as a businessman, there can be no doubt of his love for his family. He told Hannah how he thought of her night and day, and to each of his children he wrote a message full of humour and perfectly tailored to their age and character. To Elizabeth he 'wished many times many happy returns of the day. I suppose you did not hear me as the wind unfortunately blew the wrong way.' He reminded Sam that while he was absent he was his representative and asked Henry to keep his fingers from gunpowder and his lips from other explosions, Emily to be kind to her small brothers, Ellen not to speak so loudly or open her mouth so wide when she was eating and Howard not to fight. To five-year-old Washy he simply sent a kiss.[17]

In Jersey City, meanwhile, life for the family was growing steadily worse. Their season ticket for the ferry expired and, without enough funds to renew it, they could no longer cross to Manhattan. 'We have become so poor . . . that we had no meat for dinner yesterday, today we had a stew composed of potatoes with a few bones which had been carefully preserved and one penny leek.' Blackwell's return on 30 March was greeted with great joy. He had decided they should settle in Cincinnati and as he wanted to be there by May there was much to do in a short time. 'Oh what a day of business and bustle, all engaged in rubbing & scrubbing & polishing & carrying up & bringing down & turning out drawers & to add to our confusion more calls than we have ever had before in one day.'

A few days before they finally left, Elizabeth witnessed an historic event – the arrival of the *Sirius* on 22 April. This was the first fully steam-powered ship to cross the Atlantic and three days later the family went on board. Elizabeth was impressed with this 'wonder of the ocean', and especially with the engine – 'a most enormous mass of complication'. Nine days later the family all gathered at the aunts' millinery shop on Canal Street to say goodbye. As Aunts Barbara and Lucy had chosen to stay in New York, only Aunt Mary was travelling west. Uncle Charles and Aunt Eliza were returning to England (where his bigamy appears to have remained undetected) and Marian, having found a job teaching arithmetic, was to remain in Jersey City. 'We had a very nice tea but rather sad at the idea of separation, the tears would come when I wished Eliza goodbye.' The next day, in pouring rain, the depleted Blackwell family boarded their ship and set sail for Philadelphia and the West.

THREE

Cincinnati

After the family's increasingly dull existence in Jersey City the journey west was a welcome adventure. The novelty of a constantly changing scene and the drama of stranded boats and snowbound trains, as well as exposure to an entirely new group of people appealed so much to Elizabeth that their eventual arrival in Cincinnati proved an anticlimax.

The great trek west began on 3 May 1838 with the voyage from New York to Philadelphia where they made a brief stop before travelling on by train, through pouring rain, to Columbia. Here they boarded a canal boat: 'Oh what a condition! We were in a room about 6 yards by 4 stuffed full of Irish women with whole trains of squalling dirty children 16 berths & the floor covered.'[1] But the beauty of the Susquehanna River and the fascination of crossing the Juniata by aqueduct (a feat accomplished by a complicated mass of ropes and pulleys) more than compensated for the squalor of the cabin. Elizabeth spent the day on the roof of the boat enjoying the landscape and in the evening sat under the moon watching the reflections of the hills in the water.

Many of the other passengers were young farmers and mechanics. One of them, travelling west with his father in search of land, she considered 'decidedly the most decent on board'. For Elizabeth, so socially ill at ease even within her family's close circle, the journey offered a rare opportunity to meet and observe people free from conventional constraints. But however curious she may have been about her fellow passengers, she was uncomfortably aware of how little interested they were in her. This was all the more galling since she saw twelve-year-old Emily effortlessly conversing and playing board games with any number of the good-looking young men on board.

Delayed by a broken floodgate, the boat finally reached Hollidaysburg four days later. Here they boarded a train to take them across the Allegheny Mountains – a service that had only just been inaugurated. The temperature dropped dramatically as, with great difficulty, the train ground its way up five inclined planes. A problem with the engine delayed them several hours by which time night had fallen: 'We were in the wildest scenery, getting very *very* cold, deserted by all the gentlemen, who went to see what was the matter, & surrounded by squalling children. How I longed to get out as the gents did at the head of the planes and warm myself by the boiler fires for my feet were bitter cold, but the *Far West* had no door & my sex & petticoats forbad.'

Having spent the night in lodgings at the pass they continued next day through a heavy snowstorm to Johnstown where they boarded another boat. The quarters on this one were no better than the last but made a good deal worse by the numerous children sick with whooping cough and measles. Six miles short of Pittsburgh, and in the middle of the bitterly cold night, the canal became impassable forcing the passengers to disembark and struggle across marshy ground, carrying all their luggage, to a rescue ship on the Allegheny River. Elizabeth revelled in the excitement but even she was thankful for the warm welcome they received from Blackwell's old Bristol friend, Mr Howells and his family, when they finally reached Pittsburgh.

That afternoon they embarked on yet another boat for the final leg of their journey. Elizabeth spent the last couple of days on the steamboat under a dazzling blue sky enjoying the brilliant greens of a western spring and jealously watching Emily defeat a bevy of young farmers at draughts. They reached Cincinnati at 3 o'clock on 12 May. 'I was very sorry, for though pleased with the appearance of the city yet I was much grieved that the journey was over. I took leave of those I knew on board, bowed & said goodbye & went on shore with the others to seek my fortune in the West.'

During the 1830s and 1840s Cincinnati was visited by a number of distinguished English writers – Harriet Martineau, Captain Marryat and Charles Dickens among them. They were impressed with what they saw, commenting on the neat elegant houses, the roads pleasantly lined with trees, the good shops and well-kept gardens. T.G. Bradford's *Illustrated Atlas of the United States*,[2] published in 1838 (the year the Blackwells arrived in Cincinnati), listed the city's attractions: thirty churches & places of worship, a lunatic asylum and theatre; a medical college, lyceum, law school, mechanics' institute and some twenty schools. Even by the standards of a young country, it had grown with astonishing speed since its foundation in 1789 when, as Harriet Martineau observed: 'The place had been a cane-brake infested with buffalo.'[3] But forty years later, Cincinnati was quite literally on the move, as she herself bore witness: 'A house was at that moment going up the street, – a rather arduous task, as the ascent was pretty steep. There was an admirable apparatus of levers and pulleys; and it moved on, almost imperceptibly, for several yards, before our visitors began to arrive, and I had to give up watching its march. When the long series of callers came to an end, the strolling house was out of sight.'⁴

By the time the Blackwells arrived in the 'Queen City of the West', as Cincinnati was popularly dubbed, it had some 35,000 inhabitants, many of them German immigrants tempted there by the possibility of a quick fortune. Pigs were the unromantic source of the city's wealth, and Captain Marryat's description of Cincinnati as 'the pork-shop of the Union' was entirely apt.⁵ As one visitor observed: 'They live by their thousands in the streets. Neighbours take one to fatten in their houses, children mount them when they can succeed in catching them, and the police round them up to be exterminated when they propagate too much. Cincinnati is the place where they tie up dogs with choice pork sausage, which the dogs do not even eat.'⁶ Around 160,000 pigs were slaughtered each year, causing local streams to run red with their blood and the nearby countryside to reek of rotting carcases.

Apart from its lucrative pork trade, Cincinnati boasted numerous different industries – ginning, shipbuilding, breweries, mills of all kinds, tanneries, chemical laboratories and iron foundries. Indeed there was so much public confidence in the future of the city, and of the West in general, that many people considered it only a matter of time before it replaced Washington DC as the capital city of the United States. Such optimism and energy convinced Blackwell that he had found the ideal place in which to revive his fortunes and conduct his sugar beet experiments.

Furthermore, there was an aspect of their new life that held deep meaning for them all. Cincinnati was dramatically placed on the Ohio River – the border between freedom and bondage. The city itself had no history of slavery, but many of its leading citizens personally approved of it and in any case were anxious not to damage their commercial interests by upsetting the neighbouring slave states. Thus the Fugitive Slave Law of 1793 (later strengthened by the Compromise of 1850) that entitled slaveholders to pursue escapees across the river was actively upheld. Yet Cincinnati also played a vital role in the Abolitionist movement and especially in the Underground Railroad that assisted fleeing slaves to freedom. The Blackwell children had been steeped in Abolitionism since infancy. If in Bristol slavery had been only a remote concept, in New York it had become a tangible reality. Now, in Cincinnati, they were quite literally on the front line. They had only to look across the Ohio River to the beguilingly attractive Kentucky hills to see territory where slavery was an integral part of everyday life.

During their first weeks in Cincinnati the family lodged with Hannah's kinsman, Sam Browne. They found him depressed and unkempt, which was not surprising since his wife had died just three months before and two of his children were dangerously ill with measles. His daughter died five days after the Blackwells arrived, an event recorded in a curiously censorious manner by Elizabeth: 'Eliza died this morning about 5 o'clock. Mr Browne is in great distress about it, he said a day or two before in the presence of his children, that he *cared more for her than for all the rest put together.* Surely it is a judgement upon him for his wicked partiality.'

Despite this tragedy and their dislike of living with their relatives, the family soon settled in. Elizabeth gave daily lessons to her younger siblings, experimented with different churches each Sunday and began teaching music to the children of some English Abolitionists. She seized every opportunity to explore the countryside around Cincinnati but found the heat oppressive and the Ohio River little compensation for the New York harbour – 'Oh for the sea!' Although Blackwell quickly found suitable premises for a sugarhouse, it was not until 9 July that they were at last able to move into their own rented house in the centre of town.

But at the very moment when the family were hoping for an upturn in their fortunes, Blackwell began to show symptoms of the illness that had plagued him off and on for the previous three years and which throughout the remaining weeks of July recurred with alarming frequency. His family always believed that it was a recurrence of the malaria that he had originally contracted on Long Island. Whatever the cause, by 6 August he was very ill: 'We all stood round his bed that night with the most intense anxiety alternately fanning him. Towards morning he was seized with a fit of excessive restlessness tossing from side to side rolling over & over rising up & throwing himself down again. Oh t'was distressing to behold, he complained of no pain but excessive & indescribably miserable feelings.'

The next day, punctuation entirely abandoned in a frenzy of grief, Elizabeth wrote in her diary:

He is dead. Oh that I should live to write it the support of our house, the kind generous fond indulgent parent is no more. When the physicians came early this morning they thought him if anything better his pulse more regular. Oh how delightedly did we hail the gleam of hope, a dose of arrowroot laudanum & brandy was administered to him, & they all 3 agreed that salivation was the only chance left, so Mr Browne rubbed his joints with mercurial ointment several times, I spunged [*sic*] him with a solution of muriatic acid & through the day we gave him his medicines & as much chicken broth & brandy as he could take, dear dear father he always took whatever I brought him though God only knows what an effort it must have cost him. Towards evening he became worse his breathing became very irregular at one time very loud then sinking so low we could not hear it t'was a terrible sign we sent for Mr Howells & a little before ten for Dr Gross, he looked at my father, shook his head & in silence led my mother to a chair, still even then I could not give up all hope, it *seemed* as if one so loving & so clearly beloved could not die, he had one of those fits of restlessness which was followed by a calm sweet sleep. I had sat all the evening at the head of his bed with his right hand in mine how cold it was with the other I kept off the mosquitoes from him. We all knelt around his bed, *Papa's dying bed*. At 10 minutes past 10 he expired, at that awful moment, the burst of grief that proceeded from each one of us will never be forgotten.

In the intense sticky heat of Cincinnati there could be no delay in burying the dead and Blackwell's funeral took place the following day: 'The undertakers stopped screwing up the coffin to see if his family wished to bid him a final adieu, what a moment was that, I rose & went to it, I wiped the forehead imprinted the parting kiss, the features were awfully changed but still it was part of Papa & as I gave the last *last* lingering look & turned away for ever I felt as if all hope & joy were gone & nought was left but to die also.'

Blackwell's death was utterly devastating. Not only was he a much loved-husband and parent but it was his vision that had brought them all, against their better judgement, to a place that lay on the very edge of civilisation as they understood it. That he should now desert them so suddenly and so finally was impossible to comprehend.

The day after the funeral, while still in a state of numbed shock, the family made an unpleasant discovery. Blackwell, who had always kept his plans and problems to himself, had left his family penniless. Their total resources amounted to $20, leaving Elizabeth with no choice but to take up teaching again only two days after her father's death. Even worse than poverty was the revelation that Blackwell owed $1,500 to Gower Guppy & Co. Ltd, a debt which they could not hope to pay off for years. Forced to put grief to one side, the family concentrated what energy they could muster on simple survival. They were not, however, completely alone. Mr Howells rallied gallantly to their aid while their new neighbours also did what they could to help. With their influence, Sam secured work in the county courthouse and Henry a job in an exchange office. But the main burden of keeping the family afloat rested fair and square on the shoulders of the Blackwell women.

Anna and Marian were still away, so Elizabeth, her mother and Aunt Mary made the initial decisions. For genteel women who needed to earn a living, the words 'decision' and 'choice', had little meaning. In reality, there were only two possibilities: to teach or to take in boarders. Cincinnati may have been on the western frontier of settled America, but education was a high priority and a well-run school could expect to succeed. Less than two weeks after Blackwell's death Elizabeth was writing circulars advertising their new school, and at 9 o'clock on Monday 27 August 1838 she opened the doors to a handful of pupils. Aunt Mary taught the boys in the front room and Elizabeth the girls in the back, but within a few days they were both feeling the strain and longing for Anna and Marian to return. Ten days later the doorbell rang: 'I flew to the door there they were, Anna & Marian as large as life t'was a joyful and sorrowful meeting & smiles & tears sprang up on every face.'

Anna brought a whiff of refreshing unconventionality into the grieving and hard-pressed household. After church, two days later, she announced that she would in future only attend the nearest one since she 'did not care a straw for sermons as she could almost always make better ones herself so never attempted to listen to them'. Anna had grown in confidence since living apart from her family and Elizabeth, for once grateful for her company, was impressed by her eldest sister's new worldliness: 'We extended our walk round the canal conversing on ultra abolition, women's preaching etc.; Anna lent me her drama to read.' They had barely settled into their new routine when tragedy struck again. On 24 September Aunt Mary fell ill and six days later was dead. Fond though she had been of her aunt, Elizabeth had expended so much emotion over her father's death she could feel little at this latest calamity: 'With dear Papa our feelings were so intense that we could notice nothing, but now it seemed as if whatever arrived I should never feel again, not one tear did

I shed, the dreadful blow we first received seems to have rendered me callous to everything else.'

As more pupils enrolled the school began to prosper, but its growing success gave Elizabeth little satisfaction: 'Oh for a lodge in some vast wilderness far away from children.' Outside their long working hours the Blackwell sisters found their chief stimulus in Cincinnati's many and various places of worship, among them the local synagogue and Dr Lyman Beecher's lively Presbyterian church. Beecher, a revivalist in the fieriest tradition, was president of Lane Seminary, established to train young evangelists for a lifetime of preaching in the West. Beecher expected a long fight with Catholics and other 'infidels' for religious control of the vast territories rapidly opening up: 'The great battle will be fought in the Valley of the Mississippi. If we gain the West, all is safe; if we lose it, all is lost.'[7]

His considerable brood of children included Harriet Beecher Stowe, author of *Uncle Tom's Cabin*; Henry Ward Beecher, the charismatic New York preacher who in middle age was at the centre of a notorious sex scandal; and Catharine Beecher, high priestess of housekeeping and all that related to 'woman's sphere'. Her book *A Treatise on Domestic Economy*[8] was enormously influential but, with its emphasis on the importance of women's traditional role in the home, can have held little appeal for the Blackwell sisters.

Catharine was also a respected authority on female education, and it is likely that Elizabeth read her book *Suggestions Respecting Improvements in Education*[9] published in 1829 in which she set out her principles. In her view the shaping of a young woman's character to exert maximum moral influence was much more important than academic achievement. She believed, along with most of her middle-class contemporaries, that the only way to preserve woman's innate moral superiority was to keep her firmly at home within her own 'sphere', aloof from the messy world of business and politics. The notion that women could fundamentally change society for the better and help bring mankind to perfectibility was certainly a theme supported by Elizabeth. But unlike Catharine Beecher she increasingly believed that this would only happen when women were given the same educational and professional opportunities as men, thereby enabling them to realise their full potential and wield their rightful influence.

The Beecher and Blackwell families knew each other well and their lives continued to interweave over the following decades. But soon after their father's death Elizabeth and her sisters began to distance themselves from the melodramatics of Beecher's revivalism and move towards the calmer, more conventional waters of the Episcopalians. By early December Elizabeth thus decided to be confirmed. Her mother, whose Nonconformist faith had intensified since her husband's death, was profoundly distressed: 'Mr Johns called this morning so we had to tell Mamma of what I am about to do, the scene was rather disagreeable to me for I hate having to answer certain questions publicly & above all before Mamma, who began to cry & talk of my soul.'

Certainly Episcopalian services were very different from the camp meetings that her mother attended, which were usually held in the wilderness and lasted several days. These were powerful events attracting hundreds of believers, many of whom travelled huge distances in order to take part. English travellers were curious to witness this peculiarly American expression of religious fervour. Captain Marryat's description of one such meeting (at which Hannah Blackwell was present) does much to explain why Elizabeth, with her more rational approach to the world, had finally lost sympathy with her mother's faith:

The trumpet sounded, as in days of yore, as a signal that the service was about to re-commence . . . On one side of the tent were about twenty females, young, squatted down on the straw; on the other a few men; in the centre was a long form, against which were some other men kneeling, with their faces covered with their hands, as if occupied in prayer. Gradually the numbers increased . . . At last an elderly man gave out a hymn which was sung with peculiar energy; then another knelt down in the centre, and commenced a prayer . . . raising his hands above his head; then another burst out into a prayer, and another followed him; then their voices became all confused together; and then we heard the more silvery tones of woman's supplication. As the din increased so did their enthusiasm; handkerchiefs were raised to bright eyes, and sobs were intermingled with prayers and ejaculations, It became a scene of Babel; more than twenty men and women were crying out at the highest pitch of their voices, and trying apparently to be heard above the others. Every minute the excitement increased; some wrung their hands and called for mercy; some tore their hair; boys lay down crying bitterly, with their heads buried in the straw; there was sobbing almost to suffocation, and hysterics and deep agony. One young man clung to the form crying 'Satan tears at me, but I will hold fast. Help – help, he drags me down!' It was a scene of horrible agony and despair . . . Groans, ejaculations, broken sobs, frantic motions and convulsions succeeded; some fell on their backs with their eyes closed, waving their hands with a slow motion, and crying out – Glory, glory, glory.[10]

Such a scene was in stark contrast to the solitary Christmas Day Elizabeth spent having celebrated her first communion: 'After such a service I could not dine at Mr Emery's & rejoiced at the quiet in which I was left not a single person in the house beside. I had a regular Christmas dinner though not cooked in first rate style.' It was as well that her new religion gave her satisfaction since her work provided none. Her diary entries are peppered with despairing observations on the lot of the schoolmistress: 'How we long to send off the boarders! Such stories as the girls tell, such sulky looks & impertinent actions. How sick & impatient I am of my scholastic duties. By the time school was over I was almost distracted, I really think if anyone had come & offered to me I should have accepted without hesitation.'

Yet Elizabeth's acute longing for England would have made it difficult for her to surrender to any local suitor: 'Lovely, lovely England, when shall I see you again? The more I think of it the more I detest the idea of settling down in America, it would be an insuperable objection to my marrying here.' When Anna suggested that one of them should accompany some friends to England as a governess, Elizabeth found it hard to contain her excitement: 'Twas a plan which set me all in a fidget I could fancy myself already on the ocean with the foam and the blue water dashing around us. I could scarcely attend to Mr John's lecture.' But the scheme came to nothing and it was to be another nine years before Elizabeth set foot again on English soil.

Meanwhile, aged only nineteen, she was locked into a job she hated and, with no money, no lover and little prospect of adventure of any kind, the future stretched bleakly ahead. The arrival, therefore, of William Henry Channing in May 1839 brought a frisson of excitement into Elizabeth's circumscribed world. During the next few months, through his friendship she came into contact with some of the most stimulating ideas current at the time, giving her the courage to reconsider her future along unexpectedly radical lines.

FOUR

Striking Out

Cincinnati was not without intellectual life during the 1830s and 1840s, yet it remained essentially a raw, pioneering town. The streets were colonised by scavenging pigs, meals (uninhibited by conversation) were bolted and tobacco liberally spat everywhere. Elizabeth was disconcerted by the general lack of privacy and the fact that the sexes were far more segregated than was customary in England. To make matters worse, Fanny Trollope's unpopular book[1] documenting her two years in Cincinnati caused the English to be regarded with deep suspicion. But it was not so much the town's lack of sophistication that depressed Elizabeth as the sheer tedium of her daily life.

A monotonous existence was the common lot of middle-class American women at this period and one that most of them accepted without question. Once past puberty their lives revolved around household management, sewing, a little light exercise and, after marriage, a rapid succession of children. The Puritan legacy, inherited from New England, forbade public amusements such as the theatre or circus as well as cards, dancing and novels. Religion, therefore, apart from its obvious spiritual role, was for many people the only bulwark against boredom.

Revivalism and its obsession with the 'second coming' helped Hannah Blackwell to fill the void left by her husband's death. 'I spent an evening . . . with Mr Campbell and a Jewish rabbi and was much struck by their computations as to the second coming . . . all parties are agreed that the time prophesied will come to pass during the present generation – the farthest date they can bring it to will be the year 1865 . . . look abroad over all the earth and you will see that the day is fast approaching . . .'[2]

Against this background of western provincialism and revivalist hysteria, the arrival of 29-year-old William Henry Channing in Cincinnati in March 1839 was an electrifying event for Elizabeth and her two older sisters. He was everything Elizabeth sought in a man; clever, imaginative, modern and chivalrous. Born into a distinguished New England family, he followed his celebrated uncle Dr William Ellery Channing into the Unitarian ministry but was also closely associated with the Transcendentalists.

Based in New England, this group of intellectuals believed, among other things, that if people would only trust in knowledge gained intuitively from nature rather than that handed down by ecclesiastical authority, they would discover greater spiritual truth. Such a philosophy inevitably put them into direct conflict with orthodox religion, yet it was a gospel that offered hope to doubters by allowing them to question their faith without abandoning it. The Transcendentalists' most eloquent advocate, Ralph Waldo Emerson, was an admirer of Goethe, Coleridge and Wordsworth and a lifelong correspondent of Thomas Carlyle. In his first essay, *Nature*, published in 1836, he argued that because there were 'new lands, new men, [and] new thoughts',[3] society should look afresh at its laws, and ways of worship, never forgetting that it was on nature not institutions that man's soul depended for its nourishment.

It was a creed that appealed strongly to Elizabeth. Within a few weeks of Channing's arrival, she was immersed in Emerson's writing and (with Anna and Marian) had joined the Unitarian church. Her own doubts, insensitively dealt with by the Episcopalian minister, she now discovered need not be regarded as sinful but merely a stage in her spiritual growth. Moreover, Channing believed in women fulfilling their potential – unlike a number of other Christian preachers in Cincinnati who preferred to dwell on female inferiority. He swiftly established himself as leader of the small circle of intellectual New Englanders who had settled in the city and in whose company Elizabeth delighted in debating philosophy and religion: 'I well remember the glowing face with which I found Mr Channing reading a book just received "Sit down," he cried, "and listen to this!" and forthwith he poured forth extracts from Emerson's essays.'[4]

The Blackwell sisters' spiritual transfer to the Transcendentalist/ Unitarian camp was not, however, achieved without sacrifice. Catholics and Presbyterians, while disagreeing on most issues, found common ground in their deep distrust of the Unitarians. By embracing the latter, therefore, Elizabeth and her sisters not only caused their mother great distress but found themselves alienated from much of Cincinnati society, with the result that their pupils began to defect in worrying numbers. Nevertheless, despite this and her mother's anxiety over the state of her soul, Elizabeth determinedly set about establishing her intellectual independence. Her friendship with William Henry Channing and his circle was important but she also explored other opportunities to extend her mind. She attended services of faiths as diverse as Roman Catholicism and Swedenborgism[5] and subscribed to lectures on subjects ranging from women's education and morals to metaphysics and mnemonics. It was at a conference on education that she first consciously confronted the issue of women's rights while listening to a debate between a Catholic bishop opposing the free and equal education of women and a liberal lawyer supporting it.

Nor was it only with intellectual and spiritual matters that Elizabeth wished to experiment. On 18 March 1841 she wrote to Henry, 'While speaking of hunting, I want to request you not to barter away all your fire arms but keep at any rate one small gun and bring it with you to Cincin. For I very much want to learn to manage those weapons with skill and I've fixed upon you as my teacher.'[6] The various men who tried to woo Elizabeth during these years were given little encouragement despite her confession that she never remembered a time from her 'first adoration, at seven years old, of a little boy with rosy cheeks and flaxen curls', when she had not 'suffered more or less from the common malady – falling in love'. But she added significantly, 'whenever I became sufficiently intimate with any individual to be able to realise what a life association might mean, I shrank from the prospect disappointed or repelled'.[7]

The one man in Elizabeth's circle who did match up to her high standards was William Henry Channing, but he was already married. She refers to him so often and so glowingly in her letters that it is hard to believe her feelings towards him were merely those of friendship. Nor did her regard for him lessen with the years. In 1848 she wrote to Anna from Philadelphia, 'Truly William Channing is a glorious man! I find him after a seven years absence stronger, more beautiful, friendlier than ever . . . his words to me are deeper, more lasting more life-giving than those of any other human being in fact he does not seem to me like a mortal but a bright spirit from some pure world.'[8] Whatever the true nature of her feelings for him, he was for many years the yardstick by which she judged other men and to which few measured up. To her great sadness, he stayed only two years in Cincinnati before succumbing to religious doubts and returning East.

If Elizabeth failed to find an appropriate suitor in Cincinnati, her older sisters fared little better although Marian attracted a number of admirers and Anna, who by 1843 was living and teaching in Dayton, even became formally engaged to the mayor of Springfield, Ohio. When the family met him, however, they were not enthusiastic (perhaps understanding more clearly than Anna the implausibility of her marrying a country store-keeper) and the engagement slowly unravelled. This episode appears to be the nearest that any of the Blackwell girls came to wedlock. Unlike most of their contemporaries they were unwilling to risk their independence for the uncertainties of marriage. Furthermore, their close family circle provided an especially secure emotional base from which they were reluctant to cut loose.

In 1843, the school, having continued its decline, was finally abandoned and the lost income made good by taking in boarders – the family moved house five times in six years. Henry found work in a flourmill, Sam became a bookkeeper and Anna took a job teaching in Flushing, New York. The following year, Elizabeth, who had been contributing to the family coffers by teaching privately, was at last given an opportunity to strike out independently. In February 1844 she accepted the post of schoolmistress in Henderson – a small town in Kentucky and a four-day journey by steamboat down the Ohio River.

As it was considered improper for a woman to travel alone (even a Blackwell) Elizabeth was escorted by a family friend – M.H. Rose – of whom nothing is known other than he was French and that he and Elizabeth enjoyed long discussions on serious subjects. Whoever he was, it is clear that she liked him. In Louisville, where they stopped for a few hours, she bought some materials for bonnets and the gallant Frenchman showered her with presents. Despite the fog, the stops to take on fresh supplies of green wood and the 'fat, red-faced, incompetent' captain who rammed the boat into a wall, Elizabeth enjoyed the expedition. For much of the journey she stood on the deck with her agreeable companion (whose talents included playing the guitar), watching the dilapidated settlements on the riverbank slide past. But this brief idyll came rapidly to an end as they drew closer to Henderson:

> I grew almost nervous as we were approaching the station, for really all the little towns we passed looked so straggling, dingy, and uninteresting that it appeared to me almost impossible for a decent individual to inhabit them; you may imagine how I felt standing, for the last time, on a bright Saturday morning, with my last friend and remaining piece of civilisation, awaiting my destiny. The clerk approached. 'Madam, we have reached Henderson;' the boat turns, I give one glance, three dirty old frame buildings, a steep bank covered with mud, some negroes and dirty white people at the foot, and behold all that I could see of my future home. The boat touched, I was hurried off, a rough

looking man, upon my enquiring for Dr Wilson, presented his arm, 3 negroes seized my trunks, to 'tote them up,' the steamboat shoved off, & I followed my companion holding his hand to prevent myself slipping down the bank. In the middle of the mud I stopped, to see the last of our friend & civilization; we waved our handkerchiefs, till the boat was out of sight.[9]

Once ashore she found little to reassure her. Although the family with whom she was quartered was friendly enough, the solitary-minded Elizabeth was forced to share a bedroom with three young girls. Her plan to start teaching in the school the following Monday was met with incredulity: 'The schoolhouse was hardly selected, the windows were broken, the floor and walls filthy, the plaster fallen off, the responsible trustees not appointed, the scholars unnoticed.'[10] Appalled at the thought of living in Henderson with nothing to do, Elizabeth galvanised the town's dozy inhabitants into action and soon after her arrival was able to take her seat at the head of fourteen students in the new school. She taught the girls (whom she found much gentler than her Cincinnati pupils) from nine to three. In the lunch break she walked up and down under a tree in front of the schoolhouse trying not to think of home.

Although life in the schoolroom was not unpleasant, there was no escaping the fact that Henderson was unutterably dull. Two years earlier, Charles Dickens had been forced to spend a day there while travelling by steamboat to St Louis and had found the water-pump (which was constantly being detached from its moorings by rooting pigs) the only attraction worthy of his attention.[11] As Elizabeth pointed out in a letter home, it was a place where 'Carlyle's name has never even been distantly echoed . . . Emerson is a perfect stranger, and Channing . . . would produce a universal fainting-fit'.[12]

Her arrival caused a considerable stir and was described by one citizen as 'an epoch in the history of Henderson'.[13] Elizabeth noted that although she won general approval, people were a little afraid of her (a fact that clearly pleased her) particularly when they saw her reading German. She was amused to learn how much she was discussed and that her white teeth were especially admired. This was perhaps not surprising in a community that chewed tobacco almost as naturally as it breathed air. Her habit of taking long walks on her own caused great astonishment and she received dire warnings about blistered feet, wild bulls and furious dogs. The latter were a real threat as 'every negro had his pet dog, the more savage the better, and all the masters follow their example'. Although on one occasion she herself narrowly escaped being attacked by a pack of dogs, Elizabeth claimed she 'would sooner meet a dozen dogs than one negro' and never 'met a slave in a lonely place without a feeling of sudden perspiration'.[14]

But such fears served only to intensify Elizabeth's hatred of slavery, which, while existing in a comparatively mild form in Kentucky, nevertheless confronted her at every turn:

> Since my residence here I have heard of no use being made of the whipping-post, nor any instance of downright cruelty. (It was really meant as an act of hospitality when they placed a little negro girl as a screen between me and the fire the other day!) But to live in the midst of beings degraded to the utmost in body and mind, drudging on from earliest morning to latest night, cuffed about by everyone, scolded at all day long, blamed unjustly, and without spirit enough to reply, with no consideration in any way for their feelings, with no hope for the future, smelling horribly, and as ugly as Satan – to live in their midst, utterly unable to help them, is to me dreadful and what I would not do long for any consideration. Meantime I treat them civilly and dispense with their services as much as possible, for which I believe the poor creatures despise me. The mistresses pique themselves on the advantageous situation of their blacks; they positively think them very well off & triumphantly compare their position with that of the poor in England and other countries; I endeavour in reply to slide in a little truth through the small apertures of their minds, for were I to come out broadly with my simple, honest opinion, I should shut them up tight, arm all their prejudices and do ten times more harm than good. I do long to get hold of someone to whom I can talk frankly; this constant smiling & bowing & wearing a mask provokes me intolerably; it sends me internally to the other extreme, & I shall soon, I think, rush into the woods, stamp & rave, vilify Henderson, curse the Whigs, and rail at the Orthodox, whose bells have been going in a fruitless effort at revivals ever since I have been here.[15]

However depressing her circumstances, Elizabeth did her best to write cheerful letters to her mother, whose spirits were also at a low ebb. She told Hannah she could look forward to a bright future when one of her chief pleasures would be visiting Elizabeth in her beautiful residence near Boston, where she would be living with her adorable husband, her three daughters,

Faith, Hope and Charity and her four sons, Sounding Brass, Tinkling Cymbal, Gabriel and Beelzebub. But she warned her mother, 'Do not imagine however that I'm going to make myself a whole just at present; the fact is I cannot find my other half here, but only about a sixth, which would not do. There are two rather eligible young males here whose mothers have been some time electioneering for wives, one tall, the other short, with very pretty names of good family & with tolerable fortune but, unfortunately, one seems to me a dolt & the other a fool, so I keep them at a respectful distance, which you know I'm quite capable of doing . . .'[16]

In her autobiography, Elizabeth summed up her Henderson experience with a graphic anecdote. The mistress of the house where she was lodging was reclining in her rocking chair one pleasant Sunday morning on the broad veranda listening to the distant church bells and the rustling of the locust trees when her beautifully dressed daughter appeared looking fresh and fragrant on her way to church. At the same moment a slave from the tobacco plantation dressed in dirty rags approached his mistress asking for a clean shirt before attending his church: 'The contrast of the two figures, the young lady and the slave, and the sharp reprimand with which his mistress from her rocking chair drove the slave away, left a profound impression on my mind. Kind as the people were to me personally, the sense of justice was continually outraged; and at the end of the first term of engagement I resigned the situation.'[17]

Although Elizabeth clearly enjoyed her celebrity status in Henderson, the five months she spent there were for the most part disagreeable and unfulfilling. But, on the credit side, she had proved to herself that she could survive loneliness, discomfort and separation from her family – knowledge that would be of great importance to her in future decisions.

* * *

When Elizabeth returned to Cincinnati in August 1844, it was to a new home. In her absence the family had moved to Walnut Hills, a pleasant suburb some 2 miles from the centre of the city. Their finances had improved sufficiently to enable them to live in a comfortable house close to the Beecher clan and to Lane Seminary, which, with its community of ministers, scholars and students, provided them with a pleasant social life. Harriet Beecher, married to the erudite if impoverished Professor Calvin Stowe, was overwhelmed by babies and boarders, but despite the chaos of her household, she continued to write and publish – an achievement that cannot have passed unnoticed by Elizabeth. Aged thirty-five, she already had numerous articles and several successful books to her name and in the summer of 1844 was working on *Immediate Emancipation*,[18] a sketch in which she rehearsed many of the themes that seven years later were to make *Uncle Tom's Cabin*[19] one of the most extraordinary literary phenomena of all time.

Elizabeth settled back into the familiar routine of giving private lessons, attending lectures and mild socialising that, for a time at least, provided a welcome contrast to the intellectual desert she had experienced in Henderson. But her pleasure at being home soon gave way to the familiar dissatisfaction with her life and with her lack of scope to change it. Meanwhile, the fact that two of her sisters were enjoying living in New York – Anna teaching and Emily studying – served to emphasise the stagnation of her own existence. There were, however, some encouraging signs emanating from the East suggesting that Elizabeth was not the only female in the republic to be frustrated with her 'sphere'. For these women, Margaret Fuller's book, *Woman in the Nineteenth Century*, published in February 1845,[20] was the first literary attempt in America to argue their case.

Margaret Fuller was a formidable intellectual and one of the most able American critics of her time. A close friend of Emerson and Channing, she was an influential member of the Transcendentalist group and for several years edited their magazine *The Dial*, to which Elizabeth enthusiastically subscribed. Her views on women's rightful place in the world influenced Elizabeth deeply, particularly as she sought to change men's attitudes by persuasion rather than aggression. 'By Man I mean both man and woman: these are the two halves of one thought. I lay no especial stress on the welfare of either. I believe that the development of the one cannot be effected without that of the other. My highest wish is that this truth should be distinctly and rationally apprehended, and the conditions of life and freedom recognised as the same for daughters and sons of time; twin exponents of a divine thought.'[21]

This was entirely in tune with Elizabeth's own instincts. She too wished to see her sex enjoy wider opportunities and exert more social influence but not at the expense of men or the sanctity of motherhood.

It was around the time that Margaret Fuller's book was published that Elizabeth first began to think seriously of medicine as a career. A neighbour, terminally ill (probably with uterine cancer), complained to her that the examinations she had undergone at the hands of unskilled male doctors were as unpleasant as the disease itself. In this judgement, she was not alone. Most women, for reasons of modesty, were reluctant to visit a physician on gynaecological matters. Elizabeth's dying friend told her how much she would have preferred to consult a woman doctor and provocatively asked her why, with her scholarly nature and longing for purpose in life, did she not consider becoming one herself?

Elizabeth initially dismissed the suggestion on the simple grounds that she found the human body, especially its infirmities, repelling. But the idea was surprisingly hard to ignore. She later claimed that one reason for changing her mind was the need to distract herself from 'the disturbing influence exercised by the other sex'.[22] This was tacit admission of her strong physical attraction to men (and as she revealed when in her sixties, to one young man in particular) but, equally, of her despair at ever finding a husband whom she could respect intellectually. If she could not marry on her own terms, she would prefer not to marry at all. If, however, she remained single, Elizabeth knew that she would have to support herself and was emphatically not prepared to spend the rest of her life as a schoolmistress. Thus, with the Transcendentalists actively encouraging women to think more boldly of their role in society, she began to consider a medical career with renewed interest.

The sheer audacity of the project was one attraction yet there were many factors contributing to Elizabeth's decision to become a physician. Her neighbour's situation had made her conscious of an obvious need and a ready market for women doctors, and she was convinced that she possessed both the intellectual capability and the physical perseverance to stay the course, however demanding. Since childhood she had yearned to achieve something worthwhile in her life but at the same time, after years of feeling overlooked, she also wanted to be noticed.

Elizabeth did not suffer fools gladly and her unsocial behaviour had more to do with self-protection from people who bored her than with any lack of ambition. However disagreeable her sojourn in Henderson, the brief fame that she had enjoyed there had left its mark. If she succeeded in qualifying as a doctor, she would not only be achieving something of real importance but would win widespread recognition. And, unlike many women of her class whose families would have recoiled at the thought of their daughters embarking on such a course, Elizabeth knew that she could rely on her family for emotional if not financial support.

In her autobiography, Elizabeth gives the impression that the decision to pursue medicine was akin to a religious calling, instinctively sensing that such a daring step would be more socially acceptable if given the spiritual authority of a vocation. Since she never claimed that she was motivated by an urge to heal the sick, this calling had to be of a wider, moral significance: 'I felt that I was severing the usual ties of life, and preparing to act against my strongest inclinations. But a force stronger than myself then and afterwards seemed to lead me on; a purpose was before me which I must inevitably seek to accomplish.'[23]

Elizabeth, like so many of her contemporaries, assumed that the perfect society was potentially within human grasp but she also believed that it would never be achieved until women exerted a greater moral influence on the world. In order to accomplish this, they would have to fundamentally change their outlook, expand their intellectual horizons beyond household matters and prove to themselves, as well as to men, their ability to follow a serious occupation. Medicine, with its waiting female constituency, was an obvious place to start and Elizabeth was ready to lead the way. Indeed, the more she thought about it, the less she could see any logical reason why a woman should *not* be a doctor. 'Winning a doctor's degree gradually assumed the aspect of a great moral struggle, and the moral fight possessed immense attraction for me.'[24] Although she would never have confessed to it, she was also driven by a less lofty but equally strong motive – sibling rivalry. There was no question that a medical degree would mark a most splendid triumph over Anna.

To test the feasibility of her plan, Elizabeth began canvassing opinion in her immediate circle. To her disappointment, Harriet Beecher Stowe thought the project impracticable although she did concede that it might be useful if actually brought to fruition. She warned Elizabeth of the immense prejudice she would meet which, if she did not succeed in crushing, would most certainly crush her. It was a view echoed by everyone Elizabeth consulted. The reason for their objections was clear. With the exception of Oberlin College (which had opened its doors to women and African Americans in 1834) the female sex was excluded from all further education – so how could she expect to enter a medical college where, working alongside men, she would be exposed to all the embarrassment and unseemliness of the human body? It was hard for anyone, even among the Blackwells' reform-minded friends, to imagine an arena in which an educated, middle-class woman could be further removed from her proper sphere. But Elizabeth refused to be deterred: 'This verdict . . . was rather an encouragement than otherwise to a young and active person who needed an absorbing occupation.'[25] By the spring of 1845 and with as yet no idea of how to set about it, she had quite made up her mind to become a doctor.

History could offer Elizabeth little encouragement and few role models. Before the nineteenth century, the names and careers of only a handful of medical women were recorded, despite the fact that in earlier centuries the mixing of herbal medicines and the practice of midwifery were considered a natural part of any woman's life. John Evelyn, when referring to his mother and sister in his diary of 1686, could have been describing the activities of countless women of the period: 'Their recreation was in the distillorie, the knowledge of plants and their virtues for the comfort of the poor neighbours and the use of their family.[26] But until medicine acquired a sound scientific basis, it was inevitably associated with the supernatural and as a result of the sixteenth and seventeenth centuries' obsession with witchcraft, a good many women who dabbled innocently in herbal remedies were branded as witches and hanged.

The plain fact was that until medicine was transformed by science (with a few exceptions)[27] there was little anyone of either sex could do to impede serious illness. As the medical writer and practitioner Hildegard of Bingen (1098–1179) put it so aptly, herbs were God's gifts; either they produced a cure or the patients died 'for God did not will that they should be healed'.[28] The best that could be done for the sick was to soothe their pain and make them as comfortable as possible – a role to which women were traditionally more fitted than men.

But by the mid-seventeenth century, at least among the gentry, women had even been edged out of the one area over which they had previously held undisputed sway – midwifery. Forceps were introduced about this time and, as in England surgical instruments could only be legally handled by a member of the Barber Surgeon Guild, this necessarily excluded women who were rarely if ever permitted to join the guild. The eighteenth and early nineteenth centuries saw European and American women forced to retreat yet further from formal medicine as an increasingly scientific approach to the subject gathered pace. The profession became more coherently organised with the advent of medical schools, examinations and associations and within this new establishment there was no place for women.

In 1845, when Elizabeth was considering how to proceed, no woman had yet succeeded in entering a modern medical college but it was likely that she knew of Harriot Kezia Hunt (1805–75), 'a zealous little creature',[29] who had defeated enough local prejudice to build herself a flourishing medical practice in Boston. She never acquired a medical degree (her two attempts to enter the Harvard medical school were rejected), but in this respect she was no different from the majority of male 'doctors' practising between 1790 and 1840. Hunt's patients were mainly women and her remedies consisted largely of common sense, hygiene, hydrotherapy, herbal medicines, and a good deal of psychotherapy. Despite the lack of scientific training or support from professional bodies, her practice prospered, and towards the end of her life she was able to say: 'I have been so happy in my work; every moment is occupied; how I long to whisper it in the ear of every listless woman, do something if you would be happy.'[30]

Although the difficulties Elizabeth confronted in 1845 were formidable, she had one advantage over her predecessors. The obstacles that had in earlier times prevented them from being doctors were largely ill defined. With the arrival of medical schools and professional qualifications, these restraints were now clearly visible. It followed, therefore, that if only Elizabeth could gain admission to a medical college and pass its examinations, theoretically there was nothing to stop her practising medicine like any man.

Although the first medical school in America had been founded in Philadelphia as early as 1765, formal medical education had been slow to replace the earlier apprenticeship system, so that when Elizabeth was viewing her options, medical colleges were still a relatively new concept. At that time Paris was generally acknowledged as offering the best training and initially Elizabeth thought of going there. But for a young Anglo-Saxon woman of good background Paris was thought to be even more dangerous than a medical school. The combination of the two was unthinkable. A distinguished Cincinnati doctor who had visited the Paris schools, and who was consulted on the matter, declared authoritatively that the method of instruction in Paris was such that no American or English lady could stay there six weeks, and the scheme was abandoned.

Elizabeth met with more disappointment when a friend whom she understood to have pledged substantial financial help in the event offered her only a $100 loan. As she reckoned that she needed at least $3,000 to cover all her expenses over the coming years, this misunderstanding was a major setback. Rejecting the loan, she decided that her only course of action was to find a teaching job that would enable her to save enough money to pay for her medical training herself.

In the early summer of 1845 she was invited, through one of Anna's New York friends, to take up a post teaching music at a school in Asheville, North Carolina, whose principal, the Reverend John Dickson, had previously been a doctor. As it was, in any case, the normal procedure for a medical student to apprentice himself to a physician for several years before entering medical college, this seemed a promising arrangement. Like any other medical student, Elizabeth hoped to gain instruction in anatomy, chemistry, botany and the use of drugs as well as access to the doctor's library. The drawback was that Dr Dickson was no longer a practising physician and she would have to pay her way by teaching, leaving less time for study. Furthermore, she knew that even if this venture was successful, there was still no guarantee that any medical school would accept her.

But by now she was utterly resolved to study medicine and prepared to take any necessary risk. For the first time in her life, she felt driven by purpose; one, moreover, that she believed was of significance to society. Her self-appointed mission was to prove that a woman had the intelligence and tenacity to practise medicine among her fellows with as much dedication and competence as the best-qualified male. By demonstrating this, she would establish that a woman's potential was as limitless as a man's and that, like a man's, it required fulfilment. Elizabeth was convinced that when this became widely understood, society would at last be able to move forward towards that elusive perfectibility. It was a grand vision and although she realised that it could not be accomplished without immense personal effort and sacrifice, failure was not an option.

FIVE

The Carolinas

In 1845 the journey from Cincinnati to Asheville was a hazardous undertaking that took many days to accomplish. Travel by stagecoach was not only expensive and complicated but also dangerous as anecdotes of drunken drivers galloping their horses down steep mountain roads made alarmingly plain. It was decided, therefore, that Sam would drive Elizabeth to Asheville in a hired wagon drawn by the family's own horse, Fanny. The carriage was packed with her two trunks, bandbox, carpetbag, books, sewing and chessboard as well as a bucket, tin cup and two loaded pistols.

She set off for her new life at 7 o'clock on the morning of 16 June 1845 seated in front of the buggy alongside Sam, with fourteen-year-old Howard wedged uncomfortably in the back. It was an unpropitious start. The weather grew increasingly dismal and Elizabeth's head ached intensely: 'The more Sam joked, the more dolorous I became, & at last when he brought out a whole string of puns, and the clouds began to pour down torrents, I in despair changed places with Howy in the back of the carriage, & said I would try to sleep.'[1]

But Elizabeth always loved the excitement of a journey and the next day, after a good night's sleep, she prepared to enjoy herself to the full. Each day they started at 5 o'clock, rested between twelve and three and then travelled on until nightfall. Wherever they had their midday meal, Elizabeth ordered additional cold food that provided them with supper and breakfast the following morning. She considered the middle hours of the day as her 'missionary time, when I made a point of ingratiating myself with the landlady, & then I proceeded to lecture her on the importance of education, the advantages of thrift & industry, the necessity of a charitable Christian spirit & various other highly important moral subjects – it was wonderful how they all agreed to everything I said & asked me if my husband was a preacher.'[2]

Not content just with proselytising, Elizabeth liked to sing as they travelled through Kentucky and Tennessee 'to the amazement of all the rural passers by, for I considered it a piece of philanthropy to produce some little activity in the sluggish minds we met'.[3] Their nightly billets were rough and ready. At one, the woman of the house sat by Elizabeth as she undressed, examining every discarded article with wonder and not leaving her until she was finally in bed with the blankets over her head. Such invasions of privacy, however, mattered little to Elizabeth compared with the discomfort of having to manage without a commode for a whole week. After some days, they arrived at the foot of the Appalachians:

> At nightfall we reached the Cumberland ford . . . to our consternation we found the tavern was on the opposite side & not a house for some miles back, on the bad road we had just travelled. We stood by a broad rapid flowing river, the water rushing over steep rocks just below & shut in by gloomy forest covered mountains. To cross would have been madness at that dark hour so we were just meditating the feasibility of camping out, when it occurred to Sam to try & make the people on the other side hear us. He accordingly ascended a little hillock & putting his hands on his side hallooed with all his force – the rushing water & the dismal unearthly shrieking of the frogs, was the only reply. Again he shouted, but in vain – it was growing blacker every minute when a twinkling light appeared amid the trees, and a man's voice shouted hi – he told Sam to come straight across as we could make out through the blowing & rushing & shrieking around us – Sam was afraid, and urged him in vain to send someone across to guide us – after continual useless entreaties Sam turned quickly to me, 'shall I say there's a lady in the carriage too frightened to venture over?' – 'If you choose, said I,' much amused. The somewhat apocryphal statement was accordingly shouted across, and a boy on horseback speedily splashed in & we followed as well as the darkness would permit, the water coming in at the bottom of the carriage immense stones nearly upsetting us & the demon like frogs screaming horribly in our ears – I certainly was glad when I found myself in bed sinking into a comfortable doze.[4]

Elizabeth, always deeply stirred by nature, found the countryside they passed through startlingly beautiful. They enjoyed the grandest view of the entire journey from the top of Clinch Mountain. Sam recorded how he 'saw E at the summit a hundred yards before me, as I supposed triumphing in having mastered the clamber, but on closer inspection, found that she was cutting a series of capers in state of extreme exhilaration'.[5] They looked down on 'an immense ocean of hills, bounded in the extreme distance by faint blue cloud capped mountains – every rounded hill was richly wooded, here & there a little open valley – not a sign of human life but the flitting clouds giving every variety of light & shade & causing a strange vast movement over the scene'.[6]

After travelling for eleven days they finally reached Asheville, which lay on a high plateau surrounded by mountains. Because of its remoteness the small town had changed little since its foundation forty-seven years earlier. There were three public buildings to serve the town's 500 inhabitants, two churches and a courthouse complete with stocks and whipping post. Among the twenty-odd stores only a jeweller and a silversmith dealt in goods not essential to fundamental survival. The Female Academy, where Elizabeth was employed to teach music, was Asheville's most prominent institution and its principal, Dr John Dickson, one of the town's leading citizens.[7]

Despite Dr and Mrs Dickson's warm welcome, Elizabeth became deeply depressed at the thought of her brothers' imminent departure and the realisation that once they were gone she would be two weeks' journey from anyone she knew – utterly dependent on her own resources. The night before they left, she sought divine comfort:

> I retired to my bedroom and gazed from the open window long and mournfully at the dim mountain outlines visible in the starlight – mountains which seemed to shut me away hopelessly from all I cared for. Doubt and dread of what might be before me gathered in my mind. I was overwhelmed with sudden terror of what I was undertaking. In an agony of mental despair I cried out, O God, help me, support me! Lord Jesus guide, enlighten me. My very being went out in this yearning cry for Divine help. Suddenly, overwhelmingly, an answer came. A glorious presence, as of brilliant light, flooded my soul . . . a spiritual influence so joyful, gentle, but powerful, surrounded me that the despair which had overwhelmed me vanished. All doubt as to the future, all hesitation as to the rightfulness of my purpose, left me and never in after-life returned.[8]

This may have been a genuine mystical experience but was more probably the result of the strenuous mental effort to fight sinking morale and acute homesickness. Indeed, even Elizabeth questioned the source of her feelings: 'I sometimes think I am deluding myself, that imagination has conjured up this spiritual influence.'[9] It nevertheless marked the beginning of an intensely religious phase in her life even if, as a nominal Unitarian, Elizabeth did not believe in the divinity of Christ. It is unlikely, however, that she confessed such unorthodox views to her new employer, the Reverend Dr Dickson, whom she judged kind, worthy and dull.

As a Presbyterian, Dickson disapproved of light reading and games of any sort, so that Elizabeth was forced to play chess against herself, while the only books available in his household were some thirty volumes gathered under the tempting title *The Sunday School Teacher's Library*. Dr Dickson had developed an effective technique to deter the many hopeful young men who tried to court his female charges. He ushered them into his dimly lit parlour where the family was gathered for evening worship and subjected them to hours of prayers and Bible reading. After this experience, Elizabeth noted, they tended not to call again.

But if Elizabeth complained about leading 'a perfect nun's life' in the Dickson household, she was far from complimentary about the people she did meet: 'On Saturday I found myself obliged to accept the third *daily* invitation and found myself one of a *watermelon* party, which was to ride to a country house about four miles off and feast upon those detestable sweet cucumbers. After tea we played tricks with cards and seated just opposite me was such a coarse fat red-faced vulgarian that I began to doubt my own identity . . . I turned home in a fit of deep disgust at my associates yet half reproaching myself for the feeling when I had been received with the utmost hospitality.'[10]

At the root of Elizabeth's revulsion was the knowledge that the people with whom she was socialising were slaveholders. Slavery in North Carolina was practised with greater severity than in Henderson, and in Asheville slaves made up almost 20 per cent of the population. As a means of reconciling her conscience with her circumstances, Elizabeth was determined to do everything in her power to educate them despite the fact that it was illegal to teach slaves to read or write. Undeterred, she set up a Sunday school: 'I felt a little odd, sitting down before those degraded little beings, to teach them a religion which the owners professed to follow whilst violating its very first principles . . . As I looked round the little room and saw those ladies holding forth to their slaves, fancying that now they were fulfilling every duty and were quite model mistresses I longed to jump up, and, taking the chains from those injured, unmanned men, fasten them on their tyrants till they learned in dismal wretchedness the bitterness of that bondage they inflict on their brethren.'[11]

The anomaly of Elizabeth's position was brought sharply into focus when one of her Sunday school pupils died. She attended the simple funeral where she learned that her red-faced fellow guest at the watermelon party was the owner of the dead woman and was aggressively demanding his money back as he had bought her only a few days before her death. A short time later, Elizabeth witnessed the same man's father's funeral – an immensely lavish event that filled her with revulsion. Now that she was herself seeking emancipation, her hatred of slavery had become more personal and intense.

The Sunday school experiment was short-lived, as Dr Dickson would not allow Elizabeth to break the law however worthy her objective. Her frustration at not being able to speak out remained a running sore but she was at least able to make progress in her medical studies. Despite Dr Dickson's conservative manner, he fully approved of Elizabeth's ambition to become a physician and willingly gave her access to all his medical books.[12] She even performed her first dissection – on a cockchafer. For someone who remembered with disgust a school demonstration of a bullock's eye resting on its cushion of bloody fat, and who was normally sickened by the functions of the human body, dissection posed obvious problems. But when a fellow teacher presented her with a large beetle in a scent box she seized the opportunity: 'I thought it would make a capital beginning, so I laid it carefully on white paper, held it with a hair pin, and severed the head from the body with my mother of pearl pen knife – but I found no brains, and very little that was interesting inside – then I split it boldly down the middle, and laid the parts elegantly in a shell for inspection – the anatomy was by no means interesting but the moral courage exercised was of a high order, and I don't believe I shall feel more squeamish in using the real dissecting knife than I did in cutting up that beetle.'[13]

While Elizabeth was wrestling with beetles and reactionary slaveholders in the Deep South, Anna was immersed in an earnest social experiment in New England. In the summer and autumn of 1845 she lived at Brook Farm, a few miles from Boston, where, in 1841, a group of Transcendentalists had formed a utopian community. The Brook Farmers set out to prove that, despite differing social and intellectual backgrounds, a group of people could live in harmony with each other and their natural surroundings, supporting themselves entirely by their own efforts.

Fundamental to their beliefs was the notion that an individual must earn his own living and not rely on the labour of others. If the farm was successful, they hoped it would encourage others to turn their backs on an increasingly urban and industrial world and live a simpler, more wholesome life. Many of the intellectuals Elizabeth most admired were drawn into the orbit of Brook Farm – Ralph Waldo Emerson, William Henry Channing, Margaret Fuller, Orestes Brownson, Nathaniel Hawthorne, and the editor of the *New York Tribune*, Horace Greeley, among them.

Brook Farm provided a heady mixture of social and intellectual excitement for Anna, who all her life rebelled against monotony. In old age she recalled the few months that she had spent there as the happiest of her life. But the seeds of the farm's ultimate failure were sown when its supporters attempted to implement the rigorous ideas of the French social philosopher Charles Fourier. John Stuart Mill cynically described Fourier as one who set out 'to accomplish all things by means of co-operation and of rendering labour agreeable, and under whose system man is to acquire absolute power over the laws of physical nature; among other happy results the sea is to be changed into lemonade'.[14] Fourier's disciple (and Anna's occasional lover), Albert Brisbane, was responsible for importing the philosopher's highly organised system to the United States where it became known as 'Association'. During the 1840s, around forty utopian communities were founded on Association principles but, despite their participants' enthusiasm, none of them survived long.

Elizabeth was deeply attracted to the communitarian ideal and remained so long after the movement had passed its peak in America. She never entirely lost hope of setting up a Blackwell commune along Associationist lines and even tried to persuade her brothers to take up occupations that would serve such a project. She was an enthusiastic subscriber to the *Harbinger*, the magazine produced at Brook Farm and edited by W.H. Channing, who acted as the community's informal spiritual adviser. His attempts to reconcile Fourierism with Christianity produced precisely the brand of Christian socialism that came to be at the heart of Elizabeth's own philosophy. Certainly the *Harbinger*, with its offer of hope for a better, more tolerant world, contrasted starkly with the harrowing reports of human bondage she read about in the local North Carolina press.

If Anna's accounts of intellectual life in New England and her proximity to the dynamic W.H. Channing gave Elizabeth cause for envy, the months she spent at Asheville were by no means unhappy. Her medical studies were successfully launched; Dr Dickson proved a loyal supporter (despite his short legs and 'contemptible body') and his wife a warm friend and ally. But by December 1845 it was clear that the school would have to close. Apart from Dr Dickson's anti-slavery sentiments and the difficulty of his being a Presbyterian in a Methodist town, he had four sons who were considered 'great stumbling blocks in a young ladies' school'.[15] Elizabeth was again faced with the problem of what to do next.

She decided to take up an invitation to stay with Dr Samuel H. Dickson, John Dickson's younger brother and one of the most respected doctors in the South, who lived in Charleston in a large old-fashioned house surrounded by a garden full of tall evergreens.

Samuel Dickson was the most distinguished doctor Elizabeth had yet encountered – and the richest. A Yale man, he had graduated in medicine from the University of Pennsylvania before setting up practice in Charleston. When Elizabeth met him he was also a professor at the Medical College of South Carolina, which he had helped to found. Dickson was an unashamed slaveholder but Elizabeth nevertheless found much in him to admire, for he was also a self-professed 'Unitarian-Rationalist and Free-thinking-Man'.[16] Above all he believed passionately in medical education and was entirely sympathetic to Elizabeth's ambitions. He willingly acted as her tutor and gave her free access to his well-stocked medical library which, when catalogued in 1843, numbered over 1,000 volumes.[17] He also found her a job. His sister-in-law, a Mrs Du Pré, owned a girls' boarding school, housed in a fine old building overlooking the bay, where she employed Elizabeth as a music teacher for the next fifteen months.

Predictably, the school gave Elizabeth little satisfaction: 'Then what must be my situation, shut up in a nunnery of southern girls, from which all men are driven as if they had the plague, teaching seven hours a day and spending the remaining hours in a bedroom of the third story with an old rheumatic lady somewhat deaf, a good tempered but inexperienced village girl and a young lady worn out with teaching, as companions?'[18] But at least she began to make real progress with her medical studies: 'I'm studying in good earnest & am quite interested in the books that Dr has lent me; for about a week ago, I went round there, got them & had such a pleasant little visit, that I almost danced home, & I really now feel like *a medical student*.'[19]

Elizabeth's days were so filled with teaching, study and introspection that there was little time for simple amusement. But she had not entirely forgotten how to enjoy herself:

I was invited to a pleasant little party a night or two since & got some delightful ice cream & strawberries, but my intensest [*sic*] satisfaction in the eating time was derived from a fine juicy pineapple that I devoured by the seashore . . . everything conspired to make it perfect, a high wind driving about the light fleecy clouds, a long smooth shelly beach, the real boundless ocean an intense green with white crested waves which broke on the shore with a rush & a roar tossing up seaweed and foam & then my pineapple so mellow sweet and juicy, so fragrant cool and refreshing, so abounding in pleasant memories and present delight oh it was too charming. I smelt & ate & looked, jumped & shouted, kicked the foam, ran after the waves & fought the wind till my companions thought I was crazy. It was the revelry of the senses in the palace of Beauty & I shall never forget the exquisite pleasure of the moment, 'twas the gratification of many years longing, how I wished for you all![20]

A less sensual experience was listening to John C. Calhoun deliver a powerful though, in her opinion, 'erroneous' address to a rapturous audience on States' Rights. A concert she attended left an equally lasting impression. She was so affected by the violinist's performance that she wrote: 'His playing bewildered me; I did not understand it. It seemed to me like a chaos that might become a world of beauty could I only find the word that should reduce it to order.'[21] Apart from the rare ecstatic moment on a mountain peak or the seashore, Elizabeth distrusted confusion, instinctively seeking to impose order on the messy business of human existence, and on her family in particular.

It is clear from her letters of this period that Elizabeth had come to regard herself as head of the family. Her brothers and sisters were either too unpredictable or unassuming or simply too young to adopt this role and her warm-hearted mother so distracted by her children's flight to other faiths that she felt bound to concentrate her efforts on the uphill task of saving their souls. The fact that Elizabeth lived so far from her family did nothing to deter her from dispensing instructions to everyone on everything from how to conduct their businesses and friendships to which piece of music her youngest sister should practise. Henry, always on the brink of backsliding, received many anxious letters from his sister, occasionally couched in biblical rhetoric:

A lightning flash arouses the sleeping wretch to full consciousness of the awful abyss below the slender branch by which he hangs, he sees a hand stretched out to help him but the lightning flashes & he cannot reach it and clings shrieking to his frail support while the winds dash him against the rocks and the thunder rolls fearfully about. The lightning seems a messenger of wrath to fill him with horror & mock him with a hope of help he strives in vain to reach – but blessed is that light for as he struggles in agony it changes to a beam of the rising sun the stormy darkness disappears, the hand approaches and with a thrill of rapture inexpressible, the received one is clasped in the arms of his saviour . . . [22]

Often ill and prone to depression, Marian was the sister who posed least threat to Elizabeth's authority. No doubt this was partly why she was also the sister to whom Elizabeth felt closest and with whom she wanted to plan her future: 'I cannot live alone I shall want a friend & adviser in a hundred things & if you can put up with the company of a rather queer being, we will consult and act together & I know we shall find enough for fifty hands to do & I trust Dr & Miss Blackwell will find their time so full of objects of engrossing interest, that they will have no time for unhappiness or metaphysical discussion.'[23] Although Elizabeth gave Marian constant encouragement with her housekeeping and friendships, painting and poetry, she was not eager to see her married. When a year later she heard that Marian's romance with a missionary bound for India had fallen through, she wrote to her: 'Oh the idea of going to India, it seems to me so terrible, that I would charge you never to entertain it . . . the idea of your union seems to me now utterly impossible.'[24]

Anna was the sibling who continued to worry and irritate Elizabeth the most. 'What shall we do about Anna, I don't know; I live in constant fear about her for her head is so giddy, that I dread her falling into some inextricable hole . . . I wrote to her more than a month ago, but I don't know whether I may ever get an answer for I spoke very plainly though kindly and almost fear she may be offended with my unpleasant truth.'[25] Certainly Elizabeth did not approve of her translations of George Sand's novels: 'I hope sincerely Anna may get well & not translate any more French novels, unless they be better than the one she selected, I do not think *Jacques* calculated to improve the generation, either in taste, intelligence or morality.'[26]

If Anna was as exasperating as Marian was soothing, in Emily (now twenty-one) Elizabeth discovered a force to reckon with. Unlike Elizabeth, Emily was tall, but in other respects the two sisters had more in common than they cared to admit. Both were highly intelligent, single-minded and serious, with a reputation for awkwardness in society. 'How many degrees above zero is Emily's sociability?' Elizabeth asked her mother in a letter written shortly after Christmas 1846.[27] Sensing competition, Elizabeth treated Emily with a wariness absent from her dealings with the rest of the family: 'Your letters always come to me like a puff of north wind. I generally brush my hair and straighten my things after reading them.'[28]

Certainly Elizabeth was well aware of her younger sister's academic accomplishments. In a letter to Marian she wrote that she had heard that 'Mill is much improved in her manner & expanded . . . quite a genius but this I won't mention lest Emily should see it'.[29] Because of the five-year gap between them Elizabeth enjoyed a head start, but it was an advantage that she could no longer take for granted. Despite their deep mutual respect, her efforts to maintain her superiority over Emily coloured their relationship throughout their fifteen-year medical partnership and for the rest of their lives.

During the hot summer months of 1846, Mrs Du Pré took her school to Aiken, about 100 miles inland from Charleston, where it was cooler and healthier. Although Elizabeth enjoyed living there among the sweet-smelling pines, she found the incompetent Mrs Du Pré and her young charges increasingly irritating. She was also acutely aware of the passing years and more anxious than ever to press on with her medical studies. By November she was left alone in Aiken (apart from two slaves – one given to strong drink and the other to scolding), with the responsibility of handing over the school building to its next incumbent. As the hickory trees turned a brilliant yellow and the autumn winds howled around her, Elizabeth reviewed her options.

SIX

Medical Student

In late October Elizabeth returned to the cold, draughty house in Charleston where acute boredom and painful chilblains combined to make her even more determined to secure a formal medical education. At the same time Marian, clearly uncertain about her sister's commitment, confronted her with a number of probing questions to which she received a robust response:

Let me set your mind at ease with regard to professional horrors, fastidiousness, love of beauty & so forth. My mind is fully made up, I have not the slightest hesitation on the subject . . . the thorough study of medicine I am quite resolved to go through with and all opposition only makes my determination stronger. It has become one of my fixed ideas – you know I have such . . . The horrors & disgusts I have no doubt of vanquishing. I have overcome stronger distastes than any that now remain & feel fully equal to the contest. As for the opinion of people, I don't care one straw *personally* though I take so much pains as a matter of policy, to propitiate it . . . and mean to let my light shine before as many men as possible . . . You also speak of my want of bodily sympathy being an objection. If I understand what you mean, I think it would prove of the most valuable assistance possible. I suspect you were thinking of that unlucky dose of lobelia I once gave you when I grew angry because you groaned and groaned, and obstinately refused to drink the warm stuff that would relieve you. I think I have sufficient hardness to be entirely unaffected by great agony in such a way as to impair the clearness of thought necessary for bringing relief . . . but I am sure the warmest sympathy would prompt me to relieve suffering to the extent of my power; though I do not think any case would keep me awake at night, or that the responsibility would seem too great when I had conscientiously done my best.[1]

Towards the end of the year Elizabeth received some encouragement. Through the Brook Farm network she discovered that there were several physicians working in New York City prepared to offer private tuition to women. With this in mind, she wrote to Emma Willard (a pioneer in girls' education) hoping for a job in her progressive school at Troy – still some 150 miles from New York but at least closer than Charleston. Instead of offering her work, however, Mrs Willard put her in touch with an eminent Quaker doctor in Philadelphia, Dr Joseph Warrington. This was a promising introduction since the Quakers were committed to female education and Philadelphia had the best medical schools in the country.

Elizabeth wrote at once to Warrington but had to wait three long months for a reply. When it eventually arrived, it was disappointingly ambiguous. But if Warrington was not on the most radical wing of the Society of Friends, he was well meaning and sincere. In his old-fashioned Quaker prose he offered qualified support to Elizabeth despite his personal opinion that 'woman was designed to be the helpmeet for man, and that in the responsible duties of relieving ills which flesh is heir to, it is appropriate that man be the *physician* and woman the *nurse*'. He had nonetheless diligently researched the matter by asking the most liberal-minded women he knew for their views on female doctors and been surprised by their unanimous disapproval. As a result, he was not optimistic about Elizabeth's medical future: 'I confess, my dear lady, that I with thee see many difficulties in the way to the attainment – firstly, to the acquisition of the kind and amount of education thou art aware is necessary as a *capital stock* with which to begin the enterprise which has been opened to thy mind; secondly, that after years spent in the attempt the popular mind will be found barred against thy mission of love and humanity; but I beg thee to believe with me that if the project be of divine origin and appointment it will sooner or later surely be accomplished.'[2]

It was hardly the resounding endorsement that Elizabeth had hoped to hear, but Warrington's sympathetic tone and Dr Samuel Dickson's encouragement convinced her that she should nevertheless move to Philadelphia. To save money she travelled by sailing ship (despite the appalling seasickness from which she always suffered), arriving there with her carefully hoarded savings in May 1847. She found lodgings with a Dr and Mrs William Elder, who rapidly became her close friends and supporters. Elder had been a doctor before turning to the law, but by the time Elizabeth met him he was making his living by lecturing on a range of subjects from anti-slavery to anti-masonry. 'A thinking talking couple', both he and his wife were disciples of Fourier and committed Associationists.

Even more encouraging was Elder's obvious delight in discussing medical matters and his willingness to help Elizabeth with her studies.

Warrington and Elizabeth met shortly after her arrival in Philadelphia. Despite his reservations concerning women doctors he did all he could to help her, taking as much interest in her affairs as if she were a member of his own family. He allowed her to visit his patients, use his library and attend his lectures and also consulted his colleagues on the best way for her to proceed with her studies. But Warrington's kindness could not disguise the profession's deep prejudice against the whole concept of female physicians. Indeed, Elizabeth's hopes of a medical education seemed to grow daily more remote.

There were, however, a few doctors in Philadelphia sympathetic to her cause who suggested that she study medicine in Paris disguised as a man.[3] They were well intentioned but misunderstood her motives. Elizabeth was by now utterly determined to qualify as a doctor but the whole point was to do so as a woman. She did, in fact, reconsider Paris because she had heard that women were allowed to attend the free government lectures there even though they were barred from taking the diploma. But for many Americans Paris was a latter-day Gomorrah, and the idea that Elizabeth, a single woman, might live in such an evil city provoked a horrified reaction. It was not tales of sin and iniquity, however, that dissuaded Elizabeth from going to Paris; 'If the path of duty led me to hell I would go there; and . . . not think that by being with devils I should become a devil myself.'[4] She stayed because she had embarked on a political crusade and it was one that she wanted to fight and win in America.

Elizabeth applied first to each of the four leading medical colleges in Philadelphia, but the few professors prepared to meet her either prevaricated or refused her outright. She then tried the New York schools and a number of smaller colleges but met with equal failure. It soon became clear that, apart from sharing in the general conviction that woman's intellect was too weak to study medicine, the doctors were fearful of female competition, believing their profession to be already overcrowded. If women were allowed to practise medicine, there was the alarming possibility that female patients, anxious to safeguard their modesty, might defect in droves to their own sex. As one doctor put it to Elizabeth: 'You cannot expect us to furnish you with a stick to break our heads with.'[5]

Elizabeth's attempt to enter medicine also came at a time when orthodox doctors were already under pressure from alternative movements such as

Thomsonian medicine and homeopathy. Samuel Thomson (1769–1843), a layman from a poor, rural background, had caught the public mood with the introduction and clever marketing of his medical theories based on herbs and common sense. His botanical concoctions may or may not have cured people but they were certainly a great deal less unpleasant for the patient than the bleeding and blistering or the mercury, arsenic and other poisonous substances so freely prescribed by mainstream doctors.

Thomson's constituency was primarily among the poor, but homeopathy, already fashionable in Europe and developed by trained doctors, soon became popular with more affluent Americans. By the late 1840s the so-called regulars were therefore on the defensive and had little appetite for entering into yet more competition with female doctors. Indeed, one reason why the American Medical Association was established in 1847 was to protect the regulars from quacks, women and anyone else who threatened their authority or their pockets.

Unable to study either formally or informally in any of the regular medical schools, Elizabeth was at least able to receive private instruction from Dr Jonathan Allen, a farmer's son who had graduated from the University of Pennsylvania and whose gift for teaching anatomy was widely recognised. She described him as 'lymphatic' but liberal and eager to help. Dr Elder accompanied her on her first visit to Dr Allen, but as a poor but respectable family was living in the house it was decided that she would not after all need a chaperone.

Allen introduced her gently to anatomy by choosing a human wrist to dissect at her first lesson. To her surprise, she found the complex structure aesthetically beautiful and, perhaps for the first time, was absorbed by the subject rather than the campaign: 'I begin to think there is more love of science in me than I have hitherto suspected. I have certainly had lately some moments of exquisite pleasure when a momentary flash of truth has dazzled me in regard to the great laws which govern the world.'[6]

Of the many treatments on the market claiming to harness Nature's own healing powers, hydropathy was one of the most popular, attracting large numbers of enthusiasts including Anna Blackwell. For some weeks she was a patient at Dr Schiefendecker's water-cure establishment in Philadelphia, where she joined fellow reformers and Associationists in frugal meals, long, healthy walks and, above all, submission to water in all its manifestations. They drank huge quantities of it, were submerged in it for long periods and spent hours wrapped in wet sheets. The water-cure movement fitted perfectly into the reforming culture of the 1840s, promising as it did 'to proclaim and hasten the advent of UNIVERSAL HEALTH, VIRTUE, AND HAPPINESS'.[7]

Having survived the rigours of her water cure, Anna joined Elizabeth as a lodger in the Elder household. After a separation of several years, the sisters had much to discuss. Both continued to be deeply attracted to Fourier's ideas, which Elizabeth was studying closely: 'I am reading Fourier with great interest and drinking in every hint I can pick up, in relation to the *Law of the Series*, which presents to my mind the most beautiful glimpses of order & true science that I have ever yet been blessed with.'[8]. But, until her conversations with Anna, she was unprepared for the sexual implications of Fourier's theories as interpreted by his American prophet, Albert Brisbane, a 'notorious libertine'[9] and the man whom many of the idealists at Brook Farm blamed for its failure after he persuaded them to adopt Fourier's complicated system of social conduct.

Anna, in love with Brisbane and influenced by his liberal views on sex, did her best to convince Elizabeth of the virtues of free love:

Anna horrified me greatly with her doctrines, & the dreadful pictures of society she unfolded to me – simple constancy she laughed at, advocated a continual change of lovers as fancy dictates, thought it right that a woman should love one man for his beauty, another for his fortune, or rank, or talent, that it was natural and proper that a woman should unite with a man, because he could make her the mother of beautiful children; when women are better developed, their passion will be as great as man's, & that this highest material enjoyment & most beautiful act of life should be cultivated & refined with the utmost care . . . she regretted much, that she was not of a passionate nature & that all the women of our family were so deficient in that way.[10]

Anna's wistful reference to her lack of passion suggests that for her free love was more theory than practice. Elizabeth, who spent much of her subsequent career trying to redress the injustices of sexual behaviour, was instinctively traditional, as her vigorous justification of marriage in a letter to Marian six months earlier had made clear: 'I cannot bear to have the subject of marriage touched for great as its present evils are the fault does not seem to me to lie in the institution but in society . . . in a true society will not love be as lasting as life? It cannot be meant that one love should succeed another, that there is no peculiar fitness in two but that constantly changing fires should be lighted in the heart, that would be degrading & horrible.'[11]

But, with Brisbane frequently in Philadelphia and spending much of his time with Anna, even Elizabeth came to be influenced by his unconventional views. She wrote to Marian that 'he makes me think' and went on to admit: 'I have realised strange new ideas since I have been here, I feel as if I had grown years in experience.'[12] Having been finally persuaded by Anna's shocking accounts of marital hypocrisy, secret intrigues and disgusting vices, she too was ready to 'abolish marriage and everything else if you will but only let us be honest and open about it and tear off the hideous veil of falsehood'.[13] For the first time in her life Elizabeth seriously questioned wedlock as the ideal social model. Knowing how quickly she herself tired of any man to whom she was attracted, she now wondered if this was not true for most married couples: 'I began to understand how rich life might be, where these free beautiful relations prevailed, how ever varying the enjoyment, how grand the knowledge to be gained . . . the isolated household seemed a prison, marriage a hopeless slavery.'[14]

Exactly where Elizabeth's exploration of love and sex might have led her can only be guessed since it came to an abrupt halt on 27 October 1847 when she opened a letter from the Dean of Geneva Medical College in upstate New York:

> Geneva: October 20, 1847.
>
> To Elizabeth Blackwell, Philadelphia.
>
> I am instructed by the faculty of the medical department of Geneva University to acknowledge receipt of yours of 3rd inst. A quorum of the faculty assembled last evening for the first time during the session, and it was thought important to submit your proposal to the class (of students), who have had a meeting this day, and acted entirely on their own behalf, without any interference on the part of the faculty. I send you the result of their deliberations, and need only add that there are no fears but that you can, by judicious management, not only 'disarm criticism,' but also elevate yourself without detracting in the least from the dignity of the profession.
>
> Wishing you success in your undertaking, which some may deem bold in the present state of society, I subscribe myself,
>
> Yours respectfully,
> CHARLES A. LEE
> Dean of the Faculty[15]

Elizabeth 'fairly jumped for joy'.[16] Warrington had advised her to apply to a dozen country colleges with the hope that these more commercially driven institutions might prove less bigoted than their city counterparts.[17] The Dean's letter proved that the strategy had worked. Another from the students increased her delight yet further:

At a meeting of the entire medical class of Geneva Medical College, held this day, October 20, 1847, the following resolutions were unanimously adopted:

1. *Resolved* – That one of the radical principles of a Republican Government is the universal education of both sexes; that to every branch of scientific education the door should be open equally to all; that the application of Elizabeth Blackwell to become a member of our class meets our entire approbation; and in extending our unanimous invitation we pledge ourselves that no conduct of ours shall cause her to regret her attendance at this institution.

2. *Resolved* – That a copy of these proceedings be signed by the chairman and transmitted to Elizabeth Blackwell.

T.J. Stratton, Chairman[18]

But this fine principled document, which Elizabeth later had copied on parchment and was to become one of her most treasured possessions, gave little hint of the real story. In fact, the behaviour of both faculty and students was a good deal less high-minded than their letters implied. If Elizabeth's loyal ally Dr Warrington had not written to the Geneva medical professors urging them to accept her, they would have rejected her unanimously. Warrington, however, was a distinguished Philadelphia doctor, and the faculty was anxious not to offend him. The professors decided, therefore, to refer the decision to the students, confident that they would treat Elizabeth's submission with derision. And, just to make sure, the students were told that even one expression of dissent would be enough to refuse her a place in the College. It seemed an elegant solution to an awkward problem but, as one of the students later recounted, it went disastrously wrong:

For a minute or two after the departure of the Dean, there was a pause, then the ludicrousness of the situation seemed to seize the entire class, and a perfect babble of talk, laughter, and catcalls followed. Congratulations upon the new source of excitement were everywhere heard, and a demand was made for a class meeting to take action on the Faculty's communication.

A meeting was accordingly called for the evening, and a more uproarious scene can scarcely be imagined. Fulsome speeches were made in favor of admitting women to all the rights and privileges of the profession, which were cheered to the echo. At length the question was put to vote, and the whole class arose and voted 'Aye' with waving of handkerchiefs, throwing up hats, and all manner of vocal demonstrations.

When the tumult had subsided, the chairman called for the negative votes, in a perfectly perfunctory way, when a faint 'nay' was heard in a remote corner of the room. At the instant, the class arose as one man and rushed to the corner from which the voice proceeded. Amid screams of 'cuff him,' 'crack his skull,' 'throw him down stairs,' a young man was dragged to the platform screaming 'Aye, aye! I vote aye.' A unanimous vote in favor of the woman student had thus been obtained by the class, and the Faculty was notified of the result.[19]

While some of the students may have been genuinely in favour of Elizabeth's admission, it later emerged that a number of them had assumed that the whole episode was a hoax devised by students from a neighbouring college. Elizabeth, however, blissfully unaware of these intrigues, relished her moment of triumph. In personal terms, it was vindication of the contrary path she had chosen; but it was also much more. By accepting her, Geneva Medical College had publicly acknowledged the possibility of women working in the public arena. If other institutions followed, women could begin to look forward to a bright new future. With this inspiring vision, Elizabeth set out for Geneva on 4 November 1847, full of optimism and quite ignorant of the real circumstances surrounding her admission: namely that the professors regarded her as a mistake and the students as a joke.

The journey took a frustrating two days, but she finally reached Geneva late on the night of 6 November. The following day was a Sunday but, anxious not to incur the expense of another night in a hotel, she risked offending local propriety by hunting for lodgings. The first landlady she approached refused to negotiate terms on the Sabbath but offered instead to escort her to church. Had Elizabeth wished to attend church that day, she could have chosen from no fewer than nine different denominations: Episcopalian, Presbyterian, Dutch Reformed, Associate Reformed,

Methodist, Baptist, African Baptist, Roman Catholic and Universalist were all represented in the small town of under 4,000 inhabitants.[20] The Sabbath did not, however, prevent Elizabeth introducing herself to the Dean and being formally admitted to the medical department of Geneva College as student number 130.

Perched on the northern tip of Seneca Lake, Geneva was a dull little country town with only its fine views to recommend it. During Elizabeth's first few days there even these were blotted out by incessant rain, but she did at least find comfortable lodgings at a reasonable price ($2.50 including lights and fuel per week) and two days after her arrival was ready to launch herself into her studies. She had already missed a month of the sixteen-week session, she had no books and no idea where to go for lectures: 'My head was bewildered with running about the great college building – never going out of the same door I went in at.' But despite her initial confusion, she reported to Marian that 'I came home so happy and encouraged I blessed God most heartily and wanted to throw my arms round him and mend his stockings'.[21]

The reason for her cheerfulness was the unexpectedly warm welcome she had received. Her chief champion in the faculty was James Webster, the professor of anatomy, whom she described as a 'fat little fairy . . . blunt in manner and very voluble'.[22] His enthusiasm for her mission was so infectious that even the Dean, Dr Charles Lee, began to believe that Elizabeth's presence might after all prove beneficial to his college. On 9 November, she recorded in her journal: 'My first happy day; I feel really encouraged. The little fat Professor of Anatomy is a capital fellow; certainly I shall love fat men more than lean ones henceforth. He gave just the go-ahead directing impulse needful; he will afford me every advantage, and says I shall graduate with *éclat*. Then, too, I am glad they like the notoriety of the thing, and think it a good "spec." '[23]

Elizabeth arrived at a propitious moment in the college's history. Its fine new building, complete with dome and pilasters, contained a good lecture theatre and dissecting rooms, a well-equipped laboratory and an excellent collection of specimens – facilities of an unusually high standard for a mere country college. By the time Elizabeth enrolled, Geneva College had a full faculty of seven professors, several of whom were of notably high calibre. Although medical schools were still relatively new in the mid-nineteenth century, even the minor ones were generally considered a big improvement on the apprenticeship system.

Medical students were required to study for several years under a qualified doctor and then attend two full courses of lectures (the second simply repeating the first). They were expected to know Latin and natural philosophy and to write a thesis before graduation. The cost of each sixteen-week course (October to January) was $62 with an additional $20 for graduation. The curriculum was designed to cover three main areas: the basic sciences, the theory and diagnosis of disease and its treatment. In practice, lack of scientific knowledge, scarcity of corpses for dissection, limited opportunity to examine bones and organs at close quarters, large classes, and a want of clinical experience meant that the newly qualified physician left Geneva College little equipped to cure anyone.

A sample of Elizabeth's class notes illustrates some medical views current at the time:

> Enquiry should always be made as to the presence of menstruation; during its continuance, the nervous system is unusually excited, and the pelvic viscera particularly susceptible, powerful remedies should be avoided at this time, as hysteria, or unnatural affection of the menstrual function may result . . . Opium the most valuable article of the Materia Medica – differs from most other narcotics in being a safe remedy . . . Blood letting – blood a vital stimulus in disease – abstract and lessen excitement – if blood could be completely abstracted from an inflamed part, we could completely arrest the inflammation, for blood is the fuel which feeds the fire of inflammation . . . Greatest tolerance of bleeding is in congestion of the brain, 40oz can be borne . . . for children where repetition is necessary, leeches should be used . . . leeches can go where cups cannot be applied, & tenderness would forbid.[24]

The students were mostly local boys destined to become doctors only because they were thought too stupid to study law. They were a rowdy lot with little instinct for learning, as one of the students, Samuel Craddock, made plain in a letter to his sister written just two weeks before Elizabeth's arrival:

> If a student does not carry himself just so, he is hissed and cheered (by stomping) in a manner that is not at all pleasant, Last week there was a drunken Irishman fell from a wagon, and struck his head on the pavement and killed himself, and the night after he was buried, some of the students (as I have been informed) went to the graveyard to dig up his body for a subject

to dissect, but when they commenced this task they were shot at by some one who was there to watch the grave. They have tried every night since but have not been successful for the grave has been watched by other Irishmen – last night just before I went to bed I heard a number of guns fired off in the direction of the grave yard but I have not heard the result.[25]

Thrust into this boisterous, macho society, Elizabeth, unsurprisingly, was the object of much curiosity. But her quiet determination, sober dress and cool response to the paper darts aimed at her in lectures quickly won the young men's respect and produced a marked improvement in their behaviour. Most of them were several years younger than her and soon began to treat her like an older sister. Elizabeth in turn grew fond of them, although she gave short shrift to any student foolish enough to show a romantic interest: 'One poor fellow has certainly fallen into the depths – he waylays me at church for permission to accompany me home – he sits at college with his eyes fixed most inexpressibly upon me and starts and blushes if my eye meets his – he begged me to let him call upon me "from the purest and most disinterested motives," and now he is too timid to come . . . though a handsome fellow, I should be very sorry to let him touch my hand.'[26]

Elizabeth determinedly clung to her composure even under the most difficult circumstances:

A trying day, and I feel almost worn out, though it was encouraging too, and in some measure a triumph; but tis a terrible ordeal! That dissection was just as much as I could bear. Some of the students blushed, some were hysterical, not one could keep in a smile, and some who I am sure would not hurt my feelings for the world if it depended on them, held down their faces and shook. My delicacy was certainly shocked, and yet the exhibition was in some sense ludicrous. I had to pinch my hand till the blood nearly came, and call on everything; but I sat in grave indifference, though the effort made my heart palpitate most painfully. Dr Webster, who had perhaps the most trying position, behaved admirably.[27]

She was also deeply shaken by the public examination of a female patient: 'Twas a horrible exposure; indecent for any poor woman to be subjected to such a torture; she seemed to feel it, poor and ignorant as she was. I felt more than ever the necessity of my mission. But I went home out of spirits. I hardly know why. I felt alone. I must work by myself all life long.'[28]

Despite such testing experiences, Elizabeth was totally engrossed with her studies and therefore infuriated when Webster asked her to withdraw from certain lectures. The professor of anatomy was in a difficult position. He had reached the reproductive system, and even the liberal-minded Webster shrank from discussing genitalia in the presence of a young woman, especially since it was his practice to enliven these particular talks with plenty of vulgar jokes and obscenities. But he had not reckoned with Elizabeth's iron resolve.

She at once wrote him a letter pointing out that the study of anatomy should excite profound reverence; and that, while she readily understood the potential for embarrassment, surely, if the subject was approached in a pure and chaste manner, no medical man (whose mind, it was assumed, was already elevated and purified by anatomical study) could possibly raise objections. But, to make the situation easier for the professor, she would take care to sit at the back of the room. Finally, with instinctive political skill, she offered to stay away if it were the wish of her fellow students. Elizabeth waited outside the amphitheatre while Webster read out her note, and was profoundly relieved to hear the students give their noisy assent to her presence at the lectures.

Elizabeth was at Geneva to study medicine but there is little doubt that she also enjoyed her celebrity status. Paradoxically, alongside the social awkwardness and introspection that was so much part of her character there was a yearning to be centre stage. In Geneva, far from the competitive and disturbing influence of Anna, she was, for once in her life, playing the leading role and she loved it. In many respects, she spent the rest of her life seeking to recapture the exhilaration she experienced in Geneva as a triumphant pioneer – not that she was by any means universally admired. Many of Geneva's citizens regarded her as a wanton woman, a freak and a traitor to her sex. Nevertheless, despite all the difficulties, her first three months at Geneva College were among the most satisfying of her whole life.

Elizabeth condemned the January end-of-term examination as 'not much of a test' and passed it easily. But success was followed by disappointment when the letters of introduction she had been promised failed to materialise. These were of vital importance. Without them she knew she stood little chance of gaining admission to a hospital in Philadelphia, which was where she planned to spend the nine months between college sessions. The faculty may have begun to enjoy the notoriety of having a woman student but they were not yet ready to back her publicly – the promised letters were never written. On 24 January 1848, Elizabeth's landlady gave her a celebratory dinner of oysters. The following day she left for Philadelphia.

SEVEN

Facts of Life

Elizabeth stopped briefly in Manhattan to visit her old mentor, Dr Samuel Dickson (by then a professor at New York University) before returning to Philadelphia and her lodgings with Dr and Mrs Elder. To boost her finances, she gave private music lessons and sold several short stories to a monthly magazine, but her main concern was to find some way of gaining the clinical experience she knew she so badly needed. Without letters of recommendation this was no easy matter but, to her surprise and delight, the board of Blockley Almshouse (the Guardians of the Poor) gave her permission to live in the hospital for six months as an observer. Anxious not to waste any time, Elizabeth entered its grim gates on 9 March 1848.

Standing on the west bank of the Schuylkill River, on the edge of Philadelphia, Blockley was a daunting sight. The oldest institute of its kind in America, it housed some 2,000 inmates who between them harboured every conceivable physical and mental disorder. The four-storeyed buildings formed an immense square and housed a lunatic asylum, an orphanage, separate hospitals for men and women, a poor house, dissecting rooms, and a drug store. In addition a farm provided much of the patients' food and a factory their clothing.

Elizabeth was given a large room off the women's syphilitic ward on the third floor from which, through huge windows, she could see the river and Philadelphia on the far bank. Her presence inevitably caused a stir: 'It was very trying to me, all eyes and such queer eyes were fixed on every movement.'[1] To the women patients Elizabeth was a curiosity to peer at through the keyhole, but to the young doctors she was an object of contempt – a woman who had committed sacrilege by venturing so monstrously far from her proper place:

I get very little from the physicians, they keep aloof, view me with suspicion, think I am stepping out of women's sphere, have not courage to act freely before a lady, have some fear that I shall detect ignorance or malpractice etc all which reasons prove complete barriers between us and I doubt much whether they can be overcome. This feeling on their part makes me uncomfortable, I always have the sense of intrusion when I enter their wards, and though I actually have as much right there as they, unfortunately I have a sensitiveness about the matter which I cannot overcome.[2]

Despite this inhibiting atmosphere, Elizabeth was determined to extract all that she could from her stay in Blockley. She studied in her room until the hostile young doctors had finished their rounds and she felt free to visit the wards. Here she was permitted to examine the sick and (by some of the more friendly older physicians) to watch procedures such as blistering, bleeding or injecting. During her first few weeks there, she noted with disappointment that the wards contained only convalescent or charity cases: 'At present there is no epidemic in the house. If one should come it would interest me greatly. I am not afraid myself of sickness, but it is very certain if I should be ill, none of their nostrums would go down my uncontaminated throat. I should trust to fresh air, cold water and nature and live or die as the Almighty pleases.'[3]

It had taken Elizabeth only a few hours in the hospital to realise that hygiene and nature were more likely to cure the sick than most of the standard medicines with which they were regularly dosed. Having concluded that the majority of drugs were useless if not actually detrimental, Elizabeth determinedly set about learning as much as she could from her own observations since it soon became clear that no one was prepared to teach her. She diligently visited the different wards, interviewed the nurses ('who are mere hands and never think'[4]), drank tea with the staunchly Quaker matron, read in the library and whenever possible talked to the chief physician, Dr Benedict, 'the loveliest man the Almighty ever created',[5] even though he never had time to answer her questions. But such arbitrary encounters were little compensation for the lack of real instruction. She went to bed each night increasingly frustrated by how little she had accomplished.

In fact, the importance of clinical experience in a physician's training was a relatively new concept. When the hospital had moved from the centre of Philadelphia to the other side of the river in 1834, a number of doctors had opposed the decision on the grounds that the distance would make it inaccessible to medical students. The Guardians' response was telling: 'Except that the lecture is made more imposing by the subject of it being present, and possibly the students' attention to the case being fastened by the display, we know of no benefit which can accrue from it which would not equally result from the case being lectured on in the absence of the patient, from the notes of the physician, which form, in reality the basis of the lecture.'6

Despite all the difficulties and disappointments, Elizabeth's months at Blockley were of great value. She had faced hardship in life but nothing to prepare her for the experiences of the almshouse. She had learned from Brisbane and Anna that sexual intercourse was not necessarily confined to marriage; but until Blockley she had not encountered prostitutes ravaged with syphilis, victims of rape or single mothers who were themselves still children. She was also deeply shocked by the presence in the hospital of so many young servant girls made pregnant by their employers: 'All this is horrible! Women must really open their eyes to it. I am convinced that *they* must regulate this matter. But how?'7 In terms of understanding the human condition, Blockley was a steep learning curve and provided Elizabeth with much of the data she used later in her career to speak authoritatively on matters of sex and morality:

> I see frequently many painful sights, of course in so large a population of the lowest class of society much of what is loathsome in disease and shocking in morality comes before me. Within one week, a lunatic scalded himself to death, one woman cut her throat, another fell down a cellar opening and broke both legs, they died the following day, another jumped over the banisters, breaking both ankles and last night, just as I had got to sleep, I was roused by a running and screaming in the gallery and many windows suddenly hoisted. I jumped out of bed, ran to my window and looked out. There in the moat that surround the building, a depth that made me dizzy, lay a white heap covered with blood uttering a terrible sound half groan, half snort. It was a woman who had been confined in the next room to mine and had jumped out of the third story window. There she lay in the moonlight in agony while lamps held out of the windows by pale, half-dressed forms, threw a strange glare upon the terrible sight. All tongues clattered away, some wondered, some lamented and some laughed till my soul sickened . . . At last the jingling of keys was heard and the great gates, creaking on their hinges, were thrown open. The steward with two men carrying a lantern descended, lifted the girl roughly up and bore her shrieking with pain into the hospital.

I jumped into bed again, tried to think of the angels and at last fell asleep to dream it over again.[8]

In striking contrast to the Blockley inmates were the earnest Associationists whose group Elizabeth rejoined on her return to Philadelphia. Despite the failure of Brook Farm and other similar experiments, Fourier still had many followers in the late 1840s committed to his vision of the ideal society. Elizabeth was put in charge of 'social culture' although she would have preferred to be part of the more political 'indoctrination' group. She was expected to direct the ladies in their sewing – in her view yet one more act of self-denial. In any case she soon lost patience with the Philadelphian Associationists, none of whom, in her view, were of first-rate intellect. She was particularly exasperated with the women in her group whose lack of ambition and intellectual grip she considered a reflection of womanhood in general. She wrote despairingly to Emily in Cincinnati:

Oh Milly, what is to be done with the women? Woman is not as great morally as Man is intellectually . . . she sticks more to the letter of propriety, obeys more stoically the ten commandments in their narrowest sense . . . has more commonly a perverted religious sentiment quite as bad as it is good . . . It is not her intellectual inferiority I lament – I believe as a rule, an intellectual difference will always be – but if she were only grand in those qualities attributed to her, all might be well but the petty, trifling, priest ridden, gossiping, stupid inane women of our day, what can we do with them?[9]

In this diatribe against her own sex, Elizabeth failed to pay tribute to the growing number of women who *were* currently making great efforts to enhance their lives and change their status in society. Emboldened by the various reform groups in which so many of them were active – most importantly Abolitionism – these women were beginning to organise themselves into an effective lobby, demanding greater equality under the law and, by the 1840s, a political voice. On 19 July 1848 about 300 of them – white, mostly middle-class and in their mid-thirties – gathered at Seneca Falls, New York (only a few miles from Geneva) to convene the first formal women's rights meeting. Having so roundly condemned women for their triviality, Elizabeth should have been delighted. But, curiously, she made no attempt to join the new movement or take advantage of its proffered support. On the contrary, her private references to these early feminists were patronising and disparaging: 'I have curious glimpses into the American female world just now. There are several little eddies of women in various places that whirl back and forth so furiously that really placed within their sphere one would think the whole of womankind was about to rise in general rebellion and trample down all the common rules of society. Standing on the bank, however, these little eddies assume their relative value and that I fancy is a very small one.'[10]

There were several reasons for Elizabeth's view of these embryonic suffragists. Believing that women had only themselves to blame for their social predicament ('woman . . . has not felt the soul too large for the body'[11]) she was convinced that Association held the key to their future progress – not aggressive sectarianism. Furthermore, she placed herself among the prophets ('I know that I am one of the elect'[12]) whose calm, rational message would one day be heard above the common babble, guiding men and women alike to a better world. Meanwhile, she had no wish to see this grand vision derailed by a partisan group whose muddled philosophy and foolish methods only served, in her view, to alienate the male sex, thus endangering the whole female cause.

There is a further explanation for her antipathy to the women who gathered at Seneca Falls, though it is one she would have vigorously denied, for it presents a curious paradox. While unquestionably dedicated to women's emancipation, Elizabeth (in common with others who have made history by breaching the gender barrier) thoroughly enjoyed being a lone woman in a man's world. She was not eager to join a movement in which she risked becoming just one of the crowd. She liked to lead from the front, and if she needed additional resources to help her fulfil her vocation she preferred to rely on her own family.

Nevertheless, Elizabeth wrote an impassioned response to a Seneca Falls delegate setting out her formal public position:

My whole life is devoted unreservedly to the service of my sex. The study and practice of medicine is in my thought but one means to a great end, for which my very soul yearns with intensest [sic] passionate emotion, of which I have dreamed day and night from my earliest childhood, for which I would offer up my life with triumphant thanksgiving, if martyrdom could secure that glorious end – the true ennoblement of woman, the full harmonious development of her unknown nature, and the consequent redemption of the whole human race. 'Earth waits for her queen.' Every noble movement of the age, every prophecy of the future glory, every throb of that great heart which is labouring throughout Christendom, call on woman with a voice of thunder, with the authority of a God to listen to the mighty summons to awake from her guilty sleep, and rouse to glorious action to play her part in that great drama of the ages, and finish the work that man has begun.

Women are feeble, narrow, frivolous at present: ignorant of their own capacities, and underdeveloped in thought and feeling: and while they remain so, the great work of human regeneration must remain incomplete; humanity will continue to suffer, and cry in vain for deliverance, for woman has her work to do, and no one can accomplish it for her. She is bound to rise, to try her strength to break her bonds: not with noisy outcry, not with fighting or complaint; but with quiet strength, with gentle dignity, firmly irresistibly, with a cool determination that never wavers, with a clear insight into her own capacities, let her do her duty, pursue her highest conviction of right, and firmly grasp whatever she is able to carry.

It was in the next paragraph of her mission statement that Elizabeth underlined the fundamental difference between herself and the women's rights activists. While they held men responsible for their lack of fulfilment, she placed the blame squarely on women themselves:

Much is said of the oppression woman suffers: man is reproached with being unjust, tyrannical, jealous. I do not so read human life. The exclusion and constraint woman suffers, is not the result of purposed injury or premeditated insult. It has arisen naturally, without violence, simply because woman has desired nothing more . . . But when woman, with matured strength, with steady purpose, presents her lofty claim, all barriers will give way, and man will welcome, with a thrill of joy, the new birth of his sister spirit, the advent of his partner, his co-worker, in the great universe of being.

But Elizabeth left her correspondent in no doubt of her commitment to social reform, summing up her own position with a fine, statesmanlike flourish: 'If the present arrangements of society will not admit of woman's free development, then society must be remodelled, and adapted to the great wants of all humanity. Our race is one, the interests of all are inseparably united, and harmonic freedom for the perfect growth of every human soul is the great want of our time.'[13]

In May 1848, a frisson of excitement ran through the small band of Associationists in Philadelphia with the news that the dedication of their new hall was to be attended by a number of the movement's Boston luminaries – many of them ex-Brook Farmers. For a few days at least, Elizabeth was distracted from the horrors of Blockley and the inadequacies of her sex, as she was drawn into preparations for the big day. Among the Boston guests was William Henry Channing, whom Elizabeth had not seen for seven years but who had lost none of his magnetism. In a letter to Anna, she wittily described the event:

> The dedication of our hall . . . was considered, I believe the most important occasion and really on the whole, was quite a pleasant affair with speeches, music dancing, capital ice cream and a large audience who seemed to enjoy themselves much. We had Grace Greenwood there who is cutting a dash in Philadelphia and the monthlies [the ubiquitous women's magazines] and a Miss Somebody who writes poetry for the same interesting magazines and a Miss Somebody else who is esteemed very literary. Bye the bye I heard lately a most important suggestion as to the reason why young ladies contribute so largely to *monthly* periodicals . . . There was really a touch of brilliance about the evening. The Committee of arrangements went to bed in peace with all mankind. As to our worthy president, I am afraid another such week would reduce him to a state of permanent insanity. The endless calculating and planning, the world of responsibilities weighing upon him, the anxiety lest the Boston friends or the New York friends or the anywhere else friends should be disappointed or dull or anything else, the dread lest the Philadelphians should be shocked or too much enlightened or too little enlightened, the fear lest the single minded members of his little union should not come up to the expectations of everybody everywhere – oh it was too much for one frail mortal to endure . . .[14]

Although increasingly disillusioned with her fellow Associationists, Elizabeth remained steadfastly committed to the movement's philosophy, describing it as her living faith. Her plan to form a Blackwell community that (under her leadership) would succeed where others had failed became more focused. The two elder boys' successful business would underpin the enterprise financially while her mother and Marian took charge of domestic arrangements. She and Emily would work on medical and social matters,

George would be in charge of farming (Elizabeth urged him to study agriculture for this purpose), and the artistic Ellen could take care of all cultural needs. Howard, whose apathy and indifference to life exasperated Elizabeth, was more difficult to place; but in time he too would be found a niche in this ideal community into which other like-minded individuals would be drawn. Anna's role was to be Elizabeth's mouthpiece: 'I never shall be an orator – but you might be a grand one and won't you lend yourself to me? If I could only borrow your talent and fill it with my own thought and burning indignation, what a commotion I'd raise in the world!'[15]

This future dream scenario was shattered by the harsh realities of the present. The Blackwell family which, in Marian's words, had 'never been inconveniently burdened with money'[16] was in the middle of one of its recurrent financial crises as a result of Sam and Henry's commercial collapse. In 1845 they had invested in a milling business but, after struggling unsuccessfully with it for two years, Henry decided to become a sugar refiner. Leaving Sam to look after the family in Cincinnati, he went to New York to learn the business from Dennis Harris, their father's former manager. In April 1848 he returned home to set up his own refinery, but it was only in operation a few weeks before it burned to the ground.

From the smouldering ruins of his sugarhouse, Henry considered joining Elizabeth in medicine. She gave him little encouragement. However warmly she would have welcomed his companionship, she knew it would be many years before he made any money out of doctoring. And, despite Sam's and Henry's current failure, the family's hopes for a secure financial future were still pinned firmly on them, with every expectation that their next business venture would succeed. Meanwhile there were further worries. Marian suffered continually from depression and dyspepsia, while Anna, more neurotic than ever, had parted unhappily from Brisbane and was chronically short of money. In a vain attempt to recapture the magic of Brook Farm, she lived in a number of experimental communities, none of which survived for long. Emily, equally unfulfilled, earned a tiny salary from a dreary teaching job in Cincinnati; Ellen painted without profit and the two youngest boys were as yet unemployed.

Into this gloomy picture came a ray of hope in the shape of their English cousin Kenyon Blackwell. He and his recently widowed brother Samuel were prosperous iron masters in Staffordshire, and seemed anxious to help their beleaguered relations. In 1848, Kenyon made a long visit to America, spending much of August at the Elders' house in Philadelphia where

Elizabeth fed him each evening on dry bread, peaches and coffee. She thought him enchanting – intelligent, affectionate, generous and fully supportive of her ambitions. He brought her two valuable medical books and Henry the offer of a job in the ironworks. But the incurably romantic Henry, who already had a string of love affairs behind him and who was again working for Harris in New York, decided to stay in America – influenced, perhaps, by his current attachment to Harris's daughter. Whatever his motives, Elizabeth (who had earlier claimed that she could never settle in America) applauded his decision:

> You are wise to remain in New York. I cannot imagine that England would suit you as a residence any more than me and nothing I think could induce me to live there. Perfect freedom and independence is vital air to us now . . . here we can successfully trample on the barriers that hedge us in and find grand sympathy for our heresies. There, conventionalism is too strong, we could not create pure atmosphere. My belief is that I could no more have gone through a medical school in England than I could have taken Victoria's place on the throne, and we are too strong grained ever to retrace a step once gained.[17]

It was eventually agreed that Howard would work in the iron foundry and travel to England with one of his sisters. Elizabeth had reservations about any of her family returning permanently to the 'Old World'. But, given her elder brothers' difficulties in establishing themselves in a career, she recognised it as a rare opportunity for Howard, and one that must be exploited. She had firm views, however, about which of her sisters should accompany him. 'Let it be Marian not Emily who goes, she is a very beautiful woman, I cannot bear to think of her life wasting away . . . she would make a most pleasant impression on our English relations and would finally establish herself as a charming writer. But I should object to Emily going now . . . the best training she can receive is to be forced to make her own way in a situation away from home with the painful lessons it would inculcate.'[18]

Elizabeth had her own agenda. She wanted Marian to go to England because of her deep attachment to her and the belief that she had at last found the solution to her sister's persistent unhappiness. If Marian married Kenyon she would be mistress of the ironworks, perfectly placed to establish a Fourierist community among his 500 workers. Her plans for Emily were of a different order. Although instinctively wary of her younger sister and feeling nothing like the same affection for her as she did for Marian, she acknowledged Emily's outstanding academic ability as clearly as she recognised her own loneliness. If Emily became a doctor too, they might practise together and make a real impact. As her younger sister had already expressed an interest in studying medicine, it was vital from Elizabeth's perspective that she should not be distracted by a trip to Europe. Soon after returning to Geneva in October, she tried to clinch the matter:

> I have intended writing to you for a long time, as you won't write to me for I want to know what you are doing . . . your life interests me particularly, as it seems more nearly related to my own, than that of any other member of our family and if we can work together I shall be delighted for I need companionship greatly. It seemed to me once that literature and Association ought to occupy your time, but now, if your feelings still lead you in that direction, I would much sooner you should make medicine your business and let the others be incidental. I believe it would be more profitable and more useful, the wide field that opens in this direction needs laborers zealous, talented, of high character and I know not where they are to come from, for I meet with no woman anywhere, that seems to me suited to the task – but I believe you are peculiarly so in many ways. So Emily I claim you, to work in my reform – will you answer to the call and let us sketch our future together?[19]

It was a future which Elizabeth had carefully mapped out and now set before her sister. After leaving Geneva, she planned to spend a year in Paris where she hoped to make good the deficiencies of her American training. Meanwhile, she wanted Emily to embark immediately on her own medical studies so that they would be well advanced by the time Elizabeth returned to America, sixteen months later, ready to set up in practice.

As usual, lack of money was a major problem. Elizabeth urged Emily to save as much as she could from teaching while she intended to finance her own studies in Europe by borrowing $1,200 from Dennis Harris, cousin Samuel and the ex-treasurer of Brook Farm. She frankly admitted to Emily that she would incur this formidable debt 'without the smallest hesitation or feeling of uneasiness. The experience and practical knowledge I shall thereby gain, are essential to me. There is a feeling too of universality in my work, that takes off any personal feeling I should have, if the debts were purely selfish and those I have named would all be friendly creditors.'[20] On her return from Europe she expected to settle in New York, by which time she would be thirty.

At last the way ahead seemed clear and Elizabeth's once improbable vision on the verge of becoming reality. She was much too familiar with the slings and arrows of life to be complacent, but she nevertheless looked forward with renewed confidence to four more months of intensive study in Geneva followed by her triumphant graduation. The months spent at Blockley had not been easy, but when she finally took her leave of the hospital on 23 September it was with surprisingly mixed feelings: 'My last evening at Blockley. Here I sit writing by my first fire. How glad I am, tomorrow, tomorrow, I go home to my friends! And yet as I watched the beautiful sunset from my great windows, as little Mary Ann pays her willing attendance, and all seems so friendly; as I walked to Dr Benedict's with my thesis and felt the entrancing day and the lovely country, I *almost* regretted that I was going to leave.'[21]

EIGHT

Elizabeth Blackwell MD

The thesis[1] that Elizabeth presented to Dr Benedict on 23 September was required by Geneva Medical College as part of her degree. She had chosen typhus or 'ship fever' for her subject, exploiting the fact that throughout the summer of 1848 Blockley's wards were filled with Irish immigrants suffering from the disease. These unfortunate people had escaped the potato famine only to contract typhus in the appalling fetid and cramped conditions they experienced in the ships transporting them to America.

Elizabeth's dissertation, written in a clear, straightforward style (unlike most medical publications of the time) already reveals the themes that were to absorb her for the rest of her life: the importance of hygiene and sanitation and the urgent need to reform a society whose moral shortcomings were, in her view, at the root of so much human malady. She ably described the symptoms and progression of typhus as well as the extraordinary variety of treatments doctors tried on their patients ranging from doses of brandy, lead, rhubarb and opium to packs of mustard and cayenne pepper applied to the inside thigh. Significantly, Elizabeth made no reference to recent research on the differences between typhus and typhoid, preferring instead to quote Dr Samuel Johnson on the curative merits of fresh air, cold water, light exercise and nutritious food. Even at this early stage of her career, she was more interested in the underlying social causes of disease than its pathology.

She returned to Geneva on 3 October, ready to begin a new round of lectures, dissection and intense private study but also with a new preoccupation. Her recent exposure at Blockley to the bleaker side of sex led her to think more deeply about the whole subject:

Geneva is a very immoral place, the lower classes of women being often worthless, the higher ones fastidious and exclusive, so that there is no healthy blending of the sexes . . . I don't know if I've ever told you how deep this matter of licentiousness had gradually sunk into my soul, and that the

determination to wage a war of extermination with it strengthens continually
. . . I feel specially called to act in this reform when I have gained wisdom for
the task; the world can never be redeemed till this central relation of life is
placed on a truer footing.[2]

But Elizabeth's growing concern with prostitution and its effects on
society was temporarily overshadowed by a family crisis. Henry had once
more thrown his family into a state of 'great perplexity and alarm'.[3] This
time, however, it was not a bankrupt business or failing love affair that
gave them sleepless nights but his determination to join the gold rush to
California. Gold had been discovered at Sutter's sawmill near Sacramento
on 24 January 1848 but it was not until the following November that the
first ship, full of hopeful gold diggers, sailed from the east coast to
California – a dangerous voyage that could take up to six months.

Henry, a passionate liberal and incipient atheist, had fallen out with the
sternly religious Dennis Harris (whose daughter he had continued to pursue
despite her engagement to another man) and needed little encouragement to
leave the hot, disagreeable working conditions of a sugar refinery for the
promise of instant wealth and adventure. Forming a partnership with friends
he had met through Anna's Brook Farm connections, he invested his meagre
capital in a patent for a new kind of 'rocker' – a machine designed to separate
grains of gold from gravel. On hearing this news, the entire Blackwell family
united in a chorus of disapproval, using every argument they could muster to
dissuade him from sailing to California. Elizabeth led the attack with a long
letter in which she addressed her brother, 'Dear Crazy Harry':

> Your letter had distressed me exceedingly . . . I began to fear that you might
> be seized with this gold mania which has spread everywhere, whose brilliant
> visions have turned Geneva heads as well as others and been the subject of
> conversation morning, noon and night. This mad rioting after gold, gold,
> gold, this revival of the old furious Spanish folly, when men became brutes,
> insane grovelling with the ceaseless cry of gold, gold, gold trampling down
> every spark of justice, mercy and divinity in their insatiate lust for riches, is a
> thing so sad, so God-forsaken that it grieves me inexpressibly that my brother
> should be involved in it, however noble his motives may be.[4]

So deep was the family's concern over the Californian scheme that they
despatched Kenyon (through thick snow and ice) to New York in a

desperate attempt to stop it. He succeeded in persuading Henry to shelve his plans by offering him and Sam a $5,000 loan that would enable them to buy into a wholesale hardware business in Cincinnati. Henry had serious doubts about the venture but by the time he reached home in March 1849 it was a *fait accompli* and his dreams of Californian gold were lost for ever.

Against this backdrop of domestic drama, Elizabeth continued to study hard for her final examinations. In later accounts of her time in Geneva, in which her own words are often quoted, much is made of the town's hostility towards her; the women who stopped to stare at her as if she were 'a curious animal' or who held their skirts aside when they passed her in the street.[5] It was certainly true that many people considered her medical ambitions nothing short of heresy, and made their disapproval plain, but in her autobiography she herself acknowledged that, in general, she was warmly welcomed and that it was only pressure of work that prevented her from enjoying a livelier social life. Her fellow students meanwhile treated her with a respect and friendliness that touched her deeply.

Despite Elizabeth's dedication to her studies, she did allow herself one day's holiday to visit a Quaker family living close to Geneva, who had followed her progress through medical school with great interest and were anxious to meet her. Invigorated by the sleigh ride to their house, Elizabeth enjoyed the spirited talk on women's rights, homeopathy and King David's revelations but was even more intrigued by their first-hand account of the mysterious 'rappings' encountered in dozens of houses in nearby Rochester.

The cause of great public excitement, these curious sounds were first heard in March 1848 at the home of two young sisters, Kate and Maggie Fox, who, by claiming the knockings were communications from the spirit world, launched a new quasi-religious movement – spiritualism. Anna Blackwell, always susceptible to the latest intellectual fashion, was just one of many thousands of people swept up by this new promise of enlightenment and, to her mother's distress, was soon in thrall to mesmerists, table turners and the whole psychic circus. Elizabeth was more sceptical but still intensely interested in the psychological aspects of spiritualism, which from its earliest days was closely linked to the women's rights movement.

For a student of Elizabeth's calibre, the final examinations proved an undemanding test but when she finished them she admitted that 'my face burned, my whole being was excited and a great load was lifted from my mind'.[6] Henry fought his way through thick blizzards from New York to be at his sister's side on the day of her graduation – 23 January 1849. Seated up in the gallery of the church where the ceremony took place, was Miss Margaret Munro De Lancey, daughter of the Episcopalian Bishop of Western New York. That evening, she wrote a breathless account of the proceedings to her sister-in-law:

> Dear Joe – As mother is writing to Ned, I thought I would scribble a few words to you about the graduation of 'the female Student.' The Medical Commencement took place last Tuesday – a bright Sunshiny day . . . Annie and I went down early to the 'Presbyterian House' but though there a full hour before the exercises commenced yet we were unable to get a *front* seat in the gallery. We sat in the Second tier. About half past ten or eleven the procession entered the building. The Lioness of the day, Miss Blackwell met them at the door and entered with the Medical Students *without* hat or shawl. She wore a black silk dress – and cape – lace collar and cuffs and her *reddishly inclined* hair was very nicely braided. She sat in a front side pew with old Mrs. Waller until she received her Diploma. After President Hale 'made a prayer' the choir and fiddles struck up, and the audience were favored with some *extraordinary* performances in Presbyterian church music. One *woman* in the choir was (next to Miss Blackwell) the most conspicuous individual in the meetinghouse. Most alarmingly loud were the tones she uttered, and the *very* peculiar emphasis of the words in the anthem (or whatever they called it) excited any feeling *but* that of solemnity! Take it altogether – *the ladies* – carried the day! There was scarcely a coat – excepting the Students' – visible! Nothing but a vast expanse of woman's [*sic*] bonnets and curious eyes. The noise on the 'Singers' bench completed, President Hale made a brief Address to the graduating class, then donned the velvet cap and seated himself in the large chair. *As usual*, he did not know his lesson, and had to *read* his few words in Latin as he called up the graduates. Four at a time they came on the stage. The Doctor spoke. They *looked* Knowing. One of them grasped the bundle of sheepskins, all four bowed and vanished. Last of all came 'Domina Blackwell'! She ascended the steps. The President touched his cap and rose. You might have heard a pin drop. He *stood* while he conferred the Degree on her, handed her the diploma and bowed, evidently expecting she would bow also and retreat. Not so, however! She seemed embarrassed and after an effort, said to the Dr. – 'I thank you Sir. It shall be the effort of my life, by God's blessing, to shed honor on this Diploma' – then bowed, blushed scarlet, left the stage and took her seat in the

front pew among the Graduates, amid the Enthusiastic applause of all present. Her color left her cheek in a few moments and she sat calm and composed through the address of Dr. Lee. This was long but very interesting and ably written. And at the conclusion he alluded in a dignified manner to the fact that one of the present class was a female, complimented the sex generally and Miss B. in particular, and told us that she was fully qualified to practise as a Physician, and that the degree was *fully merited*. The applause was again loud, though brief. The music '*audiantur*'ed, according to the President's order, a short prayer made, the benediction given, and *Elizabeth Blackwell M.D.* and her classmates were turned adrift on the Streams of time each 'to paddle his own canoe'! The Faculty of Arts, the Medical professors, Father [Bishop DeLancey], and sundry others, as they passed out stopped and congratulated her. When nearly all the crowd had gone she put on her hat and shawl, took the arm of her brother (who came from New York to be present) and so escorted, *Miss Blackwell, M.D.* mingled with the mass and disappeared and so ended medical Commencement January 23d, 1849 – a day to be remembered – being the first instance the world has ever had, where the degree of m.d. was conferred on a Woman. She intends proceeding to Philadelphia to study a few months with Dr Bryan and will go to Paris, and on her return establish herself in New York, where, as Dr. Lee told me, she would have more practice than she could attend to – that he would insure her six thousand dollars the first year!! Nearly as good as going to California, is it not?[7]

Yours ever, M. M. DeL

The *Geneva Gazette*, determined to make the most of the occasion, was effusive in its coverage, noting the musical band of native Indians who led the procession to the church and the many women in the audience: 'it was a beautiful scene indeed to see the sparkling eyes and smiling countenances, with whispering lips and the rustle of dresses'. Recounting the actual moment when Elizabeth received her degree, the *Gazette* went into overdrive: 'It was a scene for a painter. A lady – alone! – Braving the prejudices existing against her sex . . . the first in the annals of the world to receive . . . a medical diploma! The President, as he extended it to her, bowed – as only woman can she returned the salutation. A silence deep as death pervaded the assembly – we saw a tear gathering in many an eye – her bosom heaved, almost too full for utterance. But many an ear hung listening on her lips, and we heard the heartfelt and impulsive reply "I thank you sir . . ." Thank? ELIZABETH BLACKWELL, the world cannot thank thee too much! God speed thee in thy work of mercy and as an angel spirit to cherish and to soothe, mayst thou bend over the couch of the sick and the dying!'[8]

The Dean, Dr Lee, was more circumspect in his commencement address, chiding the ladies present for subscribing to alternative therapies such as mesmerism and hydropathy before complimenting Elizabeth on her success (she had passed out top of the class) and praising the way she had proved it possible to combine intellect and perseverance with feminine grace and delicacy. He went on:

> This event will stand forth hereafter as a memorable example of what woman can undertake and accomplish, too, when stimulated by the love of science and noble spirit of philanthropy. Why should medical science be monopolized by us alone? Why should woman be prohibited from fulfilling her mission as a ministering angel to the sick, furnished not only with the softer and kindlier attributes of her sex, but with all the appliances and resources of science? If she feels called to this life of toil and responsibility, and gives evidence of her qualifications for such a calling, in humanity's name, let her take rank among the disciples of Aesculapius, and be honoured for her self-sacrificing choice.[9]

Elizabeth might well have drafted this part of the speech herself. But Lee's following words: 'Such cases must ever be too few to disturb the existing relations of society', at once dispelled any illusion that here was a man enthusiastically preaching a progressive agenda. His underlying message was clear. Elizabeth Blackwell's achievement was perfectly splendid as long as it remained a quirky exception, brought the right sort of publicity to his college and fundamentally changed nothing at all.

Understandably, Elizabeth preferred to accept Dr Lee's words at their face value. And who could blame her? After all the years of hardship, setbacks and disappointment, this was a moment of sheer glory to be relished and relived for the rest of her life. As she listened to Lee's eulogy, she must have believed that the hardest part of her mission was over and its rewards – moral and financial – within reach. In the weeks immediately following her graduation, this impression was reinforced by numerous accounts of her triumph reported in the American and international press many of them highly complimentary of both her professional achievement and personal conduct. There was even a witty tribute from London's *Punch*:

Not always is the warrior male,
Nor masculine the sailor;
We all know Zaragossa's tale
We've all heard 'Billy Taylor';
But far a nobler heroine, she
Who won the palm of knowledge,
And took a Medical Degree,
By study at her College.

They talk about the gentler sex
Mankind in sickness tending,
And o'er the patient's couch their
    necks
Solicitously bending;
But what avails solicitude
In fever or in phthisic,
If lovely woman's not imbued
With one idea of physic?

Young ladies all, of every clime,
Especially of Britain,
Who wholly occupy your time
In novels and in knitting,
Whose highest skill is but to play,
Sing, dance, or French to clack well,
Reflect on the example pray,
Of excellent Miss Blackwell

Think if you had a brother ill,
A husband, or a lover
And could prescribe the draught or pill
Whereby he might recover;
How much more useful this would be,
Oh sister, wife, or daughter!
Than merely handing him beef-tea
Gruel, or toast-and-water.

Ye bachelors about to wed
In youth's unthinking hey-day,
Who look upon a furnish'd head
As horrid for a lady,
Who'd call a female doctor 'blue';
You'd spare your sneers, I rather
Think, my young fellows, If you knew
What physic costs a father!

How much more best were married
    life
To men of small condition,
If every one could have his wife
For family physician;
His nursery kept from ailments free,
By proper regulation,
And for advice his only fee
A thankful salutation.

For Doctrix Blackwell – that's the way
To dub in rightful gender –
In her profession, ever may
Prosperity attend her!
'Punch' a gold-handled parasol
Suggests for presentation
To one so well deserving all
Esteem and admiration.[10]

The general press may have treated Elizabeth's MD as entertaining copy but the medical establishment was furious. The deep antagonism felt by most regular physicians at the mere thought of women doctors soon surfaced in the correspondence columns of the highly influential *Boston Medical and Surgical Journal*. In response to the Journal's article covering Elizabeth's graduation,[11] an enraged letter appeared over the initials D.K. – a phonetic pun on the Greek word for justice, *dike*:

Sir – . . . Whatever may be the character and acquirements of this individual, it is much to be regretted that she has been induced to depart from the appropriate sphere of her own sex, and led to aspire to honors and duties which by the order of nature and the common consent of the world devolve alone upon men. And I am sorry that Geneva Medical College should be the first to commence the nefarious process of amalgamation. Hitherto an intuitive sense of propriety has induced all civilized nations to regard the professions of law, medicine and divinity as masculine duties, and by the universal acceptation of both sexes, the sterner offices and responsibilities incident to these vocations have been considered most compatible with the physical and mental constitution of the male sex. Woman was obviously designed to move in another sphere, to discharge other duties – not less important, not less honorable, not less angelic, but more refined, more delicate. Within her own province she is all powerful. She is the pride and glory of the race – the sacred repository of all that is virtuous, graceful and lovely. But when she departs from this, she goes astray from her appropriate element, dishonors her sex, seeks laurels in forbidden paths, and perverts the laws of her Maker. When some sudden emergence or imperious necessity requires it, she is justified in rendering temporary aid to the rude avocations of men; but when no such necessity demands her service, the character and usefulness of her own sex, and the general good of society, are best promoted by a proper attention to the duties of her own province . . . As this is the first case of the kind that has been perpetrated either in Europe or America, I hope, for the honor of humanity, that it will be the last. And I trust that the high-minded members of the profession will so manifest their disapprobation of the transaction, as to teach other similar institutions the impropriety of following the example.[12]

D.K.'s letter was challenged by another anonymous correspondent, to the *Boston Medical and Surgical Journal* signing himself 'Justus', who pointed out that women had been bringing babies into the world since time immemorial and that it would surely be better for everyone if they continued to do so having been properly trained in modern scientific methods. But, while he defended women's right to administer in the delivery room, he also wrote: 'As to females engaging in the general practice of medicine, the idea is absurd; DK need have no fears of a rivalry, which he seems to dread, as about to jostle him uncomfortably.'[13]

'Justus' may have been dismissive of such anxieties but it was largely the spectre of hordes of women armed with MDs stealing their livelihoods that caused D.K. and his colleagues to protest at Elizabeth's graduation so hysterically. In a society that held women to be the guardians of moral rectitude, 'the repository of all that is virtuous, graceful and lovely', the most effective counter-attack was to underline the utter impropriety of such delicate creatures dealing with anything as messy as the human body. After all, what could be more remote from 'woman's sphere' than the image of Elizabeth Blackwell surrounded by men in the dissecting room, skilfully slicing male genitalia?

Elizabeth was not, however, entirely without support within the profession. Dr Austin Flint, editor of the *Buffalo Medical Journal*, had close links with the medical faculty in Geneva and had watched Elizabeth's progress with keen interest. He kept a refreshingly open mind about women's future in medicine, prophesying that 'before many years, there will be far less difficulty than was experienced in the present instance, in finding a Medical Institution willing to entertain favourably similar application'. But even he added, 'That females will become general practitioners is hardly to be expected, but that they may devote themselves successfully and usefully to special branches is not to be doubted'.[14] Flint backed his liberal words with decisive action by printing Elizabeth's thesis, 'Ship Fever', in the February 1849 edition of the *Buffalo Medical Journal*.

The medical establishment had no doubt about where it stood in the debate. It roundly condemned Geneva Medical College for its irresponsible actions in allowing a woman through its doors in the first place, let alone awarding her a degree. The general censure was too much for Dr Lee, who knew his college could not long survive such opprobrium. Caught in the spotlight of so much criticism, he bolted for cover. By the time his valedictory address was published later in 1849, it was accompanied by the following cowardly footnote:

The writer, while he acknowledges the validity of the argument, so far as it is founded on the general physical disqualifications of the sex for the medical profession, and the incompatibility of its duties, with those properly belonging to the female portion of the society, believes, nevertheless, that instances occasionally happen, where females display such a combination of moral, physical, and intellectual qualifications for discharging creditably and skilfully the duties that belong to our calling, that it would seem equally unwise and unjust to withhold from them those advantages and those honors, which are open to nearly all others, whether deserving of them or not. While he holds this opinion, he at the same time feels bound to say, that the inconveniences attending the admission of females to all the lectures in a medical school are so great, that he will feel compelled on all future occasions, to oppose such a practice, although by so doing, he may be subjected to the charge of inconsistency.[15]

The day after the ceremony Elizabeth left Geneva by train with Henry for New York before travelling on to Philadelphia, where she once more took up residence with the Elders. After all the excitement of her graduation, life with the worthy doctor and his wife was an anticlimax. Elizabeth complained that their house was so hard to find that few visitors called on her. They spent their evenings reading together, occasionally varying the routine with a 'wrestling match', Elizabeth had always prided herself on her extraordinary strength (Anna liked to tell the story of how, as a child in Bristol, her small sister had carried a hapless and helpless clergyman around the house in her arms having listened to him pontificate on the 'weaker' sex) but found that on her return from Geneva she was not nearly as strong as before noting: 'Mrs E and I together can trample the Doctor down, but alone we are *rather* less in strength.'[16]

Now that she had actually acquired a medical degree, Elizabeth demonstrated her faith in republicanism by formally becoming an American citizen. Considering her youthful patriotism for England, this was no small decision since she was required to renounce for ever 'all allegiance and fidelity to any foreign prince, potentate, state, or sovereignty whatsoever, and particularly to the Queen of the United Kingdom of Great Britain and Ireland, of whom she was that time a subject'. With Sara Elder acting as her referee, she took the oath on 13 April 1849.[17] Over the coming years her enthusiasm for the United States dwindled but in 1849 she was profoundly aware and grateful that America had given her an opportunity as yet unthinkable in Britain.

Elizabeth now flatly rejected many of the more radical ideas with which she had flirted when she first lodged with the Elders in 1847. The Fourierist journal, the *Harbinger*, which she had once read with such enthusiasm, by 1849 she considered 'calculated to do a great deal of mischief', particularly in its discussions of marriage. Relinquishing all previous doubts concerning this 'Divine Institution', she assured her mother she now supported it, 'whole souledly' – not only in theory but, as soon as she was given the chance, 'by example too!'[18]

Clearly, Elizabeth did not believe that her future as a doctor was incompatible with marriage although society in general may have found a more nun-like commitment easier to digest. Her passion for Fourier had waned: 'I think Associationists generally a very poor set of people & if they would commence by reforming themselves & let the Almighty take care of the world, I think they would be much better employed . . . & as to the infidel French philosophy you talk of, it's just twaddle, which I should instantly reject if any body were to stuff it into me.'[19]

Although scornful of the French philosophy she had once so much admired, Elizabeth was increasingly impatient to be off to Paris where, despite its shocking morals, like so many American medical graduates she wanted to complete her studies. But until she had raised enough money and had received the all-important letters of introduction from the various doctors to whom she had written, she remained trapped in Philadelphia. She was, however, determined not to waste her time. The razzmatazz surrounding her MD may have been highly gratifying, but she was much too intelligent to let it seduce her into believing that she was anywhere near ready to begin real doctoring. She therefore spent her days dissecting with a fellow student from Geneva, studying French and, above all, trying to gain *entrée* to Philadelphia's prestigious medical establishment. But despite her brand new degree, access to it remained as difficult as ever, as was made very clear to her when she attended a lecture at Jefferson Medical College and was directed to sit alone in an anteroom well away from the rest of the audience.

The tedious interlude came to an end when it was decided that she would sail for England in mid-April escorted by cousin Kenyon. But first she wanted to spend some time with the family in Cincinnati. It was five years since she had been home and she was anxious to see the house, so often described to her in letters, before it was sold: 'Why I've never been in a "family mansion," a real house of our own, & I think it must be a very different affair from a rented home which is only half a home. I have heard so much about the pleasant front parlour & the little lawn with its two trees & the improvements in the shape of porch & shutters, painting, papering & chimney pots, that it will make quite a gap in the family history, if I am not to see at all with my bodily eyes.'[20]

Elizabeth had earned her medical degree against all the odds but not without personal cost. She had lived in rented lodgings or other people's houses for five years with little money and few diversions. The longing for hearth and home must have been intense but she allowed herself only two weeks in Cincinnati before departing once more: 'They all came to see me off. They stood on the adjoining boat as we sailed away up the river, mother leaning on Sam, the three sisters on one side, Howy and George on the other, all hearts in sympathy. I could not keep down the tears as I caught the last glimpse of those dear, true ones.'[21]

She met Kenyon in Boston where they stayed a few days before embarkation. The highlight of her brief sojourn there was a meeting with W.H. Channing: 'I never met my old friend more fully.'[22] On 18 April Elizabeth and Kenyon set sail: 'Beautiful Boston Bay vanished in the distance. America, that land of memories, was left far behind. I took to my berth and lay there in misery five days and nights. How I loathe the ship!'[23]

NINE

European Adventure

From the ship's deck, Elizabeth watched the last faint outline of America disappear in the setting sun. But any sense of occasion was rapidly overtaken by the horrors of seasickness. For the next six days she lay in misery, tortured by the sounds, smells and constant rolling of the ship. By the time she was well enough to emerge from her tiny cabin (shared with a Virginian matron) Kenyon was ill with what was described as rheumatic fever, leaving Elizabeth to spend the rest of the voyage on her own: 'Just seasick enough not to be able to study and well enough not to bear idleness',[1] she occupied herself with a ruthless analysis of her fellow passengers:

> The majority were gentlemen who smoked, drank wine or brandy till they were very noisy, talked of races, gambling and money making. The ladies put on airs of great pretension gathered themselves into groups and turned their backs on all solitary individuals. There was the Duchess of Wellington's niece and a Lady P and a German of Barbadoes [*sic*] and family and several rich Americans opening European follies. Amongst them there was a good deal of dressing and talking of the opera and Lady this and Lady that but I listened in vain for one thought, one noble sentiment or one mark of true refinement. Oh I grew very very weary of those uncongenial people who never spoke to me but were all the time with me, for it was utterly impossible to get a quiet corner to sit in.[2]

To Elizabeth's added irritation, the crew refused to light fires on board despite the bitterly cold weather which did little to help Kenyon who was growing weaker every day. But on 30 April land was at last sighted and in the late afternoon the ship steamed up the Mersey to Liverpool with Elizabeth on the quarterdeck eager to catch her first glimpse of the country she had left seventeen years before. The customs officials failed to notice the expensive medical books hidden under her coat and, to her relief, she was charged only three shillings and sixpence duty.

Once ashore she wasted no time. Leaving her ailing cousin in a hotel (with a cup of hot chocolate), she set out alone to explore Liverpool: 'I was particularly struck by the substantial appearance of everything. Every brick wall is so high and thick and furnished with stone, the iron railings so solid, and every little shop as well as the rows of noble buildings, sets itself down with an evident determination to stand the forever.'³ Although impressed by the spaciousness and cleanliness of the market, Elizabeth thought the people ugly. 'The florid complexion so much boasted of did not strike me as being a sign of good health in connection with the humid atmosphere and feeble sun. I associated the idea of scrofula with them. I wanted to expose them to bright American sun and dry them.'⁴

The next morning, they boarded a train for Birmingham. Elizabeth delighted in the green countryside, noting with pleasure the absence of the unfinished roads and messy suburbs so commonplace in America. But a few miles west of Birmingham the rural idyll faded into the Black Country where her cousin, Samuel Blackwell, lived and directed his iron foundries at Dudley. On the short journey by carriage from the station to her cousins' house she noticed how even the flowers were black with soot and the sunlight, filtering through the thick smoke, was so pale that she was reminded of an eclipse.

Kenyon, too ill to talk for most of the journey, revived a little as they drew closer to his home and enjoyed pointing out to Elizabeth the numerous blast furnaces that lay in every direction. 'After winding through a few miles of country lanes, blackened by smoke we came in sight of an old stone ivy-covered wall inside which, half hidden by trees we could see the back of a stone building, stables etc. It stood in the midst of fields, the green hills sloping upon each side. We had reached home.'⁵

Portway Hall, built in 1674 by a Puritan (and where Oliver Cromwell's skull allegedly lay for many years), captivated Elizabeth. Its castellated roof and fine stone staircase, the formal gardens and comfortably furnished rooms perfectly embodied the romanticised picture of England she had absorbed as a girl from the novels of Maria Edgeworth. Much less picturesque were the workmen's cottages full of shabby-looking women and children with dirty faces that she observed on the 6-mile journey from Birmingham.

Elizabeth's reunion with her family should have been a joyful occasion but Kenyon's illness and Samuel's depression prompted her to write a few days later: 'decidedly I am ready to come home again'.⁶ Samuel had not recovered from the death of his pregnant wife two years earlier and was constantly sinking into a gloomy, abstracted reverie. Elizabeth, sympathetic to his plight, nevertheless found him difficult to understand:

> His manner is very strange, exceedingly nervous and uneasy. I suppose he must be about Kenyon's height but very thin and of pale complexion, eyes a light blue with a mass of curling light hair, beard of a darker hue . . . so worn a look on his countenance. He can hardly speak of his wife without tears, life has lost every ray of brightness to him and though he has most noble aspirations for the Race and longs to work for it, personally he would most gladly die. He has had many things to harass him and can find rest nowhere. He suffers constantly from indigestion and fits of exhaustion which he seeks to forget by increasing his business operations. He is continually bringing down some little momento [*sic*] of Harriet, one of her engravings for she lithographed beautifully, or some witty little composition or a piece of music that she composed . . . We do not see much of him though he comes home to dinner at two or to tea at eight.[7]

Samuel had inherited in full measure the abilities and flaws that distinguished so many of his Blackwell relations. An imaginative and energetic man, his talents as a geologist were widely recognised but in 1860 his business crashed spectacularly when he was declared bankrupt with debts so huge that they also caused the collapse of his chief creditor, the Birmingham Banking Company. Just as Elizabeth's father had tried throughout his career to discover better ways of producing sugar, so his nephew and namesake attempted to improve iron and steel production. But his investment in a string of failed experiments led only to his downfall. When Elizabeth stayed with him in 1849 there was, however, no suggestion that he was heading for failure – indeed he looked set to become one of England's foremost industrialists. His evident success coupled with his enthusiasm for philanthropic causes led Elizabeth to believe that, in her cousin, she had found the ideal patron to sponsor both her medical education and wider ambitions for social reform.

But Samuel was too preoccupied with personal grief to give much attention to her social schemes and, to add to the general despondency, Kenyon (whom Elizabeth increasingly suspected of hypochondria) had grown steadily sicker since their arrival. A doctor from nearby Dudley attended him every day making it clear that her family did not yet trust her professional judgement. She, in turn, strongly disapproved of the doctor, whom she accused of giving Kenyon: 'all manner of drugs and absurd directions which have made him very weak. For a few days the medicines were regularly thrown away and bread pills and flavoured water substituted and with judicious diet, cleanliness and kind cheerful nursing he improved rapidly but unfortunately Uncle Blackwell discovered the plot. All was over with the unfortunate effect of making Kenyon suspicious of his kind nurses.'[8]

At least Anna, who had been living some months at Portway Hall, was unchanged – enthusiastic, generous but, in Elizabeth's words, 'still different from other people'. She had found work translating Fourier and, although clearly happier living in England than in America, was still chronically neurotic. To calm her troublesome nerves she rubbed a magnetised dollar on the back of her neck each day and swallowed a tablespoonful of 'magnetic water'.

Surrounded by hypochondria, quackery and superstition, Elizabeth was profoundly relieved to spend a day visiting hospitals and physicians in Birmingham. The calls were organised by a young friend of Samuel's, Charles Plevins, whom Elizabeth much admired for his reforming zeal. Anxious about her dress for the occasion, she borrowed Anna's velvet sack and sables so that she made a 'very plain but rich' impression. The doctors, suppressing any scepticism they may have felt towards a female MD, gratified Elizabeth by appearing to treat her with genuine respect. At the General Hospital, she visited every ward both male and female, watched an operation performed without chloroform (the surgeon disapproved of it) and heard detailed accounts of the most interesting cases. She concluded that the students looked much the same as their American counterparts but remarked on their quicker movements and better quality coats. The Birmingham experience was encouraging and, with the promise of further introductions to physicians in London, Elizabeth began to look forward to her visit there with confidence.

Howard had settled well into his job at his cousins' ironworks, where he spent much of his time experimenting with new methods of making steel. Elizabeth visited him at the foundry (noting that the nature of the work forced him to wear black clothes) and was impressed by what she saw:

> I went one afternoon to see the casting [which] was very curious. Twice a day the melted iron is drawn off from the bottom of the great brick towers they call furnaces. Strong men with faces as black and scorched as a coal were

busy, armed with iron poles, guiding the sea of fire that rushed out into the moulds that covered a great extent of ground, drawing out the white-hot masses of cinders and dirt, and splashing cold water over the front of the furnace to enable them to stand there. We remained at the farther end, but the heat was so great that we had to cover our faces. Suddenly with a loud noise, the flames burst out from the furnaces, ascending to the very top, immense volumes of black smoke rolled over our heads, and the rushing noise grew louder and louder. I thought some accident had occurred, and looked out for the safest retreat, when I found it was only the clearing of the furnaces by sending a powerful blast through them, which was always practised after a casting. Within a square of 12 miles one sixth of the iron used in the world is said to be made.[9]

Despite such stimulating diversions, Elizabeth was relieved to leave the charged atmosphere of Portway Hall for London on 16 May – especially since the delightful Charles Plevins had offered to escort her. After she had secured the promised introductions, she felt free to indulge in tourism and walked with Plevins some 5 miles through the heart of London past Westminster Abbey and the new Houses of Parliament ('an immense pile, the ornaments too delicate for its size'[10]) up Regent Street to lunch with his aunt in Devonshire Street.

This was an utterly new experience for Elizabeth. A footman wearing crimson plush breeches, white stockings and a claret-coloured coat with gold buttons conducted them to the opulent drawing room – its walls hung with figured crimson velvet. Mrs Wilson, a handsome brunette with highly rouged cheeks and black eyes, appeared wearing a blue and black satin dress and lace headdress. She was altogether too mannered for Elizabeth's taste: 'I sat still and talked very quietly, thinking to myself that if I were condemned to live there one week I should overturn the lady and smash everything to atoms.'[11] Elizabeth was particularly incensed by the stream of wealthy visitors who called to sympathise with Mrs Wilson for having scratched her throat by swallowing a mouthful too hastily 'and so was an *invalid*'. 'We descended to lunch, ladies sitting down in their bonnets. The dining-room and library had ceilings beautifully painted to imitate the sky with clouds; the whole house was hung with paintings. The lady's manner grew gradually pleasanter; she seemed to like me, admired my hand, and insisted on my drinking a glass of wine – the first I ever took. I told her so and she was much pleased by her influence.'[12]

Elizabeth had survived her first encounter with the English upper classes but her next social engagement in London, a pharmaceutical *soirée*, was much more to her liking. Her host was Dr William Carpenter – a man of impeccable medical and reforming credentials. Open to new ideas across a broad spectrum, he was a prolific writer on scientific subjects and an eminent biologist and microscopist. His sister Mary had recently opened a ragged school for working-class children in the slums of Bristol and was developing radical new ideas for dealing with young delinquents. It was through acquaintance with Carpenter's wife (a granddaughter of Sir Henry Cort, who had transformed iron manufacture with his invention of 'puddling',) that Samuel and Kenyon were able to provide Elizabeth with an introduction to the family:

> I have just returned from Dr Carpenter's delightful little party. It really is absurd to say the Unitarian's faith is nothing but negative. Here under its influence, is just such a party assembled as I have met with so much pleasure in the days of yore. A little less Transcendentalist certainly and a little more style but still the same spirit. The ladies were in regular ball costume . . . Dr C gave us a very beautiful piece of Mendelssohn's on the organ; he and his wife sang together with great feeling. His microscopes, said to be the most beautiful in England were there. His preparations were exquisite: the lung of a frog most minutely injected, a piece of sharkskin which seems covered with innumerable teeth, and piles of other specimens.[13]

At this gathering, where science and society combined so agreeably, she met a number of leading London intellectuals – among them the 'Transcendental bookseller'[14] John Chapman, later to become the owner and editor of the *Westminster Review*. He spent much of the evening with her but 'seemed a little undecided what tone to take'.[15] Chapman, a notorious womaniser with a penchant for recording the clinical details of his lovers' menstrual cycles, may have been wondering whether to share with Elizabeth his fascination for female physiology (in 1857 he qualified as a doctor specialising in gynaecology). But if Chapman had a curious attitude to female bodies, he did, at least – as befits the one-time lover of Marian Lewes (George Eliot, née Mary Ann Evans) – have a genuine respect for female minds.

Within a few days of arriving in London, Elizabeth had not only received introductions to leading doctors and hospitals but had also moved effortlessly into a stimulating social circle. It is surprising, therefore, that she should have determined to leave all this for Paris, where she had no connections and would be forced to study in a foreign language. In making this decision, however, she was not alone. Between the end of the Napoleonic Wars and 1860, thousands of doctors and students flocked to Paris to continue their medical studies, among them some 700 Americans.[16] They were lured there partly by the sheer pace of innovation – tissue pathology, clinical statistics and the invention of the stethoscope were just some of the developments that had taken place recently in France and were transforming medical practice. But an even greater magnet for the students was the simple fact that medical education was more accessible in Paris than London – and free.

In France where regulations were less stringent, students did not suffer from the chronic shortage of corpses needed for dissection that so thwarted medical education in England. Furthermore, American students, brought up on the Declaration of Independence, deplored the English practice of promoting men with money and family connections over those with talent. They believed that in France preferment was gained on merit alone. It was the openness of the French system as opposed to the opaqueness of the British that appealed to them, persuading them to forgo the advantages of the English language and a more familiar culture for months, sometimes years, of study in Paris.

But before setting out on their Parisian adventure, the majority of them spent at least a few weeks in London as medical tourists and were generally enthusiastic about the experience. They had seen nothing in their own country to compare with the great London hospitals or the medical museums such as the Hunterian, whose collection of anatomical specimens Elizabeth visited under the personal guidance of its curator, the great palaeontologist (and coiner of the word dinosaur) Sir Richard Owen. Many of the leading British physicians were impressive figures and as one American student put it: 'London has been the theatre of action of the remarkable names that adorn the history of our noble science . . . when I, for the first time traversed the courts, museums, wards and operating rooms of those majestic hospitals, I felt that I was treading upon consecrated ground.'[17]

St Thomas' was the best known of the London hospitals that Elizabeth visited in the spring of 1849. The senior surgeon conducted her through all the wards (both male and female), invited her to examine patients and attend one of his clinical lectures. He even showed her the 'everlasting brew house' where, with diplomatic modesty, Elizabeth omitted to sign MD after her name in the visitors' book until he encouraged her to do so. She was showered with invitations to attend post-mortems, lectures and the various departments of the hospital but had to refuse them all as she planned to leave for Paris two days later.

Having always considered herself a recluse, Elizabeth was surprised to discover just how much she liked having her days packed with social and professional appointments: 'engagement treads upon engagement, so that I've hardly a moment to think. I thought such excitement would have bothered me intensely. It did at first bewilder, but now I've roused myself to meet it and I really enjoy it. I've never had such an experience; I must have walked 10 miles a day. I come home sometimes hardly able to move a foot; I wash and dress, and in an hour I'm up again and fresh for as much more – the more I have to do, the more I can. I believe I've never yet begun to call out my power of working.'[18]

Given how extraordinary the whole notion of women doctors was to the British medical establishment, Elizabeth was treated with remarkable deference by most of the physicians she encountered during her brief stay in England. But it is hard to judge whether she was just lucky to meet a number of unusually broad-minded men or if they regarded her merely as an American curiosity, worth humouring for the sake of good manners. Whatever their real views concerning Elizabeth's medical degree, it is unlikely that any of them thought it possible that her example could ever be replicated in England.

On 21 May 1849, having bade farewell to her solicitous escort, Charles Plevins, she boarded a ship for France. It poured with rain the whole way across the Channel (denying her a view of the white cliffs of Dover) but the journey was not wasted. An English couple gave her detailed advice on how to deal with the unscrupulous French who, they warned, cheated the English unmercifully, believing them all to be rich.

The next morning, while waiting for the custom house official, Elizabeth watched with fascination the market women in their white caps ('the common people wear no bonnets') and the stout, muscular fisherwomen clad in a single short petticoat that barely reached their knees. But despite such novel scenes, Elizabeth's first impressions of France were not favourable. She noted that the countryside, dominated by peat bogs, dwarf willows and shabby villages, was poorly cultivated in comparison with England. The customs men in Paris who searched her trunk (for illicit butter and cheese) were rude, and the city itself she considered 'very odd'.

She disliked its narrow streets and the tall old-fashioned houses devoid of all expression. In fact, she was 'utterly disappointed in Paris . . . it seems to be far behind London in everything as the country is behind England'.[19]

Her immediate problem was to find somewhere to live. Convinced that she had been cheated in the hotel where she stayed her first night, she set out early the following morning 'with a map in my hand and hope in my heart',[20] to find Hugh Doherty, a dedicated Associationist whom her Philadelphia friends had assured her would help her to get settled. Through Doherty's contacts she found small, gloomy rooms for a modest rent in the rue de Seine and began to consider her immediate future.

She had arrived in Paris at an extraordinary time. Just fifteen months earlier the 1848 February revolution had spawned the Second Republic and set off a series of political upheavals throughout Europe. Americans had followed these popular uprisings with keen interest but few can have been more enthusiastic in their support for republicanism than the little Fourierist group in Philadelphia.

Before Elizabeth left America, they entrusted her with a signed resolution to present to the most romantic republican of them all – Alphonse de Lamartine. A poet, historian, politician and statesman, Lamartine was the leading figure in the short-lived provisional government that came to power after King Louis-Philippe's abdication on 24 February 1848. However, by the time presidential elections were held ten months later, public opinion had swung decisively in favour of Napoleon Bonaparte's nephew, Louis-Napoleon, who was swept to power with a huge majority. But for those of Elizabeth's political persuasion, Lamartine remained the great hero – a fearless defender of liberty and, in his own words, a stern critic of the 'Napoleonic religion' and 'cult of force'.[21]

A few days after her arrival in Paris, Elizabeth received permission to present her American friends' resolution to Lamartine in person:

> Of course I dressed with great care, and arrived just at the appointed hour. I was asked if I was a lady from America, for Lamartine is to most people *in the country* . . . The door opened and Lamartine entered; very tall and slender, but the most graceful man I have ever seen, every movement was music; grey eyes and hair. He has a gentlemanly voice (Uncle Charles's), clear, melodious, perfectly well bred. In fact his exterior harmonised perfectly with his poetry. He understood English. Slowly and distinctly I explained the commission which had been entrusted to me. He asked me if the resolution referred to the

fraternity of the race, and seemed to understand at once the whole matter when I replied in the affirmative . . . He said he was very happy to receive these expressions of sympathy. He would read the letters carefully and send me an answer, which I promised to transmit to America. He accompanied me very politely to the stairs, bowed, and we parted. I was in no way disappointed; there was perfect harmony in the man and his surroundings. Doubtless he is a true man, though unable to work into practice the great thoughts he cherishes.[22]

The elegance and brilliance Elizabeth so much admired in Lamartine she had yet to discover in his city. But she had come to Paris as a doctor, not a tourist, and her first priority was to plan her medical future. Her initial enquiries brought discouraging results. She had expected to attend public lectures but was firmly told by the professors whom she consulted that this was impossible. Nor was she able to arrange any private instruction. She had, however, been given an introduction to Pierre Louis, the great physician whose use of statistical methods to measure the success of different therapies paved the way for modern clinical trials. To her astonishment, the day after she sent him her card, Louis appeared without warning at her lodgings. Having established that she was not a crank, his advice to her was clear and unequivocal. She should enter La Maternité, the biggest state-run maternity hospital in the country, where girls from all over France were trained as midwives. Elizabeth summed up the pros and cons in a letter to Marian:

I must enter La Maternité as an élève, be shut up for . . . months without even stirring out for the laws are very strict and I suppose necessarily so for young French women and no exception can be made for me. Friends, I believe will be allowed to visit me once a week. My companions will be ignorant and degraded but I believe the duties of the élèves not to be menial. If I will consent to this imprisonment, I will be in the best school of midwifery in the world. In three months I shall witness 1000 cases and be constantly practising. I shall hear lectures from the most distinguished professors living and in this one branch find the utmost desire gratified. Will it not be worth the sacrifice and is it not wise to seize such an opportunity? I think so and have resolved to take this step at the beginning of July when the year commences.[23]

Elizabeth was essentially a pragmatist. She well understood that her hard-won MD was of little substance until underpinned with practical, clinical knowledge and La Maternité offered to give her exactly that. But for a woman of nearly thirty who had so recently fought her way into a professional career, it was not an easy choice.

Having settled her future, Elizabeth determined to make the most of her few weeks of freedom and systematically set about immersing herself in Paris. She attended a synagogue, a séance and accompanied her landlady to mass in the local church: 'I felt fully the impressiveness of this scene to the uneducated people, no thought awakened but the emotional religious sentiment powerfully addressed; and this every night, when the solemn ceremonial contrasts so strongly and soothingly with the traffic of the day. The children are nursed in this atmosphere until it becomes a part of their nature that no reasoning can ever change.'[24]

Anna's arrival in June with a friend from Dudley transformed Elizabeth's solitary existence. Anna had come to Paris primarily to be magnetised but was so enchanted with the city that, within a few days, she decided to live there permanently. The three women explored everywhere, absorbing not only the tourist sights but also the volatile political atmosphere. After the unrest of the previous year, the counter-revolutionary forces of the President, Louis-Napoleon, had re-established control, much to Elizabeth's indignation.

On one occasion near the Tuileries she witnessed a tense confrontation between the people and the army. The soldiers stood with drawn bayonets, the cavalry mounted, ready for action, while the people, crowding the streets and bridges, listened to political activists making impassioned speeches. To her surprise and satisfaction, she noticed several women among the more eloquent speakers. But while deeply sympathetic with the popular cause, Elizabeth was unimpressed by such displays of Gallic excitability – 'I confess the whole exhibition seemed to me peculiarly French'. She had not been in France long but was ready to declare: 'I find more clearly every day that the genus of the French nation does not suit me, and my love for the Anglo-Saxon race, and my admiration for our wonderful Fatherland, increase by the comparison.'[25]

On 29 June Anna took Elizabeth to the theatre as a parting treat. The following day they drove by carriage to La Maternité, housed in the old convent of Port Royal, surrounded by a high stone wall. They entered the hospital through a small door and in the dark, gloomy entrance hall Anna bade her sister an emotional farewell leaving her in the hands of the chief midwife, 'an amicable but excitable little hunch-back lady'.[26] Elizabeth was accepted into the hospital on exactly the same terms as the other students as not even the American Consul's best efforts had succeeded in extracting the smallest concession to either her status as a qualified doctor or her relative maturity.

She was quartered with twenty of them in a large airy dormitory that was rarely quiet: 'how French girls do chatter! How they do go into sudden fits of ecstasy or rage! Once at least in the day we have a grand storm, Madame Blockel coming in for some trouble or other, in which she and the accused out-scream each other, and appear to be mortal enemies for a few minutes, and the best of friends immediately after.'[27] At night, while Elizabeth tried to sleep, her boisterous companions enjoyed a game they called 'promenading the bedsteads':

> You must know that our bedsteads are of iron, and placed on rollers so movable that a slight impulsion will speed them a considerable distance . . . the favourite freak is to place a bedstead at the end of the room and drive it with great violence down the centre. The rolling noise on the brick floor is tremendous, and accompanied by a regular Babel of laughter, shouting and jokes of every description. Some get on top of their beds, which consist of three thick mattresses, and jump up and down like mad things; others get up a wild dance in one corner of the room, which grows continually faster and noisier, and the strife of tongues is truly astonishing . . . the frolic ends as suddenly as it began, when, fairly full of fun, they suddenly jump into bed, say good-night, and in five minutes all are sound asleep.[28]

If Elizabeth was fascinated by her high-spirited fellow students, they were equally intrigued with her. Some of the girls expressed surprise that, despite coming from America, she was not black but having overcome their disappointment showered her with warm affection and kindness. Elizabeth in turn admired their hard work, cheerfulness and dedication to their studies even though many of them had received little previous education.

Despite the strangeness of her new environment, Elizabeth settled quickly into the hospital's strict routine. It was a long, hard day starting at 5.30 a.m. and two or three times a week she was on duty all night. But for the first time since beginning her medical studies she had unrestricted and intensive exposure to patients – an opportunity that she was determined to exploit to the full. Fortunately the tough regime did not blunt her powers of observation and life at La Maternité provided plenty of rich material for her letters home. Meals were eaten to 'the music of Madame Blockel's voice . . . a somewhat important personage, superintending our meals and our dortoirs; she is a little red-faced, squint-eyed being, with tremendous projecting teeth, and dressed always in rusty black with a black cap. She is good natured, liked by the girls, but has a tremendous vocal organ, which is always sounding forth at its highest pitch.'[29]

The senior midwife was the most important figure in the lives of the young élèves and she quickly won Elizabeth's admiration:

The lectures have now commenced. From seven to eight Madame Charrier gives her lesson every morning; I sit beside her in consideration of my foreignness . . . Three pupils are called down every morning, seated on a long bench in front of Madame Charrier's table, and undergo an hour's examination . . . If they answer promptly and well, her satisfaction is extreme, her face grows beautiful and her 'Bien! Tres bien!' really does me good, it is so hearty; but if an unlucky pupil hesitate, if she speak too low, if intelligence or attention be wanting, then breaks forth the most admirable scolding I ever listened to. Alternately satirical and furious, she becomes perfectly on fire, rises upon her chair, claps her hands, looks up to heaven, and the next moment, if a good answer has redeemed the fault, all is forgotten her satisfaction is as great as her anger . . . [30]

The lectures Elizabeth received from the hospital doctors, though less dramatically presented than Madame Charrier's, were highly competent and perfectly complemented her daily clinical contact with patients. But Elizabeth, while recognising the hospital's merits, remained in general sceptical of the French, noting in a letter home that a dentist who had treated her was 'a man decidedly dirty but agreeable – a very common combination of qualities in France'.[31] Nor did she approve of the 'fat, red-faced priest' attached to the hospital: 'I have taken a great dislike to his sensual-looking worship, and will not give him the slightest opportunity to make my acquaintance.'[32]

There was, however, one Frenchman to whom Elizabeth was attracted from their first meeting. Hippolyte Blot was a handsome young physician who presided each week over the vaccination of the latest batch of babies. On these occasions Elizabeth sat next to him watching the infants, brought for the incision bound like mummies in their coarse swaddling clothes, and noticing how every time she asked him a question he blushed, passed his hand through his hair and stared at the baby in a very 'un-Frenchmanlike' manner. By late August, Blot had plucked up enough courage to ask Elizabeth for English lessons. She was pleased: 'I think he must have been meditating this request for some time; it hardly had the air of a spontaneous thought. I like him. I hope we may come a little more closely together.'[33]

Several months later her wish came true. It was not, however, incipient romance that drew them together but an appalling tragedy. On 4 November Elizabeth became increasingly aware of an irritation in her left eye and immediately feared the probable cause. That morning, while she had been syringing the infected eye of a baby, some of the liquid had squirted into her own. By nightfall both her eyes were swollen and full of discharge. The following day Blot confirmed that she had contracted ophthalmia.

TEN

Crisis

Ophthalmia neonatorum was so widespread among babies born of mothers infected with gonorrhoea that, until an effective treatment was developed in 1881,[1] it remained the single biggest cause of childhood blindness. Within a few hours of birth the baby's eyes became grotesquely swollen and emitted a purulent discharge. If the corneas perforated (as in the worst cases) the result was blindness. Hippolyte Blot had seen more than enough of this form of ophthalmia in La Maternité to linger long over diagnosis of Elizabeth's infection, and after examining her eyes on 5 November at once abandoned all other work to devote himself entirely to her care.

Her eyelids were cauterised, leeches applied to her temples, and cold compresses, belladonna ointment and opium pressed on her forehead. She received footbaths, mustard plasters and purgatives but probably the only treatment to give real benefit was the hourly syringing of her eyes with water. Anna arrived at her bedside the first evening expecting to see a slightly inflamed eye but was so appalled by the sight of her sister that she burst into tears.

She broke the news to the family in a long letter in which she vividly described Elizabeth's suffering but emphasised how she bore it 'like a martyr with wonderful patience and fortitude'. For all Elizabeth's outward self-control there is no doubt that she underwent real torment, both physical and mental. Anna recounted how she 'frequently found her in such excruciating pain that speech was impossible and a paroxysm of nervous distress and pent up feeling . . . made her weep bitterly causing her eye intense pain'.[2] Even worse than the pain was the threat of blindness and the realisation that all the grinding years of self-denial and hard work could be laid utterly to waste.

But as Elizabeth was convinced that nothing less than divine purpose had directed her towards medicine, the possibility that her embryonic career might be shattered by arbitrary disease (especially one caused by gonorrhoea) was inconceivable to her. This unshakeable faith in her destiny unquestionably helped her survive the ordeal. While those around her prepared for the worst Elizabeth never doubted that she would be cured. Furthermore, she managed to rationalise the whole disaster as 'an illustration of that grand law of the solidarity of the human race which someday will repay by its infinite production of happiness the misery it seems now to inflict on the innocent'.[3]

Throughout her illness, she received devoted attention from her colleagues at La Maternité. Every hour round the clock she was awakened to have her eyes washed and every two hours Blot, using fine pincers, peeled off the membranes constantly forming over the lens: 'How dreadful it was to find the daylight gradually fading as my kind doctor bent over me, and removed with an exquisite delicacy of touch the films that had formed over the pupil! I could see him for a moment clearly, but the sight soon vanished, and the eye was left in darkness.'[4]

The current between them – already flowing several months – became rapidly stronger during the acute phase of Elizabeth's illness. Blot admired her braid of long hair and wondered how she could arrange it so beautifully while unable to see. He even talked of religion, hinting, much to Elizabeth's satisfaction, that if he were ever to become a believer, he would choose the Protestant faith. Although Anna wrote to the family of Blot's 'brotherly' devotion to Elizabeth, it seems clear that their feelings for one another had evolved into something deeper than friendship.

After a few days the infection slowly subsided but Elizabeth was forced to lie in bed with her eyes bandaged for three long weeks before the relatively undamaged right eye gradually began to open. Anna, fully aware of the gravity of the situation, threw herself into looking after her sister, convinced that her best hope of recovery lay in magnetisation:

As it was impossible to get a magnetizer admitted I, of course, have done my best to supply the lack and magnetize her with all the strength I can muster three times a day . . . indeed the magnetic action is so evident that I feel impelled to exercise it though the effort is quite beyond my strength. My time is entirely occupied in going down and getting back, six journeys a day besides the daily journey to my kindly magnetizer without whose constant aid I could not have borne all this fatigue, anxiety and exhaustion which follows my constant action upon poor E's eye. I have indeed lost again almost all the flesh I had gained of late in consequence of this constant outlay of vitality.'[5]

Anna had for many weeks been attending Baron Du Potet's magnetic séances. The Baron, a disciple of Anton Mesmer, devoted his whole life to therapeutic magnetism, astonishing Parisians with his mesmeric feats. The Academy of Science, though, after conducting a formal investigation into magnetism dismissed it as charlatanism.

Du Potet, like his mentor, believed that the body harboured invisible magnetic fluids which when disturbed or depleted caused illness. To effect a cure the magnetiser had to pass the magnetic aura from his own body to that of the patient and then direct the substance to the diseased organs with magnets or, in the case of a very gifted practitioner like Du Potet, with just his hands. A few weeks before she became ill, Anna had even made Elizabeth accompany her to a séance at the Baron's house on the one day (in four months) that her sister had been allowed out from La Maternité so convinced was she of his theories. Elizabeth, though instinctively sceptical (particularly, perhaps, since Anna was so enthusiastic), gave a typically droll account of the proceedings to her friends in Philadelphia:

> Now I must describe a magnetic séance to you; but I beg that you will receive the description with becoming seriousness, for I have a decided respect for M. Dupotet [*sic*] and if any risibility should be excited it will proceed from your own nervous imagination, and not from my sober portraiture . . . It is a large somewhat darkened room hung round with curious pictures, and lined with very curious people. Mesmer occupies a large frame carved with firebrands and anchors and other significant images; he looks fixedly at a pale lady hanging opposite to him, who has evidently undergone several magnetic crises . . . It is a very original assembly . . . there was a lady with a small hole in her cheek, a child with a crooked neck, the painter to the King of Sweden and the son of the English Consul to Sicily. There was one remarkably fat dame, seated just within the folding-doors, who had powerful fits of nervous twitching, which gave her a singular appearance of pale, tremulous red jelly. But though no miracle was wrought, the faithful audience hung with intense interest on every manifestation of simple magnetic power . . . the red jelly became more tremulous at every fresh magnetisation; and when the séance closed everybody shook everybody's hand, and found it good to have been there.[6]

Although the medical establishment had judged magnetism to be worthless, Elizabeth did not herself reject it out of hand. She recognised that a force existed but, unlike Anna, could not accept it as a 'grand universal truth'.[7] Certainly she had not expected so soon after the séance to find herself on the receiving end of the 'vital fluid' and from the hands of her own sister. But even Anna, for all her faith in magnetism and her deep distrust of orthodox doctors, was forced to concede that medical treatment in Paris was considerably less intrusive than in America and that Elizabeth was receiving the best possible care.

Elizabeth was not able to leave La Maternité until after Christmas 1849 and even then, nearly two months since the onset of the disease, she was far from well. In February Anna wrote home: 'Poor E hopes on and thinks she will recover her sight but I confess that my hopes of so good a result have vanished.' For the first few weeks after Elizabeth's release from the hospital the two sisters lived quietly together in Anna's lodgings at 1 rue de Fleurus. Unable to read, write or even knit, Elizabeth was forced into an idleness that was utterly alien to her. Daily walks in the adjacent Luxemburg Gardens helped pass the time, as did the regular visits from Blot who went to their apartment to examine her eye and continue his English lessons. It is impossible to know what took place between them at a deeper level but in the context of any long-term attachment, Elizabeth must have been painfully aware of the permanent disfigurement around her eye caused by the infection. As for the eye itself, instead of a pupil there was now only a 'grey, flinty looking substance quite opaque and a good deal protruded'.[8]

Despite such depressing circumstances, Elizabeth remained steadfastly optimistic about her future. Still determined to become 'the first lady surgeon in the world',[9] she set about making plans for resuming her studies as soon as her eye was recovered enough for her 'not to keep running into people'. Dr Paul Dubois,[10] the senior obstetrician at La Maternité had been so impressed by her progress before her illness that he had tried to persuade her to remain at the hospital for a whole year. This was not an appealing prospect to Elizabeth (who in later years described Dubois as an old fox), but she was delighted to be told by him that she would become the best obstetrician in America, male *or* female. After he visited her, while she lay sick in the infirmary, she was confident that she had so thoroughly convinced him of society's need for women doctors that in future he would do all he could to further her career. With Dubois as a powerful sponsor and Blot at her side always ready with thoughtful advice, Elizabeth believed that her phoenix could yet rise from the ashes.

But for once in her life, mind over matter was not enough. Her sick eye remained stubbornly sightless and prone to inflammation while the good one was still very weak. Apart from attending a few lectures and being read to by Blot, she was unable to attempt serious work and thus prevented from putting any of her well-considered plans into action. This enforced inactivity grew daily more oppressive as she helplessly watched her precious time and money dwindle away. Cousins Kenyon and Samuel came to the rescue, as they had so often before, with much-needed funds to replenish the sisters' diminishing resources.

Anna was earning a little money from translation and journalism and, as part of her efforts to make a living as a writer, she planned to publish a history of famous musicians. But first she wanted to serialise the book in America and wrote to William Elder asking him to promote the project with several leading magazines in Philadelphia. In the summer of 1850 she also lobbied Henry who during this period was spending his days on horseback, riding through vast tracts of the American West for weeks on end selling pots and pans in small townships and to pioneering farmsteads. Anna believed that he was therefore in an ideal position to approach the new journals springing up throughout the West and suggest they employ her as their Paris reporter. 'Whoever engages me as a correspondent must understand that I will try to make my letters what they wish for; either purely gossip, purely political or mixed according to the need of their paper. But of course I should like to have full scope for my *heresies* if they have no objection.'[11]

There was certainly plenty to write about. The political situation in Paris remained highly volatile and Anna firmly believed her clairvoyant's prediction that foreign troops would enter Paris in March, that Louis-Napoleon would be ousted and the Bourbon pretender placed on the throne by popular will. As Elizabeth noted dryly in a letter home: 'Anna is looking forwards with some anxiety to the coming weeks and means to have her passport all ready to fly off at a moment's notice. She will have to fly alone however, for the Doctor will certainly not accompany her on account of a revolution.'[12] Elizabeth's personal crisis had taken the edge off her former political zeal, lending a certain world-weariness to the views she expressed on the current situation:

It seems strange sometimes to be living in such an unquiet place but it has ceased to trouble me or to excite my strong emotion. For though the struggle is a grand one in which Europe is now engaged, the little individuals on each side who are carrying on the warfare are so mean, that whichever side triumphs, disappointment must follow. The people don't know what it is they want. They are worshipping an unknown God and it will be very long before they know him. Then though I hope dearly that the people may triumph, I know they will make a bad use of their triumph; experience has calmed my enthusiasm for apparently great movements. I have to guard the precious fire for the slow sure work of gradual reform.[13]

While his sisters struggled with life in the old order, Henry was absorbing the new. His journeys took him through impressive landscapes that led him to meditate on the radical evolutionary theories that by the middle of the century were circulating more widely. Darwin did not publish *The Origin of Species* until 1859 but Henry (having almost certainly read Robert Chambers' enormously influential *Vestiges of the Natural History of Creation*[14]) was contemplating his own origins in a manner guaranteed to make his poor mother ever more fearful for his soul:

I have traversed rolling hilly country, level flat country, heavily timbered land, sand barren covered with small oak bushes, broad prairies almost out of sight of a tree some as level as a ten pin alley, others gently undulating and sprinkled over with little swells just as the ocean currents left them here and there even with beds of washed pebbles of great grey rocks sticking up, fellows who just saw the light of day through the green spectacles of the vast ocean when you and I a long time ago were – where? Have you any idea where? I would give a good deal to know wouldn't you? In the absence of anything positive, I prefer to believe the theory of *development* and will assume that you and I were beginning life just then in the shape of two streamers of sea weed which father and mother, a little ahead in the scale of being, reposed under our shade in the form of a periwinkle and an oyster or some rudimentary form of animal existence.[15]

Elizabeth, sharing her mother's anxiety over Henry's leanings towards atheism, can have been little reassured by such reflections. More happily, she was delighted to hear that Emily had taken up her former teaching post in Henderson, Kentucky, having finally decided to follow her sister into medicine. Elizabeth was convinced that Emily, despite her lack of social graces, would be a great success in Henderson and that if she survived the loneliness, would soon lay up enough funds to begin her studies.

Visits from other members of the family brought some much-needed cheer to the beleaguered sisters that bleak February in 1850. Howard was enchanted with Paris, finding it an idyllic contrast to his smoky existence at the Blackwell ironworks in south Staffordshire. Elizabeth, who thought him much improved, slipped easily into her familiar big sister mode: 'He seemed much more teachable than formerly and was really obliged to us for our plain talking and structuring on little improprieties. I found him a little leaning to conservatism at first, rather too much wishing to worship Napoleon and dilate upon the benefits of strong government but I found that he is quite right at bottom.'[16]

The same month Kenyon also made a welcome visit. It was on this occasion that Anna introduced him to Marie de St Simoncourt ('The lady is not rich, nor regularly handsome but has a beautiful nature'[17]) with whom he fell passionately in love and married four months later. Despite such romantic distractions, Kenyon agreed to explore the possibilities of Elizabeth continuing her studies in one of the major London hospitals. By April he was able to write to his cousin with the first good news she had enjoyed in many months. Enlisting the help of Elizabeth's old acquaintance, Dr William Carpenter, he had thoroughly researched all the options and now recommended that she accept an offer from James Paget (later Sir James) to enrol in St Bartholomew's hospital where the latter was Dean. Elizabeth responded immediately and was delighted in May to receive confirmation that her application, having passed through all the relevant committees, had been accepted and she was to be admitted to St Bartholomew's the following November 'to attend as a student in the wards and other departments of the hospital.'[18]

Now that she had firm plans for the future, Elizabeth was ready to take her friends' advice and look for a complete change of scene to speed her recovery. Although sceptical of magnetism, she was much more sympathetic to another health cult greatly in vogue – hydropathy. Acutely aware of the failings of conventional medicine, she had for some months been 'desirous of obtaining that bedside knowledge of sickness which will enable me to commit heresy with intelligence in the future if my conviction impels me to it'.[19] She decided, therefore, to use the time before she went to St Bartholomew's to explore hydropathy at first hand by spending some weeks at Grafenberg, on the border of Germany and Czechoslovakia, where the fashionable of Europe gathered to take its famous water cure.

Hydropathy had its roots in ancient times but its modern founder and high priest was a Silesian peasant, Vinzent Priessnitz, who, as a boy, claimed to have cured his broken ribs simply by applying cold damp cloths to them.

At his greatly expanded farmhouse on the slopes of the Grafenberg, he developed a whole range of treatments based on water, fresh air, exercise, simple food and sleep that had by the middle of the century become immensely popular – especially in America. Elizabeth already knew something of hydropathy from Anna's experiences in Philadelphia but Priessnitz's centre, the birthplace of the whole water cure movement, was an altogether more extravagant venture and a triumph of entrepreneurship.

Travelling on her own, Elizabeth stopped long enough in Berlin to fall under the spell of Correggio's painting *Jupiter and Io* – 'the most beautiful picture I ever saw – her head thrown back the face expressive of divine bliss . . . such ecstasy as only the embrace of a deity could give. It is too beautiful to be called voluptuous yet it is the most powerful representation of the love sentiment in women that I have ever seen.'[20] Whether or not Elizabeth ever allowed herself to imagine what her future might have been with Hippolyte Blot, there is real poignancy in the image of her standing before this painting, emaciated by illness, her eye horribly disfigured, yet overwhelmed by such an unashamed celebration of sexual passion.

Apart from the beauty of the mountains, there was little sensuality awaiting her at Freiwaldau, the small village at the bottom of the Grafenberg, which she reached on 22 June 1850. It was, she remarked, 'a very watery place . . . There is a fountain in the market place, a rapid stream running through the town, every hill sends forth its little rills and a misty atmosphere like a soft wet blanket overspreads everything . . . I find you can occasionally be dry but still dryness is certainly an unnatural state and the exception here.'[21]

Elizabeth's first problem was to find lodgings – no easy matter. A German countess informed her that Priessnitz's establishment was full but that in any case it was not suitable for her to stay there alone since it was full of men walking around in their shirtsleeves. Undaunted, Elizabeth engineered an interview with the great man himself, who suddenly appeared unannounced in her hotel room: 'He examined me closely with his little blue eyes all the time I was explaining my wishes. Then in his abrupt manner, he told me he could make me quite strong in about six weeks, and the cure would do no harm to my eye. When I told him Grafenberg was quite full, he said, "You can come my child; come this afternoon" and off he went.'[22]

The high temple of water cure proved to be an enormous though undistinguished white house that reminded Elizabeth of a cotton manufactory in the Deep South. When she expressed dismay at her sparsely furnished bedroom under the rafters, she was told she should not complain as her neighbours were all aristocrats and that in any case she would be out in the woods all day.

At 6 o'clock the following morning Elizabeth's cure began in earnest. Invariably Priessnitz's first action was to make his new patients jump into a tub of cold water. Having observed their skin reaction, he would then devise a programme of treatment for them. After Elizabeth had endured this initial test she was subjected to wet packing, a plunge bath, a half bath, cold, wet bandages and innumerable glasses of water. The whole programme was repeated at midday and again at 4 o'clock. In between the treatments, patients were expected to spend their time outside roaming the woods and climbing mountains – preferably in bare feet. Apart from water and exercise, the essence of the cure was a regular routine, plenty of sleep and relief from worry so that patients were forbidden to discuss their ailments with one another.

Much of this had more to do with common sense than sophisticated science and resonated strongly with Elizabeth's own instincts. Yet she found much to criticise in Priessnitz's particular regime: 'The *abreibung* [rub down] deadens my fingers, the sitz bath gives me the colic, the wet bandages impede digestion, and tonight I went to bed with quite a feverish attack, which gave me unpleasant dreams the whole night.'[23] The living conditions were also far from perfect. The stench from the cows (tethered under the great hall where everyone ate their frugal meals of sour bread and milk) was mixed with that of the lavatories, kitchens and sodden blankets stretched out all over the house to dry.

Elizabeth had long been accustomed to physical discomfort but the social scene at Grafenberg presented her with a much tougher challenge – high society:

I found myself quite mistaken on the character of the place. It is in fact a fashionable summer resort for the widespread Germany . . . there is no end to the counts and barons and generals and little princes of the Lichtenfels. Instead of walking about bare-footed and wearing all my old dresses some attention to dress is indispensable. I find I have brought altogether too small a wardrobe for the demands of the place. The Countess von Westhalp wishes to introduce me into a fashionable English circle in Freiwaldau headed by Lady Darley. Doesn't it sound queer in Grafenberg? And we have

our balls and our theatre and every sort of miniature folly. Here in the
house we have our gymnasium, billiard room, library, theatre and what else
I shall discover I know not. In fact Grafenberg is the rage of Germany.
Priessnitz has five hundred under his care and with their friends they
amount to hundreds more.[24]

One of the grandest subscribers to Priessnitz's water cure was Princess
Obolenska, who sent a tall black-whiskered Russian envoy to ask Elizabeth
to call on her next time she was in Freiwaldau: 'I paid my visit, a professional
one, after all. I had to put up with four gulden, instead of the honour; but she
was a simple, pleasant lady, and we parted on the pleasantest terms. This
was, in fact, my first regular professional consultation.'[25]

But any hopes Elizabeth had of becoming one of Priessnitz's success
stories were dashed when a serious inflammation developed in her diseased
eye. With great difficulty she managed to travel back to Paris where she put
herself in the hands of Louis August Desmarres, the most innovative eye
surgeon of his day, whose skill with the scalpel was legendary. He forced
her to accept the truth she had so long denied – her eye would never
recover and must be surgically removed. This news was the bitterest of all
the blows Elizabeth had yet suffered for it finally put paid to her long-
cherished ambition of becoming a surgeon.

After the (expensive) operation was performed on 15 August, and the
long-dreaded glass eye put in place, she recuperated alone in a boarding
house, an exhausted Anna having removed herself to the country to take
refuge from the stresses of her family and the heat of the city. The despair
Elizabeth felt at this cruel turn of events was well under control by the time
she emerged again into the outside world. There was no public display of
anguish, only renewed determination to continue to work as a doctor and
reformer and put the whole traumatic episode behind her.

The surviving correspondence does not reveal much about Elizabeth's
feelings on parting from Hippolyte Blot at the time she left for Grafenberg,
thus leaving unanswered the tantalising question of whether their bond was
a serious one, tragically derailed by illness, or just a whiff of romance
destined to evaporate the moment Elizabeth left France. She wrote to
Emily: 'I shall miss him exceedingly when I leave Paris for there is a most
affectionate sympathy between us – but a reformer's life is not a garden of
roses.'[26] Whatever the truth, within two years of Elizabeth's departure Blot
was married and his wife expecting their first child.

Despite the appalling experience of her illness and the monastic conditions she had endured in La Maternité, Elizabeth looked back on the months she spent in Paris with surprising satisfaction. Circumstances had forced her to remain on the threshold of the medical scene, but she had, at least, witnessed at first hand the 'spirit of investigation that pervaded young and old'.[27] There was, she reflected in a letter to her old mentor, Dr Samuel Dickson,[28] a permanent sense of excitement among the Parisian medical profession with one or other of their number always on the brink of a major new discovery, a brilliant theory almost proved or a novel treatment awaiting assessment. Professors, she stated, were given ample resources for research but also found time to deliver imaginative lectures (sponsored by the government) to enthusiastic audiences. Most importantly, La Maternité had provided Elizabeth with a wide range of practical experience without which she would never have gained the confidence to set up her own practice.

* * *

Elizabeth arrived in London on 3 October and was immediately enveloped in smog. It was not just the filthy atmosphere that depressed her: 'As I continued to make my observations on people and things, on the dingy look of every building, the ugliness of the people, their rude unpleasing manners, their vulgar dress, the monotonous hard working life and finally, when after a week's visit to Portway I settled down in my present unpoetical lodgings, I asked myself with astonishment, is this the same London that I saw a year and half ago or is it a different person examining the same objects?'[29]

She took rooms at 28 Thavies Inn on Holborn Hill close to St Bartholomew's Hospital, where she duly presented herself soon after her arrival. Along with a dozen other new students (who seemed to be 'gentlemanly fellows') she was invited to breakfast by James Paget. Mrs Paget commented:

Well we have our 'Lady Doctor' here at last, and she has actually attended two of James' lectures, taking her seat with perfect composure. The young men have behaved extremely well, and she really appears likely to go on her way quite unmolested. She breakfasted here one morning with several of our students, and last evening we had a few medical friends to dinner, and she joined us in the evening. Her manners are quiet, and it is evident her motives for the pursuit of so strange a vocation are pure and good. So let us hope she will become useful in her generation.[30]

Paget was one of the outstanding medical men of his generation. Only twenty-nine when appointed warden of St Bartholomew's first residential college for students, he had already gained a reputation as an inspiring teacher and powerful advocate of the new professionalism developing within the medical establishment. He underlined to his students the scientific basis of medicine but was also at pains to remind them of their humanitarian duty to their patients. That duty required them to record and learn from their failures as much as from their successes. In a strikingly modern message he made it clear to them that, as well as becoming teachers, they must expect to remain students for their entire career.

After his apprenticeship to a Yarmouth surgeon, Paget had been unable to acquire the patronage then considered essential in England for a successful medical career and was consequently largely self-taught. He learned by following ward rounds, copious reading and spending his spare time dissecting as many corpses as supply would allow. It was perhaps memories of his own early struggle to acquire a medical education that led him to support Elizabeth's efforts so robustly. But despite clear mutual regard, no close friendship developed between them. They were, in fact, very different people. Paget, one of the founders of modern pathology, was utterly committed to science and not afraid to speak his mind: 'I know of no book which has been a source of brutality and sadistic conduct, both public and private that can compare with the Bible.'[31]

Elizabeth, on the other hand, rooted in Christianity, was increasingly critical of orthodox medicine especially as she perceived its application in England: 'I do not find as active a spirit of investigation in the English population as in the French . . . I cannot wonder that the students throng to Paris instead of this immense smoke hidden London. Here there is no excitement, all moves steadily onward constantly but without enthusiasm, no theory sets the world on fire til it is well established. Everything is stamped by good sense and clear substantial thought.'[32]

Although disillusioned with the drugs and the other conventional therapies Elizabeth saw administered to patients in St Bartholomew's ('I must confess that this study of the old practice is both difficult and disgusting to me – but it is essential and I shall be diligent'[33]), the 'heresies' she had so far investigated – mesmerism and hydropathy – also failed to convince her. She did consider the Swedish system of medical gymnastics introduced into England by Augustus Georgii (whom she met) highly promising and looked forward eagerly to exploring homeopathy, but she knew that if she abandoned regular medicine for more experimental treatments she risked being branded a female quack and all her efforts on behalf of women to gain acceptance by the medical establishment would be annulled. 'I have come to this conclusion – that I must begin with a practice which is an old-established custom, which has really more expressed science than any other system; but nevertheless, as it dissatisfies me heartily, I shall commence as soon as possible building up a hospital in which I can experiment; and the very instant I feel *sure* of any improvement I shall adopt in my practice, in spite of a whole legion of opponents.'[34]

Despite such mutinous thoughts Elizabeth was pleased with her progress at the thoroughly orthodox St Bartholomew's. Each day she spent about three or four hours on the wards diagnosing disease, watching the progress of cases and accustoming her ear to the stethoscope. The students treated her with respect and a number of the leading physicians went out of their way to be helpful. Dr Clement Hue, one of the more eccentric doctors working there, was always ready to show her interesting cases and even took her through the underground passage to Christ's Hospital School to taste its famous pea soup. She was particularly fond of Dr William Baly whom, she recorded, taught her more than anyone else. He had trained in Europe and was engaged in research into four of the biggest killers of the time – cholera, dysentery, scurvy and tuberculosis – all of which were rife in the poorer parts of New York City where Elizabeth was to set up practice a few months later.

Not all the physicians at St Bartholomew's Hospital were so accommodating. The Professor of Midwifery and Diseases of Women and Children sent a note to Elizabeth telling her that he entirely disapproved of women studying medicine and wanted her to know that his lack of support was not from disrespect to her as a woman but a condemnation of her objective. Almost certainly, the professor was as concerned about the potential competition from women entering his field as he was for their propriety.

Elizabeth had always been fundamentally more interested in social reform than scientific medicine and now that she could no longer train to be a surgeon, she began to contemplate the human condition with renewed vigour. She was horrified by the prostitutes she saw everywhere in London:

The terrible fact of prostitution has weighed upon me fearfully since I came to London for I believe in no city in the world does it show itself so publicly as it does here. At all hours of the night I see groups of our poor wretched sisters, standing at every corner of the streets, decked out in their best, which best is generally a faded shawl and even tattered dress, seeking their wretched living . . . My great dream is for a grand moral reform society, a wide movement of women in the matter, the remedy to be sought by action in every sphere of life – radical action, not the foolish application of plasters that has hitherto been the work of the self styled moral reform society. Leave the present prostitute, we can, alas, do nothing for her but redeem the rising generation.[35]

Elizabeth may have envisioned 'a great movement of women' but her opinion of her own sex in general, and of Englishwomen in particular, remained deeply unflattering. After dining with the Pagets she observed: 'I was very much impressed at the style of the ladies but really Englishwomen are not as sensible as I thought they were. Here was a rather grave dinner party, about twenty gentlemen and three ladies beside myself. These ladies were in full dress short sleeve dresses so low that more than a third of their bosom was visible; stiffening that made their petticoats balloon and all manner of scarves and flyaways. Women so dressed out don't look like rational beings and consequently they cannot be expected to be treated as such.'[36]

Paradoxically, she remained equally sceptical of those women who *were* attempting to behave like rational beings and expand female horizons by involving themselves in the women's rights movement – including her own sisters Marian and Ellen. Marian had finally escaped her domestic duties in Cincinnati and had moved east with the youngest Blackwell daughter, Ellen. In October 1850 both of them attended the first women's rights convention in Worcester, Massachusetts, the proceedings of which Marian sent to her sister in London. Despite the fact that Elizabeth's hero, William Henry Channing, sat on the platform and was one of the most prominent speakers, she was no more impressed by this latest feminist manifestation than she had been by the Seneca Falls meeting.

She considered their thinking hopelessly muddled and, in any case, could never herself sympathise with an 'anti-man movement'. Irritated to find that her name had been placed on the industrial committee without her permission, she told Marian frankly, 'I must keep my energy for what seems to me a truer movement'.[37] Marian, immensely proud to have been elected on to the education committee at the Convention, cannot have been greatly encouraged by Elizabeth's response to her request for contributory material: 'I feel a little perplexed by the main object of the Convention – Women's Rights. The great object of education has nothing to do with woman's rights or man's rights, but with the development of the human soul and body.'[38] Ironically, only a short time before making this crushing comment, Elizabeth met the woman who was to become her dearest lifelong friend – Barbara Leigh Smith, arguably the most charismatic leader of England's own nascent women's rights movement.

ELEVEN

'A Jolly Brick'

Barbara Leigh Smith and her friend Bessie Parkes appeared one dreary
November afternoon at Elizabeth's lodgings bearing flowers, paintings and
– ideas. Elizabeth was enchanted with them: 'They belong to "young
England" – girls of highly respectable families who have imbibed in some
unknown manner the best reform spirit of the day. Vigorous, thoughtful
minds that will not be contented with a selfish frivolous life and are
struggling hard to change the senseless customs which fetter them.'[1]

Both women, aged twenty-three and twenty-one respectively, came from
distinguished Unitarian families and, despite their youth, were already
deeply immersed in reform issues. Bessie's father, Joseph Parkes, was a well-
known liberal lawyer and her great-grandfather no less a radical figure than
the scientist and discoverer of oxygen, Joseph Priestley, whose politics had
forced him into exile in America in 1794. She was also a cousin of Samuel
Blackwell's late wife, Harriet Twamley, and it was through this connection
that she first learned of Elizabeth's arrival in London. She wasted no time in
alerting Barbara: 'Language cannot tell you what an exceedingly jolly brick
Miss Blackwell [is] . . . such a tale of energy, and hope; of repulses from
men and scorn of her own countrywomen.'[2]

Barbara's background was more unusual. She too came from a long line
of reformers; both her grandfather and father had been members of
parliament for Norwich and closely identified with such issues as anti-
slavery, the repeal of the Corn Laws and promotion of free trade. But,
although the Smith family was rich and successful, Barbara and her four
siblings were set apart from other children of their class as they had all
been born out of wedlock. Their mother Anne Longden (she used the
pseudonym Leigh) was a milliner whom, for whatever reason, Ben Smith
never married although he was clearly devoted to her. Surrounded in
childhood by a close, liberal-minded circle of friends, Barbara was largely
protected from the social ostracism that so often went hand in hand with
illegitimacy but could never entirely escape the fall-out from her father's

eccentric conduct. One telling example was the refusal of Ben Smith's own sister, Fanny Nightingale, to recognise his children, with the result that Barbara was allowed no contact with her first cousin, Florence.

Bessie Parkes had literary aspirations. She wrote poetry and essays on such themes as girls' education and, together with Barbara, established the *English Woman's Journal* in 1858, which remained under her editorship for five years. Although Elizabeth admired her warmth and energy she regarded her new friend with some reservations: 'She will not wear corsets, she won't embroider, she reads every heretic book she can get hold of, talks of following a profession, & had been known to go to an evening party, without gloves . . . she is really a very noble girl, but chaotic and without definite aim.'[3]

Ben Smith's behaviour was also unorthodox in another respect. On Barbara's twenty-first birthday, he presented her with a portfolio of stocks and shares that yielded an annual income of £300, thus giving her a financial independence that was exceptional for a young unmarried woman at the time. She determined to use her money creatively in support of reform causes close to her heart – a course from which she never wavered for the rest of her life.

When Elizabeth first met her in 1850, she had already published a number of articles, the first exhorting the local residents of Hastings (where she mostly lived) to invest the same energy into health and environmental issues as the Church of England put into distributing Bibles.[4] She had also published a piece echoing Mary Wollstonecraft's argument that the well-established notion of female 'innocence' was in reality plain 'ignorance'.[5] A striking redhead, Barbara's looks were as arresting as her politics and she won Elizabeth's instant admiration.

Barbara and Bessie moved in precisely the affluent, liberal circles that Elizabeth wanted to penetrate and they transformed her social life at a stroke. Suddenly, the small, impecunious woman doctor with a glass eye and American accent found herself in the middle of London's intellectual scene and she loved it: 'I have passed several delightful evenings with Mrs Follen, the whole family of the Twamleys are unending in their kindness; the de Morgans, Morells, Chapmans receive me fully and if I stayed in England I think I could lead the large important class they represent constantly forward in reforms.'[6]

John Chapman, whom she had first met in London the year before and who was shortly to become the owner and editor of the radical magazine, the *Westminster Review*, invited Elizabeth each week to his literary gatherings. Had she known the details of his exotic sex life she might not have accepted his hospitality so enthusiastically. Although married with two children, he expected his wife to tolerate cheerfully his various lovers living under the same roof, among them Marian Evans (George Eliot), the assistant editor of the *Review*. A few years later, Chapman had Barbara Leigh Smith in his thrall. He almost persuaded her to set up house with him, only to be thwarted at the last moment by the fury of the Smith males and by Barbara's own irritation at his request that she should give up work once they were living together.

Others in Elizabeth's social circle led more sober lives. Augustus de Morgan was the first professor of mathematics at University College London, John Morell a writer and government inspector of schools and Charles Twamley, a lawyer. As Elizabeth's acqaintance expanded she commented: 'Now I find these people vary in religion and everything else yet all are alive and open to progressive ideas if they are not shocked back. There seems to be a very large class of this kind who are not united in any special effort but in whom the true ideas are germinating which will come in time, perhaps in their children, for things move slowly in England.'[7]

One introduction that gave Elizabeth particular pleasure was to the American children's author, Elizabeth Lee Cabot Follen, whose late husband had been the first lecturer in German at Harvard (and responsible for introducing Christmas trees to the United States). Elizabeth wrote pointedly to Marian, whom she still hoped would act as her future housekeeper, 'Miss Cabot [Mrs Follen's sister] is charming in her affectionate attention to her sister, her right feeling and the unthinking contentment with which she takes second place'.[8]

Of all the new people whom Elizabeth met through Barbara Leigh Smith, none was more earnestly philanthropic than Lady Noel Byron, widow of the poet. A clever but reserved woman, her marriage to Lord Byron in 1815 was a curious match from the start and survived little more than a year. After their separation, she became interested in social reform supporting, among other great issues of the day, education, the cooperative movement, Abolitionism and Italian republicanism.

Lady Byron's views on education are clear from a description she gave Elizabeth of a school she had helped to set up in 1834 and they strike an extraordinarily modern note: 'No creed. No scripture books. No continual sedentary indoor employment. No *under*-demand on any of the faculties.

No over-excitement of feelings by prizes or other artificial stimulants. No definite boundary between work and play, the former as much as possible a pleasure, the latter not a contrast with lessons. No corporal chastisement. No over-legislation.'[9]

By the time the two women met in 1851, Lady Byron was fifty-nine, 'a slender, rather small, but venerable-looking lady with fair complexion, delicate features, and grey hair'[10] – and an exceptional understanding of scientific matters for a woman of her time. In April Elizabeth stayed a few days at her house in Brighton where the writer and critic Anna Jameson (who had also escaped an unhappy marriage) was a fellow guest. Elizabeth was impressed by the fact that since parting from her husband Jameson had managed to support herself entirely from her writing but also admired her 'warm Irish heart, exquisite appreciation of art, and deep interest in all high reform.'[11]

One evening during Elizabeth's visit to Brighton, the actress Fanny Kemble appeared: 'throwing open the door and declaiming a tragic Shakespearean quotation, dressed in rose-coloured satin, with a crimson mantle trimmed with white fur, a large bouquet in her bosom, her jet-black hair braided low down, with large black eyes, and a grand, deep-toned voice. She sat on the sofa beside Lady Byron – a most strange contrast. She was really magnificent in *Macbeth*, dressed in black velvet trimmed with ermine, and Mrs Jameson, who sat beside me, was in raptures.'[12]

The demurely dressed Elizabeth must have presented an equally strange contrast to the flamboyant actress. But, however different in personality, the two women had one searing experience in common – both had witnessed slavery at first hand. Fanny Kemble, although herself an Abolitionist, had been married to one of the wealthiest slaveholders in America, Pierce Butler. Early in their marriage, she had attempted to publish an anti-slavery treatise but was prevented from so doing by her husband. In 1838 she spent a distressing four months on his plantations in Georgia still convinced she would be able to persuade him to emancipate his slaves. When she failed to accomplish this, the marriage also failed and she returned to England to resume her acting career. She recorded her experiences in a memoir: *Journal of a Residence on a Georgian Plantation*.[13]

It is likely that Lady Byron, safe in the knowledge that Elizabeth was a qualified doctor, confided to her the scandalous circumstances surrounding the break-up of her marriage, namely Byron's incestuous affair with his half-sister Augusta Leigh. When she wrote to Elizabeth 'I regard the recognition of the same morality for men and women as absolutely necessary to the progress of civilization and Christianity'[14] she did so with some authority. Elizabeth regarded her new friend with profound respect. She had, after all, been the wife of one of the great romantic icons of all time. Yet marriage to Byron had also brought with it awareness of bi-exuality, incest, promiscuity – even, possibly, sodomy.

Elizabeth, whose only telling experience of sexual proclivity was gained from treating prostitutes at Blockley and La Maternité, believed that in Lady Byron she had discovered a remarkable survivor of male licentiousness and one whose bizarre experiences made her a particularly valuable interlocutor with whom to debate mankind's moral progress. In their correspondence, which continued until Lady Byron's death in 1860, Elizabeth consciously set out both her social theories and personal ambitions (hoping, no doubt, for Lady Byron's patronage). She repeatedly tried to convince her older friend that society could not advance until women (reformed and properly educated) took their place alongside men as equal partners.

But although devoted to change across such a wide social spectrum, Lady Byron was surprisingly reluctant to accept this image of women's future role: 'I do not desire equality of power and privileges. Where a woman's capacity is such as to raise her to an equality with men, I honour the exception, but I would not make it the rule. I do not attempt to give reasons – they would have no weight with you.'[15] Despite Lady Byron's disastrous marriage – or perhaps because of it – she still believed that a woman's highest calling in life was her husband: 'In striving to develop the Divine in Man's nature, a woman rises above even her own strongest temptation – to find God in him.'[16] This was too much for Elizabeth whose response, although deferential, was framed in steel:

> I have read and re-read your note with deep interest. The view it presents is a most important one, for the ideal of which you speak, is the highest ideal now presented to Women practically, it is the fundamental thought which directs their education and determines their social position. It is then of immense importance to know that the ideal is the true one. 'A life devoted on one – to the highest objects for that one' *is* that Woman's noblest ideal? To me such a view is fearful. Were the Divine incarnate in men, were their lives an expression of a grand soul, I could understand the reason of such a thought but when I examine the condition of the World . . . I must consider such a relationship between Man and Woman as *idolatry*. Beautiful sometimes, but a false worship *always*.[17]

When Lady Byron tactlessly suggested that women doctors were best fitted to play a secondary role in medicine she met the full force of Elizabeth's well-honed arguments. Firstly, she pointed out, there was nothing in the studies themselves to prevent a woman from pursuing medicine, only the deep-seated prejudice prevalent in colleges and hospitals, which 'obliged her to force her way through opposition, suspicion and vulgar curiosity'. Secondly, she confronted a longstanding objection to women entering the profession by referring (if opaquely) to menstruation asserting that 'the health of *healthy* women is never so variable as to prevent study, or render proper attention to medical practice difficult'. Finally she argued that a woman could only be an effective physician ministering to female diseases when she had been well trained in *all* aspects of medicine. The fatal error, she concluded, was to rank human beings according to *sex* instead of *character*.[18]

Lady Byron's more conventional view of women's role in society did not prevent her from making every effort to introduce her new friend to eminent doctors and surgeons and to discuss in depth with her projects such as self-supporting dispensaries. In response, Elizabeth summarised her social philosophy, underlining her disapproval of charity and making it clear that the cooperative movement still remained at the heart of her thinking.

She also shared with Lady Byron her ambition to found a hospital that would not only be a centre of science but also one of 'moral growth' so that her patients could be cured spiritually as well as physically. Attached to the hospital would be a church, workshops and studios forming in effect 'a whole society'. As yet uncertain how far it would be possible to mix men and women in this ideal hospital community, Elizabeth was nevertheless convinced that in the near future men and women would work closely together in all aspects of human endeavour. Was it mere diplomacy or heartfelt conviction when she wrote: 'How I wish I had the experience of human nature that you, dear Lady Byron, must have gathered in your active life.'[19]

As Barbara Leigh Smith was unable herself to introduce Elizabeth to her cousin, Florence Nightingale, this was left to a favourite aunt, Julia Smith, who arranged for the two – only a few months apart in age – to meet some time towards the end of 1850. Unfortunately, there is no record of this first important encounter but it is easy to imagine their mutual delight. Since the age of seventeen, Florence had been striving to find some meaningful way to use her remarkable talents but, at the time she met Elizabeth, had nothing but frustration to show for her efforts.

On 17 April 1851, Elizabeth visited the Nightingales' country house, Embley Park, in Hampshire: 'The laurels were in full bloom. Examined the handsome house and beautiful grounds. Walked much with Florence in the delicious air, amid a luxury of sights and sounds, conversing on the future. As we walked on the lawn in front of the noble drawing room she said, "Do you know what I always think when I look at that row of windows? I think how I should turn it into a hospital ward and just how I should place the beds!" She said she should be perfectly happy working with me, she should want no other husband.'[20]

Although at first sight they appeared to have so much in common, Elizabeth and Florence's vastly differing views on doctors and women's role in medicine led in later years to an inevitable rift. It was not just matters of policy that separated them. Such powerful personalities were never likely to coexist harmoniously, but an added irritant from Elizabeth's perspective was the massive fame Nightingale attracted after the Crimean War.

Elizabeth would have been scarcely human if she had not felt some pangs of jealousy at the extraordinary outpouring of emotion centred on her well-born, affluent contemporary who had never had to suffer the financial hardships she had been forced to endure while acquiring her medical status. In the early stages of their acquaintance, however, both women, so determinedly flying in the face of convention, were delighted by the friendship. Elizabeth had long considered hygiene a more effective remedy for disease than most drugs but acknowledged in later years that it was primarily to Nightingale that she owed her 'awakening to the fact that sanitation is the supreme goal of medicine, its foundation and its crown'.[21]

For many weeks Elizabeth had been watching with fascination Joseph Paxton's extraordinary structure of iron and glass rise in Hyde Park. On 1 May 1851 she witnessed the opening ceremony of the Great Exhibition as the guest of her cousin Samuel Blackwell, a prize-winning contributor to the mining section. This astonishing display of Britain's industrial achievements, together with the pomp and glitter of the occasion, only added to Elizabeth's perception that London was the place to live – despite the fact that she was now a naturalised American citizen.

Elizabeth had been at St Bartholomew's for six months and knew that, whatever the shortcomings of her medical education, she must soon move on. As usual, poverty dictated her choices. Since she had no hope of raising enough money to practise in London, she had only one realistic option – to go back to America and seek her fortune there. As Anna commented: 'Elizabeth has come to be quite an English woman in feeling and could very gladly stay here were it not that to set up in England would require more capital than she has at command. But she will no doubt return here eventually.'[22] Anna was right. Elizabeth had no intention of giving up permanently her agreeable life in England. And with Barbara's firm support in particular, she felt certain she would be able to establish herself successfully in London within a few years.

But for now there were other good reasons for crossing the Atlantic. Prejudice against women studying medicine in America appeared to be waning (two female medical colleges had been recently founded in Philadelphia and Boston), theoretically creating promising new opportunities for a woman already qualified. There was also the family to consider. It was six years since Elizabeth had spent more than a few days with them and she felt they needed her. Her brothers continued to struggle with their business, Marian remained dyspeptic and depressed, Ellen rudderless, and it was clear that Emily, now desperately seeking a medical education herself, would welcome her support. Perhaps the time had now come to turn the dream of a family community into reality.

Having definitively decided to return to America – at least for the next few years – Elizabeth spent her last weeks in England studying what she could of social conditions and taking leave of her friends. On 23 June she accompanied Florence Nightingale to visit the German Hospital. Opened in 1845 with just twelve beds, it was designed to serve the 30,000-odd (mostly poor and illiterate) German immigrants working in the East End of London. The Protestant nuns who provided the exceptionally good nursing at the 'German' came from the Kaiserswerth Institute near Wessendorf, where a few weeks later Florence based herself in search of medical training. The visit also proved to be one of real significance to Elizabeth who six years later was to establish a similar infirmary in a poor (predominantly German) immigrant quarter of New York.

On 17 July she paid a farewell call on St Bartholomew's. She was pleased that several of the doctors believed her presence in the hospital had been such a success that more female students might soon be admitted. It was, in fact, to be nearly 100 years before this happened. James Paget told Elizabeth how sorry he was to lose her while his wife described her as 'a benefactor to the human race'.[23] In later years, Paget gave a more guarded assessment: 'The celebrated Dr. Elizabeth Blackwell – a sensible, quiet, discreet lady – gained a fair knowledge (not more) of medicine, practised in New York: then tried to promote female doctordom in England.'[24]

Four days later Elizabeth left London for Dudley. She enjoyed an excursion with Howard – riding up Worcestershire Beacon on a donkey and sliding all the way down – but spent her last day in England more characteristically observing social conditions in a cotton mill in Manchester. Cousin Samuel and Howard saw her off from Dudley on 26 July – 'dear Howy running up the railway bank as I rushed off in the train' – and by nightfall she was aboard the *Constitution* sailing down the Mersey, 'another important page in life fairly closed'.[25]

TWELVE

Medical Practice

The New York to which Elizabeth returned in August 1851 had become a seething metropolis of half a million people – a vastly expanded city from the one to which her father had first brought his family nearly twenty years earlier. Bankers, brokers, railroad barons, publishers, property developers and traders of every kind were intent on claiming their share of the current economic boom. Broadway was so densely packed with people and omnibuses that it was claimed it might take half an hour to cross from the shilling side (east) to the dollar side (west). The city was full of new hotels (some of them catering for as many as 800 guests), theatres, shops and splendid private houses.

As New York extended northwards, the stretch of Fifth Avenue between Washington Square and Madison Square became the most desirable place to live. Here the rich built lavishly carved houses in the newly fashionable brownstone that gave Manhattan its uniform appearance. But at the other end of the spectrum were the flimsy, squalid tenements put up to house the thousands of mainly Irish and German immigrants flocking to the city in the wake of the potato famine and the short-lived revolutions of 1848.

For an unknown woman doctor attempting to set up practice in this hustling society, the first prerequisite was a good address. With the help of her mother, Marian and Ellen, who were in New York to greet her, Elizabeth found lodgings at 44 University Place close to Washington Square and just one block east of Fifth Avenue. They suited her well: 'I like the room, it has an air of pleasant gloom about it, which Marian and I agree is calm and soothing, rather philosophic'.[1] Attached to her new rooms was a greenhouse: 'We have a good deal of use out of it. In fact I keep my girl there and when it gets too hot she retreats into the water closet which leads out of it and which is quite a jewel of a water closet having a cool window and large enough to hold her cot bedstead and preserving its atmosphere in a state of perfect purity.'[2]

Elizabeth now had the qualifications, the consulting rooms, the maturity (she was thirty) and even a maid – but no patients. Horace Greeley, the editor of the *Tribune* and (at this stage of his life) a staunch supporter of women's rights, did his best to help her by printing a piece in his newspaper lauding her achievements and advertising her practice. But even this generous announcement did nothing to tempt the female patients that Elizabeth had been so sure would come flocking to her surgery. The novelty of a woman doctor and the deep-seated prejudice against such a concept were, of course, major factors but there was also another problem – Madame Restell.

Dubbed 'the most evil woman in New York', Madame Restell was also the most skilful, hygienic and wealthy abortionist in town. In 1831 Ann Trow (as she was then) arrived in New York a poor immigrant from England. Soon widowed and with a child to support, she discovered a means of earning her living that within a few years transformed her into one of the most notorious women in America. It could, however, be argued that she was as much concerned with enabling women to gain more control over their lives as Elizabeth. Certainly Madame Restell, unlike most other practitioners, was prepared to justify abortion on ethical grounds, asking: 'Is it moral for parents to increase their families, regardless of consequences to themselves, or the well being of their offspring, when a simple, easy healthy remedy is within our control?'[3]

In 1847 she was imprisoned for a year but was back in business soon after her release, and so successful that she was able to build one of the most splendid houses in New York on the very plot of land (opposite St Patrick's Cathedral) that the bishop had earmarked for his own palace. Society needed Madame Restell's services but emphatically did not wish to recognise her existence. And the fact that she described herself as a 'woman physician' did little to encourage those respectable New York women *not* wanting an abortion to seek Elizabeth's medical expertise.

Socially, Elizabeth's life was as disappointing as it was professionally. Emily summed up the situation in her usual blunt manner:

I am very glad you have made so pleasant a circle of acquaintances in London. I fear that will be the most unsatisfactory point in your New York residence. I don't believe there is any pleasant society to be found there and the commonness you speak of in Mrs McDaniel [ex Brook Farmers, friends of Anna's and Henry's] is, I believe, an American characteristic. I think you will not find the same educated and refined class in New York, as you are probably accustomed to meet in England, though I suppose they are more simple and unprejudiced.[4]

While Elizabeth waited in vain for patients to knock on her door, she did, at least, have time to consider Emily's future. The caginess that existed between the two sisters had never entirely evaporated so that Elizabeth's attitude towards her sister's medical ambitions fluctuated between a real longing to have a professional companion and *angst* that her pre-eminence as a pioneering woman doctor might be challenged by a clever younger sister. Emily, sensing this ambivalence, confided to her diary: 'I ask myself often if I do not expect too much sympathy and companionship from Elizabeth.'[5]

In matters of family rivalry, Elizabeth had reason to be nervous, for Emily was extraordinarily able. But, unlike her older sister, she was racked with self-doubt: 'My soul rises in one intense aspiration for a heroic life, till I almost fear its very intensity is selfishness.'[6] In her search for a medical education, she proved as single-minded as her sister. Despite suffering all the same setbacks and rejections as Elizabeth (she was even refused by Geneva College), she persevered until finally accepted by Rush College in Chicago in November 1852.

Eight months earlier Elizabeth, desperate to stimulate business and to occupy her mind, gave a series of lectures on girls' education which was published later in the year under the title *The Laws of Life with Special Reference to the Physical Education of Girls*[7] – her first significant publication. Preparing for these lectures was not easy. She could not afford the subscription to a library and had to ask Emily to send her material. But her labours were rewarded. She found a small but appreciative audience among the Quakers – so often at the forefront of female emancipation – who subsequently formed the core of her practice. Although she confessed to Emily how much she disliked extempore teaching, she was encouraged by the enthusiastic response of her class.

Given Elizabeth's own history and the arguments she had so recently put to Lady Byron regarding women's role in the modern world, the message delivered in these talks was remarkably conventional. Yet she failed to see any conflict between her radical actions and traditional teaching. Indeed, throughout her long life, her strong instinct for reform was counterbalanced by an equally robust conservatism. This double helix structured her very being but was deeply perplexing to those feminists who assumed her to be a fellow-traveller.

In her lectures Elizabeth was adamant that girls' education needed reform, but at no point did she suggest that this change was necessary in order to prepare women for professional life, or work outside the home. In fact, she appeared closer to supporting the accepted middle-class view that motherhood and moral suasion were the only proper female missions in life. To her rapt students, she presented an image of the delivery room saturated with sentimentality: 'The mother forgetful of weariness and suffering, lifts her pale face from the pillow, and listens with her whole soul. The physician, profoundly penetrated with the mystery of birth, bends in suspense over the little being hovering on the threshold of a new existence. For one moment they await the issue – life or death! The feeble cry is the token of victory. The mother's face lights up with ineffable joy, as she sinks back exhausted, and the sentiment of sympathy, of reverence, thrills through the physician's heart.'[8]

The underlying theme of these talks was one to which Elizabeth so often returned – the perfectibility of the human race. Physical vigour played an essential part in this quest for if the body were properly treated and trained from an early age, spiritual health would develop naturally – *mens sana in corpore sano*. A young girl should not be overstretched academically, slump over her desk or sit on hard benches. Most importantly, she should practise kinesipathy, the system of gymnastics developed by the Swede Per Henrik Ling, whose emissary Elizabeth had met in London.

> By the age of 16 or 17, under *proper training*, she would have acquired a strong graceful and perfectly obedient body. Her senses would be acute. Accustomed to the exercise of their powers on beautiful objects appropriate to them, they would be truthful in their perceptions, and ready to receive the fullest extent of scientific training. She would speak fluently several languages, write a good hand, sketch with ease and correctness; sing with accuracy; for all these requirements and many others, would be necessarily obtained by pursuing a complete system of physical development.[9]

To Lady Byron, Elizabeth had vigorously rejected the notion that menstruation might prevent women studying medicine. In her lectures, however, she modified this position by suggesting its onset be delayed for as long as possible, thus appearing to conform to the widely held view that it was essentially hazardous – an undesirable symptom of female weakness. In her view, of course, most women *were* weak. And until they improved themselves physically, intellectually and morally, she argued they could neither pursue the kind of challenging career that she had chosen nor expect men to treat them as equals. For all the feminist arguments she had put so persuasively to Lady Byron, in reality she believed that only a very few women were currently capable of leading their woolly-minded sisters to a higher, more fulfilling existence.

In response to an invitation to attend a women's rights convention later that year in Syracuse, Elizabeth set out her views on the status quo of her sex in a manner that can have only infuriated the suffragist lobby:

I believe that the chief source of the false position of women is, the inefficiency of women themselves. The deplorable fact that they are so often careless mothers, weak wives, poor housekeepers, ignorant nurses, and frivolous human beings. If they would perform with strength and wisdom the duties, which lie immediately around them, every sphere of life would soon be open to them. They might be priests, physicians, rulers, welcome everywhere, for all restrictive laws and foolish customs would speedily disappear before the spiritual power of strong, good women. In order to develop such women, our method of educating girls, which is an injurious waste of time, must be entirely remodelled.[10]

This was *not* what the architects of the feminist movement wanted to hear from one who, as the 'first woman doctor', should have been their finest trophy. And it was certainly not an opinion shared by Lucy Stone. One of the most prominent and eloquent speakers on equal rights, her approach to female liberation could scarcely have been more different from Elizabeth's. Yet within a few years the two women were to become sisters-in-law. Lucy Stone and Henry Blackwell met in 1850 when she went to his hardware store in Cincinnati to cash a cheque. Initially Henry thought she would make the perfect wife for his brother, but when Sam showed little enthusiasm he decided to court Lucy himself. This he did with great ardour until she finally agreed to marry him in 1855. Elizabeth did not approve of the match. Although small and demure in appearance, Lucy's forthright methods of pursuing her objectives were precisely those that Elizabeth thought most damaging to women's future prospects.

Certainly, she did not hesitate to make plain to Lucy her views on women's rights conferences: 'To my mind, the time, if ever it existed, for such conventions, is already past and their continuance is a waste of time to those whose time is of value and an injury rather than a benefit to the cause.' Such gatherings, she believed, were mere talking shops incapable of transforming ideas into action and therefore nothing but a 'slur on the dignity of the Woman Cause'.[11] But in Lucy, Elizabeth had met her match: 'It seems to me that you could not consider them a "waste of time" if you had noted their results with which I am *more* than satisfied. The ideas of the movement have been received with remarkable readiness and applied practically far more than we had reason to expect.'[12]

Lucy, like so many other women, had become a feminist via the anti-slavery movement. Born in Massachusetts into a modest farming family, she had, against her father's wishes, enrolled in Oberlin College, Ohio. After graduating in 1847 she caused a further stir by announcing to her family that she planned to join the lecturing circuit, talking on abolition and women's rights. At a time when it was unthinkable for a woman to speak from a public platform, this was no feeble undertaking.

But, convinced of the rightness of her cause and fearless of public ridicule, Lucy travelled from one small town to another, up and down the eastern seaboard and across the Midwest preaching her message. She met with intense hostility. Hosed with icy water, refused a room in which to speak or sleep, insulted as a woman who smoked cigars and swore like a trooper, her choice of career was not one for the faint-hearted. Elizabeth admired her personal courage but was nevertheless quick to pass on to Henry a damning account, received from Dr William Elder, of a lecture Lucy had delivered in Pittsburgh: 'It seems that her last lecture on "Our Country and its Needs" was a complete failure and though her women's rights lectures had abundantly answered, the last failure was so entire that they declared she would not pay her expenses if she returned. He says he never saw such a complete revulsion of feeling from one lecture and he was really anxious she should redeem her credit. His interest was really a kind one. Is it worth speaking of? Keep a good heart dear Henry.'[13]

In July 1852, Emily joined Elizabeth in New York. They viewed their reunion with some apprehension since they had not met for four years, yet were planning a lifelong professional partnership. In the event, both were pleased with the encounter. After five days of incessant talking, Emily wrote in her diary that she liked Elizabeth, finding her less 'particular and fidgety'[14] than she had expected. For her part, Elizabeth wrote enthusiastically to Lady Byron that the week she had just spent with her sister was the most exciting she could remember.

Emily had travelled east in the hope of being accepted at Dartmouth Medical College but, after rejection there, she returned to New York uncertain what to do next. Horace Greeley came to the rescue with some judicious string pulling and, several weeks later, Emily was walking the wards of Bellevue, one of the finest hospitals in New York. For the next couple of months she studied every day at the hospital and at last began to feel like a proper medical student. Occasionally she and Elizabeth took a day off: 'Last Sunday E and I took a pleasant little excursion to Staten Island. We sat among the pines on a hill overlooking the bay and read Hawthorne's *Blithedale Romance*. I find E a very noble disposition and a good head. She has nervous streaks that seem to me to point out delicate health.'[15]

Finally, in November, Emily was permitted to register at the Rush College in Chicago as a bona fide medical student. After just one week there, she recorded her first great trial: 'I know not yet whether it is the first of a terrible series or whether I shall be able to smile three months hence at its record. Yesterday I attended at Dr Evans' strong desire, his demonstration of the external generative organs . . . I was glad to find myself in command sufficient to prevent even my colour from changing, but I fear, now the trying lectures have commenced, that the pleasant feeling the class has hitherto manifested will begin to change.'[16]

This initial embarrassment was swiftly overcome. By January 1853 (having completed her study of syphilis and moved on to ruptures) Emily had decided to become a surgeon and already concluded that operations, although the showiest aspect of surgery, were not necessarily the most difficult. 'The determination of cases suitable for operation and the after treatment are even more serious and far less satisfactorily settled than the manner of performing operation.' She had also resolved to specialise in the reproductive system, spurred on by the conviction that 'some means might be found placing conception under the control of the individual . . . the part of woman in such matters ought to be more under her control, more dignified and individual than it is'.[17]

Elizabeth, meanwhile, was slowly beginning to build up her practice, which, as she readily admitted, relied largely on the Quaker community. A number of her customers, however, behaved in a decidedly un-Quakerish manner:

Some of my patients will fall in love with me, do what I will they absolutely haunt me, make the most absurd speeches, look at me with most enamoured eyes and three of them in unguarded moments, kissed me! Yesterday came a very determined lady to consult me. I saw to my horror that I was captivating her and as I stooped down to make a necessary measurement she suddenly kissed my head with some absurd sentimentality. I charged her three dollars. I've no objection to kissing a healthy, handsome man occasionally, but love passages with women are diabolical!![18]

The increased flow of patients improved Elizabeth's income but she was still heavily dependent on borrowed money. A literary prize produced an unexpected windfall of $100. Marian, Emily and Ellen had all submitted anonymous stories to a leading literary magazine, taking it upon themselves to include one Elizabeth had written some years earlier. To the embarrassment of the magazine (when they discovered the sisters' identities) and the chagrin of Emily (who failed to win anything) Marian, Elizabeth and Ellen won the first three prizes. But this was only a brief shaft of light in the general financial gloom.

To make matters worse, Elizabeth was lonely. At thirty-one, the possibility of marriage seemed ever more remote and while she was used to being on her own, her recent social success in London and the fact that her key supporter, Marian, now spent most of her time in Jersey City living with wealthy Dutch friends, threw into sharp relief her current isolation. As 1853 approached, Elizabeth made a double resolve that she hoped would lift her professional and social life out of the doldrums. She would open a dispensary and buy a house.

THIRTEEN

Hard Times

Elizabeth had experienced plenty of bigotry and prejudice in her life but even she was shaken by the degree of isolation forced upon her during her early years as a physician. Emily, with characteristic directness, suggested that it was her 'English nature' that held her back but Elizabeth blamed 'strong prejudice on the part of women . . . heightened by the vulgarity of the medical movement'.[1] But if she was disillusioned with the reality of doctoring, her belief in the perfect society survived remarkably intact. As she explained to Lady Byron: 'I do believe that this faith in the oneness of Humanity, with the resolution to press on to a high Ideal of the Future, has taken a deep root, and will develop itself in more worthy forms than have hitherto appeared. This is my hope and I do cherish it for otherwise my work here, would be very cheerless.'[2]

It was not only the medical profession that ignored her – she also felt socially outcast especially since even old friendships seemed to have evaporated. William Henry Channing, the man whom (with the exception of Hippolyte Blot) she valued above all others, fell sharply from favour: 'He has never been near me since your book arrived, he has taken no notice of the letter which I think may have reached him and Mrs Channing has never sent me a line or message of thanks as remembrance though a year has elapsed since [their son] Frank was under my care for three weeks, I sparing no trouble to aid him. So I think it is a worthless family in a social point of view. They absorb kindness but make no return. I am very sorry but so it is; Mr Channing disappoints me more and more in every relation of life.'[3]

Elizabeth suffered physically as well as mentally during these grim early years in New York. In winter she could not afford enough food or fuel to keep warm while throughout the summer she toiled long distances (even when the heat made 'the brain seem too large for the head') to attend her handful of patients. To add to her woes, she received hostile letters and had to fend off men propositioning her late at night as she walked home alone after visiting patients. All in all, her New York existence was a bleak contrast to the stimulating life she had enjoyed in London and a pathetically poor reward for the long years of privation. Dedicated though she was to the task of reforming society through the empowerment of women, even Elizabeth needed the occasional diversion – 'I should like a little fun now and then, life is altogether too sober'.[4]

'Although she viewed orthodox medicine with increasing cynicism, Elizabeth remained acutely aware that as a pioneer woman doctor she dared not risk being labelled a quack by dabbling in the so-called heresies. Even so, she could hardly remain immune to the extraordinary craze for spiritualism rampant in New York during the early 1850s that she had first encountered near Geneva just before her graduation. Margaret and Kate Fox, now celebrities, were attracting huge audiences in Rochester and later New York City with public displays of their unusual talents. Many prominent citizens (among them Horace Greeley and the novelist James Fenimore Cooper) fell under the sisters' spell after witnessing the rappings and knockings at a private party given for the girls soon after their arrival in Manhattan. Elizabeth, still doubtful, was nevertheless intrigued by the whole affair. In reply to a letter Lady Byron had sent her on the subject of magnetism she wrote: 'Magnetism . . . connects itself in my mind with a most curious movement now taking place in America to which I want to call your attention because beneath all the absurdity and frequent deception there is a curious truth which demands earnest attention. I refer to what is called the spiritual manifestation, a fruitful subject for newspaper ridicule, for the contempt of the learned and for the anger of sectarian piety. But nevertheless a remarkable fact which no so called explanation can explain!'[5]

In fact, Elizabeth's old acquaintance Dr William Carpenter (who had first recommended that she study at St Bartholomew's Hospital) had investigated a variety of popular phenomena such as dowsing, table turning, and the magic pendulum, determined to prove that such supernatural curiosities could be explained by conventional science. In 1852 he produced his theory of ideomotor action, demonstrating how the power of suggestion could influence muscular movement independently of will.[6]

The following year Michael Faraday (whose lectures Elizabeth had attended with Lady Byron at the Royal Institution in London) made a thorough and carefully controlled study of table turning. In an ingenious experiment involving impeccably honest sitters and cardboard sheets, Faraday satisfied himself that the only force moving the table was human, even though the humans themselves were entirely unaware that they were exerting it. Faraday's findings were published in America[7] but science, however elegantly expounded, made little impression on those (like Anna Blackwell) eager to be seduced by the paranormal.

Elizabeth continued to sit on the fence: 'I know no reason why this communication with the spirits is in itself impossible but it does not approve itself to my conviction.'[8] She was similarly ambivalent in her attitude to scientific method in general, for while she always publicly supported science, she was quick to condemn it whenever it conflicted with her own sense of morality. Above all, she wanted: 'a field of medical discovery in which we may labour without doing violence to our taste in the dissecting room, without exercising injustice morally by vivisection and without destroying any sentiment of delicacy and reverence for humanity by the disgusting experiments on human beings by which the French savants have disgraced the scientific enquiry'.[9]

In contrast, Emily was a natural scientist whose misgivings about the medical profession tended to evaporate once she was peering down a microscope. Her detachment in the operating room was admirable if faintly chilling: 'I went to the first severe operation, amputation of the thigh, with some nervousness but neither in that nor in any other case I have seen have I felt the slightest unpleasant feeling. I believe I shall have no difficulty about that, and when once engaged in observing or helping, all feeling of its being cruel or even disagreeable vanishes. I could not feel the slightest pity for the dog at the time and the blood affected me no more than so much warm water. If it had not been for principle, I would have cut him up without scruple if there had been any object to be gained.'[10]

Neither sister had any illusions about the efficacy of contemporary medicine nor were they motivated by a burning desire to ease the suffering of the sick, as Emily made clear in a letter to Elizabeth:

I know you look on medicine with something of contempt, and there is certainly nothing attractive in the care of miserable, forlorn, sick people. I always feel that the best thing that could be done with a hospital were to blot it and its inmates out of existence, when I think of them as people. It is only as scientific illustration that I can take the least interest in them, unless it were possible to raise them and that is a difficult matter. Generations will progress but it is difficult to improve one already formed. I should not think anyone a good physician who was fascinated by the practice of medicine at present. But I look upon it as a great means.[11]

Towards the end of February 1853, having completed her first term in Chicago, Emily returned to New York anxious to ease Elizabeth's depression. Another (uncharacteristically frivolous) concern was the shabbiness of her bonnet, which she did not want to replace in 'dirty little Chicago'. Initially, the sisters were glad to be reunited but, as Emily recorded in her diary, it was not long before the old doubts concerning their compatibility resurfaced: 'I do not feel perfectly clear that I can establish myself in New York and work in concert with E. On many accounts I should like to but whether I could not work more effectually elsewhere I have not yet decided.'[12]

Emily was able to resume her part-time studies at Bellevue Hospital but for most of the nine-month gap between semesters was forced to study alone. It was during these long, tedious months that the two sisters began to plan a project that they believed could transform their careers – the opening of a dispensary. Shortly after returning to New York, Elizabeth had applied to work in the women's department of one of the large city clinics but was unceremoniously rejected. Stung by this rebuff, but realising that it was likely to be one of many, she concluded that the only way forward was to launch a clinic of her own. She had little notion of how to set about such a project but early in 1853 received a blueprint from the founder of the Rush Medical School and Emily's medical protector, Dr Daniel Brainard.

Brainard's scheme was designed to mitigate, as much as possible, the deep suspicion and distrust he knew such a venture would attract. He proposed that Elizabeth ask the most influential men she knew to act as the clinic's trustees and consulting physicians. These men, he underlined, must be prepared to use their influence in her support and not desert her the moment anything went wrong. She should rent rooms in a poor quarter of New York and advertise the dispensary in newspapers read by the Irish and German immigrants who were likely to form the bulk of the practice. Brainard also cannily suggested that she should gain the confidence of one or two Catholic priests. If enough subscriptions could be raised, medicine should be dispensed free.

It was good advice. After much deliberation and planning, the clinic finally opened its doors in March 1854, having been incorporated several months earlier as 'The New York Dispensary for Poor Women and Children'. Apart from providing medical care for the poor, the clinic was intended to be a place where well-qualified female physicians could find the clinical experience they so desperately needed and also to provide training for nurses. Although in its early version the dispensary was never more than a modest success, it marked a turning point in Elizabeth's professional fortunes as it formed the genesis of a much more ambitious project, the New York Infirmary for Women and Children, opened three years later.

The dispensary was situated on East 7th Street close to Tompkins Square – a Lower East Side landmark that for much of the nineteenth century formed a focus for radical thought and political demonstration. Tompkins Square was part of *kleindeutschland*, a neighbourhood crammed with flimsy tenement buildings that a New York mayor once described as being 'so slightly built that they could not stand alone, and, like drunken men, require the support of each other to keep them from falling'.[13]

For Elizabeth, brought close to despair by the sluggishness of her practice and the medical profession's refusal to acknowledge or support her in any way, the dispensary offered distraction and some opportunity at least to practise her skills. The few deprived women who turned up at the small, damp room seeking treatment showed a refreshing lack of interest in the middle-class obsession with 'appropriate' female behaviour. On the contrary, most of them considered it an unexpected bonus to be able to consult a woman doctor about women's problems.

Furthermore, since such destitute immigrants were in as much need of guidance in basic hygiene, ventilation and healthy diet as they were of medical care, Elizabeth was able to dispense exactly the brand of holistic social medicine in which she so fervently believed. For two hours, three afternoons a week, simple remedies were supplied along with advice on how to find jobs, seek help from charities, run hygienic households and deal with drunken husbands. It was fortunate that Elizabeth spoke some German as the majority of the patients were from Germany and spoke little or no English – and so poor that a fund was set up to provide the most destitute among them with small loans until they could find work.

The money for this initiative came mainly from the Quakers who also formed the majority of trustees on the dispensary board. The board's most influential member, however, was not a Quaker. Horace Greeley was a dedicated Fourierist and proprietor of *New York Tribune* which, since its foundation in 1841, had supported all the issues closest to Elizabeth's heart – Abolitionism, Association and the progress of women.

Greeley, therefore, was a natural recruit and by the time he joined the dispensary board had already been of invaluable help to Elizabeth and Emily. At the time when Emily was first trying to gain a foothold in Bellevue

Hospital, she described visiting him at his home to seek his help. 'Greeley was in his bare parlour writing at a table which was the substratum of a mountain of papers – papers on the chairs everywhere . . . he looked up with his blue eyes under their colourless lashes and brows and told me, writing all the while that Mr Draper thought it could be done.'[14]. By the late 1850s the *Tribune* was a major force on public opinion, its circulation easily outstripping that of all its rivals. Greeley's backing was exactly the kind of support Elizabeth and Emily needed if they were ever to succeed.

Greeley was joined on the dispensary board by his assistant editor at the *Tribune*, Charles A. Dana, who had been a leading figure in the Brook Farm experiment and cut his journalistic teeth on its journal, the *Harbinger*. Dennis Harris, Samuel Blackwell's old foreman, who had sailed on the same ship with the family from Bristol in 1832 and was now himself a successful sugar refiner, proved a more conservative if no less dedicated trustee. Although he was never regarded with much affection by the Blackwell siblings, he continued to offer them loans, jobs and general support over many years until his death.

However, in August 1853 Emily received the unwelcome news that Daniel Brainard, who had been so helpful to the sisters with their plans for the dispensary, would shortly be leaving for Europe and would therefore no longer be at the Rush Medical College to act as her patron. Consequently she was not surprised, if bitterly disappointed, to learn when she returned to Chicago in November that the college authorities had decided not to admit her for the second semester. Wasting no time, she packed her bags and took a train to Cleveland where, to her relief, she was allowed to enrol in the Western Reserve Medical School. Three months later, on 22 February 1854, she formally qualified as a physician but with none of the drama or ceremony that had marked Elizabeth's graduation. One of the doctors did present her with flowers after her examination remarking: 'it is not often that roses bloom in winter, and it is not often professors have such a student.'[15]

Emily may not have attracted the same celebrity as her sister (by 1854, the novelty of women doctors had faded as more graduates emerged from the women's medical schools in Philadelphia and Boston) but she could, at least, benefit from Elizabeth's experiences. Like her, she had never doubted that she must go to Europe to complete her studies and for many months had been considering how best to accomplish this. All too aware of the difficulties Elizabeth had faced, she was resigned to disguising herself as a man in order to gain admission to a good hospital. In the event, she was able to avoid such subterfuge when a medical friend of Lady Byron's recommended her to one of the most talented and innovative doctors of the century, James Simpson, Professor of Medicine and Midwifery and the Diseases of Women and Children at Edinburgh University, who agreed to accept her as a student in the spring of 1854.

When Emily first met James Simpson (he was made a baronet in 1866) he was already famous well beyond his native Scotland. Indeed, many people regarded him as the saviour of mankind for the simple reason that in 1847 he had transformed surgical practice with his championing of the first effective and relatively safe anaesthetic – chloroform. It is hard now to imagine how the alleviation of pain could have been a controversial issue but the use of anaesthetic was passionately resisted in many quarters, not so much on medical as on moral grounds – particularly when given to women in childbirth. One of the main objections (invariably raised by men) was the understanding that under the influence of chloroform a woman might become sexually aroused – a fate clearly worse than death itself: 'I may venture to say, that to the women of this country the bare possibility of having feelings of such a kind excited and manifested in outward uncontrollable actions, would be more shocking even to anticipate than the endurance of the last extremity of physical pain.'[16] But by the time Emily arrived in Edinburgh the chloroform debate was more or less over, won by Simpson's own persuasive evangelism and pragmatic public opinion.

In the letters Emily wrote to Elizabeth during the eight months she spent with Simpson, she gave an intriguing account of the man and his work. Although greatly admiring his innovative treatments, his ability to examine patients effectively and the extraordinary skill with which he diagnosed their condition, Emily was not so overawed by her famous teacher that she was incapable of analysing his practice with cool objectivity: 'He is so excessively rapid that I felt convinced he cannot always do justice to his patients and by further watching the practice I feel sure I shall find many cures where his success is less than he thinks or where he fails . . . he is very enthusiastic, quite sure that he can cure anything and that comforts his patients at least.' She shrewdly observed the placebo effect of Dr Simpson's reputation 'which dazzles his patients till they feel they must be relieved by him'.[17]

Emily learned more in a month assisting Simpson than she had from all her previous studies, but was still frustrated by the meagre opportunities she was given to examine patients herself. She painstakingly described his various treatments in letters to Elizabeth but was acutely aware that descriptions, however detailed, were no substitute for practical experience. Having closely observed Simpson at work, she understood all too clearly that it was only by repeated physical examination of patients that she and Elizabeth could ever hope to become expert in the field of women's diseases. She was at least able to send Elizabeth some of the latest pessaries and obstetrical instruments which, on arrival in New York, were examined with great curiosity by puzzled customs officials. From Elizabeth, however, they only prompted the sad admission that her current practice gave her little opportunity to use such relatively sophisticated apparatus.

In May 1854, when the dispensary had been in operation just two months, Elizabeth's efforts to keep it afloat were given an unexpected boost by the appearance of an exuberant young Prussian woman Marie Zakrzewska, destined to become one of the most effective of all the first generation of qualified women doctors. She was only twenty-four when she first met Elizabeth but her roller-coaster life already overflowed with accomplishment and disappointment.

She was born in Berlin, the daughter of a Prussian army officer who was dismissed from his post (for his liberal views) while she was still a small child. Her resourceful mother took over as the family breadwinner by enrolling in the Berlin School of Midwifery, whose course included a six-month residency in the charity hospital. Because the twelve-year-old Marie suffered from eye problems, she was allowed to live there with her mother and became a great favourite of one of the senior doctors. Although her eyes were bandaged, she accompanied him each day on his rounds precociously absorbing the medical talk that flowed about her.

It was an unusual experience for a child but one that left her determined to enter professional medicine. Throughout her teens Marie worked in her mother's practice so that by the time she decided to become a midwife herself at the age of eighteen, she already had years of obstetric experience. She was fortunate to catch the eye of the Professor of Midwifery at the Berlin school, who was so impressed by her ability that he even involved the King of Prussia in his efforts to gain her admission to his college. In the teeth of intense opposition, he succeeded in having Zakrzewska (then only twenty-two) appointed chief midwife in the hospital and the professor of education at the school. Unfortunately for his protégée, he died within weeks of her taking up the job and without his protection she fell prey to all the familiar jealousies and prejudices. Six months later, unable to withstand the hostility of her colleagues, she resigned.

While working at the hospital, Marie had seen a copy of the first report issued by the Female Medical College of Pennsylvania from which she wrongly concluded that in America women could train to be doctors on the same basis as men. This misleading scrap of information persuaded her to emigrate to the United States. With no money, a nineteen-year-old sister in tow and not a word of English, she arrived in New York on 22 May 1853. Disillusionment quickly set in as no one she asked knew anything about any female medical college. They were, however, quick to tell her that all women physicians were abortionists, quacks or clairvoyants.

With an immigrant's instinct for survival and her own entrepreneurial flair, Zakrzewska set up a business making small worsted articles and silk wigs that was so successful she was soon employing thirty girls. But small-time trading was no substitute for medicine. In the spring of 1854 she sought advice from the Home for the Friendless, who put her in touch with Elizabeth Blackwell.

The timing of their encounter was ideal. Elizabeth, still profoundly lonely and finding the dispensary hard to manage on her own, complained to Emily: 'This medical solitude is really awful at times and I should even turn thankfully to any decent woman to relieve it if I could find one.'[18] She was quick to realise that a woman of 'decided medical genius'[19] had turned up on her doorstep and offered not only to act as Zakrzewska's preceptor but also to help her enrol in a medical college. The two women, so different in character, had much to offer each other and for a time at least, the symbiosis worked well.

By the autumn of 1854, Elizabeth had succeeded in arranging for Marie to study at Emily's Alma Mater in Cleveland. The German's departure coupled with mounting practical and financial difficulties decided her to close the dispensary but with the firm intention of reopening it on a more ambitious scale once Emily returned from Europe and Zakrzewska had graduated from college. The suspension of the dispensary was disappointing but at least her private practice was at last beginning to expand and she could proudly claim that in 1854 she had earned $615.

Nevertheless, it was clear that the odd prolapsed uterus, mammary abscess or case of dysentery would never provide her with enough income to pay the bills. For this reason and because she had spent so many years in rented accommodation, Elizabeth longed to buy her own home. She paid an annual rent of $500 for her rooms but reckoned that if she bought a house for $700 and took in tenants, she could have both a home and additional income. There was another good reason for buying a property. It was increasingly clear that New York landlords (aware of the activities of Madame Restell and assorted women spiritualists) were not prepared to rent rooms to a woman advertising herself as a female physician.

Although hampered by poverty for so much of her life, Elizabeth rarely had difficulty in borrowing money when she needed it. On this occasion it was the Alofsen family, friends of the Blackwells' since their Jersey City days, who arranged the necessary capital. In the spring of 1854 she bought a house at 79 East 15th Street close to Union Square, which for the next six years she shared with a constantly shifting population of lodgers and siblings.

The purchase of the house gave Elizabeth peace of mind but did not lessen her social isolation. This loneliness, coupled with her intense dislike of household chores, led her to consider adopting a child whom over the years she could 'train up into a valuable domestic'. Having cast her eye over hundreds of orphans at the House of Refuge on Randall's Island, she picked out a seven-year-old Irish girl, Catherine Barry. 'She was a plain and they said stupid child, though good, and they all wondered at my choice. I thought otherwise. She wanted to come with me, no difficulty was made, I gave a receipt for her, and the poor little thing trotted after me like a dog.'[20]

Some twenty months later and with the benefit of hindsight, Elizabeth remembered the acquisition of Kitty in a more philanthropic light:

I was very lonely and I found my mind morbidly dwelling upon ideas in a way neither good for soul or body. Then it was revealed to me that a little human soul that I could develop into beautiful maturity would be my cure . . . a forlorner specimen of neglected childhood could hardly be found . . . her whole soul seemed to be asleep. The child was utterly friendless, no record of birth or appearance on the island, a mere stray child. It is a perpetual pleasure to me to watch this child's growth. I have had and shall have a great deal of trouble with her for she is full of intense vitality but the results are worth the trouble.[21]

It was a companionship that lasted until Elizabeth's death in 1910, although Kitty always lived a curious twilight existence. As Elizabeth's adopted child, she became the focus of her emotional life yet never entirely escaped the subservient role for which she had been originally earmarked. Her softening influence, however, was noticeable on Elizabeth from the start:

Instead of being stupid, I find that now she is withdrawn from blows and tyranny that she is very bright, has able little fingers that are learning to dust and wash up and sew and has much perseverance and energy for so small a child. She is a sturdy little thing, affectionate and with a touch of obstinacy which will turn to good account later in life. Of course she is more trouble than use at present and quite bewildered me at first, but still I like on the whole to have her and it is quite pretty to hear her in the morning, sitting up in bed, waiting for permission to get up, and singing *Oh Susanna, don't you cry for me, I'm going to Alabama, with me washboard on me knee* which seems to be the Ireland version of Lucy Long. So you must imagine me now attended by small Kitty, attired in my coloured Paris straw bonnet and a black silk cape of mine that hangs over her like a mantle.[22]

While Kitty's childish charms gave new warmth to her guardian's austere life, in no way did they deflect Elizabeth from her career. Even at her most impoverished, Elizabeth always appears to have afforded a servant who, no doubt, after Kitty arrived, was instructed to care for her as part of her duties. In her new role as a single mother, Elizabeth continued the uphill struggle to be recognised as a mainstream doctor aware that, on the other side of the Atlantic, Anna was becoming ever more addicted to alternative therapies.

* * *

By the end of 1854 the whole Blackwell family was in crisis. During the summer Anna settled in Malvern (a much cheaper option, to the relief of her family, than London or Paris), drawn there by a clairvoyant who had 'described her whole inside to her in the most satisfactory manner'.[23] From Malvern she wrote to Bessie Parkes Rayner (now engaged to cousin Samuel Blackwell), lamenting Marian Evans' elopement with George Lewes: 'It is too bad for a woman of her worth to have so thrown herself away'[24] – a surprisingly conservative judgement from an ex-Brook Farmer and one as eccentric as Anna.

Emily judged her eldest sister 'cracked' but was nevertheless concerned about the deep rift that had opened up between Anna and the rest of the family, who strongly disapproved of her extravagant and, as they saw it, idle existence. She, in turn, had become passionately anti-American: 'I recognise all that is praiseworthy in the American character although I regret their want of honesty, their boastfulness, their prosaic ignorance, their slang, nasal particularization and general unhealthiness and find their agreeableness as companions much impaired by these peculiarities.'[25]

Anna was not the only Blackwell to cause Elizabeth and Emily distress. In England, Samuel and Howard's iron business hovered on the verge of a spectacular crash, involving more than £1 million while Kenyon's wife, Marie, lay desperately ill in Edinburgh. That autumn, Dr Simpson performed a controversial gynaecological operation on her from which she made a poor recovery and nearly died. As Elizabeth dryly pointed out: 'It is the heroic, self-reliant and actively self-imposing practitioner that excites sensation and reputation. The rational and conscientious physician is not the famous one.'[26]

Emily, forced to postpone her move to Paris, nursed Marie round the clock: 'I took a stick of nitrate silver and blistered the whole surface of the abdomen after allowing the blister to rise I stood by her the rest of the night quieting the pain which was extreme by light poultices and linseed laudanum.'[27] In the middle of this double drama, Emily heard that Dennis Harris, on whose financial backing she counted for her European studies, was close to bankruptcy.

Nor was the situation much better for the family in America. Henry and Sam's hardware business was so unprofitable that they had decided to wind it up as soon as they could find a buyer. The unpredictable Ellen was proving a constant anxiety to her family and, much to Elizabeth's alarm, had declared herself a vegetarian: 'That naughty Ellen will not eat meat and bowel weaknesses, headaches, debilities will torment her.'[28] Far more worrying than Ellen's diet, however, was Henry's announcement of his engagement to Lucy Stone.

Several years after their first fleeting encounter in the hardware store they met again at an anti-slavery convention after which Henry wrote: 'I decidedly prefer her to any lady I ever met always excepting the Bloomer dress[29] which I *don't* like practically tho' theoretically I believe in it with my whole soul.'[30] He courted her vigorously but despite admitting her love for him, she declared she could never abandon her women's rights ideals for marriage. This hard-line attitude only softened when Henry performed a deed of such heroism that Lucy's defences crumbled and she promised to become his wife.

In August 1854, Henry, torn as usual between commercial ambition and reforming drive, deserted his hardware business to speak at an anti-slavery convention in Salem, Ohio. A despatch arrived in the middle of the proceedings informing the conference that a young slave girl was travelling with her owners on a train heading west to Tennessee which would stop briefly that evening in Salem. This news presented the assembled Abolitionists with a perfect opportunity to test legislation recently passed by the Ohio Supreme Court decreeing that any slave brought into the state by his master was free if he declared his wish to be so. The 1,200 delegates gathered at Salem station to await the train. A committee of four men, including 'a respectable coloured man' was appointed to see the conductor and ask the girl if she wanted her freedom:

> When the cars arrived I found myself along with them. We found the little girl, only eight years old, with her mistress and baby, and the coloured man asked her whose child she was. Getting no answer, he asked the lady who promptly told him 'twas none of his business'. The child was asked if she wished to be free and replied 'yes' whereupon I said the child was now legally free under the law, and must go with us. I took the child's arm and commenced lifting her from the seat seeing that the passengers in the cars seemed to sympathise with the owners, and that there was no time to be lost. At that moment a young Cincinnatian collared me and remonstrated with me. I let go of the child who was instantly caught up by the other members of the Committee and passed out and carried swiftly off into the town in the arms of a coloured man. And shook him off. So soon as I found the child safe, I returned and explained to the astonished Tennesseans the motives of our conduct, and after a very animated and angry discussion of a few minutes, the bell rang, the cars started and the assembled multitude gave nine hearty cheers.[31]

For Lucy it was a 'divine and glorious impulse' that impelled Henry to 'a deed so right and beautiful'. Not everyone shared this view. The local papers gave hostile accounts of the incident, claiming that Henry had physically assaulted the woman, knocking her baby to the floor. Slaveholders from across the Ohio River came to his store in Cincinnati to stare at him so that they might recognise him should he ever set foot in Kentucky, where a $10,000 reward was offered for his capture. Even his family, dedicated as they were to the Abolitionist cause, were dismayed by his actions, not least because the whole affair had a disastrous effect on his already ailing business.

In their disapproval of Henry and Lucy's engagement, the three elder Blackwell sisters were for once united. Emily summed up their reaction:

'Henry's engagement was not very welcome but few marriages are ever all we could desire. I believe the foundation of her career is really noble. I hope that intercourse with our family may induce her to lay aside some of the ultra peculiarities that are so disagreeable to us, certainly we will not allow it to break the strong feeling that has always existed among us if possible.'[32]

No Blackwell was present at the wedding that took place on 1 May 1855 at Lucy's home in Massachusetts. It was a conventional ceremony (except for the omission of the word 'obey' and the fact that Lucy kept her own name) but preceded by a most unconventional statement read out by Henry and subsequently printed in various newspapers. This declaration made it clear that their marriage did not imply acceptance of any of the traditional or legal ties of wedlock. Henry utterly rejected the current laws that gave a husband:

(1)   The custody of his wife's person;

(2)   The exclusive control and guardianship of her children;

(3)   The sole ownership of her personal and use of her real estate unless previously settled upon her, or placed in the hands of trustees, as in the case of minors, lunatics, and idiots;

(4)   The absolute right to the product of her industry;

(5)   Also the laws which give to the widower so much larger and more permanent an interest in the property of his deceased wife than they give to the widow in that of her deceased husband;

(6)   Finally, against the whole system by which 'the legal existence of the wife is suspended during marriage', so that in most States she neither has a legal part in the choice of her residence, nor can she make a will nor sue or be sued in her own name, nor inherit property . . .[33]

Elizabeth had done her best to dissuade Henry from making such a declaration: 'You haven't the vulgar vanity to wish to make a fuss about your marriage, and do not take the human nature out of it by crushing it with platforms and principles . . . the bad taste seems to me to result from the dragging of one's private, personal affairs into public notice.'[34] But despite Elizabeth's intense dislike of using private occasions for political ends, she accepted that Henry had at last found happiness and warmly welcomed the couple into her New York house on their wedding night.

Nine months after Henry and Lucy's wedding, Sam Blackwell married Lucy's best friend – Antoinette Brown. A gentler, more feminine creature than the militant Lucy (she enjoyed wearing bright, flowery hats), Antoinette nevertheless made her own striking contribution to female emancipation: on 15 September 1853 she had become the first woman in America to be ordained a minister. Impressed by this bold achievement and by her compassionate nature, the Blackwell siblings warmly welcomed her into their fold although Elizabeth could not help wishing privately that she spoke with a less pronounced American accent.

Born in 1825, Antoinette had wanted to be a preacher since childhood. At the age of twenty she entered Oberlin College, where she first met Lucy Stone and where she was eventually allowed to study theology with the male students. There was, of course, no question of her being allowed to graduate in the subject. Even in this reform-minded institution, St Paul's command 'Let your women keep silence in the churches for it is not permitted unto them to speak'[35] was taken literally.

Although Antoinette had expected opposition, she was saddened by the lack of encouragement from Lucy who, radical though she was, clearly thought Antoinette's quest hopeless: 'You will never be allowed to do this. You will never be allowed to stand in a pulpit, nor to preach in a church, and certainly you can never be ordained.'[36]

In a manner reminiscent of Elizabeth's approach to medicine, Antoinette pursued her goal with quiet conviction, determined (despite St Paul) to enter the Church as a properly trained, orthodox minister. Her experience reflected that of her future sister-in-law in other respects, for while women were often her sternest critics, men, including the familiar figures of Horace Greeley, Charles Dana, William Henry Channing and Gerrit Smith, were among her staunchest champions.

Eventually, a small Congregationalist community in South Butler (an impoverished village in upstate New York) invited her to become their pastor with an annual salary of $300 – a sum so paltry that, until Antoinette appeared in their midst, they had been unable to recruit anyone for the post.[37] But just as Elizabeth, on qualifying, had become rapidly disenchanted with regular medicine, so too Antoinette realised after her ordination that she was at odds with many fundamentals of her faith. She found it particularly difficult to threaten her near-destitute flock with eternal damnation or to condemn an unmarried mother's dead baby as her Congregationalist creed demanded. Disillusioned and exhausted, she resigned her ministry nine months later, eventually transforming her allegiance to the Unitarians. After the bruising experience at South Butler she did not seek another parish, preferring to work closely with the women's rights movement and among the poor of New York City.

Sam Blackwell (while travelling on a business trip between Cincinnati and Boston) had first met her in South Butler while she was still a minister: 'She received me very pleasantly, took me to her room and I forgot my drenched boots and the rain and wind without, while busily talking with her for three hours . . . We had a general confab, commencing with Woman's Rights and ending with metaphysics and theology . . . She has evidently thought much on the great themes of her profession and of the age, and has that breadth of sympathy and hearty toleration which are so clear an evidence of a magnanimous and cultivated mind. I enjoyed the visit exceedingly.'[38]

When Sam, dressed in Henry's wedding waistcoat, married the Reverend Antoinette Brown on 24 January 1856, Lucy noted, 'he alone of all men in the world has a Divine wife'.[39]

FOURTEEN

'Trust a Woman as a Doctor – Never!'

Over the next few years Elizabeth continued 'to struggle with life as only a Blackwell can struggle'.[1] For while Henry and Sam were discovering the joys of marriage, Emily intellectual stimulus in Europe and Marie Zakrzewska fulfilment at medical school, she remained entrapped in her dull, unrewarding life in the heart of overcrowded New York, longing to breathe the fresh air of the countryside. Furthermore, Marian's shortcomings as a housekeeper forced her to spend much of 1855 catering for her eight lodgers, six of whom were lusty young medical students whose blatant pro-slavery sentiments distressed her even more than their large appetites. She did, at least, draw comfort from watching Kitty blossom into a warm, loving child and from the steady growth of her practice. But her efforts to establish a foothold in any of the city hospitals or find wider professional support continued to fail dismally.

When Dr Marion Sims (arguably the most famous American nineteenth-century gynaecologist) founded his Women's Hospital in New York during the spring of 1855, Elizabeth had high hopes that she would become closely involved. Her optimism soon faded: 'I fear the new Woman's Hospital which they are trying to establish here, will interfere with any plans we may endeavour to carry out. Dr Sims has never called to see me and is evidently straining to keep in with the conservatives.'[2]

A more encouraging signal was the New York Hospital's agreement in January 1855 to allow eight women through its doors to attend lectures and make clinical visits. At first sight this seemed to indicate real progress, but as the students all came from a hydropathic institution run, in Elizabeth's view, by a notorious quack, she feared that ultimately they could do the cause more harm than good.

Frustrated by these setbacks, as well as the continued suspension of the dispensary, she made two bold decisions late in 1855. First, she would discard principle and advertise her medical services commercially and second, plan the clinic's resurrection along completely different lines.

Because of the problems women faced in establishing professional links with hospitals, Elizabeth began to reassess the whole purpose of her little dispensary. Abandoning philanthropy, she now saw it primarily as a means of delivering medical education and clinical experience to women. More convinced than ever that female involvement in medicine was fundamental to social reform on a larger scale, she believed that the dispensary's new role would therefore be one of real significance.

By the mid-1850s increasing numbers of women were graduating in medicine (or homeopathy) from a variety of institutions but the courses and facilities available to them in comparison with those for men were still of a lamentably low standard. Raising the quality of medical education for women rapidly became Elizabeth's prime vocation, so that routine doctoring (which had never much interested her anyway) was now significant only as a means to an end: 'I have no turn for benevolences; I feel neither love nor pity for men, for individuals. They may starve, cut each other's throats or perform any other gentle diversion suitable to the age without any attempt to stop them on my part for their own sakes. But I have boundless love and faith in Man, and will work for the race day and night. And as I have now based my charity on principle of great significance and universal value I really take immense interest in the dispensary.'[3]

A fully equipped hospital for women and children staffed by female physicians had, in fact, long been part of Elizabeth's master plan, but it was specifically because of the intransigence of the New York hospitals that she decided in December 1855 to turn the concept into reality. In a drawing-room talk she gave to a small group of sympathisers on the importance of medical education for women she underlined the point: 'The most serious difficulty to be overcome by women students is the closure of all avenues of practical instruction to them. There are many colleges open, as we have seen, where they may listen to lectures with more or less profit and in due time receive a legal permission to practise – but the hospitals, where alone they can become really acquainted with disease, and learn how to treat it, are all closed to them.'[4]

Fortunately the dispensary already had a charter (granted by New York State in 1854), so that all Elizabeth needed in order to expand it into a fully fledged hospital was money. Fired with enthusiasm for her new project, she launched a sewing group whose mission was to produce articles for a fund-raising fair. In view of the problems Elizabeth had experienced in finding small sums to keep the original dispensary operating, her proposal to raise $10,000 from the sale of babies' bootees seems astonishingly naïve.

But luckily for the future of the scheme Marie Zakrzewska, having graduated from the Western Reserve Medical College (and resisted an offer to work with the Cherokee Indians), returned to New York early in 1856. She moved into Elizabeth's house in April and took over the fundraising campaign with Teutonic thoroughness. She at once saw that Elizabeth's original plan was much too ambitious and suggested that they aim for a more manageable institution. First they had to find suitable premises. An old Dutch house in Bleecker Street proved ideal. The rent was $1,300 per annum and Zakrzewska proposed that they raise enough to guarantee payment for three years plus a further $500 for furniture and equipment. On 1 May 1856, in an impressive leap of faith, both women vowed that the New York Infirmary for Indigent Women and Children would open exactly one year later.

Emily, who had returned to London after studying in Paris (where she spent part of her time at La Maternité), supported the hospital entirely but felt strongly that it should be established in England. She was convinced that English public opinion in relation to women and medicine had changed dramatically since Elizabeth had lived there – not least because of Florence Nightingale – and was now determined to work in London. She had written to Elizabeth about Nightingale leading a team of nurses to the Crimea: 'You will have seen all about Miss Nightingale in the papers. She has quite made a reputation accepting the superintendence of the nurses. I am sorry I shall not see her when I go to London. As soon as I heard the Government was organising boats to go to Scutari I wrote to London to make enquiries about it to find if there were any opportunities to get a post that would make some reward, and help our work a little. But I have pretty well decided that there is nothing to be done, as I shall not of course accept a subordinate position.'[5]

Barbara Leigh Smith (Florence Nightingale's illegitimate first cousin) had strongly encouraged Emily to go to the Crimea, but Elizabeth had thought it an outrageous proposal: 'I am surprised at Barbara Smith's insane suggestion to you – she is generally a person of excellent sense but I suppose the enthusiasm excited was very great and that must excuse her. For Florence Nightingale I should think the episode might be an instructive and in everyway useful one. She will probably sow her wild oats in the shape of unsatisfied aspirations and activity and come back and marry suitably to the immense comfort of her relations.'[6]

Emily rejected the Crimea as a career move but was now determined to explore the possibilities of practising medicine in London. In May 1856, she wrote to Nightingale seeking advice. She received a typically robust if ambivalent response:

> General Hospital Balaclava
> May 12/56

I would have replied sooner had I had any opinion to give worth you having. But I have been 1½ years away from England and I cannot therefore give any judgement upon the state of opinion there now relative to women undertaking medicine and surgery.

So far one can safely say that the first woman who undertakes it will have a hard struggle and will probably face sacrifice either in spirits or in pocket. But pioneers must always be prepared to throw their bodies into the breach.

Rather would I ask that pioneer whether she has sufficient confidence in herself that she is the right one to initiate that cause which sooner or later must find its way. She must have the natural talent and experience and undoubted superiority in her knowledge of medicine and surgery and I would rather be inclined to wish that she might gain her experience elsewhere than in England. She must be entirely above all flirting or ever desiring to marry, recollecting that to her, the apostle of the cause, her cause must be all in all. She must be above all personal feelings, hope and fears.

A mistake such as ignorance of her profession, using her profession for the sake of social advancement or feminine affection would check that cause for fifty years.

Pray remember me most affectionately to your sister whom I shall never forget and believe me

Yours most truly though I have never had the pleasure of seeing you,

F Nightingale

My time and thoughts are here so more than taken up by almost over-whelming labor [*sic*] that I have not given a particle of either to the consideration of any future scheme for myself, nor have I been able to do so. I thank your interest and offer of help most sincerely in any future work of mine.[7]

The letter is interesting because it underlines the basic difference between the Blackwell sisters and Florence Nightingale on the whole question of women and medicine. While Elizabeth and Emily strove to persuade society that female doctors were a natural part of God's creation, Nightingale wished to set them apart from other women and turn them into a quasi-religious order. It was probably as well that Emily did not join her in the Crimea for it is hard to imagine how a working relationship between them could ever have succeeded.

Elizabeth was tempted by Emily's suggestion to join her in England but in the end turned it down. In America, notwithstanding all the frustrations and disappointments, there were clear signs that the medical profession was slowly opening up to women. The first women's medical colleges had been in existence some five years and there was now a small but steady stream of female doctors qualifying each year from an increasing number of institutions. Elizabeth therefore judged it foolhardy to abandon such hard-won progress for an unsure future in England where, despite Emily's optimism, it was still far from certain that there were enough people ready to accept the notion (let alone the reality) of women physicians.

In any case, life was improving for Elizabeth on other fronts. Her dream of forming a Blackwell commune was briefly realised in the autumn of 1856 when, with the hardware business finally sold, the family headquarters moved from Cincinnati to her house in New York, thus ending an especially bleak period of her life. She already had Kitty for companionship but her delight in having her mother, siblings and new sisters-in-law, Lucy and Antoinette, living with her after so many years of loneliness is palpable from her letters of the time.

There was, however, one notable gap in the family circle – Emily. Her declared intention to stay in England was a major blow to Elizabeth who, despite the jealousies and tensions that existed between them, well understood how much she needed Emily (and her surgical skills) if her hospital were to succeed. She knew that she was not herself an instinctive doctor – a fact she admitted in a letter to Marie Zakrzewska many years later: 'You are a natural doctor and your best work will always be in the full exercise of direct medical work . . . you know I am different from you in not being a natural doctor; so, naturally, I do not confine myself to practice. I am never without some patients but my thought, and active interest is chiefly given to those moral ends for which I took up the study of medicine.'[8]

Marie was not only a natural doctor, she was also a fearless fundraiser. On W.H. Channing's advice she went to Boston in search of investors, but even in this 'hothouse of all reforms' it was an uphill struggle to persuade people to put money into a scheme as bizarre as a hospital staffed entirely by women. The objections were endless: women doctors would be so suspect that the police would constantly interfere; death certificates issued by them would not be recognised; and their patients (coming from the dregs of society) would be too rough for them to treat or control.

Even those broadly in support thought it would be impossible to raise enough money to launch such a doomed enterprise. Undaunted by all this pessimism, Marie managed to raise $650 in Boston and, on her return to New York, threw herself into the city's most liberal circles where, as she put it, 'there was a quiet revolution going on in all strata of social life'.[9] Not sharing Elizabeth's reservations about some of the more avant-garde ideas then in currency, she was happy to join any group (including the Free Lovers) who might help her solicit support for the hospital.

Free love was unlikely to have been among the topics discussed at Elizabeth's Quaker-dominated weekly sewing group, which continued to produce vast quantities of mats, pin-cushions and baby clothes for the bazaar that they hoped would raise most of the money needed to furnish the hospital. The fair was due to take place just before Christmas but, with 79 East 15th Street already overflowing with homemade artefacts, an unexpected problem emerged. No one in New York could be persuaded to rent a church, hall or room of any kind to a group of individuals whose declared purpose was to raise money for women doctors.

Yet again it was the Quakers who came to the rescue. One of the dispensary trustees found a half-finished loft up three long flights of stairs. His wife sent a crystal chandelier from her own drawing room to light it. Others loaned rugs for the floor and covered the walls with greenery. In the event the fair (open for four days) was a gratifying success, raising (what seemed to them all at the time) the immense sum of $600.

As a result of their energetic fundraising, Elizabeth and Zakrzewska were able to secure the Bleecker Street house in March 1857 and (at a cost of $100) twenty-four iron bedsteads. Bleecker Street itself was respectable enough but the rear of the house backed on to the notorious Five Points, a district dominated by poor Irish immigrants and steeped in human misery. Charles Dickens caught the essence of Five Points in his *American Notes* published in 1842: 'From every corner, as you glance about you in these dark streets, some figure crawls half-awakened, as if the judgement hour were near at hand, and every obscure grave were giving up its dead. Where dogs would howl to lie men and women and boys slink off to sleep, forcing the dislodged rats to move away in quest of better lodgings. Here too, are lanes and alleys paved with mud knee-deep; underground chambers where they dance and game . . . hideous tenements which take their names from robbery and murder; all that is loathsome, drooping and decayed is here.'[10]

That spring Elizabeth, Zakrzewska and their faithful band of followers set about transforming the old Bleecker Street house into a working hospital. The third floor was devoted to maternity cases while the second was divided into two wards each containing six beds. Downstairs there was a waiting room (furnished with comfortable sofas) and an examination room; in the attic bedrooms were created for students and servants. Linen and furniture were donated from a great variety of sources so that the final effect was a curious mixture of antique elegance and cheap utility. Open-grate coal fires provided heating throughout the house.

Zakrzewska's talents were considerable but from Elizabeth's point of view she had one insuperable shortcoming – she was not a Blackwell. Thus it was with enormous relief that she received the news that Emily, having failed to obtain a licence to practise in London, had decided to return to America. She arrived a few months before the official opening of the hospital which took place on 12 May 1857 – Florence Nightingale's birthday. Elizabeth's choice of this particular date may have been a tribute to her old friend but it was also politically astute. So great was Nightingale's fame by the spring of 1857 that any connection with her name (however tenuous) could only help an institution whose existence was as precarious as the New York Infirmary for Indigent Women and Children.

Elizabeth's choice of speaker at the opening ceremony was also shrewd. Henry Ward Beecher (Harriet Beecher Stowe's brother and the man whom Hannah Blackwell always hoped would retrieve Henry's lost soul) was the best-known preacher in New York. His charismatic sermons attracted thousands of worshippers to his Plymouth church in Brooklyn each week and his presence at the formal opening of the Infirmary (well covered by the press) undoubtedly lent a touch of celebrity and glamour to the occasion.

Others also spoke. William Elder, Elizabeth's stalwart supporter, reviled the fogeyism and humbug of the medical profession while the Reverend Dudley Tyng (thrown out of his church for his anti-slavery sermons) arrived at the last moment, clutching his carpet bag, to praise the women doctors for their holistic approach to their patients. Although on the day the three women kept a low profile, Elizabeth, wearing her doctorial sack, briefly took the floor to read out a progress report and, more important, to send a reassuring message to a wider, still cynical public: 'The full thorough education of women in medicine is a new idea and like all other truths requires time to prove its value. Women must show to medical men, even more than to the public, their capacity to act as physicians; their earnestness as students of medicine before the existing institutions with their great advantages of practice and complete organisation will be opened to them. They must prove their medical ability before expecting professional recognition . . .'[11]

Two days after the opening Marie Zakrzewska sent an account to Harriot Hunt in Boston:

> Elizabeth Blackwell seemed to feel some sort of gratification at the day of the opening though she tried hard to conceal [it]. Emily B. was pleased. It seems to me so strange that some natures always will be in opposition to themselves, these two women for instance, have all right to be satisfied with their work and efforts as it resulted, and they are, but still they won't acknowledge it either to others nor to themselves, they do persuade themselves, I believe, that they are not . . . They are to me a combination of contradictions. In spite of all I love them and feel sad that nothing can cheer them up. Or do they perhaps show their joy in their bedroom when nobody sees them? I do not know but one thing is certain, they do wrong not to reward their friends by showing them a pleased countenance.[12]

Elizabeth *was* capable of expressing joy – the dance of delight at the summit of Clinch Mountain, the beach at Charleston, the ferry rides of her girlhood in New York. Nevertheless, her Puritan upbringing remained a strong influence on her so that, whatever emotions surged through her breast on the day of achievement, no hint of triumphalism was allowed to show.

The Infirmary was a success from the start. Within a month the beds were all full and a steady stream of mostly Irish and German patients (many of whom had attended the East 7th Street dispensary) turned up each day at the outpatient clinic. Poor women and children were given free care – the better off were charged $4 a week. The 1858 annual report noted that in its first eight months the Infirmary treated 866 patients in the dispensary; forty-eight bed cases and twelve house calls were made. The following year these numbers doubled. Before long students from the women's medical schools in Philadelphia and Boston were working at the hospital between college semesters – exposed at last to real patients – and unskilled women were taken on for training as nurses. Thus Elizabeth's aim of providing clinical education for women was on target from the very beginning of the Infirmary's existence.

It was, however, immensely hard work. Apart from caring for the sick and pregnant women, the three doctors also had to instruct the students, supervise all the catering and cleaning, keep track of the hospital's ever-precarious finances, beg and buy medicines and attend their private patients – their only source of real income. Nor did they confine their activities to the Infirmary. Much of their work took place in the nearby slums to which they were often called in the middle of the night to deliver babies and where they did their best to introduce some basic notions of hygiene by giving away soap and sponges to their patients: 'We had no fear about going to these squalid places, and there really was no need of fear either. The greatest politeness and attention was given to our students when they were once accepted.'13

But, in general, public perception of women doctors remained one of deep suspicion. When a woman died in childbirth at the Infirmary, that underlying mistrust rapidly turned into an ugly demonstration:

> It was not an hour after this sad occurrence before all the cousins who had relieved each other at the bedside appeared, with their male cousins or husbands in working attire and with pickaxes and shovels, before our street door, demanding admission and shouting that the female physicians who resided within were killing women in childbirth with cold water. Of course an immense crowd collected, filling the block between us and Broadway, hooting and yelling and trying to push in the doors, both on the street and in the yard; so that we were beleaguered in such a way that no communication with the outside was possible. We could not call to the people who were looking out of the windows in the neighbouring houses, our voices being drowned by the noise of the mob. At this juncture the policeman who had charge of Bleecker Street and one from Broadway came running up to the scene. On learning the complaint of the men, they commanded silence and ordered the crowd to disperse, telling them that they knew the doctors in that hospital treated the

patients in the best possible way, and that no doctor could keep everybody from dying some time.[14]

A few weeks after the Infirmary opened, Emily successfully performed her first operation. As Elizabeth perceptively noted in a letter to their brother George: 'I think a reputation in surgery will be sure to make her fortune in time, for it will be the very thing that will overcome the distrust women still feel in employing women doctors.'[15] The actress Fanny Kemble (whom Elizabeth had met so memorably while staying with Lady Byron six years before) provided a sharp reminder of just how reluctant middle-class women still were to entrust their bodies to doctors of own sex. Elizabeth and Zakrzewska approached her while she was in New York, hoping to persuade her to give a benefit performance of Shakespearean readings in aid of the hospital: 'She received us courteously, listened with kindness to an explanation of the object of our visit and the needs of the infirmary; but when she heard that the physicians of the institution were *women* she sprang up to her full height, turned her flashing eyes upon us, and with the deepest tragic tones of her magnificent voice exclaimed: "Trust a *woman* as a DOCTOR! – NEVER!"'[16]

Ironically, while the vast majority of middle-class women continued to show little enthusiasm for female doctors, a growing number of their husbands began to encourage the idea, realising how much they preferred their wives to be examined by a woman than by a man.

The battle to win hearts and minds was conducted on many fronts – in the press, at social gatherings and by word of mouth. It also received great encouragement from the number of distinguished medical men prepared to act as consultants to the Infirmary. The support of physicians such as Valentine Mott (an innovative ambidextrous surgeon) was vitally important in persuading the public that women doctors (or doctresses as they were often derogatorily described) were not some freak of nature but respectable young women striving to do a decent job.

With the hospital up and running, Elizabeth grew restless. The pioneering phase of her initiatives always appealed to her more than their mundane maintenance and, in any case, after years of grindingly hard work in New York, she was ready for a change. As she explained in a letter to George (the only Blackwell still living in the West), 'I now know American possibilities thoroughly – I feel the freedom, the comparative simplicity and the slow, steady growth of practice which we shall enjoy here. I also feel the want of society, the difference of nature, and the trying climate, which we meet here. Life in New York is monotonous and very hard to us and it will continue so, for it arises partly from our position which is without money or connexions, partly from our nature which, with the best endeavour, cannot enter into close relations with the society we meet.'[17]

It was clear that, despite the launch of the Infirmary and the steady growth of her private practice, Elizabeth still yearned for England. In May 1857, just a week after the opening of the hospital, her friend Barbara Leigh Smith arrived in New York. Considering Elizabeth's lack of sympathy with the American women's rights movement, it is curious that she should have formed such a close bond with one of Britain's most articulate feminists, but it was nevertheless the deepest friendship she ever made. Barbara not only gave her unwavering emotional and financial support but, even more important, continued to provide introductions to the liberal, moneyed circles where Elizabeth's ideas were most likely to find favour.

Barbara travelled in America with her recently acquired French husband, Dr Eugene Bodichon – seventeen years her senior. They had met in Algiers where, together with her father and two sisters, Barbara had spent the winter of 1856. A gifted artist, she had been stirred by the wild North African landscape, and, more unexpectedly, by the tall, eccentric doctor with a social conscience. Bodichon had chosen to stay in Algeria (where he had originally been posted as an army surgeon) rather than sign an oath of allegiance to Napoleon III – an act of principle entirely approved of by Elizabeth.

The Bodichons and Elizabeth, with ten-year-old Kitty in tow, spent some days together visiting Niagara Falls. The other tourists must have thought them an unusual quartet. Eugene Bodichon (who with his deep brown eyes and dark complexion looked more Arab than French) towered over the pale, slight figure of Elizabeth. At thirty, Barbara was a handsome redhead whose preference for practical outdoor clothes (when sketching or sightseeing) shocked the sensibilities of middle-class America almost as much as the burnous worn by her husband.

The two women had plenty to talk about. Since they had last met, Barbara had fought a number of important campaigns on behalf of her sex. Realising how little women understood the law as it related to them, she had published a pamphlet, *A Brief Summary in Plain Language, of the Most Important Laws concerning Women*[18] (1854) – a readable digest of a lengthy work on the subject published the previous year.[19] The clarity of *A Brief Summary* threw the legal plight of women into stark relief, making it an uncomfortable read. Elizabeth, in her determination to preach one morality for both sexes, took particular note of the section on seduction in which Barbara pointed out that in law: 'If a [single] woman is seduced she has no remedy against the seducer; nor has her father, excepting as he is considered in law as being her master and she his servant, and the seducer having deprived him of her "services". This reveals, once again, that it is not the woman herself who is represented as having a grievance: she exists legally only as the "property" of her father, from whom another man has stolen the woman's "services".'[20]

In 1857 Barbara published another pamphlet on a subject equally close to Elizabeth's heart entitled *Women and Work*, in which she strongly argued that fathers had no right to cast the burden of the support of their daughters on to other men: 'It lowers the dignity of women; and tends to prostitution, whether legal or in the streets. As long as fathers regard the sex of a child as a reason why it should not be taught to gain its own bread, so long must women be degraded.'[21]

Barbara strongly encouraged both sisters to return to England and open a hospital along similar lines to the New York Infirmary, as she believed that there was now enough British interest in women medics to enable them to continue their work there. But much as Elizabeth wanted to do so, she knew it would be professional suicide if she misjudged the timing, for it was clear that England, despite the Florence Nightingale phenomenon, still lagged far behind America in its attitude to medical women.

She was not, therefore, prepared to cross the Atlantic permanently until she had firm backers who could give financial security to any such project. She had long hoped that her close friendship with Lady Byron would result in major sponsorship: 'Earnest words once spoken by you are spoken forever. Had I never heard from you again, my trust in your friendship would have been entire. I have felt my friendship to you and the recognition of that strange fact, has become one of the deep calm joys of my life.'[22] But it was not to be. Lady Byron never offered more than her substantial social network and the occasional generous donation. The final disappointment came after her death in 1860 when she left no money to the Infirmary in her will.

In 1858, however, a new, mysterious character emerged on the scene whose great wealth, Elizabeth hoped, would enable her and Emily to repeat their American success in England. A friend of Barbara Bodichon and Lady Byron, the Comtesse de Noailles had exactly the right credentials – she was enormously rich and passionately interested in women's health. As reports from England suggested that the Comtesse was much excited by Elizabeth's achievements, it was too promising an opportunity to miss, but with the Infirmary still struggling to make ends meet, a journey to Europe was hard to justify. A problem with Elizabeth's glass eye, however, provided the perfect excuse: 'I shall be obliged to visit Europe in a short time on account of my eyes. Boissonneau has entirely failed in fitting me, though he has tried in three different packets and he thinks some change must have taken place in the organ which needs a new measurement. My stock is just out and I cannot get it renewed in this country so the journey seems inevitable though I can ill afford the expense, I shall put it off as long as possible to gather as many fees as I can into my slender purse, but in July or August I must go.'[23]

On 18 August 1858, Elizabeth and Kitty sailed for England. If her reconnaissance proved successful, Elizabeth intended that they stay there for good.

FIFTEEN

Civil Wars

Elizabeth left for Europe in August 1858, determined to settle once and for all the vexed question of whether she and Emily should work in America or England. Emotionally she had already chosen England: 'I am so tired of physical privations that it does seem to me I would rather work where I could make most money and have good food and clothes and that I think would be in London.'[1] But she knew that she would have to present a watertight case to Emily who, since her rejection in London two years earlier, remained unconvinced that British attitudes to women doctors had changed enough to justify such a move.

Elizabeth did not linger long in London. After depositing Kitty in a progressive, co-educational boarding school (of which Barbara Bodichon was a patron) she hastened to Paris. Not only did she need to replenish her stock of glass eyes (the enamel ones supplied to her by Monsieur Boissonneau, although aesthetically attractive, quickly wore out), she also wanted a new wardrobe. She planned to persuade the British public of its need for female physicians through a series of lectures, and she knew that her appearance would be closely scrutinised. Any hint of eccentricity (Anna sometimes wore a nightcap under her bonnet) or poverty would only confirm the majority view that a woman doctor was a freak of nature – a traitor to both her sex and sphere:

> I have been considerably perplexed on the subject of dress. In the first place it is a real slavery to be subjected to Anna's time and taste but I did not want to quarrel. Now I don't think Anna's taste in dress good. Fortunately however being in the country she was obliged to deputize and introduced me to a Mrs Buxton, a very lady like Englishwoman who has taken up dressmaking to retrieve her husband's affairs . . . as soon as I told her of my position, she took at once a great interest in the matter . . . she is determined I shall make a thoroughly lady-like appearance and get all the support possible from dress . . . she says I must consider it as capital invested and not economise injudiciously.[2]

Although her brother Howard was prepared to foot the bill, Elizabeth clearly felt pangs of guilt over so much self-indulgence and the need to defend herself to Emily: 'I have quietly judged everything she has proposed . . . they are really what I need if I am to carry out properly in London the plan we proposed before I started and I now therefore agree to this expense because I do think without it I shall not be faithful to what I've undertaken and if it all falls through, I shall bring back the clothes and we'll divide them between us.'[3]

Elizabeth was also anxious to look her best when she eventually met the woman on whom she was pinning her hopes for a secure professional future in England – the Comtesse Anna Maria Helena de Noailles. It was through Lady Byron and Barbara Bodichon that Elizabeth had first learned of the Comtesse's interest in funding a rural hospital for women where her sanitary theories could be put into practice. The Comtesse, an English-woman, had an impeccable pedigree. On her mother's side she was a Baring and the half-sister of Lord Cromer and Lord Revelstoke. Her marriage to the Comte de Noailles in 1849 had been unhappy but had nevertheless given her the name of one of France's most illustrious families. The Comte's death, three years later, had left her a rich, childless widow of twenty-eight with a consuming interest in matters of health and sanitary reform.

The Comtesse was a genuinely benevolent woman who throughout her life gave generously to many good causes, but she was also self-centred and manipulative. Her wealth and social position allowed her to indulge her natural eccentricity unchecked – often to the detriment of the very people and enterprises she was seeking to aid. She was a woman used to getting her own way whose violent temper was quick to surface when her wishes were thwarted.

During a visit to the Paris Salon in 1863, she was captivated by a portrait of a young Italian peasant girl and wished to own it. Distressed to discover the picture had already been sold, she decided instead to buy the child. The father was paid off and seven-year-old Maria transported (without explanation) from the back streets of Paris to the grandeur of the Comtesse's town house in the Champs Elysées.

Although well treated in a material sense, the little girl was the unfortunate focus of her adoptive mother's theories on health and education: some very sensible, others bordering on the obsessive. She was not only sent to a convent school in England with her own cow, so that she might have fresh milk each day, but – unlike the other children, who wore a uniform – made to dress in a Grecian tunic especially designed by the Comtesse. This was the capricious woman whose patronage, Elizabeth believed, would enable her and Emily to replicate their New York success in England.

But before being allowed to meet the Comtesse herself, Elizabeth was interviewed in Paris by her sister-in-law, Mrs Lionel Standish (née Angelique de Noailles) who was eager to see women enter medicine because of the 'moral degradation' she had observed among her friends when they were treated by male doctors for female diseases. As she listened to Elizabeth describe Emily's successful amputation of a breast, the 'stout, full-blooded black-eyed Frenchwoman became radiant with intense satisfaction . . . for it proved to her . . . what she wanted to believe, yet could only accept intellectually . . . viz the necessity of letting the midwife drop and striking unflinchingly for the highest [professional] position. This one fact gave her real faith in the Physician.'4

The meeting was a success but Elizabeth and Mrs Standish did not agree on everything. The latter subscribed to the Nightingale view that women physicians should never marry, declaring that she would be shocked to see Doctor Blackwell dancing in a ballroom with garlands on her head. For Elizabeth, this notion that a woman doctor was only socially acceptable if prepared to sacrifice all worldly pleasure and personal gain was profoundly irritating, and made her want to 'expand [her] lungs and rush into the wild woods'. Nevertheless, she was generally encouraged by the encounter, admiring Mrs Standish for knowing 'as much of England and Anglo-Saxon nature as a Frenchwoman ever can know'.5

Early in the new year Elizabeth returned to England. She immediately went to see Florence Nightingale in Great Malvern, where England's favourite heroine was taking one of her regular cures. It was over seven years since they had last met and they had much to discuss. Each woman wanted something from the other. Indeed Florence had a specific proposal to put to Elizabeth – she wished her to become superintendent of the Nightingale nursing school. Since her return from the Crimea, she had been haunted by the Nightingale Fund – a sum of £44,000 raised by an adoring public to establish an 'Institution for the training, sustenance, and protection of Nurses'. The war had ended four years earlier yet the nursing school was still not established and the Fund remained untouched.

The Fund had become an embarrassment to Nightingale after her work with the statistician Dr William Farr convinced her that the nursing operation in the Crimea had made little impact on the mortality rate of the army. In fact more soldiers had died in her hospital during the war than in

Elizabeth Blackwell in her early thirties.

Hannah Blackwell, the family matriarch.

Henry Ward Beecher with his sister Harriet
Beecher Stowe, *c.* 1870. The Blackwells and
Beechers were neighbours in Cincinnati.

William Henry Channing, Unitarian
minister, Transcendentalist and reformer.

Anna Blackwell, eldest of the Blackwell siblings.

Dr Emily Blackwell. Her medical partnership with Elizabeth lasted fifteen years.

Henry Browne Blackwell, Elizabeth's brother and avid campaigner for women's suffrage.

Lucy Stone Blackwell, Henry's wife. Elizabeth disapproved of her women's rights activism.

Geneva, New York. The medical school with its dome is seen top centre.

Horace Greeley, editor of the *New York Tribune* and presidential candidate.

Hippolyte Blot, the French doctor with whom Elizabeth fell in love.

The south façade of La Maternité, the hospital where Elizabeth studied in 1849.

Barbara Leigh Smith Bodichon by Samuel Laurence.

Florence Nightingale, pictured at about the time she and Elizabeth met again in 1859.

St Bartholomew's Hospital, London. The print dates from 1845, five years before Elizabeth arrived to study there.

The Comtesse de Noailles, the eccentric philanthropist from whom Elizabeth received intermittent support for over forty years.

Dr Mary Putnam Jacobi. Her strict scientific methodology was in contrast to Elizabeth's more 'Transcendental' approach to medicine.

Women medical students attending a post mortem, 16 April 1870.

Above: Sophia Jex-Blake, leader of the British women's medical movement.

Left: Dr Elizabeth Garrett Anderson, *c.* 1865, the year she became Britain's first woman doctor.

Elizabeth Blackwell in middle age.

Susan Durant, sculptor, and mother of an illegitimate baby for whom Elizabeth took on responsibility.

Josephine Butler, the leading social reformer.

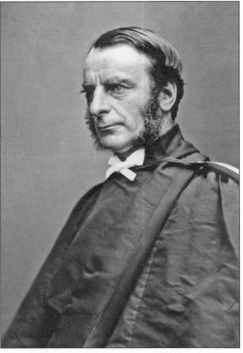

Charles Kingsley, Elizabeth's close friend, *c.* 1870.

Rock House, Hastings, Elizabeth's home for her last thirty years.

Elizabeth and Kitty in their sitting-room at Rock House.

any other. Farr's statistics produced devastating evidence to show that no amount of good nursing could have countered the appalling overcrowding and lack of sanitation and hygiene that were the real causes of so many deaths at Scutari. As a result of this shattering discovery, by the beginning of 1859 Nightingale was more interested in improving hospital construction and management than in the training of nurses.

In order, therefore, to escape the shackles of the Nightingale Fund, she needed to find a competent medical woman to run the nursing school. Elizabeth was her first choice. She was in every respect an obvious candidate for the job except for her exasperating insistence on the importance of educating women doctors and maintaining a private practice: 'I have just returned from an interview with Miss Nightingale at Malvern in relation to a school for nurses which she wishes to establish . . . My old friend's health is failing from the pressure of mental labour . . . I think I have never known a woman labour as she has done . . . Of course we conversed very earnestly about the nursing plan in which she wished to interest me . . . Unfortunately she does not think private practice possible in connection with her plan. If so it would be impossible for us to help her.'[6]

For her part, Elizabeth was enough of a politician to realise that whatever work she and Emily eventually undertook in England, its chances of success would be greatly improved if linked to the name of Florence Nightingale. If she could persuade Florence to support her own medical projects, many of the daunting financial and public relations problems that she faced would melt away.

Shortly after the Malvern visit Elizabeth travelled to the Riviera for her long-awaited meeting with the Comtesse de Noailles. The Comtesse and Nightingale, her two most promising English backers, could scarcely have been more different but they did share one link – a passionate belief in the overriding importance of sanitation. The Comtesse's own health theories were based on a mixture of the serious sanitary themes being vigorously debated during the mid-century, her own (often acute) observations on such matters as supplies of fresh water and milk and pure whimsy. Each night, for instance, she tied cashmere stockings round her head with a piece of fur hanging over her eye to ward off neuralgia.[7]

Elizabeth had never before dealt with anyone as aristocratically eccentric as the Comtesse. She soon discovered, however, that they shared a common approach to social reform, agreeing on the vital role of sanitation and hygiene, better education for girls and the wisdom of siting hospitals in the countryside.

After five days together in Menton, it was decided that their goal should be the establishment of a small hospital in the country near London under Elizabeth and Emily's direction, specialising in women's diseases. It would be staffed entirely by female physicians and have a medical college attached.

From Elizabeth's point of view this was all highly satisfactory, but when she stated her intention of earning income through private practice in London, the Comtesse was outraged. She believed, like her sister-in-law, that women doctors should be nun-like in their vocation and certainly not expect fees for their ministrations. Ignoring this unpleasantness, Elizabeth wrote to Barbara Bodichon relating how the Comtesse (although embroiled in a family quarrel and 'excited almost to insanity'[8]) was so enthusiastic about the project that she intended to sell her Brighton house in order to fund it. She planned to give £1,000 towards the hospital and £5,000 to the endowment of a sanitary professorship – a post Elizabeth planned to fill herself. She at once wrote to Nightingale outlining their hospital plan and asking her advice. The reply was not encouraging:

> That all Hospitals will ultimately be in the *country* I have emphatically said, both in and out of print. In this therefore I am not likely to differ from Madame de Noailles – but I should say that the way to hinder, not to help this desirable consummation, would be to begin with a small pottering Women's Hospital 'on a Farm in the country'. . .
>
> Think what £5000 is! (about £150 per annum) for a Hospital!! . . . I would not act as one of your advisers, because I entirely deprecate the principle of the thing proposed to you . . . nothing would ever induce *me* to undertake anything where I could not have jealous and warring elements (and *men* too) to keep my staff up to their work . . . *I* should feel certain of failure in doing what *you* propose to do (supposing even that I had your physiological and medical knowledge) with the opposition of the authorities.[9]

In the light of this letter, Elizabeth changed tack. Still hoping to find a way of benefiting her own mission from the Nightingale fame and Fund she decided (in the short term) to abandon the idea of establishing a hospital in the country and look for a compromise with Nightingale: 'Your idea of a Nurses' college seems to me *the thing* wanted now and it must be in connection with a great [i.e. London] hospital.'[10] She then suggested that the best of the nursing students (having completed their course) should enter a proper medical college from which they would graduate as fully fledged doctors.

Although Nightingale had herself suggested that a few head nurses might eventually be trained as doctors, she now suspected that Elizabeth intended to use her Fund as a Trojan horse for setting up a training programme for women doctors in a major London hospital – an arrangement quite unacceptable to her and to the medical establishment. Her own opinion of women doctors was made plain in a letter she wrote to the philosopher John Stuart Mill, dated 12 September 1860:

> I refer to an American world, consisting of female M.D.s etc, and led by a Dr. Elizabeth Blackwell, and though the latter is a dear and intimate and valued friend of mine, I reassert that her world talks a 'jargon,' and a very mischievous one – that their female M.D.s have taken up the worst part of a male M.D.ship, of thirty years ago – and that, while medical education is what it is – a subject upon which I may talk with some *connaisance de cause* – instead of wishing to see more Doctors made by women joining what there are, I wish to see as few Doctors, either male or female as possible, for, mark you, the women have made no improvement – they have only tried to be 'men,' and they have only succeeded in being third-rate men. They will not fail in getting their own livelihood, but they fail in doing good and improving therapeutics. I am only stating a matter of fact. I am not reasoning, as you suppose. Let all women try. These women have, in my opinion, failed. But this is no *a priori* conclusion against the principle.[11]

By March 1859, it was clear to both women that any working relationship between them was impossible. Elizabeth recounted her version of events to Barbara Bodichon: 'She wishes, I see, to absorb me in the nursing plan which would simply kill me, if it did not accomplish my medical plan, and I am desirous of committing myself to the "education of the physician", before taking any part in her schemes . . . this I see she is very desirous I should not do, but I consider it rather the turning point of my being able to help her.'[12]

Unsurprisingly, Florence Nightingale viewed their exchange rather differently: 'I saw and corresponded with pretty nearly all the hospital authorities and female superintendents *in esse* or *in posse* that could be applied to the Fund. . . . The most promising, that of the "London" *qua* hospital and of Miss Blackwell *qua* superintendent, has fallen through. And I am bound to say that the Hospital showed itself far more accommodating than the lady.'[13]

Since the two women had first dreamed of working together eight years earlier, the gulf between them had widened – too far now ever to be a viable possibility. Ideologically they had much in common but it was inevitable that two such strong personalities would clash. Nightingale was driven to find practical solutions to the multitude of problems that she saw existing in health administration, particularly in relation to the army – always her first concern. She had been to war, witnessed thousands of men die in the most horrible circumstances and then been confronted by the terrible truth that vast numbers of those deaths might have been prevented if only elementary sanitation had been introduced to Scutari from the outset. It was in this context that she viewed Elizabeth's efforts to educate women physicians as an irrelevant distraction.

Elizabeth, for her part, held fast to her vision of a more equal (and consequently more moral) society in which women physicians would play a crucial role. While wanting them to make their own distinctive feminine contribution to medicine she never wavered from her conviction that they must always be as rigorously professional as the most able of their male colleagues. It was her self-appointed mission to ensure that these women received the best medical education available so that they did not merely evolve into an inferior medical species. The idea, therefore, that she should work in a subordinate position for a woman who (however famous) did not share this ideal was simply not feasible. Nightingale may have been the most powerful woman in England after Queen Victoria but, as Elizabeth must have frequently reminded herself, she did not have the letters MD after her name. Nightingale summed up their differences thus: 'I remember my impression of your character – that you and I were on different roads, (although to the same object). You to educate a few highly cultivated ones – I to diffuse as much knowledge as possible.'[14]

The *British Medical Journal* was in no doubt where it stood in the matter. In a long leader, it huffed and puffed with indignation:

Is it compatible with the attributes of woman, that she should arm herself with a medical education and medical diplomas, and put herself forward to practise medicine? Certainly not . . . Does any one hint that there is no greater incompatibility with feminine attributes in the proceedings of Dr. Elizabeth Blackwell than in those of Florence Nightingale in her attendance on the hospitals of Scutari and the Crimea? There is, we fear, a wide difference between the two cases. The mission of Florence Nightingale was one of mercy and benevolence: she went, that she might afford to the sick and wounded the treatment which woman alone could give them. The mission of the lady doctors of medicine is – what is it? We lament to record our conviction that it is one of arrogance and self-glorification.[15]

If Elizabeth found relations with Florence Nightingale problematic, her dealings with the Comtesse de Noailles were no easier. Elizabeth had miscalculated the malleability of her patron. Having been confident that she could 'shape' her to do what she wanted, she was unpleasantly surprised by the Comtesse's reaction to her view that their work should be initially based in London. The Comtesse was furious, and immediately backed away from her promises, proclaiming she had no interest in any hospital not established in the countryside (she believed that in seven cases out of ten, women's diseases could be cured by fresh air alone) and even less in the education of women doctors. Elizabeth, although deeply disappointed, remained sanguine: 'Were she not half crazy, I should be very angry with her, as it is, I really pity her for having missed doing a noble thing for once in her life'.[16]

Without the Comtesse's support Elizabeth knew there was little prospect of her being able to stay in England. But she still hoped that her lectures might generate enough interest and money to launch a small hospital. During the spring of 1859, however, it became increasingly clear that, despite their approval of women *nurses*, the British had little interest in women *doctors*. The lectures that Elizabeth delivered in London (and other major cities) were mostly well received, but neither they nor the widely distributed hospital prospectus ignited the public's imagination (or pocket) sufficiently to give Elizabeth grounds for remaining in England. But on one young woman, at least, her gospel did have a profound and lasting effect – Elizabeth Garrett.

Elizabeth Garrett had read an article by Anna Blackwell about Elizabeth and Emily in *The English Woman's Journal* (the feminist magazine edited by Bessie Rayner Parkes) that had touched a chord. On 2 March 1859 she was among the audience gathered to hear Elizabeth's first London lecture in the St Marylebone Literary Institution – decked out for the occasion with flowers from Barbara Bodichon's garden. Elizabeth was a good speaker, well practised at presenting her case with style and simplicity. Her message, radiating common sense rather than revolution, made a deep impact on the 22-year-old Garrett. After the lecture, they met at Barbara Bodichon's Blandford Square house in what proved to be a decisive encounter for the younger woman.

Before she met Elizabeth Blackwell, Garrett had never thought of medicine as a career for herself. By the time she returned to her family in Suffolk some weeks later she had decided to become a doctor. Elizabeth, perhaps recognising something of her own spirit in Garrett, thought her plucky enough to see it through. The two women came from similar social backgrounds but with one major difference. Samuel Blackwell had died a failed businessman leaving his family in penury in a foreign land. Newson Garrett, though, made a fortune from his malting business and remained very much alive to give his pioneer daughter unstinting financial support in the difficult years that lay ahead. In 1865 Elizabeth Garrett became the first woman to gain a British qualification licensing her to practise medicine.

By the early summer Elizabeth knew that she must return to America. Apart from the unravelling of her English plans, a decisive factor was Zakrzewska's acceptance of a job in Boston which left the beleaguered Emily to run the Infirmary on her own. But Elizabeth was not returning to America empty-handed. There were significant achievements to show for her time in England – not least Elizabeth Garrett's decision to take up medicine.

An even more immediate cause for celebration was her own success in becoming the first woman to be placed on the newly formed British Medical Register. This was set up as a result of the 1858 Medical Act, which made registration with the Medical Council compulsory for anyone wishing to practise medicine or surgery within the British Isles. Fortunately for Elizabeth, doctors holding foreign degrees (sex not specified) were allowed to register if they had been in practice in Great Britain before October of that year – a loophole promptly closed once the profession realised it had let in a woman. Florence Nightingale's disapproval of women doctors had not prevented her from writing Elizabeth a letter of introduction to the liberal-minded Sir Benjamin Brodie, who also happened to be the president of the Medical Council. His influence was probably crucial since, although Elizabeth's 'medical practice' in Britain in 1858 amounted to little more than a few consultations, her name appeared in the first Medical Register published in 1859. It was a welcome and very public feather in her cap.

The months in England had also given Elizabeth the chance to strengthen old friendships and broaden her social network. She may not have been as famous as Florence Nightingale but it was highly gratifying to receive admiring letters from such eminent figures as Marian Lewes: 'Your note accompanying Barbara's [Bodichon] is a permission for me to tell you that you are one of the women I would love from all the rest in the world to know personally.'[17]

But, from Elizabeth's perspective, the biggest prize of all was the Comtesse de Noailles's agreement to fund a small sanatorium near New York in conjunction with the Infirmary. By providing the money to acquire a country property (but being physically too far removed to interfere with its management) Elizabeth's fickle patron had come up trumps. Elizabeth saw at once the possibility of realising her Associationist dream by combining professional and family life in a country commune:

Now in relation to the sanitarium [*sic*], I want to suggest, as it will be solely under our control and the class of patients neither dangerous nor troublesome, as it is especially designed to establish all hygiene appliances as gymnasium, swimming bath, gardening and daily exercises so that there will be facilities for educating the little ones in health [apart from Kitty she now had two baby nieces], and as moreover it is important that it should be near our business in New York, why cannot we realise the family farm and advantageously buy a tract together each having an independent portion? . . . Think of this, and see if some plan cannot be struck out, by which, while carrying out the Comtesse's intention, we can also make it a family blessing. Indeed I believe Mad. De N would consider you all as suitable inmates of her sanitarium.[18]

Despite the failure of the hospital project, Elizabeth was, therefore, not entirely downhearted when she sailed for America in August 1859 accompanied by Kitty and Ellen (who, having studied for some months with John Ruskin, had finally given up her attempts to earn a living in London as an artist). Although more certain than ever that she wanted to settle permanently in England, she was content to wait until the seeds that she had planted there had been given a chance to ripen. The small committee[19] that she had organised to handle donations and publicity for the hospital would continue to spread the word. They had also agreed to undertake the vetting of any young woman who wanted to study at the New York Infirmary. All in all, Elizabeth was satisfied that she had successfully launched a campaign that within a few years was bound to bear fruit. When it did, she would return to England, assume leadership of the women's medical movement, and stay there for good.

Meanwhile, there was work to be done in America. Emily had been holding the fort, running the Infirmary and looking after Elizabeth's private patients as best she could but with little pleasure. The rewards for her labours were certainly very few. With the East 15th Street house crammed full of boarders, she slept in the attic and ate meals (of mostly cold food) in the cellar, sometimes treating herself to a small piece of meat cooked over an alcohol lamp. Her life was unutterably dull. As a woman doctor she remained socially unacceptable – never receiving personal invitations even from those who publicly supported the Infirmary. On her return to New York, Elizabeth was determined to breathe new life into this gloomy existence and Emily's faltering resolve.

In a long letter to Barbara Bodichon, written a few days before Christmas 1859, she gave a shrewd analysis of how matters stood for her and Emily:

In the first place then let me speak of plans and prospects. I have now fully determined on another three years work in America . . . Were it a question only for myself I should act differently and unhesitatingly settle in London in accordance with your plans, and confine my attention to private practice, making my way gradually and slowly into a respectable position as physician – this is all I should do – for I have no genius for medicine, only those substantial qualities which will in the long run ensure a respectable success. And were I alone settling in London, in my position, and with the difficulties for women that are still unconquered, this respectable private position is all I should accomplish.

Joined however with an equally intelligent partner, I can accomplish much more – more for our own success; more for other women. In the first place, as to our own medical practice. We are now fair average practitioners, with rather less than the average medical initiation, but considerably more than the average judgement and common sense. Now it is an important question with us how to cope with the distinct medical difficulties of our profession, and become authorities in the profession, instead of having in every emergency to yield to others. This is the real point of difficulty for us now to conquer not only for ourselves but for other women. We must be able to say in every dangerous case 'I understand this fully, I recognize all the symptoms, I foresee the issue, I know all the dangers to be guarded against, I have watched many such cases. The usual remedies are unavailing, I shall now do so and so.' The same with surgical practice, we must have actually done it all again and again in order to be able to speak and act with authority. Now private practice will never give us this experience. Directly a case becomes dangerous, when a surgical operation becomes necessary, in ninety-nine cases out of a hundred the family will call in a man and they are right to do so; for not only has the man more experience, but more boldness, unscrupulousness, and consequently efficiency. The fact is until women have a very large experience, their conscientiousness will stand in their way . . . they will never I think stand on the same level. Now it is our problem how to reach this higher level – for let us once reach it and it will not be conquered only for ourselves. We are not willing to remain as hygienic or common sense medical advisors only . . . as it is inferior men walk over us and will continue to do so all our lives, because they *are* men unless we can solve our problem. It is this perception which interests us so in our hospital. We see it as our only chance, the sole way by which we may gain that amount of positive medical knowledge, which is indispensable for our purpose. All our family, almost all our friends, think we are wasting our time and taking wrong methods in labouring so heartily at this poor little lazar house. But they cannot see how with our women's nature and our outside professional position, we cannot push private practice as a man can and can never attain more than unsatisfactory results.

Last week at the infirmary we had a case of convulsions, high application of the forceps, and perforation of the cranium, one of the most formidable complications of obstetrical surgery. Now in private practice the case would have been instantly taken out of our hands. But here our kind consulting surgeon stood by, and I supported Emily with all my power and she had a grand experience – accomplished it all herself and the woman is getting well! If we kill a few it does not matter. The authorities receive our certificate without question . . . and then we are really not as bad in the killing line as the male hospitals.[20]

Elizabeth's understanding of the Infirmary's vital role in winning women a proper foothold in medicine had on her return to America given her renewed energy. Moreover, any sense of *déjà vu* was soon dispelled by two major events: the removal of the Infirmary to elegant new premises – and the Civil War.

In her absence, Elizabeth's board of trustees had decided to raise an endowment of $50,000 with the aim of placing the Infirmary on a firmer footing and establishing an educational fund. On 18 April 1860 the hospital moved into a fine house on the corner of Second Avenue and Eighth Street:

I think we shall like it very much when we have got in shape. It is a large handsome house such as we might have found in Russell Square and the neighborhood may also compare with that square only a little better (fashionably). The owner was . . . a well known Paris lawyer and he finished it off with much taste – tasselated marble hall, silver, preserved papers, fine glass windows etc. We keep the first floor as reception, lecture rooms etc. The next floor we are throwing into a fine sweep of wards. We are opening the basement to the street for dispensary purposes and I think that when complete it will be suitable and substantial commencement of a medical centre for women, with more promise than any we have yet seen. Here Emily and I will live and superintend the growth of the work and carry on our own practice.[21]

The move to Second Avenue was undertaken against a backdrop of mounting political tension as America moved inexorably towards civil war. Many factors – economic and political – contributed to its outbreak but, as Abraham Lincoln himself observed, everyone understood that slavery was somehow the cause.[22] Lincoln's election to the Presidency on 6 November 1860 spelled the end of compromise politics and triggered the secession of seven slave states. Not that Lincoln was, at this stage, an Abolitionist: 'I am not, nor ever have been, in favor of making voters or jurors of Negroes, nor of qualifying them to hold office nor to intermarry with white people.'[23] Indeed he would himself have willingly sought compromise with the South if by doing so he could have preserved the Union and the Constitution. But on one vital issue he was implacable – he refused utterly to condone the expansion of slavery into the newly acquired western territories. Elizabeth reported her view of the situation to Barbara Bodichon:

. . . it will not be a war of principles but a compulsory struggle for self-preservation. Anti-slavery sentiment has very little part in it and there is a very wide felt feeling and irritation at the mistaken views and actions of the abolitionists . . . I think the great majority of the country are perfectly willing to accept almost any compromise with slavery, if they could ensure safe commercial relations . . . I cannot get rid of the suspicion that the whole fuss will end in some base patching up of the business . . . Nevertheless this is a great country, and I cannot but feel an interest in it, although the people are strange to me and their souls very shallow.[24]

The opening shots of the Civil War were fired when Confederate guns attacked Fort Sumter in Charleston Harbour on 12 April 1861. Elizabeth was quick to recognise the war's potential for furthering the cause of medical women, hoping that it might accomplish for her and Emily what the Crimea had achieved for Florence Nightingale. If, under the Blackwell sisters' supervision, suitable women could be successfully trained as nurses for military hospitals, their wartime achievement would do more to accelerate women's right to practise medicine than years of peacetime endeavour.

On 23 April, Elizabeth invited some fifty women from many of New York's leading families to a meeting at the Infirmary to discuss how they might best aid the war effort. It was clear that the female contribution would be twofold: the collection of supplies and money, and hospital nursing. There was certainly no shortage of enthusiasm. In the opening days of the war, Northern women energetically packed up anything they could lay hands on, from cakes and jam to blankets and books, to send to the troops. There was also, as Elizabeth put it, 'a perfect mania amongst them to act Florence Nightingale'. The question was how to deploy this great army of women volunteers to maximum effect without irritating the authorities. Elizabeth knew only too well, both from her own experience and from hearing at first hand of Nightingale's trials in the Crimea, that if the women's patriotism was not properly channelled, their efforts would simply be dismissed by the government as troublesome interference.

Anxious to avoid this at all costs, Elizabeth was the prime mover in setting up the Women's Central Relief Association (WCRA) designed to bring together in one organisation all existing female-run charities and voluntary aid societies. In a letter addressed to the women of New York and published in the city's newspapers, 'Ninety-Two of the Most Respected Ladies' offered to undertake this task of coordination and to guarantee that no single group would be given prominence over another. The WCRA came into formal existence at a meeting of 4,000 New Yorkers (3,000 of them women) at the Cooper Union on 26 April.

Among its stated aims was the initiation of a sensible dialogue with army doctors, to create a central depot for hospital stores and to set up an office to register and examine volunteer nurses. Ironically the president (Dr Valentine Mott), vice-president (the Reverend Henry Bellows) and half the board of this 'women's' association were men, but at least the chairmanship of the committee responsible for dealing with the nurses was given to a woman – Elizabeth Blackwell. Out of Elizabeth's WCRA initiative grew the highly effective United States Sanitary Commission, given formal sanction in an order signed by Lincoln on 13 June 1861. The thousands of women volunteers who worked under the auspices of the USSC collected food, bandages, clothes and medicines, served as nurses in army camps and hospitals, organised free board and lodging for soldiers on leave and, largely through the 'Sanitary Fairs', raised some $6 million in aid of the war.

But for Elizabeth and Emily, who had played a seminal role in the formation of this great organisation, there was to be no credit. The Nightingale effect had made little impact on the United States army, whose authorities regarded the whole idea of female nurses in military hospitals – especially those processed by a voluntary organisation – with deep suspicion. This despite the fact that their own resources were hopelessly inadequate. The army medics were particularly antagonistic to Elizabeth and Emily: 'The doctors would not permit us to come forward. In the hospital committee . . . they declined to allow our little hospital to be represented and they refused to have anything to do with the nurse education plan "if the Miss Blackwells were going to engineer the matter". Of course, as it is essential to open the hospitals to nurses, we kept in the background. Had there been any power to support us, we would have fought for our true place, but there was none.'[25]

In fact, Elizabeth's position was undermined from the start when, a few days after the outbreak of war, the government appointed Dorothea Dix as superintendent of nurses. Dix, a 59-year-old Boston schoolteacher, had no formal medical training but as a result of her successful campaigning on behalf of the indigent insane she had made powerful friends in the capital. On the outbreak of war she went immediately to Washington DC to lobby for the establishment of an army nursing corps under her leadership. Elizabeth was understandably bitter: 'The government has given Miss Dix a semi official recognition as meddler general – for it really amounts to that, she being without system, or any practical knowledge of the business.'[26] Although relegated to the sidelines, Elizabeth's committee worked hard during the first six months of the war processing the avalanche of applications they received from aspiring nurses. It selected ninety-one nurses for training who were sent to either the Bellevue or New York Hospital for one month's training before posting – under Dix's direction – to a military hospital.

The formidable set of conditions that these women had to meet in order to pass Elizabeth's selection board reflected Florence Nightingale's views.

Each woman had to be between thirty and forty-five years of age and of a strong constitution. She had also to present testimonials to her morality, sobriety, honesty and trustworthiness, accept subordination to Dix and the medical authorities – and wear a dress without a hoop. It was greatly in an applicant's favour if she were physically plain. The fact that Elizabeth had absorbed many of Nightingale's theories did not prevent her from criticising *Notes on Nursing* published by Nightingale in 1860. Indeed, her comments reveal the depth of their rift: 'I have read Miss Nightingale's little nursing book . . . and I see . . . how impossible it would have been for me to do her work. The character of our minds is so different, that minute attention to and interest in details would be impossible to me, for the end proposed – nursing. I cultivate observation with much interest for medicine – but I have no vocation for nursing and she evidently has. It is a capital little book in its way, and I shall find it very useful. You noticed her little sneer at the hospital! How difficult it is for people to understand others' work.'[27]

Nor did she admire Nightingale's literary talents: '[The book] has great faults. It is ill tempered, dogmatic, exaggerated. It will not at all increase her reputation. Nevertheless the book is good, it is very suggestive, contains a great deal of excellent practical sense and is a very readable book. Piquant quite, and a readable book on nursing is a valuable thing. Florence cannot write a book in the usual meaning of the word. She can only throw together a mass of hints and experiences which are useful and interesting, but she is not able to digest them into a book which will remain as a classic . . . so her little nursing book is very welcome to me because I expected nothing higher.'[28]

Elizabeth's transparent jealousy is not difficult to understand. As a result of the Crimean War, Florence Nightingale had won instant fame, ensuring that her views would always command universal respect and attention. In contrast, Elizabeth's experience of war was primarily one of frustration and lost opportunity. Instead of being at the centre of the nursing effort where she could have contributed so much, she was humiliatingly ousted from the very organisation that she had helped conceive. Provoking though this was, Elizabeth did not regard her rejection as a mortal blow. Even before the outbreak of the Civil War she had confessed to Barbara Bodichon that 'The Woman medical question has become too narrow ground for me to stand on in America because it is essentially gained here'.[29] Despite establishment prejudice – military or civil – she knew that she had put in train a process that was unstoppable.

SIXTEEN

'A Deed of Daring'

If professionally Elizabeth had a disappointing war, she did at least have the satisfaction of meeting Abraham Lincoln. In 1864 she twice visited Washington where her old friend Dr William Elder was working as a statistician in the Treasury (and where, she was pleased to note, some 300 young women were employed as clerks). Elder, whose job was clearly not too demanding, took Elizabeth on an extensive tour of the city that included a visit to the White House. They particularly admired the President's reception room, although Elizabeth thought it a pity that he had only the one:

Just as we were going out Judge Kelly of Philadelphia met us and said 'why don't you go up and see the President' . . . Dr Elder and I are always ready for any deed of daring in that line so up we went and Judge Kelly swept aside the usher and opened the door of a large comfortable square room on the second floor, announced Dr Elder and Miss Blackwell of New York and left us! A tall ungainly loose-jointed man was standing in the middle of the room. He came forward with a pleasant smile and shook hands with us. I should not at all have recognized him from the photographs – he is much uglier than any I have seen . . . His brain must be much better in quality than quantity, for his head is small for the great lanky body and the forehead very retreating. Dr Elder remarked that I was the second woman who had become a citizen of the United States and I added that I believed Queen Victoria reserved the privilege of shooting me. 'Why yes' said he, 'that was the chief cause, I believe, of our war of 1812' and then he plumped his long body down on a corner of the large table that stood in the middle of the room caught up one knee looking for all the world like a Kentucky loafer on some old tavern steps, and began to discuss some point about the war . . .[1]

The purpose of Elizabeth's visit to Washington other than sightseeing is unclear, although she did spend an hour with Dorothea Dix 'making acquaintance with the lady and observing her style'.[2] Despite her disapproval of Dix, she did her best to cooperate with her and was pleased to hear news of the nurses selected and trained by the New York committee. One of these, a frail German girl, had managed to slip away from the Dix organisation to serve on the front. After Gettysburg 'she spent two days and nights on the field of slaughter, wading with men's boots in the blood and mud, pulling out the still living bodies from the heaps of slain, binding up hideous wounds . . . in an enthusiasm of beneficence which triumphed equally over thought of self and horror of the hideous slaughter'.[3] Of the urgent need for nurses Elizabeth could be in no doubt as she watched the endless stream of wagons filled with wounded soldiers pass beneath her hotel bedroom: 'The driver walked by the horses making them creep along to try and avoid the rough jolts which make the poor wounded suffer so dreadfully'.[4]

An Abolitionist since childhood, Elizabeth could at least take comfort in Lincoln's proclamation granting freedom to slaves in the rebel states: 'That on the first day of January AD 1863 all persons held as slaves within any State or designated part of a State . . . shall be then thenceforward and forever free.'[5] This at least gave some purpose to the soldiers' suffering. On a second visit to Washington in November 1864 (when she visited several Sanitary Commission-sponsored schools for black children) Elizabeth reported delightedly to Kitty on the new order:

> I cannot tell you with how much satisfaction I traversed the state of Maryland as a free state. It seemed to me that already it began to look more thrifty with more land under cultivation and the houses and gardens trimmer and more home like. In Baltimore, there were all the old coloured men busy as before on the sloops and about the wharves, grown grey in toil, but now, thank Heaven, no longer slaves. And the coloured teamsters driving their long lines of horses with their curious expletives, as Dickens described them, Hi ho ho jiblen, hi jigggy jibblin, jo-o-o! But all freed men. It was an immense satisfaction to reach the Capital City in a free state.[6]

Not every Northerner shared her euphoria. In three days of the worst civil disorder in American history, the poor (mostly Irish) of New York had vented their fury on rich whites and poor blacks alike in three days of violent rioting in July 1863. The riots resulted from the government's attempt to draft 300,000 men into the Union army. The fact that the rich could buy a substitute for $300 (despite their principles, both Henry and Sam Blackwell took advantage of this) did little to make the draft more acceptable to the New York poor. Black men were hanged, drowned and mutilated and the Colored Orphan Asylum looted and burned by rioters screaming 'Burn the niggers' nest'.[7] Horace Greeley, whose newspaper roundly condemned the protesters, was a prime target. The mob set the *Tribune* building alight, although Greeley himself managed to escape down a back staircase and hide under a table in a nearby restaurant.

Although it was well known locally that the Infirmary housed black patients, it was left unharmed. However the nearby explosions and fires that lit up the sky frightened the other patients into demanding that the black women be forced to leave. Elizabeth and Emily remained resolute. Any patient was free to depart whenever she wished but they insisted that the black women remain. Order was finally restored in the city when troops arrived – a few days after the battle of Gettysburg – forcing the rioters to retreat to their tenements.

Elizabeth and Kitty first heard news of the riots in the peaceful countryside of New Jersey, from where they hurried back to New York to help defend the Infirmary. It was in the wooded landscape of Montclair that Elizabeth had chosen the previous year to build a cottage with the money received from the Comtesse de Noailles. While the property proved a welcome escape from the summer heat of New York, it never fulfilled Elizabeth's more ambitious expectations, becoming neither the hub of a family commune nor the sanatorium envisioned by the Comtesse. Yet again lack of funds forced Elizabeth to compromise her plans as she could only afford to open the house for a few months each year.

Although she occasionally invited a few infirmary patients to Montclair, Elizabeth had long been troubled by the fact that it had taken her two years to spend the Comtesse's donation and even now she knew that it was not being deployed entirely as Madame Noailles had intended. Nevertheless she had justified not returning it on the grounds that at some point in the future the capital sum could be used to support the women's medical cause in England. In any case, the Comtesse was so excited by this modest 'sanatorium' that she at once started to plan a larger institution in Philadelphia, at the same time urging Elizabeth to tell her patients to follow her example and go barefoot: 'What is true for the feet is true for the whole body.'[8] How much financial detail Elizabeth disclosed to the Comtesse is not known, but it is clear that without the $8,500 that she received in 1867 from the sale of the Montclair house and its surrounding land she could not have afforded to settle permanently in England.

It was not only the sanatorium that failed fully to materialise. Her vision of a tightly knit family settlement was also thwarted, although Henry and Lucy, with their small daughter Alice, lived next door and by the early 1860s most of the family were based in New Jersey. The ties between the Blackwell siblings in middle age were as intricate and binding as when they were children, and their separation into American and English camps a source of continual regret to them all.

Since childhood Elizabeth's own loyalties had swung back and forth across the Atlantic so that the antagonism between England and the Union States sparked by the Civil War caused her real distress. Officially Britain was neutral but the Prime Minister, Lord Palmerston, made it clear that he favoured a permanent division between North and South while William Gladstone, in a famous indiscretion, spoke out publicly in favour of the South. His view of the Civil War (shared by many of his fellow countrymen) was influenced by the loss of thousands of jobs in the cotton mills – a fact that did nothing to lessen Union anger at Britain's doubtful neutrality.

In 1860 Elizabeth had written to Barbara Bodichon 'It is evident to me that the English government is fast resolving to fight the North . . . the arrogance of the English press has only been equalled by the insolence of the Northern press and now the English press is publishing such astounding lies and misrepresentations about the state of things in the North that matters are evidently coming to a crisis. I think both countries very wrong!'[9] A year later the situation had not improved: 'It is a painful position we occupy – asked not infrequently, "well what do you think of your England now?" . . . with part of our own family furiously American and part as furiously English, and disapproving as we do of the conduct of both countries. It is a terrible trial of feeling.'[10]

Since moving east, Henry had characteristically tried a number of imaginative ways to earn a living, including setting up farmers' libraries across the Midwest. But much of his and Sam's activity centred on the complicated Western land deals that he was convinced would one day make his fortune, leaving him free to devote his energies to reform politics. In his lack of commercial judgement, however, Henry proved himself a true Blackwell. Just as land prices began to rise, he handed over his real estate business to his youngest brother, George. Always the least idealistic of the

Blackwell siblings, George in due course became a highly successful property speculator and millionaire. The only member of the family to make real money, he was largely responsible in later years for keeping his more philanthropically minded sisters financially afloat. Early in 1861 Lucy had returned briefly to the women's rights front, but her efforts were brought to an abrupt end with the outbreak of the war – the suffragists having agreed to suspend their activities until it was over. She spent the next few years in New Jersey, suffering from endless migraines and trying to keep her family solvent.

Although the state of Sam's finances was generally little better than those of his brother, there was no questioning the happiness of his marriage: 'The truth is I fall in love with you anew every time we separate . . .'[11] Nettie touchingly wrote to him while on a three-month lecture tour of upstate New York. She had resumed her public speaking career after the death of their second baby (by 1869 they had five daughters) but like Lucy had been forced to return to domesticity when the war began.

Elizabeth, whose brave words claiming emotional self-sufficiency failed to disguise a yearning for married love, recognised Sam and Nettie's happiness in one another and appreciated its rarity:

> Though I have quite out-lived the pain, and gained strength by the necessity of self centred life, it is still a fact which I am analysing with intense interest. Ah love is a very grand thing, ever more and more precious to me, as I more fully understand its wonderful power, and I study it more carefully, more reverently as I recognize the priesthood of woman in love. I often wonder that women are so careless of the love in their life, cherishing it with so little care, so indifferent to the comprehension of other's nature, so ignorant of the quality of their mutual relation. Most people alas are very faithless to the trust of the love committed to their keeping.[12]

Although Elizabeth approved of Nettie's wifely devotion, she emphatically disliked her preaching: 'Nettie has much annoyed us by preaching in New York . . . under the name of Blackwell. It's very hard to have to bear the crude untasteful proceedings of other women on our shoulders, and it has been a serious evil to us . . . still I believe no burden is really crushing.'[13] While always deeply involved in her siblings' lives, Elizabeth's special responsibility was to her adopted child. By the end of the Civil War, Kitty was a young woman of eighteen who, in Elizabeth's view, had more than repaid her investment in her, as she had remarked to Barbara Bodichon four years earlier:

> It might seem as if I had been very unfortunate in my experiment of adoption, at least many persons think so, and yet in truth, that child has been, and is, so great a blessing to me, that I hardly know what I should have done without her. And, so sure am I of myself and my needs in this way, that I am fully resolved in carrying out my original plan, by adopting two or three more. But they must be of good stock. I want good English children – so look out for me dear Barbara. A little boy or girl about two years old, who has no other home will find a true home with me, and I am prepared to receive it at any moment.[14]

Despite this outburst of maternal enthusiasm, it is hard to view Elizabeth as a natural mother. Her love for Kitty was entirely genuine but it was also selfish and did not stop her from continuing to treat the child as part servant, part daughter. Unlike a fully fledged Blackwell, Kitty was expected to address her 'aunts' and 'uncles' as Miss Marian or Mr Henry, while Elizabeth signed her letters 'your doctor'. Kitty's health was not perfect. Her weak eyes and bad hearing (as well as acute shyness) inevitably stunted her education and provided Elizabeth with a permanent excuse not to let her roam – in any sense – too far.

In truth, Kitty was Elizabeth's creature. She gave and received love without question, proved herself an able housekeeper and, although highly intelligent, never questioned her foster mother's authority. In other words, she behaved exactly like the Victorian ideal of the perfect wife. Elizabeth, who had spent her whole life advocating both the sanctity of motherhood and the right of women to work, failed utterly to see the irony of preventing her own adopted daughter from finding fulfilment in either role. Kitty was neither allowed to choose a career (the idea that she should train as a gymnastics teacher came to nothing) nor given the opportunity to meet eligible young men. No doubt Elizabeth convinced herself that Kitty's deeper needs were perfectly met by the Blackwell family circle and in helping her guardian to accomplish the great task of reforming society.

And in this latter ambition, Elizabeth could justifiably feel that by the mid-1860s she and Emily had made real progress. The practice of medicine by women in America was no longer in question but an established fact. In the decade following her own early struggles in New York some 200 female physicians had graduated and were practising in one form or another all

over the United States. The Infirmary was so successful that in 1862 half
the pregnant women wanting to give birth there had to be turned away
and, just a few years later, over 7,000 patients were recorded as having
passed through its doors to receive treatment of one kind or another.
Furthermore, the Infirmary received official recognition from the state
legislature when, along with all other dispensaries in New York, it received
an annual grant of $1,000.[15]

Encouraging though all this was, the fact remained that there was still not
a school in the whole country where women could obtain a high-quality
medical education. While ten or so colleges had absorbed a few female
students, the best of them still kept their doors firmly shut to women; and
those colleges founded especially for women in Philadelphia and Boston
(where Marie Zakrzewska was working) were, in Elizabeth's view, merely
perpetrators of female inferiority. 'They have each quite a large number of
superficial people engaged in pushing what I think a sillier and sillier scheme
. . . the products are worthless . . . I have yet to see the first decent doctor
come from either of those schools.'[16] Equally, she had only scorn for the
New York Medical College for Women, a homeopathic institute opened by
Clemence Lozier in April 1863: 'Nothing could be more shallow and
unprincipled than their whole course . . . it was a vulgar little class of
women, led by one of the commonest type of woman's right's women. They
did the most indiscreet the most tactless and impertinent things.'[17]

The problem of how best to give women a proper medical education was
never far from Elizabeth's mind. On 19 December 1863 she gave an address
(jointly authored with Emily and published in 1864) at the Infirmary to a
group of sympathisers on the subject in which she vividly described the
plight of the female doctor: 'Consider how women stand in this matter;
how alone, how unsupported; no libraries, museums, hospitals, dispensaries, clinics; no endowments, scholarships, professorships, prizes, to
stimulate and reward study; no time-honored institutions and customs, no
recognized position; no societies, meetings, and professional
companionship; all these things men have, none of them are open to
women. One can hardly conceive a more complete isolation.'[18]

In a dry assessment of the situation, Elizabeth condemned the inadequacy
of the average girl's education that left her so ill-equipped to deal in later
life with the discipline of any serious work, let alone medicine. And while
agreeing that the sympathetic nature so universally attributed to women
was indispensable to a good doctor, she argued: 'It is knowledge not

sympathy which can administer the right medicine; it is observation and comprehension, not sympathy which will discover the kind of disease.'[19]

If the men's colleges would not accept women and if the women's colleges were hopelessly inadequate, there was only one possible course of action. The New York Infirmary must open its own medical school. Elizabeth envisioned an institution where the course of study would be so rigorous that it would rival the best medical education on offer anywhere and the examinations so thorough that no one (male or female) could ever doubt the competence of its graduates. Not that Elizabeth ever wanted simply to replicate male doctors. As she had pointed out to Barbara Bodichon in 1861: 'I do not look on a good medical training as having power to make men of women, but as a most valuable educator of their own natures . . . It is very possible that women so trained will not act just as men would nor supply the places now occupied by medical men. But they will find their own place and work and I think it will be very valuable work.'[20]

In 1864 two committees were formed in addition to the Infirmary's main board. One of these dealt with hospital matters, the other was given the task of carrying through the college project. In September that year, Elizabeth wrote to Barbara Bodichon: 'The combination of very thorough long continued drill with the highest aims, and exalted criticism, is so rare, nay so unknown in women's education, and yet so indispensable for the growth of the race, that it is the San Greal [sic] of my life, the deep unchangeable undying interest.'[21] Sensing that in the proposed medical school she would at last see this dream given real substance, she again brimmed with energy.

* * *

Because Elizabeth rarely complained or even spoke to anyone about the loss of her eye (after a few hours she found the artificial one tiring to wear) it is easy to underestimate the profound impact it made on her life – and especially on her relations with Emily. Unable to practise surgery or, indeed, any sustained work that required close inspection, she had been forced to defer (against her natural inclination) to her younger sister on most medical matters. A serious attack of eye inflammation in 1860 prompted the sad admission: 'My eyes [are] so much weakened that I dare neither read a book, nor write a lecture. The sight is perfect but the eye becomes fatigued with any continued exertion and the reading of even a chapter in a book is quite out of the question . . . I do not consider it possible that it will ever be prudent for me to do much study from books, and the plan of a professorship which I have always looked forward to, must be given up.'[22]

This depressing situation made her all the more anxious to exert her influence in the areas where she could still wield authority – strategy and hygiene. But while she took the lead in the public campaign to launch the medical college, she was less successful in her crusade to promote hygiene as the most important subject on its curriculum. Always more drawn to social welfare than pure medicine, this natural bent combined with the influence of Florence Nightingale and her eye problems led her, by the early 1860s, to give further serious thought to the role of hygiene in medicine and how it should be taught to women medical students: 'The question I have been pondering lately is a modification of the present system of medical education and the establishment (by legislative sanction) of a Doctorate of Hygiene, in the belief that family practice would speedily, by the good sense of the community, be transferred to these new Doctors.'[23]

Rightly sceptical of the value of most drugs then prescribed to the sick, she wanted 'to reduce them to their proper place', making them subordinate to the much more important therapeutic and hygienic agents – 'Water, Air, Food, Electricity'.[24] Anxious, however, not to stray too far from orthodox medicine, she also wanted to increase the time students spent studying medicine and to maintain their enthusiasm for scientific research. She summed up her thoughts in a letter to Barbara Bodichon:

. . . you see my great objective would be to turn the young doctors out, thorough practical hygienists; to convert the great army of the medical profession into active agents for diffusing hygiene knowledge and to direct the impulse of pecuniary reward and scientific investigation into researches on the meaning and conditions of Health. Recognizing fully the value and place of drugs, and graduating my young doctors in Medicine as well as Hygiene, I should nevertheless put the two subjects into their true position, in which I believe the latter stands much higher than the former.[25]

This championing of hygiene at the expense of other subjects may have been one element in the growing tension between Elizabeth and Emily during the 1860s. Another was Emily's continuing disillusionment with medicine: 'She has taken an extreme dislike to it and though she performs her duties conscientiously, she only does in medicine what is unavoidable

. . . she will never practise in England.'[26] It seems likely that Emily's intention to give up medicine had more to do with a growing intolerance of Elizabeth's dominating ways than a rooted dislike of doctoring. Once the Atlantic separated the two sisters, there was no more talk of Emily quitting medicine.

But whatever their professional differences, two deaths – one notoriously public, the other intensely private – caused them to unite in grief. Lincoln's assassination at Ford's Theatre on 14 April 1865 touched Elizabeth deeply:

> I cannot explain how our private lives have all become interwoven with the life of the nation . . . neither is it possible to estimate the keen personal suffering that has entered into every household and saddened every life with this last wicked blow which has fallen upon us . . . the great secret of our dead leader's popularity was the wonderful instinct with which he felt and acted the wishes and judgements of the great mass of the people. He did not lead; he expressed the American heartbeat . . . it has been to one a revelation to feel such influence and see such leadership. I never was thoroughly republican before; there was always a shade of conservative aristocratic tendency. But I am so thoroughly now, heart and soul. It seems the grandest of all governments where the people are willing and the leader is transparent to their will.[27]

For all her carping about American society, Elizabeth identified wholeheartedly with her adopted country at a time of such trauma. Her brother Howard, however, had definitively thrown in his lot with the Old World – and with his sister Anna. In the wake of cousin Samuel Blackwell's business collapse, he had abandoned the Staffordshire ironworks and found employment with the East India Company prospecting mines north of Bombay. But despite a generous salary, he decided not to stay in India and returned to look for work in England, intending eventually to set up house with Anna. The news of his death, at the age of thirty-five (from what was then described as an internal rupture) reached New York on 5 March 1866, prompting Emily to write in her diary: 'The circle is broken. Ah dear Howard – poor Anna!'[28] His death was a shock to the whole family but for Anna it was cataclysmic. 'It is wonderful that the heart does not break outright under such a shock – such an utter emptying of one's life of all that gave it value. Unconsciously I had built on that beloved life as on a rock. Every thought, hope, prospect, plan centred on him. Our lives had been so long and intimately interwoven that there is nothing about me little or large, of the inner or of the outer existence that was not to me more full of him than of myself.'[29]

The Blackwell sisters did not lack passion but having shunned marriage were forced to seek other ways of finding emotional satisfaction. Emily and Marian, in middle age, lived with female companions; Elizabeth, Emily and Ellen all adopted children, while Elizabeth and Kitty lavished extravagant love on a series of pet dogs. For Anna, separated by thousands of miles from most of her family, earning a fragile living in Paris as a journalist, Howard had become brother, husband and child rolled into one and the centre of her life.

In response to Anna's deep distress, Elizabeth and George sailed to Europe in May 1866 to spend much of the next six months in Paris comforting her as best they could. Grateful, perhaps, for this enforced holiday, Elizabeth wrote of her intense pleasure at studying the piano once more: 'You know I have taken up music systematically because my eyesight is really so unreliable that reading is out of the question as an amusement and I must have some relaxation.'[30]

Notwithstanding Howard's death and Anna's depression, Elizabeth enjoyed Paris to the full, remarking on how much the city had improved under its present government. To Kitty (left behind in America) she wrote detailed accounts of the current fashions and of the modest social events hosted by Anna at which George (wearing polished boots and Howard's dress suit) made polite conversation to suitable young ladies. If, for once, work took second place to pleasure, a meeting with Mary Putnam was a potent reminder of just how much had been achieved for women doctors since Elizabeth's days at La Maternité but also of the task that still lay ahead.

Mary Putnam represented a new breed of female doctor – one markedly different from Elizabeth. Daughter of the publisher George Putnam (whose firm published Elizabeth's 1852 *Laws of Life*), she had been drawn to medicine by her passion for science. In 1860, at the age of seventeen, she had spent some months at the New York Infirmary. Three years later she obtained a qualification from the New York College of Pharmacy before going on to graduate in 1864 from the Female Medical College of Pennsylvania. She also studied for a time in the New England Hospital for Women and Children that had been founded in 1862 by Marie Zakrzewska. But none of this experience – all gained before she was twenty-four – satisfied Putnam. She wanted a serious scientific education and knew that the only place she could hope (as a woman) to find it was in Paris. With great persistence, she talked her way into the École de Médecine from where she graduated (with high honours) in 1871. She did not go unnoticed by the *British Medical Journal* whose Paris correspondent recorded:

A young woman – I cannot bring myself to say a young lady – may be seen daily, at half-past twelve, and for some hours thereafter, dissecting in one of the pavilions of the École Pratique. She seems to be about twenty-five years of age, and wears . . . a lady's round hat, and a blue garment having the general effect of a Frenchman's blouse. On Friday last she was dissecting the thigh of a female subject, while at the same time a male fellow-student was dissecting the opposite limb . . . The anatomical scene now described takes place daily in Dr. Fort's pavilion. A punning friend, when there with me the other day, said – pointing to the professor – *'C'est fort'*; and then added – pointing to the mixed dissecting group – *'Et c'est trop fort'*; and another of our party added, *'Et le tout est degoutant'*.[31]

Putnam believed in science in a way that her older mentor never could. Elizabeth always set out to promote science but when it conflicted with her religious instincts, it was the science that she rejected. For Putnam, however, science *was* a religion: 'Immersion in technical studies is like arsenic eating – once begun, you must go on, and at a continually increasing dose. I am really astonished to find how this absorption grows upon me.'[32] Putnam's commitment to science led her to become arguably the most distinguished American woman physician of the nineteenth century, whose professional achievements ranked highly among those of either sex.

Although their profoundly different approach to medicine caused them to spar in later years, Putnam always gave full acknowledgement to Elizabeth's pioneering courage and left an affectionate account of their meeting in Paris:

When she went away, she actually kissed me for the first time during the period of our long and friendly acquaintance! I was quite astonished but very much delighted. I hope to improve gradually my acquaintance with her sister Anna, a very interesting but peculiar person. I was much amused to have the Dr describe to me the way in which she had been incessantly snubbed and criticised by this sister, who is several years older, and of a very positive and rather domineering temperament. She is a great Spiritualist much to the Dr's disgust and thinks she is continually receiving communication from the brother who has recently died; and with which she expected the Dr to sympathize.[33]

Putnam liked Anna when she called on her some months later, though she found her 'absurdly spiritualistic'. She was also much amused to receive a lecture on how to breathe: '[Anna] is very critical and can hardly be with a person for more than five minutes without criticising them for something. Hence I considered myself fortunate to escape with an adjuration to alter my manner of breathing. She has become an enthusiastic convert to Catlin's idea on the danger of breathing through the mouth, and talked a great deal of eloquent nonsense to prove to me that I must make a powerful and conscientious effort to breathe through my nose.'[34]

Mary Putnam was not, however, the first woman to earn a medical degree in Paris – that distinction went to Elizabeth's English protégée Elizabeth Garrett, whose medical apprenticeship had for the most part taken place in the Middlesex Hospital in London. The licence that she received from the Society of Apothecaries in 1865 entitled her to practise medicine legally but did not have the same status as a medical degree. Determined not to settle for second best, she was intent on acquiring a full MD despite being consistently refused permission to sit the examinations set by any of the English Boards entitled to award one. Turning to Paris, Garrett asked the British Ambassador, Lord Lyons, if he would promote her application to take the six examinations of the Paris MD. This he achieved (thanks to the personal intervention of the Empress Eugénie) and in June 1870 Garrett became the first woman to earn a medical degree from the Sorbonne.

For Elizabeth, there were bitter-sweet elements in the success of these two spirited young women. The fact that her vision and determination had shown them the way was a source of deep pride and satisfaction. Yet, at some level, she must have suspected that their very success heralded a waning of her own influence. A younger generation of pioneer women doctors was emerging and one which had its own ideas of where they were going in medicine – ideas that did not necessarily reflect her own.

But during this short stay in Paris Elizabeth, for once, was determined to enjoy herself and nothing gave her more pleasure than her reunion with Hippolyte Blot. Old feelings were quickly rekindled:

The intimate friendship of a man of one's own age with whom a great deal of human feeling exists and of whom you are very fond, has a very great charm and is giving to the last part of my stay an intensity of life that is very refreshing to a half starved soul. He has a wife and two charming children . . . Last Sunday was a brilliant day. I paid them a little visit at their country house that was really a time to remember. Do not imagine however that I shall come back with regret. I am only delighted to know that I have such full power of enjoyment in me and I mean to try if I cannot put more brightness into our New York life.[35]

Blot was not the only man to re-emerge from Elizabeth's past with the whiff of romance about him. When she travelled back to America in October 1866, she was accompanied by the recently widowed Herman Bicknell, whom she had first met in 1850 when they were fellow students at St Bartholomew's Hospital. The colourful and exotic Bicknell brought a dash of glamour into her existence that chimed well with her new determination to enjoy life. In 1862 he had visited Mecca undisguised – allegedly the first European to do so. He repeated the exercise in Qum seven years later, when it was reported that only his knowledge of Muslim ritual saved him from being lynched by a furious mob. He had served as an army surgeon in Hong Kong and during the Indian Mutiny but abandoned medicine in 1861 to devote himself to travel and the study of oriental languages.

The panache with which Bicknell took on the world both impressed and amused Elizabeth. He climbed the Matterhorn, translated Hafiz and wrote poetry himself – some of it even dedicated to Elizabeth under the pretence that it was a translation of the work of a Persian academic. A liaison between the two of them was probably never a serious option but it did occur to Elizabeth that Bicknell might marry Ellen (still struggling to earn a living as an artist) not least, perhaps, because Bicknell's father, Elhanan Bicknell, was William Turner's patron. The matchmaking came to nothing but Elizabeth and Bicknell retained their close friendship – full of warmth and fun – until his death from cancer in 1875 at the age of forty-five. He had succeeded in revitalising a part of Elizabeth that had for many years lain dormant: her interest in the opposite sex. As Kitty dryly noted, in later life Elizabeth was rarely without a devoted younger man in tow.

On returning to America, Elizabeth reiterated her determination not to stay longer than two years. She wanted to see the medical school launched but had already decided that Emily should take charge of it: 'Emily . . . does grandly at the centre of this movement – towers head and shoulders above her students . . . and exercises a certain imperiousness as head of the establishment which is not unbecoming . . . I am more than willing that she should assume this headship and have long assisted her in acquiring it . . . She fully approves of my going to Europe to reside and only wishes I could go sooner . . .'[36] These last words were true for reasons that Elizabeth did not care to acknowledge. Emily was finding it increasingly difficult to accept her sister's controlling nature and constant need to assert her seniority. The time had come to dissolve their fifteen-year partnership and go their separate ways – but not before they had successfully launched their medical college.

The Women's Medical College of the New York Infirmary was formally opened on 2 November 1868. It was a day of intense satisfaction for both sisters but, predictably, it was Elizabeth who stepped forward to deliver the inaugural address.[37] She charted the struggles of the last fifteen years ('the way has been very dark') to the present triumphant inauguration of a medical education for women that was designed to prove equal to the best on offer anywhere. The 'two perpendicular cliffs' they had faced for so long – money and professional support – were largely scaled. Although the new college had not yet reached its endowment target of $100,000, it had attracted financial support from a wide public and several prominent businessmen – thanks chiefly to the success of the Infirmary.

As for the quality of the teaching, Elizabeth had only to point to the many eminent names listed in the College's prospectus. As a reflection of her determination not to sacrifice professional standards to principles of gender, only three members of the eighteen-strong faculty were women. Elizabeth held the chair of hygiene (the first in the country), Emily that of obstetrics and diseases of women and Lucy Abbott (a graduate of the Female Medical College of Pennsylvania) taught clinical midwifery.

The standards set at the new medical school were exacting from the start. The students all had to pass an entrance examination and were then required to follow a three- rather than the more normal two-year course of study. Clinical experience was to take precedence over the lecture theatre, studies would be progressive (not merely repeated) and, most important of all, there would be an independent examining body of distinguished physicians who would ensure that only genuinely qualified students graduated. This bold strategy was a gamble. Elizabeth and

Emily were well aware that they might lose many talented women unable to afford the longer period of study while others (hampered by an inferior education) would be deterred by the high academic standards demanded and simply opt for easier medical qualifications elsewhere. Insistence on such stringent standards therefore carried great financial risk but characteristically neither sister was prepared to contemplate compromise.

Among the very first students to enrol in the College was a tempestuous young Englishwoman, Sophia Jex-Blake, then aged twenty-eight. She had originally intended to be a reforming educator but after living some months with her friend Lucy Sewall (a doctor at the New England Hospital for Women and Children in Boston) she had decided instead to become a doctor herself. After being rejected three times by the Harvard Medical School, she went to New York in March 1868 where she met the Blackwell sisters and spent a few weeks working informally at the New York Infirmary – an experience that persuaded her to return six months later (with her faithful maid, Alice) to begin the three-year course in earnest. The day before the official opening of the School she wrote to her mother: 'The term begins tomorrow, and I am glad to say that Alice and I have just succeeded in getting things into some sort of order in time. Besides laying down carpets, buying a stove and kitchen pots and pans, a bedstead and chairs, etc., I have been providing winter stores in American fashion, and yesterday bought two barrels of potatoes, 30 lbs. of butter, etc., etc., to say nothing of flour and wine . . . The Blackwells are very pleasant, and though I have no special friends here, I shall be so busy and cosy that I expect to get on capitally.'[38]

A week later she wrote again to her mother describing her daily routine:

I go to the dissecting room at 9 a.m. and work till about 11.15. At 11.30 comes a lecture on Anatomy and Physiology on alternate days, – and I get home to lunch a little before one. Alice always has things ready and nice for me, and I rest for about half an hour after lunch, before going to the afternoon lectures which begin at 2pm and continue (except on Saturday) till 5 – three lectures of an hour each. I have just put in a petition to Dr. Emily Blackwell (who manages everything and is very nice) for five minutes space between each two lectures for opening windows and a walk up and down the corridors, to which she instantly assented as desirable . . . I believe that I never was so strong in my life before – isn't that grand?[39]

Sophia Jex-Blake's delight in her new life as a medical student was short-lived. Two days after writing this letter, she received news that her father was dying and immediately left for home.

Eight months later, with the launch of the medical school safely accomplished and her partnership with Emily legally dissolved, Elizabeth herself left for England. The fact that relations between the two sisters had finally reached breaking point was a major factor in convincing Elizabeth that the time was now right for her to establish a career in London and achieve her ambition of leading Englishwomen into medicine.

SEVENTEEN

Medical Sisterhood

Elizabeth arrived in England on 28 July 1869 still uncertain whether she would be able to live there permanently. In fact she was to stay until her death over forty years later. Before acquiring her own home at 6 Burwood Place (off Edgware Road) in April 1870, she based herself primarily in Barbara Bodichon's spacious house in Blandford Square, St Marylebone.

Although her earlier campaign to establish women doctors in Britain had failed, she was convinced that this was only a temporary setback. A decade later she was more than ready to try again, knowing that this time she could point to the success of the New York Infirmary and Medical College as solid evidence of what women could achieve given the opportunity. In any case, breakthrough in England had already been achieved when in 1865 the Society of Apothecaries had granted Elizabeth Garrett a licence to practise medicine. Since then even the most diehard conservative could no longer dismiss women doctors as an absurdity.

But the battle was far from won. Just as Geneva Medical College had refused to accept any more women in the wake of Elizabeth's graduation, so too the Society of Apothecaries, appalled at having let Miss Garrett slip through the system, revised its constitution in 1867 to exclude any more women from taking its examinations. Until 1877, when five new names were finally added to the list, there remained just two female doctors on the British Medical Register – Dr Elizabeth Blackwell and Dr Elizabeth Garrett.

In view of her unique contribution to opening up the medical profession for American women Elizabeth fully expected to spearhead the British effort, but in this she was to be disappointed. By the time she arrived in London, Sophia Jex-Blake, until so recently one of her own students, had become the leader of the movement. But if Elizabeth failed to take control of Britain's first generation of women doctors she nevertheless remained a powerful role model, regarded by them with deep respect. She had, after all, been qualified for twenty years and on the British Medical Register for ten. She was living proof that a woman could succeed as a doctor, and her decision to live in England gave crucial encouragement to those hoping to follow in her footsteps.

If Sophia Jex-Blake took up the cause on behalf of all Englishwomen wanting to be doctors, Elizabeth Garrett was a remarkable example of individual success. Echoing Elizabeth's New York experiment twelve years earlier, in 1866 she opened a dispensary in the slums of St Marylebone in London, staffed by women for the treatment of women. Again following the Blackwell pattern, this dispensary evolved into a hospital – the New Hospital for Women – formally opened by the great Tory philanthropist Lord Shaftesbury on 2 February 1872.

Although Elizabeth was listed as a consultant to the New Hospital for some thirty years, her connection with it was more honorary than professional. Her long experience of dealing with the problems faced by such an institution should have made her an invaluable ally for Elizabeth Garrett, but the latter kept her at arm's length. As the only two qualified women doctors living in England, both of them realised the importance of presenting to the world a united front, but behind this façade there lurked a good deal of professional jealousy.

The New Hospital was just the latest manifestation of Garrett's extraordinary success. After she had obtained her Paris medical degree in 1870 her private practice continued to expand. Physicians of the calibre of Sir James Paget were prepared to consult with her. She became visiting medical officer to the East London Hospital for children and, amid great publicity, in November 1870 was elected to the London School Board. On top of all this she had found deep happiness with her husband, James Skelton Anderson (a wealthy ship owner) who, remarkably for his time, saw no reason why his wife should not continue her career after their marriage in 1871.

Even the *British Medical Journal*, normally implacably opposed to women doctors, was prepared to admit that 'everyone must admire the indomitable perseverance and pluck which Miss Garrett has shown'.[1] By any standards her achievement was impressive; it was, nevertheless, a solitary one that did little to draw other women into its wake. In her efforts to succeed as a doctor yet avoid all unnecessary confrontation with the medical establishment Dr Garrett Anderson was essentially following the Blackwell model. She believed, as did Elizabeth, that steady, quiet success was the most effective way to erode prejudice.

Sophia Jex-Blake, however, was anything but quiet. Clever, ebullient, often endearing, yet also tactless and hot-tempered, she was a very different creature from both Elizabeth Garrett Anderson and Elizabeth Blackwell. The latter recognised her ability but deplored her methods, convinced that her stormy outbursts would, in the end, only undermine the cause to which they were all devoting their lives. One of Jex-Blake's schoolfriends wrote a description of her at the age of fourteen that applies equally well in adulthood: 'Sophy is certainly excessively clever but unfortunately knows it, and makes a point of showing it off upon every possible occasion. She is truthfulness itself and can really be trusted. Very passionate but very penitent afterwards. Affectionate.'[2]

Jex-Blake's enforced departure from New York had in no way dented her determination to study medicine. Wanting, however, to remain closer to her mother after her father's death, she decided not to return there but to seek qualification as a doctor in her own country, with the added bonus that once achieved this would entitle her to a place on the British Medical Register (after Elizabeth had slipped through the net in 1859 with her American MD, holders of foreign degrees were not permitted to register).

Although Edinburgh University had turned down Elizabeth Garrett's application to study medicine in 1862, Sophia Jex-Blake (who at that time had been completing her own education in Edinburgh and become closely involved in her friend's failed quest) had reason to believe that, seven years later, the University might change its policy. In March 1869 she sought permission to attend medical lectures but was rejected on the grounds that the University could not reasonably approve such an upheaval within its medical department in the interests of just one woman.

Undeterred, that autumn Jex-Blake tried again, having by then gathered around her a group of four intelligent women equally eager to study medicine. This time she was successful, and, after all five of them passed their matriculation examinations, they were allowed to enter the University as undergraduates on 2 November 1869 – by coincidence the first anniversary of the opening of the Blackwells' medical college. Elizabeth Blackwell reacted swiftly: 'I do indeed congratulate you undergraduates with all my heart . . . it seems to me the grandest success that women have yet achieved in England; it is the great broad principle established that conducts to every noble progress . . . I feel as if I *must* come up to Edinburgh in the course of the winter to see and bless the class!'[3]

But it was a false dawn. When the women's seriousness of purpose became fully apparent, reinforced by their unexpected academic success (one of their number *won* but was not *awarded* a chemistry scholarship), antagonism towards them hardened. The opposition was led by the formidable Professor (later Sir) Robert Christison, one of the most respected physicians of his generation and a man with whom no one crossed swords lightly. He liked to quote (in Latin) from the 1337 statutes of the Spanish College of the University of Bologna: 'And since Woman is the origin of sin, the weapon of the Devil, the expulsion from Paradise and the corruption of ancient law, and because all conversation with her must be carefully avoided, we forbid and expressly prohibit anyone from introducing any woman, however honourable, into the said College.'[4]

Christison was backed by the *British Medical Journal* which claimed that the whole idea of young men and women studying anatomy together 'is simply intolerable to our British sense of decency, and to our notions of the relations which should pervade the two sexes . . . the attempt of women to undertake the practice of medicine . . . never has prospered: we do not believe that in the nature of things it can ever attain more than a very limited development'.[5]

Enormous difficulties were now thrown in the women's path. Not only did they have to arrange all their courses at great expense (they were not allowed to attend the same classes as the men) but they had also to fight for admission to the Royal Infirmary and permission to sit the requisite examinations. One leading professor even suggested publicly that women seeking to study medicine were 'basely inclined',[6] implying that they intended to become abortionists. In all this, Sophia Jex-Blake was the group's undisputed leader, working tirelessly to overcome each new obstacle as it arose, giving financial support to the less well-off women and at the same time trying to keep up with her own studies.

The women's campaign, widely covered in the press, began to capture public attention. One event in particular excited popular sympathy. On 18 November 1870 the (now seven) women walked to the Surgeons' Hall expecting to sit an anatomy examination. Instead, they found their way blocked by a mob of hostile students who hurled mud and abuse at them. They nevertheless managed to enter the Hall and take their examination in the presence of a sheep which had been pushed into the room by the rioters. While the experience was deeply unpleasant for the women it was also a publicist's dream. The image of a small group of earnest female students assaulted by several hundred hooligans left its mark on public opinion and attracted many new supporters to the women doctors' cause.

Unfortunately, all this new-found goodwill seemed to be at risk when Sophia Jex-Blake, in a crowded public meeting, accused her chief adversary, Robert Christison, of personal involvement in the riot. He sued for libel and won. Although he was only awarded a farthing damages, Jex-Blake was landed with legal costs of nearly £1,000. Letters of support together with more than enough money to cover the debt poured in from all over the country and from all sections of society, not least the working classes.

Despite the public's positive reaction, Drs Blackwell and Garrett Anderson strongly disapproved of the whole affair. And there was worse in store. Having no doubt spent too much time on the campaign and not enough on her studies, in October 1872 Sophia Jex-Blake failed her first-year examinations. This was awkward enough for the women's cause, but two years later, in a letter to *The Times*, she blamed the examiners' bias for her failure. To call into question the integrity of six distinguished medical men was considered rash – even by Jex-Blake's most loyal supporters – and produced precisely the sort of ugly confrontation that Elizabeth Blackwell and Elizabeth Garrett Anderson had in their own careers striven so hard to avoid.

But in any case, by the time Jex-Blake's accusation against her examiners was published on 20 June 1874, the women's long-drawn-out battle with the University had reached its dismal conclusion. In a final attempt to force it to provide them with full tuition, access to the Infirmary and admission to examinations, the seven women took legal action, in 1872, against the University Senate – *Septem contra Edinam*. Elizabeth wrote to Jex-Blake strongly disapproving of this dramatic move and received an emollient response: 'I need not say how doubly glad I shall be to give every explanation and information to you to whom all of us medical women owe so much gratitude and respect as our pioneer and forerunner'.[7]

Jex-Blake did indeed give 'every explanation' to a large meeting in London on 25 April 1872 chaired by Lord Shaftesbury at which both Elizabeth Blackwell and Elizabeth Garrett Anderson were present, seated among the dignitaries on the platform.[8] Although radiating disapproval of Jex-Blake, Elizabeth could at least share her pleasure at seeing male medical students in the hall – not on this occasion there to deliver insults but to act as stewards.

Three months after Jex-Blake's lecture, the Lord Ordinary of Scotland handed down his judgment. He had concluded that 'it is impossible to hold that ladies are students with no rights whatever whereas males are students with legal and enforceable rights. To admit them as students and yet deny their right to be taught would be absurd . . . And lastly it follows that the pursuers are entitled equally, as a matter of right, to demand full and complete medical degrees.'[9]. This judgment fulfilled all the women's hopes but eight months later it was overturned in the Appeal Court and the long battle was finally lost. In 1869 Edinburgh University had made history as the first British university to admit women undergraduates, now, three and a half years later, it had once again shut them firmly out.

The cautious approach to reform favoured by Elizabeth Blackwell and Elizabeth Garrett Anderson was shared by most of the early British feminists. However much they wanted progress for their sex, many of them did not even themselves believe that female professional performance could ever fully match the male equivalent. Indeed Elizabeth Blackwell, for all her determination to see women succeed in medicine, thought that 'they will never stand on the same level.'[10] Jex-Blake's audacious campaign therefore infuriated a good many of the early suffragists and none more so than Dr Garrett Anderson, who bluntly told her that her 'want of judgment and want of temper'[11] had done great harm. Garrett Anderson went further by writing to *The Times* on 5 August 1873: 'Nothing succeeds like success; and if we could point to a considerable number of medical women quietly making for themselves the reputation of being trustworthy and valuable members of the profession, the various forms which present opposition now takes would insensibly disappear, and arrangements would be made for providing female medical students with the advantages which it appears hopeless to look for at present in this country.'[12]

In the same letter, she recommended that any woman wanting to study medicine should go abroad and acquire a foreign degree, ignoring the fact that not everyone had her linguistic abilities or a rich father to support her. Neither did a foreign degree qualify its holder for registration in Britain. Jex-Blake produced a robust response, published in *The Times* on 23 August 1873:

> . . . it is infinitely better that Englishwomen should study medicine under the direction of their own countrymen, in their own language, and amid the social and hygienic conditions which will occur in their own future practice, rather than in a foreign land, from lecturers who teach in a strange language and in hospitals where all the arrangements and theories vary from those of this country . . . We live under English law, and to English law we must conform, so far as lies in our power . . . I can imagine few things that would please our

opponents better than to see one Englishwoman after another driven out of
her own country to obtain medical education abroad, both because they know
that, on her return after years of labour, she can claim no legal recognition
whatever, and because they are equally certain that, so long as no means of
education are provided at home, only a very small number of women will ever
seek admission to the profession . . . Let me, therefore, conclude . . . by
protesting as strongly as lies in my power against this idea of sending abroad
every Englishwoman who wishes to study medicine; let me entreat all such
women to . . . 'fight it out on this line,' and neither to be driven out of our
own country for education not to be induced to cease to make every effort in
our power to obtain from the Legislature that measure of justice which we
imperatively need . . .[13]

As it turned out, Jex-Blake's bold strategy proved the more successful.
Two events took place in the mid-1870s that eased women's access to the
all-important Medical Register. In June 1875, the General Medical Council
(responsible for the Register) was requested by the Privy Council to report
on the whole question of whether women should be allowed to enter the
Profession. There followed three days of intense debate before it could
finally bring itself to draft a recommendation. All the familiar arguments
were raised, including the claim that women were simply not intelligent
enough to study medicine because they had smaller brains. One draft
conclusion reflected such views: 'The Medical Council are of opinion that
the study and practice of Medicine and Surgery, instead of affording a field
of exertion well fitted for Women, do, on the contrary, present special
difficulties which cannot be safely disregarded.'

But by the last day of their discussions pragmatism had prevailed. The
Council concluded that (however distasteful to some of its members) the
women's medical movement was a fact of life and in its final report added
this crucial statement: '. . . but the Council are not prepared to say that
women ought to be excluded from the profession'.[14]

Mealy-mouthed though this statement might be, it nevertheless
represented a great victory for the women. A year later came further
triumph. When the Appeal Court had upheld Edinburgh University's
objection to admitting women, it had done so on the grounds that the
University was not legally empowered to teach or examine them. Late in
1874 Elizabeth Blackwell started a lobby group to promote legislation to
deal with this problem:

I have tried to enlist some help in forming a society which shall work to introduce a short act into Parliament decreeing that nothing in any charter of University or Examining Board, shall prevent the examination of women simply on the ground of sex. I believe that agitation for such emancipation of woman's intellect and encouragement of her serious efforts and aspirations would be a good thing and would lead to valuable results but I fear that I shall not find efficient co-workers for the people who sympathise in these views are often already overworked; but I shall not attempt any new measure of which I must bear the chief responsibility as I find that I cannot bear such responsibility as I did twenty years ago.[15]

Fortunately, one very 'efficient co-worker' proved to be her old friend Russell Gurney MP, a distinguished lawyer and a Quaker. He had acted as a trustee of her hypothetical hospital in 1859 while his wife had been one of its most active fundraisers. On 11 August 1876 the Russell Gurney Enabling Bill became law, making it possible for all the medical examining bodies to admit women as candidates but with the proviso that they could not be compelled to do so. By seeing this Act through Parliament, Russell Gurney had removed one of the most formidable barriers facing potential women doctors.

Fully aware that its 1875 report represented the thin end of the wedge, the General Medical Council put forward various proposals designed to limit the damage. One concerned the training of this alarming new tribe of Amazons poised to wreak such havoc on the medical establishment: 'That in the interest of public order, the Education and Examinations of Female Students of Medicine should be conducted entirely apart from those of Male Students.'[16]

In view of this uncompromising statement, it was as well that the London School of Medicine for Women – the brainchild of Sophia Jex-Blake – had opened its doors to fourteen students eight months earlier, on 11 October 1874. Following her defeat in Edinburgh, Jex-Blake had diverted her energies into setting up the school in Henrietta Street (off Brunswick Square), despite initial opposition from Garrett Anderson, who feared that its graduates would always be considered inferior. Elizabeth, equally sensitive to this danger, was nevertheless pleased to accept a place on the School Council:

[The school] is really organised by Miss Jex-Blake's energy and the fact that Dr Anstie [the Dean] has been able to induce her not to let her name in any way appear, is a good omen for she is such odium with the profession that her name would have damaged the chances of the school and this voluntary suppression of herself, makes me hope that we may retain her energy and avoid her tactlessness. She has asked me if I would be Professor of Hygiene should the chair be formed. But as she opposed Mrs Anderson's proposition to lecture on Diseases of Women on the ground that for the present, men had better occupy the chairs, I think it would not do to offer me a chair, even if my head were clear enough to accept it . . . [17]

By 1874 the intense mutual dislike between Dr Garrett Anderson and Sophia Jex-Blake was clear to all. Their correspondence bristled with hostility:

Dear Mrs Anderson,

If I kept a record of all the people who bring me cock and bull stories about you, and assure me that you are 'greatly injuring the cause,' I might fill as many pages with quotations as you have patience to read, but, beyond defending you on a good many occasions, I have never thought it needful to take much notice of such incidents, still less to retail them to you.

Nor do I much care to know whether or no certain anonymous individuals have confided to you that they lay at my door what you call 'the failure at Edinburgh' . . . It can, I say, serve no purpose whatever to go into this sort of gossip . . . but . . . I am more than willing to say that if, in the opinion of a majority of those who are organizing this new school, my name appears likely to injure its chances of success, I will cheerfully stand aside . . .

In conclusion let me say that I never said it 'did not signify' whether you joined the Council . . . I think it of very great importance, both for your credit and ours, that there should, as you say, be no appearance of split in the camp, and I should greatly prefer that your name should appear on the Council with Dr Blackwell's and those of the medical men who are helping us.

> Believe me, Yours Truly,
> Sophia Jex-Blake[18]

Despite this mutual distrust, Garrett Anderson accepted Jex-Blake's less than gracious invitation to join the Council and, having done so, worked energetically for the School until the end of her life. Elizabeth, although sharing many of her younger colleague's misgivings about both Jex-Blake and her medical school, was delighted to be once more actively involved in such an enterprise: 'I feel much interest in this school as a true though small beginning and shall do all I can to help it on. It will perhaps furnish me the opportunity (without personal responsibility) which I have looked about for ever since I have been in London to help on the medical work but which Miss Anderson has hitherto refused positively to assist in.'[19]

A few days before the school opened Elizabeth, now clearly in her element, gave Barbara Bodichon an update:

> I am very busy about the Medical College in the delicate work of reorganizing the affair and securing proper safeguards against the headlong energies of its most active member [Jex-Blake]. I have gained two important points already and if I can secure two others one of which is the proper management of the finance I shall feel secure in remaining, and recommending the College. Hitherto I have been obliged to suspend my opinion. We shall always have a certain amount of trouble with Miss J.B. but things look rather promising for getting sufficient controlling force to keep her cleverness and energy in their proper place. I have been obliged to work single handed in this matter of cautioning our Council and securing certain measures, for Mrs Anderson has too much on hand and is morally weaker than I thought. But all are working harmoniously.[20]

But Elizabeth knew perfectly well, as did everyone else involved with the new school, that despite the distinguished group of medical men who had agreed to teach in it (many of whom as a result suffered severe censure from their own institutions) its future hung in the balance until two vital conditions could be met. The first was recognition of the School by at least one of the many boards eligible to do so and a willingness to examine its students; the second was affiliation with a hospital (with a minimum of a 150 beds) at which its students could receive their clinical training. Until these two vital pieces were in place the young women's hopes of becoming registered doctors rested on nothing more than a wish and a prayer.

After various disappointments, the first of these difficulties was finally resolved in 1876, when the King's and Queen's College of Physicians in Dublin agreed to accept students from the London School of Medicine for Women for examination providing they met with all the normal requirements. One of these was, of course, adequate clinical training, thus making the search for a hospital willing to link itself to the School pressingly urgent.

In the women's campaign to enter British medicine, three Parliamentarians stand out as knights in shining armour. Russell Gurney was one and W.F. Cowper Temple, who attempted to pass a bill entitling women with foreign medical degrees to be registered, was another. The third was Sir James Stansfeld. Like so many reformers, Stansfeld was a Nonconformist, but he was also the only boy among seven sisters – a fact that may have contributed to his consistent championing of female causes. In 1877, deploying admirable diplomacy, he brokered a deal with the Royal Free Hospital, thus ensuring the long-term survival of the London School of Medicine for Women. As Sophia Jex-Blake's biographer, Dr Margaret Todd, so delightfully put it, 'Mr. Stansfeld, Mr. Cowper Temple, and Mr. Russell Gurney were all the kind of friends with whom one would go tiger-hunting'.[21]

The year 1877 was momentous for Jex-Blake. Having earned a medical degree in Berne in January, she went on to gain a licence from the King's and Queen's College of Physicians and a coveted place on the Medical Register. But an even greater satisfaction was the fact that by March 1877 the three essential requirements for aspiring women doctors had been achieved: a medical school, affiliation with a hospital and access to examinations and registration.

Shortly after these triumphs, however, Jex-Blake was faced with a bitter personal disappointment. As Elizabeth so readily acknowledged, the London School of Medicine for Women was largely the result of her energy and resolve, but now that it was successfully launched many on its Council believed that it should be run by a less controversial figure and removed her from office. Thus deprived of the School's key executive position, Jex-Blake returned early in 1878 to Edinburgh, where she established a successful practice. But the hardest blow was yet to fall. In 1883 her arch-enemy, Elizabeth Garrett Anderson, was elected Dean of the School. Although Jex-Blake remained a Trustee and Governor she ceased to take an active part in its running. Four years later she founded a new one – the Edinburgh Medical School for Women.

In 1875, shortly after the London School opened, Elizabeth Blackwell was appointed Professor of Diseases of Women 'chiefly because we did not wish that specially to fall into the hands of men and it seemed it rested with me to rescue it.'[22] Finding the post too much of a tie, however, she resigned in December 1877. She did remain on the governing body of the School until 1899, although bouts of bad health and European travel, plus an increasing antagonism towards Dr Garrett Anderson, caused her active involvement with it to fluctuate over the years.

There was one issue, however, that always brought her full attention back to medical school matters. Of the bewildering number of ethical questions with which she became involved on her return to England, opposition to the use of animals in research or teaching was among those closest to her heart. At the merest hint of vivisection or vivisectors being introduced into the School her interest and fighting spirit were instantly aroused.

Elizabeth's return to London neatly coincided with the launch of Englishwomen's crusade to enter medicine. Although perhaps disappointed that she did not play a more central role in its ultimate success, she could at least take credit for laying down important groundwork in 1859 when she had so energetically put the case for women doctors to a still sceptical British public. Since her own graduation the movement had grown beyond all recognition on both sides of the Atlantic but her status as its original pioneer was unchallenged and commanded profound respect – if not always love – from all concerned with it.

Proud though she was of her personal achievement, Elizabeth recognised that the real reason for the success of the women's medical movement, both in America and Britain was, as Sir James Stansfeld put it, '. . . that the time was at hand'. He went on: 'It is one of the lessons of the history of progress that when the time for a reform has come you cannot resist it, though, what you may do is to widen its character or precipitate its advent. Opponents, when the time has come, are not merely dragged at the chariot wheels of progress – they help to turn them.'[23]

EIGHTEEN

'Social Evil'

As far as her own medical practice was concerned, Elizabeth's return to England marked a major turning point. Although she continued to see private patients for a few years and briefly taught at the London School of Medicine for Women, the remainder of her professional life was devoted primarily to her first love – social reform. Christian socialism remained at the heart of her philosophy for, unlike many of her contemporaries whose faith had been profoundly shaken by the evolutionary theories emerging in the mid-century, she never found reason to reject either Christianity or the notion of a perfect society.

Of all the many issues with which she became involved over the next three decades, social purity or, to put it more bluntly, sex, was the one that absorbed Elizabeth most. It was, to say the least, an unusual preoccupation for a single Victorian woman but she believed that, as a female physician and a Christian, it was her special calling to speak out on a subject so fundamental to the human condition – specially since nowhere, in her view, was divine law more flagrantly flouted than in matters of sexual relations.

Among the countless social problems that existed at the time of William Gladstone's first administration, the relentless spread of syphilis was one of the most horrible, not least because of the deadly way it reached beyond the grave to affect its victims' children and grandchildren. It devastated the human body, producing rashes and lesions, attacking the heart and nervous system and, in the worst cases, resulting in paralysis, insanity and death. Of particular concern to the British government was the rise of the disease within the armed forces – syphilis having been cited by the Royal Commission, set up in 1857 to investigate the army's health, as one of the chief causes for its poor performance in the Crimean War.

There was a widespread belief that while sex was essential for men, respectable women merely endured it in order to procreate or please their husbands. The only way to compensate for this unequal state of affairs was for society to accept that men (particularly single soldiers and sailors) must satisfy their needs with prostitutes. It followed, therefore, that the most effective way to stem syphilis was to attempt to control not male lust but the prostitutes who serviced it. A further twist to the argument held that men must have access to clean prostitutes in order to safeguard both the virtue and health of decent women. As a result, the Contagious Diseases Acts were passed in 1864, 1866 and 1869 and remained on the statute books until they were finally repealed in 1886. Devised as a pragmatic measure to protect the health of the armed forces, they arguably became the most burning women's rights issue of the century.

The Acts were modelled on a system of state-regulated prostitution that already operated throughout much of Europe. They were first applied to the areas around eleven ports and garrison towns where any woman suspected of prostitution could be arrested and, if she refused to submit voluntarily to an internal examination (with all the pain and degradation that involved), be taken to court and imprisoned indefinitely. If, on the other hand, a prostitute agreed to the examination and was found to be infected, she was forcibly detained and treated in a custom-built 'lock' hospital for a maximum of three months.

The first Act of 1864 was strengthened with subsequent amendments so that by 1869 the number of towns included within its jurisdiction had risen to eighteen, the maximum stay in hospital for an infected woman had been extended to nine months and all registered prostitutes were forced to undergo regular examinations by special police. Added clauses did, at least, provide for moral and religious instruction to the women while in hospital and an end to examinations once they had left the district, but the proposal that any *man* knowingly infecting a woman should be sanctioned, was defeated in Parliamentary committee.[1]

This double standard was enshrined in a report produced by the Royal Commission (appointed by Gladstone's government in 1870) to look into the whole question of the Acts, which stated that there was 'no comparison to be made between prostitutes and the men who consort with them. With the one sex the offence is committed as a matter of gain; with the other it is the indulgence of a natural impulse'.[2] This entirely ignored the fact that it was lack of alternative work that so often forced women into prostitution – simply in order to eat.

Elizabeth arrived in England on 29 July 1869, a few days before the third Act received royal assent on 11 August. The Contagious Diseases Acts ran counter to everything that she stood for. Not only were they designed to control rather than suppress prostitution but they also gave legitimacy to the notion that men and women lived in separate moral worlds. However, just as gaining entry into medical school (over twenty years earlier) had presented a concrete challenge that had ultimately proved easier to overcome than indiscriminate prejudice, so too, the Acts now offered a tangible target and one that she, along with a great many others, resolved to attack and destroy.

Ever since she had first encountered prostitutes in the Blockley Almshouse in Philadelphia and a few years later in 1850 been appalled by the sheer number of pathetic creatures haunting the streets of London, Elizabeth had envisioned

> . . . a grand moral reform society, a wide movement of women in this matter; the remedy to be sought in every sphere of life – radical action – not foolish application of plasters, that has hitherto been the work of the so-called 'moral reform societies' . . . Education to change both the male and female perverted character; industrial occupation, including the formation of a priesthood for women; colonial operations, clubs, homes, social unions, a true Press, and many other things have been among my visions and the whole so combined that it could be brought to bear on any outrage or prominent evil. I should seek to interest the Queen, and place her, as the highest representative of womanhood, at the head of this grand moral army.[3]

The campaign to repeal the Contagious Diseases Acts provided Elizabeth with a perfect platform from which to promote such schemes and within a few weeks of arriving in England she was fully immersed in it.

Her introduction to the debate took place in Bristol in October 1869 where, together with Herman Bicknell (with whom she been holidaying in the Lake District), she attended the Social Science Congress.[4] Mary Carpenter (a pioneer in juvenile reform and sister of Dr William Carpenter) persuaded her to take part in the session in which extension of the Acts to the civilian population was to be debated. Because of the subject matter the discussion was closed to women, but in the eyes of the organisers Elizabeth's MD made her an honorary man and she was allowed to attend.

Passions were so strongly aroused during the debate that the chairman several times threatened to leave if the gentlemen (many of them clerical) did not behave in a more orderly manner.[5] As the only woman present in the packed hall, Elizabeth felt honour bound to resist extension. But to speak out publicly on such a subject before so many men was, even for her, a daunting prospect. As she admitted in her autobiography, she was therefore greatly relieved when Professor Francis Newman – brother of the Cardinal – stood up to lead the opposition.[6]

The Lancet (in common with most of the medical establishment) strongly supported the Contagious Diseases Acts and published a scornful account of the repealers who spoke at the meeting:

> It would be difficult to name any subject that more requires to be considered in a thoughtful and calm spirit than that as to the expediency of applying some legislative measure with the object of limiting the spread of certain forms of contagious diseases; and yet some clerical gentlemen at Bristol the other day seem to have entered on it with more than the usual degree of passion and prejudice which too often characterise the cloth . . . that the object contemplated by legislation is abstractedly considered, a good and laudable one, we do not doubt. That, rightly regarded, and properly carried out, the sanitary supervision of fallen women is capable of being made to them a merciful measure, and a work of compassionate charity, quite in accord with the true spirit of Christianity, we have also no doubt.[7]

The ever-inventive Herman Bicknell (a Catholic) tried to lighten the intense atmosphere of the Congress by inviting Elizabeth to co-host an ecumenical breakfast. Among those present were several Hindus, a Communist and George J. Holyoake, who in 1842 had become the last man in England to be imprisoned for atheism. Elizabeth was struck by Holyoake's observation: 'What an extraordinary, odd notion that of a soul is! I wonder how it could have arisen.'[8] Charles Kingsley was chairing the Educational Committee at the Bristol meeting. Pointing to Holyoake, he remarked to Elizabeth, 'That man, many years ago I put into prison for blasphemy; now I am begging him to come down and visit me at Eversley!'[9]

Kingsley (whose *Water Babies* had been published five years earlier in 1862) delighted Elizabeth by at once telling her that she was 'one of his heroes'.[10] This was not mere flattery for, as he wrote in a letter to John Stuart Mill explaining his withdrawal from the women's rights movement, the only one of their issues to which he could give his full support and sympathy was their quest for medical education.[11] His views on women's role in social reform – and on many other matters – so perfectly dovetailed with Elizabeth's own that a close friendship between the two of them was inevitable: 'Of woman's right to be a medical practitioner, I hold that it is perhaps the most important social question hanging over us. I believe that if once women can be allowed to practise as freely as men, the whole question as to the relation of the sexes, according to natural laws, and therefore according to what I believe to be the will and mind of God, the author of nature, will be made clear . . .'[12]

Elizabeth and Kitty often visited Kingsley and his wife at his Eversley Rectory and, later, at the Chester Deanery. She lunched with them in the cloisters of Westminster Abbey a short while before he died (on 23 January 1875) – an event which prompted Kitty to write, 'Aunt Bessie has lost one of her best friends in England, England has lost one of the most liberal of her clergymen and women one of their truest friends.'[13]

But for all Kingsley's eagerness to see women active in medicine, he was convinced that until they had acquired proper scientific training they 'should not meddle with these sexual questions'.[14] No doubt he had in mind the remarkable campaigner Josephine Butler when he wrote this – a woman who devoted her life to meddling in 'sexual questions' and to great effect. From 1869, she led the long fight to repeal the Contagious Diseases Acts and in the process focused public attention on hitherto largely ignored problems associated with prostitution, such as the lack of work for destitute women, widespread paedophilia and the double standard of morality applied to the two sexes.

Shortly after the Bristol meeting, the National Association for the Repeal of the Contagious Diseases Acts was organised though, through a misunderstanding, women were initially excluded from its membership. Consequently the Ladies National Association was formed and Josephine Butler invited to lead it. It is hardly surprising that it took her three months to decide whether or not to accept the task for she knew that to do so would not only attract opprobrium on herself but also on her whole family. For most people, it was utterly unthinkable that a woman of her social standing (she was a cousin of Earl Grey, Prime Minister 1830–4) could even contemplate involving herself in such sordid issues, let alone speak about them in public.

But Josephine Butler was not without experience of the seamier side of Victorian life, having several years earlier opened a refuge for prostitutes in Liverpool where her ordained husband (and steadfast supporter) was headmaster of Liverpool College. Mrs Butler, a deeply religious woman, was also looking for distraction from the tragedy of her small daughter's death five years earlier (after falling from the stairs in their house) and by the end of 1869 had made up her mind that, whatever the personal cost, she would devote herself to defending the humanity of 'fallen' women. She also understood that a much wider principle was at stake – one that applied to women of all social classes, for as she pointed out: 'By this law, a crime has been *created* in order that it may be severely punished, but observe, that has been ruled to be a crime in women, which is not to be a crime in men.'[15]

For all her devotion to the cause, Josephine Butler never regarded *men* as the enemy and in this respect her brand of feminism was similar to Elizabeth's own: 'I wish it were felt that women who are labouring especially for women are not one-sided or selfish. We are human first; women secondarily. We care about the evils affecting women most of all because they react upon the whole of society, and abstract from the common good. Women are not men's rivals, but their helpers. There can be no antagonism that is not injurious to both.'[16]

Having aligned herself wholeheartedly with the repeal movement, Elizabeth went into action. Soon after the Bristol meeting she wrote to Florence Nightingale requesting some statistical information. She received the usual brisk reply although the 'My Dear Friend' had now been replaced with the more formal 'Dear Miss Blackwell':

> What is wanted is not the opinion of physicians, however eminent. It is not a professional or medical question at all. It is a question:
> (1) of what is *fact*,
> (2) of what is expedient and practicable. What is wanted is a *clear connected statistical detail* showing:
> What is the amount of syphilis among a population 'unprotected' then, what is the amount under 'protection' and lastly what results when 'protection' is withdrawn.[17]

Nightingale deplored what she saw as the 'amateur' efforts of the repealers: 'I feel a sort of despair at the working of the Association in which hardly anything but *opinion* is invoked. The other side is no better.'[18] But there was no doubting her own position on the matter: 'I wish *so* well to every opponent of the CD Acts that I regret that they do not take it up (e.g. as I did Army Sanitary Reform – i.e.) not as subsidiary or magazine or newspaper work but as the most serious work of life to strain every nerve for, as a General does in a campaign, with professional ability and devotion

– without which they will do little good and I regret that I am entirely unable, overdone as I am with business, for this most urgent war and most dreadful crisis ever known in the history of civilized mankind.[19]

In another letter to Elizabeth written a few months later, she went to the very heart of the matter: 'Be a woman ever so vicious, she has inalienable personal rights, which none but such idiots as social legislators would venture to interfere with.'[20]

On Barbara Bodichon's advice, Elizabeth canvassed Marian Lewes's support for the campaign but without success: 'Barbara must have been under some misunderstanding, I think, as to my having been much occupied lately with thoughts on this 'permanent subject for sorrow.' Referring to the Franco-Prussian War (1870–1) she went on: 'Like so many of my neighbours, I have had my sympathy drawn forcibly away to another kind of misdoing and suffering which has burst out upon Europe in a more sudden, torturing way.'[21]

While Marian Lewes's reaction was disappointing, Elizabeth Garrett Anderson's refusal to join the repealers was a much more serious blow. In a long letter to the *Pall Mall Gazette* (25 January 1870) she strongly supported the state regulation of prostitutes – a position that emphatically did not win her friends in the burgeoning women's movement. They had expected her, as England's first woman doctor, to be a powerful advocate against the Contagious Diseases Acts. But in her own dispensary she had seen the ravages of venereal disease as most of them had not and accepted the reality that prostitutes, once infected, had few options: 'Hospitals as a rule do not admit them; dispensaries cannot cure them; even soup-kitchens for the sick will not help to feed them; missions and refuges scarcely reach them; they are without health, without character, without habits of industry and self control, without friends, without money.'[22] She was convinced, along with the vast majority of her medical colleagues (including Sophia Jex-Blake) that the Acts were the prostitute's best hope of retrieval and the only way to prevent the infection of innocent people.

Elizabeth believed equally strongly that by introducing legislation to deal with the *effects* of prostitution, the government had entirely missed the point: 'We may as well expect to cure typhoid fever whilst allowing sewer gas to permeate the house, or cholera whilst bad drinking-water is being taken, as try to cure venereal disease whilst its chief cause remains unchecked.'[23] And the chief cause was in her view – fornication. But her refusal to accept bacteriology as an alternative to 'divine law' led her to conclusions that were either simply wrong: 'Promiscuous intercourse inevitably tends to give rise to varying forms of venereal disease no matter what precaution may be taken',[24] or deeply offensive (to the modern mind at least): 'The special danger of specific disease also arising from the congress of different races, is a well-known fact'.[25]

Elizabeth wanted the government to suppress prostitution by law: 'Vice in both sexes increases far more rapidly, and assumes an intensity of corruption unknown to us, whenever the state accepts, registers, and guards prostitutes, instead of repressing promiscuous intercourse . . . Meanwhile, corruption increases to such an appalling extent, that belief in the possibility of purity in men no longer exists in the minds of men or women . . . Male lust must be restrained, in order to check female obscenity.'[26]

But she was realistic enough to recognise that legislation would never succeed unless supported by public opinion. She therefore saw it as her clear duty, like some latter-day prophet, to make society understand the terrible threat posed to it by prostitution. Through the Moral Reform Union (which she founded with Mrs S. Woolcott Browne in 1881), the Social Purity Alliance, the National Vigilance Society and numerous publications, she set forth her uncompromising views. 'Social evil' was a travesty of divine law and as such, if left unchecked would result in nothing less than the annihilation of Christian civilisation: 'From these purchased women, this human merchandise, come the frenzied menads [*sic*] of bloody revolution, human tigers who delight in destruction and torture. They are growing up among us here, as elsewhere, moral dynamite ready for explosion.'[27] Intellectually Elizabeth had left Nonconformism behind with her youth but she never lost her instinct for its rhetoric when she wanted to reach out to her public with the most powerful means at her disposal.

Even that indispensable piece of Victorian equipment – the magic lantern – was mobilised in the great moral crusade. One of Elizabeth's colleagues in the Social Purity Alliance, the Reverend Robert Bullen, offered to deliver his slide show on Pompeii wherever he was wanted (subject to his clerical duties) because 'he was able boldly to introduce the subject of Social Purity, while amusing and instructing his audience, for Pompeii has left in her ruined temples of Isis and Venus, and in the moral meaning of the domestic architecture of the Romans, a text writ large, from which to advance their subject'.[28]

Elizabeth did not confine her campaign to Britain. She contributed regularly to *The Philanthropist*, a New York-based journal that dealt with issues of moral purity. In a letter to its editor, Aaron Powell, she set out her manifesto for the abolition of prostitution. Men and women must work closely together since 'injustice or narrowness at once arises when men alone, or women alone, attempt to guide what must be a sacred, joint work'.[29] As society's highest priority must be the protection of the young, she recommended that the age of consent be raised to seventeen and that anyone sexually abusing a minor should be prosecuted.

She also came up with a startling new concept – that 'a certain number of superior women [be introduced] into the police organisation, to act, amongst other duties, as heads of stations where women offenders are brought'.[30] The idea that female officers would not only improve the plight of women offenders but also raise the tone of the police force, showed Elizabeth at her most imaginative.

Although she generally preferred to concentrate on the moral rather than the economic aspects of prostitution, Elizabeth did advocate that brothels should only be closed when alternative work had been found for their inmates. Key to her strategy for defeating prostitution was the belief that all citizens – not just the police – must be involved in the campaign and that only those individuals with an impeccable moral pedigree should be eligible for election to public office.

The Liberal Member of Parliament Sir Charles Dilke (once tipped to succeed Gladstone) was, in her opinion, emphatically not one of them. In 1886 he was at the centre of a notorious divorce case in which he was accused of going to bed with two women – one of whom was married – simultaneously. His immaculate record in social reform could do nothing in Elizabeth's eyes to redeem his alleged sexual crimes. At the 1886 annual general meeting of the Moral Reform Union (founded as an organ to fight the Contagious Diseases Acts and to provide information on matters of sexual morality) she put her name to a resolution condemning Dilke: 'That in the opinion of this meeting, it is a grave public scandal that any man should be permitted to occupy an honourable and responsible public position who, upon any grounds whatever, allows himself to be accused in a public court of justice, in the course of proceedings to which he is himself a party, of gross and disgusting criminal immorality, and does not at once seize the opportunity afforded him of meeting the accusation with his solemn denial, and of offering himself for cross examination.'[31]

If, in Elizabeth's view, Dilke epitomised the moral degradation of public office, his fellow Liberal Sir James Stansfeld MP (hero of the London School of Medicine for Women) was a shining example of moral probity. Josephine

Butler possessed great gifts of leadership but she could not have won her long crusade without the support of a number of extraordinary men, most notable among them James Stansfeld. He gave up a cabinet post in Gladstone's government to dedicate himself to the repeal cause – a cause which Gladstone himself (despite his enthusiasm for saving prostitutes) never fully embraced. It was fitting, therefore, that it was Stansfeld who finally won victory for the repealers with his resolution to abolish the Contagious Diseases Acts – carried in Parliament on 16 March 1886.

But for Elizabeth this triumph was by no means the end of the matter. She believed that any relaxation on the part of the national repeal societies as a result of their parliamentary success was premature. As she pointed out in an address to a group of medical women in 1897, 'in a House of six hundred and seventy members, only two hundred and forty-five voted on the side of a great moral question [while] two hundred and eighty-nine absented themselves . . . the mighty forces of evil, of selfishness, of ignorance, of timidity, of hypocrisy, and of lust were sure to rally' – and, when they did, the very fabric of Christian civilisation would be threatened.[32]

Elizabeth deeply admired Stansfeld although they did not always agree. Writing to Lucy Stone Blackwell she expressed the wish that her fellow repealers should recognise the importance of hygienic measures in fighting venereal disease: 'I do not believe that these acts will ever be repealed with no attempt made to check a loathsome disease, which does exist, and which the growth of Sanitary Science requires should be checked. I want our repealers to recognise this fact, and whilst repealing these immoral and unjust laws to insist upon a law applicable to all making the communication of syphilis an offence to be judged in camera . . .'[33]

This, however, was a step too far for Stansfeld: 'I cannot personally approve the suggestion that the communication of syphilis should be made a criminal offence viz: 1st because the Law has no business with such filth; 2nd because nothing would come of it, save possibly the unjust persecution of some women.'[34]

The year before the Acts were revoked, Josephine Butler focused her attention on child prostitution. As the outcome of her own researches on the Continent and an investigation into a Chelsea brothel, the traffic of young children to Europe (the so-called white slave trade) was uncovered in all its horror. But the paedophile clients of this high-class establishment (run by a Mrs Jeffries) were too much part of the establishment to be exposed in court (they allegedly included Queen Victoria's first cousin, King

Leopold II of the Belgians) so that after pleading guilty Mrs Jeffries was given a modest fine and allowed to walk free – the evidence surrounding her case having been successfully kept hidden from public scrutiny. Frustrated by this cover-up, Butler joined forces with W.T. Stead, the founder of modern sensationalist journalism and editor of the *Pall Mall Gazette*, with the intention of exposing the trade in girls – some of them purportedly as young as three years old.

On 6 July 1885, Stead published the first of four articles entitled 'The Maiden Tribute of Modern Babylon'. Under lurid headlines such as: 'Strapping girls down', 'Delivered for Seduction' or 'I Order Five Virgins' he described the actual purchase of a thirteen-year-old girl for prostitution. Public outrage at Stead's revelations prompted the government to rush through legislation designed to protect young girls (the Criminal Law Amendment Act 1885) that had been languishing on the parliamentary back burner. The new Bill raised the age of consent from thirteen to sixteen, allowed for a child's evidence to be admissible in court without an oath and imposed new penalties on anyone using drugs to commit rape or procure a girl for prostitution.

It was as well that the new law was safely enacted before it emerged that it was Stead himself (with the help of a reformed prostitute), who had 'bought' the child and that the whole story had been fabricated to prove the case. After the girl's father brought charges of abduction, Stead was tried and sentenced to three months' imprisonment. During the trial, Elizabeth attended a protest prayer meeting held on Stead's behalf at which Josephine Butler rallied those present to march to the Home Office to demand fair treatment for him:

The meeting rose, Mrs Butler & Mr Varley with Mrs. Booth, Bramwell Booth etc leading the way, & the audience falling in behind filed into the Strand, then made for the Pall Mall office. The Staff came out amused to find out what the cheering meant. Mrs. Browne and Aunt B. arm in arm were nearly at the end of the procession, behind two girls in Salvation Army bonnets. From Pall Mall the 500 made for the Embankment & straight to the Home Office. People began to stare, & much jeering took place when an occasional Salvation Army member was seen in the line. Aunt B. says at the Home Office a sentry with drawn sword came out of his box & looked bewilderedly on the ladies & gentlemen's orderly mob. Then three more came and gazed, & finally, a policeman came and asked their business. He said only 20 cd go in, so the rest waited in the street & shortly Mr Varley addressed them from the steps, saying Mr Lushington informed them nothing cd be done, & that they (the deputation) had been insulted. But they would go to the Queen . . . At this point, the crowd was ordered by various policemen to 'move on, move on!'[35]

In another gesture of support for Stead, whom she described as 'the bravest man in England',[36] Elizabeth, together with her ally, Mrs Woolcott Browne, visited the Cold Bath prison, where he was held, to leave her visiting card.

Elizabeth's sense of herself as a prophet of social reform is nowhere more apparent than when she railed against the evils of sexual abuse and exploitation. Intelligent, articulate and armed with a lifetime of medical experience, she should have been one of the more effective voices in the late nineteenth-century debate on prostitution. But her insistence on moral perfection plus her lack of sympathy for individual need or suffering, make many of her assertions – at least to the contemporary ear – hollow and unsympathetic.

The sensible and perceptive things she did have to say about prostitution and venereal disease were too often smothered by pseudo-science and religious rhetoric. The idea that an amoral bacterium might be the cause of syphilis and an equally unprincipled antibiotic its cure would have been as repugnant to Elizabeth as the disease itself. It was fortunate for her, therefore, that the villain of the piece (*syphilis spirochaete*) was not identified until 1905 by which time, at the age of eighty-four, she was no longer actively engaged in the debate.

NINETEEN

Social Challenge

On 23 February 1870, Elizabeth wrote to Kitty: 'I am settled in England. I have not the slightest intention of returning to America and D.V. will never cross the ocean again . . . I would sooner live here on an attic floor upon £200 a year, than go back to American life. I am deeply interested in the people and things around me; I have found most important work to do. I am appreciated here and I know that my position does not depend on money (though of course money widens my life) . . . I belong here and here I shall stay.'[1]

Her enthusiasm for life in England, however, was soon tempered by social disappointment. Despite her celebrity as 'the first woman doctor', she found it much harder to establish herself in London than she had expected. The stimulating circle that she had met through Barbara Bodichon melted away when her friend departed for Algiers in the winter, leaving her lonely and insecure. Not that she was unrealistic about the lot of a single woman: 'My letters, of course, will vary in cheerfulness of tone, as an unmarried woman of limited means necessarily does not find life always very bright.'[2] But, as it was partly the promise of a more congenial social life that had drawn her so determinedly back to England, her sense of alienation was a bitter pill to swallow. Deprived of Barbara Bodichon's patronage, she discovered that winning acceptance in London society was every bit as challenging as gaining entrance to medical school had been a quarter of a century earlier:

My most troublesome occupation since I last wrote was going to the reception at the Motleys because I had to make my best black silk as grand as possible, go at 11 o'clock, and not get to bed till 2 o'clock in the morning. But I did it as a duty. It was a brilliant affair. The King of the Belgians was there, and dukes, marquises and lords in plentiful supply, foreign ministers; an eastern prince in turban and jewels any number of orders, diamonds and decorations. Browning the poet and Miss Thackery I was glad to see. The toilettes were brilliant but not artistic to my eye. Mine was the only black, and of course not décolleté but I opened it and had plenty of white lace, slit up the sleeves and had lace ruffles and some white and purple lilac in my hair so I think I passed unobserved from singularity. I said a few words to the Jays and Lady Lyall and talked to the Smalleys and Conways but it was not customary to introduce so I was almost entirely a stranger . . . I shall go to that sort of thing as a duty when the opportunity presents itself but it has not the slightest attraction for me as far as the snobbery goes.[3]

Invitations to the ancient universities were more to her liking. At Corpus Christi College in Oxford she sat on high table next to the Professor of Chemistry, Sir Benjamin Brodie,[4] and noted with pleasure that among her fellow guests were Miss Thackeray, Mrs Gaskell and Thomas Arnold. Cambridge, where she was the guest of Dr William Bateson, Master of St John's College, was equally engaging. Arriving there on a brilliant but piercingly cold day in December 1869, she at once fell in love with the town: 'It was along the river bank that we took our first walk giving a sense of park like beauty as well as architectural magnificence, that I was quite unprepared for. The immense extent of velvet lawn, the grand old elms, hundreds of years old, the graceful little bridges spanning the winding stream, all lit up by brilliant sunshine, made my first glimpse of Cambridge one I shall never forget . . . I watched the first boat with its healthy looking students shoot by and of course a vision of Tom Brown instantly came over me.'[5] Here at last was the England of which she had so long dreamed and of which she so much wanted to feel a part.

Cambridge society proved as agreeable as its architecture although even in the august setting of the Master's Lodge at St John's, Elizabeth was unsettled by her lack of décolleté: 'The ladies were in low necks and trailing satin dresses but I think I looked a great deal better in my well fitting black silk which I opened in front and wore handsome Valenciennes lace.'[6] She particularly enjoyed meeting Professors Sedgwick and Sidgwick. The former, having shown her around the geological museum invited her to dinner at his rooms in Trinity: 'saying that as I had enjoyed his bones, I ought to taste his flesh'.[7] Henry Sidgwick, with his keen interest in women's education (he was the driving force behind Newnham College, opened in 1880) was, despite his agnosticism, a natural ally. In fact, with the launch, three months earlier, of the first female college in Hitchin, women's education was the hot topic of conversation: 'In the afternoon Mrs Bateson and I went to a meeting of ladies at Mrs Fawcett's (the blind minister's wife)[8] to consider the best way of opening Cambridge lectures to women in Cambridge itself . . . I gave them an account of Vassar[9] which seemed to interest them.'[10]

Hitchin College, founded by Emily Davis and Barbara Bodichon, was a big step forward. Its students were taught by Cambridge dons and prepared for the same examinations as the male undergraduates. But, despite Bodichon's misgivings, it had been established 30 miles away in Hitchin – a great mistake in Elizabeth's view. She believed that in a matter so fundamental to their future as education, women should never allow themselves to be fobbed off with second best – intellectually or geographically.

Pursuing this theme, she wrote to Bodichon: 'It is this same shackled spirit that has placed the College at Hitchin when it would have been so grand at Cambridge. It is the perception of this spirit in the present workers that brought me to England, resolved that your father's daughter should not stand alone in her large hearted views of work!'[11] Two years later, a compromise was reached when the College was moved to Girton – a great deal closer to Cambridge than Hitchin but still a safe 2 miles from the heart of the University and its male undergraduates.

While Elizabeth's experiences at Oxford and Cambridge were delightful, they did not reflect the real substance of her life in England. In the wake of Barbara Bodichon's departure to Algiers in May 1870, she wrote to her brother Sam: 'I am settling down now to an independent London life for the first time, for Mme Bodichon left a week ago and I now realize how much I miss her. She leads so full and active a life and shared it so fully with me that her friends and occupations seemed to become mine to a great extent. But her departure breaks up the centre and I am thrown on my own resources. It seems almost like beginning life again for I have not the establishment or the Art interest that hold her circle together so of course I am now to a great extent thrown out of the way of meeting those who were pleasant acquaintance.'[12]

Kitty's presence would have eased her loneliness but she had been left behind in America to help Marian look after the elderly Mrs Blackwell – a decision that Elizabeth clearly regretted. Given her lifelong dedication to broadening women's options, it is ironic to find her tempting Kitty to England, in terms that a Victorian husband might well have used to a stereotype wife '. . . and you can help me so much by taking charge of all my things and telling where they are and reading and occasionally stitching for me and doing errands and keeping my rooms in first rate order and above all loving me very much'.[13]

Elizabeth badly wanted Kitty with her in England but knew that it would be a wrench for the girl (now twenty-two) to leave America and particularly her beloved friend Alice Stone Blackwell, Henry's daughter. Knowing how much Kitty adored children, she wrote to her: 'When I have made my fortune, I shall let you adopt first one and then another tiny urchin, so that you shall have a little family always about you!'[14] It was, therefore, mainly with Kitty's interests in mind that Elizabeth decided to foster a baby boy in the autumn of 1870.

Mystery shrouded the child from the start. In May Elizabeth wrote to Kitty: 'I have agreed to receive a little baby patient, whose parents are obliged to be away. A little Harry, a charming little fellow of eight months old, who will be under my care, probably for some years.'[15] There was good reason for Elizabeth's deliberately vague reference to the boy's parents. He was the illegitimate son of Susan Durant and Baron Henri de Triqueti – both of them distinguished sculptors who had undertaken major commissions for Queen Victoria. Triqueti, married and twenty-three years Durant's senior, was not the only older man in her life. In 1864 she had begun a passionate affair with the historian George Grote (then seventy) to the great distress of his wife, herself a noted suffragist, to whom he had been happily married for forty-two years. Grote's enthusiasm for women's university education (he was vice chancellor of London University from 1862 until his death in 1871) was no doubt given extra impetus by his infatuation with the gifted Miss Durant.

Described in one obituary as a woman who 'embraced with ardour all the great questions of the day, whether connected with the progress of science or the enfranchisement of women . . . [and gave] every possible assistance to the improvement of female education',[16] Susan Durant showed not the slightest desire to sacrifice her profession or independence for marriage. In a letter thanking a friend for a house-warming present, she wrote: 'Tell Mr Wallis I am very proud of my *wedding* present which I consider the dessert service to be and am saucy enough to think I have the best of it, being *minus* the husband!'[17]

Born in 1827, Susan Durant was one of the more unusual women of her generation. She cleverly contrived to lead a Bohemian life yet appear conventional enough to become a great favourite of Queen Victoria. In view of the Queen's uncompromising views on morality and 'this mad, wicked folly of Women's Rights',[18] this was no mean feat.

Durant discovered her talent for sculpting as a young woman while wintering in Rome with her parents. But unlike so many other women of her class with artistic leanings, she was not prepared to settle for amateur dabbling. Announcing her intention to become a professional sculptor, she trained in the Paris studio of the highly successful Baron Henri de Triqueti but rapidly went on to establish herself as a gifted sculptor in her own right, exhibiting regularly at the Royal Academy from 1847.

In 1856 she collaborated with her old teacher on a monument for Queen Victoria's uncle, Leopold, King of the Belgians. While working on this project with the Baron in Paris, she met Harriet Beecher Stowe – an encounter that resulted in a fine bust of the author[19] – then at the height of her fame. By this date, Durant already knew several members of the Blackwell family. She was an intimate friend of Kenyon's wife, Marie Blackwell, dined frequently with Anna and had met Ellen while the latter was herself studying art in London with John Ruskin.

In 1866, the same year that Durant completed a medallion of the Queen, she made a posthumous relief of Howard Blackwell for the grieving Anna. 'I shall try to go and see Miss Blackwell. The medallion of her brother Howard is finished and I hope they will consider the likeness successful.'[20] It is likely that it was around this time that she first met Elizabeth. When, three years later at the age of forty-two, Durant found herself pregnant by de Triqueti, Elizabeth, newly arrived from America, was the obvious person to whom to turn for help in such a delicate situation.

A child born out of wedlock to a woman of Susan Durant's age and social background would, under any circumstances, have been a scandal but her close relationship to the royal family made her predicament doubly sensitive. She had executed medallions of the Queen and Prince Albert, advised the princesses on how to wear their hair and taught sculpture to the rebellious Princess Louise. Indeed, she had become so intimate with the inner royal circle that while working at Osborne she was invited to lunch with the Household – a rare regal gesture of approval for a mere artist. There was clearly no place in this royal tableau for Paul Harvey, as her small son came to be called. Elizabeth's discretion, tact and professional expertise were never more in demand.

By the time Kitty arrived in England in August 1870, Durant had helped Elizabeth find a suitable house near Hyde Park just two minutes walk from her own home, which she shared with her elderly father. It was the perfect solution. As the baby's 'guardian', Durant could come and go as she pleased ('she was in and out of the house half a dozen times a day and seemed just like one of the family'),[21] Kitty found fulfilment as a surrogate mother, and several nursemaids looked after the child's basic needs while Elizabeth took on overall responsibility for the household. With her secret safe, Durant was able to continue her career untroubled and in 1872 completed a bust of Queen Victoria for the Inner Temple. This convenient arrangement might have lasted for many years but for the tragedy of Durant's premature death. In December 1872 she took Paul to Paris to see his father, and died of pneumonia on 1 January 1873. Baron de Triqueti's death followed a year later.

Kitty was overwhelmed with grief. Her own uncertain origins may have contributed to the special bond she formed with this charismatic woman and her lovable little boy: 'Miss Durant is like a sister she is so kind and thoughtful, I'm sure I don't know what I should have done without her, away from the family as I am.'[22] But an even worse blow for Kitty than her friend's death was the permanent removal of Paul from her care. Kenyon Blackwell had died unexpectedly in 1869 and Marie swiftly married the man with whom his family suspected she had long been having an affair. As Madame Drousart, Marie took firm charge of Paul, bringing him up in her Paris home and refusing to let Elizabeth and Kitty have further contact with him. As Elizabeth's arrangement with Durant seems to have been entirely informal, she had no legal claim to continue looking after the boy and no doubt his legal guardians considered him better placed in Paris close to his paternal relations. Elizabeth believed the cause for Marie's irrational behaviour was the fear of losing the generous funds provided for the boy's care.

Twenty years later, on 30 September 1893, Paul resurfaced. Through a chance encounter with an old friend of Susan Durant's, Elizabeth traced him to the War Office where he was working as a civil servant:

Poor dear fellow! He was sent to school at 8½ in England . . . Thence to Rugby, then to Oxford. He has spent his holidays alone. It is really cruel . . . it has been very solitary, and he has so craved affection. He nearly broke down again and again. I felt no more shy of big Paul than of little Paul, and just took possession of him. He belongs to me more than to any creature in the world, and I consider him my best possible birthday gift . . . Monday, before we left the dining-room, I turned him round, and said 'you have not seen this.

This is your nursery high-chair.' He took it out, tried it, said, covering his face with his hands; this is too much, all these years! All these years & no one told me I had such friends![23]

Once reunited, Kitty and Paul never again lost touch. He went on to a distinguished career as a diplomat (he was knighted in 1911) and in retirement compiled and edited the Oxford *Companion to English Literature* (1932) and *Companion to Classical Literature* (1937). Kitty became godmother to his only child, Susan, often taking care of her when her parents were abroad.

Despite their very different personalities, Elizabeth and Susan Durant had much in common. Each maintained her independence through a professional success acquired, not by radical demonstration, but, as Elizabeth would have put it, by quiet, steady example. And while both women were committed to achieving a wider, more satisfying existence for their sex, neither had any desire to see men nor, indeed, their institutions destroyed in the process.

Their partnership worked well on a domestic level and so did their collaboration in the world of public affairs, where each had already left such a marked imprint. In the summer of 1870 the Franco-Prussian War broke out – a war that was to change the face of Europe for ever. Marian Lewes cited her concern over it as the reason why she could not join the anti-Contagious Diseases Acts campaign, for although Britain was not directly engaged in the conflict she, like so many of her fellow countrymen, watched it unfold with horror and sympathy. Despite their natural anti-French bias, the British could not help identifying with the terrible humiliation suffered by France and her appalling human loss.

In respect of the war, Elizabeth and Susan Durant shared divided loyalties. Elizabeth, weaned on anti-Catholicism, felt a natural affinity with the Prussians. But countering this basic instinct were her intimate memories of Paris – the city where she had fallen in love, lost an eye and where her sister, Anna, now lived. Durant experienced a similar emotional dilemma. While working on the royal medallion portraits of the royal family, she had spent many weeks with the Crown Princess of Prussia (Queen Victoria's eldest child, Vicky) at her court in Potsdam and the two had become close friends. On the other hand, the father of her son lived in Paris where she had spent many happy months and had formed lasting friendships. Their response was to combine forces in gathering supplies for the wounded on both sides of the conflict.

Organising relief for the victims of the Franco-Prussian War was just one of various attempts Elizabeth made during the months following her return to London to find a significant role for herself. The urge to lead was an instinct deep within her that showed no sign of waning as she grew older. Although she was active in the women's medical movement and the campaign to abolish the Contagious Diseases Acts, both organisations already had formidable leaders. In order to recapture the excitement of her pioneering days, she needed to find a cause behind which *she* would be the undisputed driving force. But just as she never quite achieved the social status in England that she craved, nor did she succeed in gaining complete control of any of the many enterprises with which she became involved.

She was, however, enormously active. Propelled by her conviction that Christian civilisation was under terminal threat from fornication and prostitution, she joined a plethora of committees, set up societies, lectured, wrote and travelled. Perhaps if she had been prepared to accept a more diverse model of society her public work might have had greater influence. As it was, her refusal to accept human frailty as an integral part of the social equation resulted in too many of her causes fading away or in her own premature exit from their committees. Yet, if some of Elizabeth's most cherished organisations such as the Moral Reform Union, the Social Purity Alliance or the National Vigilance Society seem quaint from the perspective of the twenty-first century, the National Health Society was founded on timeless principles and, in terms of lasting influence, was the most successful of her English projects.

In May 1871, while Kitty played upstairs with little Paul, Elizabeth held a meeting at her house in Burwood Place, close to Marble Arch. Barbara Bodichon was present, as well as Anna Goldsmid, a former supporter of the thwarted 1859 hospital scheme. Ernest Hart was also there. The son of a Jewish dentist, he had been a successful ophthalmologist before turning to medical journalism. Since 1866, he had been editor of the *British Medical Journal* – well known for its dislike of female physicians. Hart, however, made clear his personal support for them by marrying one. He was also a highly respected authority on matters of public health.

The purpose of the meeting was to form 'A National Health Society, whose object shall be the promotion of health amongst all classes of the population'. The following December, Elizabeth reported to Mary Putnam Jacobi with evident satisfaction: 'My little Health Society meets at my house every Thursday afternoon. It is at present only an opportunity for which I try to gather materials for future work, using my influence to create an interest in Sanitary topics, and instruct those who come. I am not sure yet in which direction it will chiefly grow.'[24]

Despite a slow start, the Society fulfilled Elizabeth's most ambitious hopes. It successfully lived up to its motto 'Prevention is better than cure' by disseminating health, hygiene and common sense around the country well into the twentieth century. Perhaps Susan Durant had a hand in securing the Society's patron – Princess Louise. Durant had sculpted a medallion of Queen Victoria's unruly daughter in 1865, brilliantly conveying the young woman's restless, questioning spirit. Princess Louise had once turned up unannounced in Elizabeth Garrett's consulting rooms, much to the annoyance of Queen Victoria, who despised the whole concept of women doctors. The Princess's patronage was therefore a welcome bonus to the fledgling society. In fact, it had little trouble in attracting prominent reformers and intellects. Among its early subscribers were Elizabeth's hosts in Cambridge, Dr and Mrs Bateson, the sanitary engineer Edwin Chadwick, William Farr the statistician who had worked so closely with Florence Nightingale and, inevitably, the Comtesse de Noailles – still dangling large sums of money before worthy causes only to withdraw them on some obscure whim.

By 1879, the National Health Society could report that in the previous year: 'Sixty-three lectures to audiences of different classes have been delivered, chiefly to Mothers' Meetings and Working Men's Clubs . . . and there is strong evidence that the desire for this sort of instruction is increasing amongst the class of persons whom it is most desirable to interest. Miss Barnett's lectures on cooking have all been illustrated by practical demonstrations, the dishes prepared before the audiences being tasted by them after the lecture.'

Nor did the Society confine its interests to the lecture room: 'In the summer the Committee again applied to the School Board to allow three play-grounds in the east of London to be opened on the Saturday holiday, the Society undertaking to pay 5s. a week for caretakers for each playground. The Board, however, refused to allow the playground in Great Castle Street to be opened on account of the Jews residing in the neighbourhood, whose prejudices might be offended, and only to permit the others to be opened on condition that the Society should engage and pay a policeman to keep order during play hours.'[25]

Prizes were awarded by the Society to schoolgirls for, among other things, swimming and knowledge of physiology. Indeed, the Society took a strong view on girls' health and particularly the threat to it from certain fashions – a subject to which they devoted one of their pamphlets:

> *How to Be Strong and Beautiful: Hints on Dress for Girls*
> The evils from which girls suffer arise mainly from three sources. 1st the great <u>weight</u> of clothing fastened round the delicate organs of the waist; secondly insufficient <u>warmth</u>, or warmth distributed unequally over the body; and thirdly the <u>pressure</u> upon the heart, lungs and other vital organs by unyielding bodices. No weight should hang round the waist of a growing girl . . . delicate girls should also wear warm drawers, combined if possible with a vest in union dress . . . the chief source of evil is, of course, stays . . . loose stays are also a source of evil. The weight of clothing causes them to slip down from their natural place at the waist and press upon the soft parts of the pelvis, tending to cause mischief there which may affect the happiness of the whole future life.[26]

Other NHS pamphlets included titles such as *In a Sick Room*; *Hints on how to avoid Catching Fevers and other Diseases*; *Dust and Dirt*; *Cheap Cooking* and *Healthy Houses*. Elizabeth herself contributed a pamphlet entitled *On The Religion of Health*, published in 1878. It was a tract that came from her heart, leaving no doubt on which side of the religion versus science debate she stood: 'Obedience to divine law is the highest wisdom of the human race. Wherever God's laws are clearly visible, stamped in immutable characters, so plain that every human being who is willing to read them can do so, then the wisdom, the happiness, nay, the simple common sense of the race, lies in obeying them.'[27]

The National Health Society had been largely Elizabeth's brainchild but its remit was too broad for her to maintain her grip on it indefinitely. Although she kept up a connection with the Society until 1897, inevitably a rift arose. In an undated letter to Barbara Bodichon, written some time in the early 1880s, she complained: 'I have no control of them now . . . have remonstrated with them about bringing vaccination into the work of Health Society as I strongly hold that such a disputed point should not come into the work of a Society which has far more than it can do in promoting accepted sanitary truths.'[28]

One sanitary truth that Elizabeth was especially keen to promote was birth control. Deeply influenced by the theories of Thomas Malthus, she believed that overbreeding was one of the major causes of poverty. She was, however, horrified at the idea of artificial contraception, claiming that it would lead to dire physical consequences for women and increased immorality. The pieces of sponge or India rubber that were the recommended devices of the day played no part in Elizabeth's notion of the perfect society. Nor, for that matter, did physical infirmity: 'All forms of chronic disease, are so many disqualifications for marriage, and particularly injurious are any scrofulous or consumptive tendencies or any danger of insanity. Two persons, both possessing one of these diseased tendencies, should be forbidden by law to intermarry, for the offspring are certain to be either idiots, cripples, or defective in organization.'[29]

Elizabeth's views on the importance of the health of 'the race' over that of the individual had not mellowed and were even extended to Kitty. Indeed, the fact that Kitty endured deafness and poor eyesight throughout her life gave Elizabeth exactly the excuse she needed to prevent her adopted daughter from ever contemplating a family of her own. On the rare occasions that any man paid the slightest attention to Kitty, Elizabeth reacted with panic and transparent self-interest.

The extent of Elizabeth's dependence on Kitty was underlined in the autumn of 1872 when she fell seriously ill with gastric problems. Kitty nursed her devotedly, regularly reporting back to the family in America on her progress, noting however, 'Doctors can't bear to allow that they are ill'.[30] It is not clear exactly what was wrong with Elizabeth but whatever the cause of her illness, she believed that London's dreadful pollution was a major factor and that she must find somewhere else to live. A leisurely journey through Europe with Kitty and Marian seemed the ideal way both to convalesce and consider future plans.

TWENTY

Grand Tour

Elizabeth, Kitty and Marian left England on 30 April 1873 to spend the first six months of their travels in Switzerland, sightseeing, sketching and enjoying the fresh mountain air that made such a delicious contrast to the London smog they had endured all winter. Kitty also studied French because, as she explained to Alice, 'I like it and because I desire to be able to talk freely to Pauli if ever Heaven should restore our dear boy to us'.[1] Only anxiety over money marred their pleasure. Not only did Susan Durant's death mean the end of the income Elizabeth received for housing Paul, but she also learned soon after leaving England that the American bank handling her Chesapeake railroad bonds had failed.

By November, however, she felt financially secure enough to lead her small party to Rome where they established themselves for the winter in a cold, bleak apartment on the Via Quattro Fontane overlooking the Barberini Palace. Although Elizabeth was ostensibly on holiday, her interest in social politics remained as sharp as ever. Kitty recorded how each day she bought *La Capitale*, an 'ultra-liberal' paper that advocated universal suffrage and free education. But in general, Italian politics left Elizabeth unimpressed: 'I do greatly wish that poor Italy had a cleverer set of rulers than the present leaders of public affairs seem to me. There is an immense lack of intelligent agricultural and manufacturing activity . . . though the country is laden with debt and its currency miserably depreciated, the great thought of the people seems to be given to increasing and building up its army. What with the priests and the soldiers, and the hosts of officials, there seems to me an unduly small proportion of the people to carry on honest industry and industrial enterprise.'[2]

Kitty particularly enjoyed looking at sculpture in Rome as it reminded her of Susan Durant but Elizabeth, who thought the Apollo Belvedere by far the finest male statue she had ever seen, recalled another friend, 'Something in the expression of face reminded me of Channing in his best days'.[3]

When they returned to London the following April it was to rented rooms, the house in Burwood Place having been permanently given up. A few weeks later, Kitty left for a much-anticipated holiday in America (she was still, she proudly claimed, 'a yankee to the backbone'[4]) leaving Elizabeth alone to resume her various reform activities – and to re-engage with Anna.

Elizabeth, always more at ease with Marian than any of her other siblings, had been glad of her amiable companionship in Europe. Anna was a different story. The tension that had existed between the two sisters since childhood was now aggravated by Anna's ever-deepening obsession with spiritualism. In 1870, she had fled the Franco-Prussian War to find refuge with the Countess Medina de Pomar (later Countess of Caithness), who believed herself to be the reincarnation of Mary Queen of Scots. Such eccentric friends, in Elizabeth's view, were emphatically not a salutary influence upon her sister: 'I feel little doubt that [Anna] could be won back in great measure to ordinary earthly life, if she had some of her family near at hand. We exchange visits almost every other day, and she freely criticizes me . . . I have even consented to initiate myself into her good graces, by going into a reverie for two hours, with my hands on a round table!'[5]

Three years later, by which time Anna was living in a small cottage at Wimille on the north coast of France, Elizabeth was less conciliatory: 'Her ridiculous theories . . . put me completely out of patience . . . it is a pity she is so autocratic that it would be impossible to live with her; even meek Marian does not want her to come to England, for as she says, every other will has to be laid aside if peace is to be kept. I take it for granted always, as a matter of course, that I shall never have an independent opinion, never dissent from any proposition and never discuss any topic on which there can be the possibility of difference of opinion whilst I am with Anna.'[6]

Anna's spiritualist mania came to a bizarre climax when she collaborated with a Madame Deville, whom she first met in the late 1870s. Claiming that she was descended from King James II and therefore the rightful queen of England, the woman convinced Anna that after the King fled to France in 1688, he had buried substantial treasure under a cottage at Triel (near Paris) now in her possession.

It took little effort on Madame Deville's part to persuade Anna that, with the help of the spirit world (and her money), the treasure would be quickly uncovered. Absurd though the scheme was, to Anna it all seemed perfectly logical. Ever since her father's failure, she had felt cheated of her rightful place in the world and bitterly resented her enforced poverty. Now, at last, compensation was at hand. The fantasy might have been harmless enough if it had not absorbed Anna's entire capital (most of it inherited from Howard) and fourteen years of her life. Her family did their best to disentangle her from the clutches of Madame Deville but it was only when she had finally spent all her money that she reluctantly agreed to give up the quest.

In 1882, Elizabeth and Kitty visited the Triel cottage to inspect the excavations for themselves. Elizabeth peered through a hole to see 'the old woman's adjoining domain of mystery, and the two contiguous hovels and blind alley, under which the great treasure chamber is now supposed to lie'.[7] When introduced to the 'princess' the following day, she was not impressed: 'a short, fat, thick featured older woman with gray hair, in a shabby dressing gown . . . one of the forlornest specimens of death in life it has been my misfortune to see'.[8]

Despite condemning Anna's addiction to spiritualism, Elizabeth was not entirely immune to it. She dabbled in experiments with psychic phenomena during the 1870s and in 1889 joined the Society for Psychical Research (chaired by Professor Henry Sidgwick), whose stated aim was to make 'an organised and systematic attempt to investigate various sorts of debatable phenomena which are *prima facie* inexplicable on any generally recognized hypothesis'.[9]

Elizabeth's belief in an afterlife grew stronger with her advancing years. In 1902, at the age of eighty-one, she wrote to a friend:

> I notice two currents of thought of much importance. The first is a very widespread and growing disbelief or uncertainty about a future life. I probably realise this more than you do because my doctorship brings me so much in contact with such numbers of young people who are throwing off religious beliefs and scientific people who have long done so. Yet a thorough conviction of the reality of continued existence and the necessary effect that character must have upon that future life, is really of tremendous practical importance. So I think that any experimental tests that a reverent foresight can devise, to enlighten and strengthen the instinctive belief of Humanity by facts, and gradually accumulated experience, is not only a legitimate but a very important effort.[10]

Expanding on this theme, Elizabeth tried to form a 'Council of Elders', which would settle the whole question of life after death by devising experiments to prove its existence. Her own contribution consisted of preparing a sealed statement whose contents would be revealed by her spirit after her death to a preselected group of friends.

T.H. Huxley was one of several eminent figures with whom Elizabeth corresponded on such matters; Alfred Russel Wallace (who in parallel with Charles Darwin developed the theory of natural selection) was another. As early as 1871 Wallace had attempted to convert Elizabeth to spiritualism by offering to introduce her to a famous medium, but Elizabeth was more interested in his theories of land reform. Nine years later in 1882, Wallace published *Land Nationalisation: Its Necessity and Aims*[11] in which he argued that all large land holdings should be bought up by the State and rented out in an elaborate but fair system. He argued that 'landlordism' was the cause of the 'widespread and crying evils – political, social, material and moral' afflicting the nation and that the only solution was to put in place a 'properly guarded system of Occupying Ownership under the State'.

Although Elizabeth joined Wallace's Land Nationalisation Society, she was more interested in forming colonies along the lines of the utopian communities that she had seen established in America during the 1840s. She had known many of the individuals involved in those experiments and she also knew that most of them had soon failed. But despite this, ever since as a young woman in Cincinnati she had come under the influence of Transcendentalism, she had remained wedded to the co-operative ideal. By the early 1880s, however, it was no longer Fourier's philosophy that served as her inspiration for Association, but Christian socialism. She set out her ideas in a pamphlet published in 1882: 'A true church, then, suited to the needs of this age, must be a self-governing, industrial community, guided by Christian principle, holding and managing its own lands, varied industries, and colleges. It should send off outshoots from time to time, new self-governing colonies at home and abroad . . . . A grand work is before all the Churches to join their members together under the noble banner of Christian Socialism.'[12]

In her pamphlet she cited the Familistère of Guise, which she had visited in 1872, as a successful example of such a colony. At this community, set in 18 acres along the River Oise, some 900 men lived, most of them employed in an iron foundry. Elizabeth was particularly drawn to the way the settlement regulated itself through citizens' councils, seeing this model as the solution to what in her view was 'excessively bad' local government in Britain. Her overall impression of the Familistère was more mixed: 'I attended the prize giving at the schools, saw the theatre, workmen's club and choral society, witnessed a ball, and visited the manufactory. The organisation was a great object lesson both in its success and its defects; full of interest to those who seriously study this important subject of improved social relations. The life of the Familistère, however, was intense, and rather overpowering to me.'[13]

Three years later, having finally decided that for health reasons she could no longer live in London, she launched a scheme which she called 'Associated Neighbours'. She prepared a circular letter setting out her aims:

> I have always lived in large towns, endeavouring to put ideas into practical shape: and I dread the waste of experience, the absence of social stimulus, and the possible growth of selfishness, that may arise from the isolation of a country life.
>
> I am therefore desirous of meeting with other persons holding the same views, who wish to make their home on the sea coast of England, hoping that we may agree to choose the same neighbourhood for our residence . . . Each member would establish the independent home most congenial to him, but would unite in the endeavour to secure justice and loving kindness in the relations which grow out of the individual household, meeting together to consider how these principles could be best carried out in daily life.[14]

This plea attracted little response but her determination to pursue the Association ideal remained as strong as ever. In 1884 she asked Alice to send her several copies of Melusina Fay Peirce's book: *Co-operative Housekeeping; How Not to Do It and How to Do It*,[15] remarking that 'In spite of its many faults and crudities, there is a white heat of passion about it, *founded on truth*, which is impressive, and excites attention'.[16]

Elizabeth shared her thoughts on the subject with Emily: 'I hope to send you Mr Wallace's book, which is very worth reading. I quite agree with you however, that Association is the only solution for the great evils of the present system. But Association can only be reached gradually and the advantage of many of the partial movements of the day (land nationalization agitation amongst them) is that they are gradually preparing for Association.'[17] Alfred Russel Wallace himself, however, was not persuaded that her ideas were viable: 'Your scheme will involve a large (a *very* large) amount of energy, labour, time, and money, all spent with no appreciable permanent benefit. For if, with a few carefully chosen inmates, the association should so far succeed as to work on for ten or twenty years, what appreciable result on society or on the mass of poverty wretchedness and crime, of the country would be produced? I fear the whole efforts of the association would have to be expended in keeping itself in existence.'[18]

William Morris was another critic of her blueprint: 'I cannot think that the establishment of communities isolated more or less from general society will solve the difficulty: in the first place I don't think anything will hold them together except some religious or quasi religious belief; they assume that each is to be a holy band higher than the rest of the people: on those terms I do not desire to see them succeed; they would be mere monasteries practising the counsels of perfection.'[19]

Undeterred by such criticism (her brother George also attacked the economic basis of her ideas) Elizabeth channelled her energies into yet another new organisation – the Home Colonisation Society. In a letter to Barbara Bodichon, she outlined its purpose: 'to prepare for drawing together in a neighbourhood . . . three conditions being essential to membership viz: (1) Joint ownership of land; (2) profit sharing in industry; (3) just morality between men and women'.[20]

She persuaded the veteran cooperator and Christian Socialist, Edward Vansittart Neale, to chair the committee but, at its first meeting on 19 October 1882, clashed with him over issues of morality in the Society's proposed colonies.

Elizabeth's ideas on Home Colonisation received fresh impetus when she and Kitty attended a lecture in St James's Hall in London given by the American political economist Henry George. His widely read book *Progress and Poverty*,[21] explored the reasons why these two conditions always seemed to develop in tandem. Not only did the solutions he put forward perfectly match the cooperative aims of the Home Colonisation Society, but the enthusiasm with which they were greeted that evening encouraged Elizabeth to pursue her own colonial ideas more vigorously. Kitty described the scene: 'The platform, body and galleries were filled. The hall seats 4,000. The meeting was enthusiastic with just enough dissent to make it spicy. I had the front middle seat and heard every word of all the speeches. Cheer upon cheer greeted George before and after the speech . . . there must have been forty reporters of London and other papers at the table in front of me . . . the mass of the audience rose, handkerchiefs and hats were waved as they cheered and cheered till they were forced to stop from hoarseness.'[22]

But it was not until 1890 that, under the leadership of Herbert V. Mills (author of *Poverty and the State*[23]), the Home Colonisation Society could claim any tangible progress. Mills proposed to establish privately a model colony for the unemployed whose success, it was hoped, would inspire the government to invest in further such schemes. As a result of this policy, the Society backed the Salvation Army's community at Hadleigh in Essex and two years later set up one their own at Starnthwaite Mills in the Lake District, where Elizabeth spent a week soon after it opened. The Hadleigh project lasted well into the twentieth century but Starnthwaite Mills failed after a few years.

Although with this latter colony's collapse Elizabeth's lifelong search for the perfect community came materially to a halt, she always kept faith in its possibility. On New Year's Eve 1898 she wrote in her diary: 'Now also my old interest in Co-operation is revived by the latest efforts to plan a truer organisation of towns! Perhaps after all, my great desire to live and die on righteously held land, may be gratified!!'[24]

It probably never crossed Elizabeth's mind that it was her own inability to negotiate that prevented so many of her projects from succeeding more fully. Throughout her life, her persistent refusal to compromise produced mixed results. When fighting for women's medical status and education, it was undoubtedly an asset. But, as both Alfred Russel Wallace and William Morris pointed out to her, sectarian communities based on a rigid moral code and woolly economic principles could have little impact on the vast national problems of poverty and unemployment that they – and she – were seeking to address. It is a curious facet of Elizabeth's character that, considering her long experience of human nature, even in late middle age she was unprepared to sacrifice one jot of her youthful idealism for pragmatic results. But then, to borrow from her contemporary Anthony Trollope, '*She Knew She was Right*'. This conviction was her greatest strength and her greatest weakness.

* * *

Resolute though Elizabeth was in anything to do with medical or social policy, she was remarkably indecisive when it came to settling on where to live. Between returning from Italy in April 1874 and leaving again for Europe in October 1876, she and Kitty moved at least ten times. Living in the heart of the city gave Elizabeth a pleasurable sense of being in the thick of things but, as Kitty put it, 'to be clean in London is a luxury'[25] so that she also longed to be by the sea or in the countryside. Thus, with the faithful Kitty continuously packing and unpacking, and with Marian often in tow, they stayed in a variety of boarding houses, shuttling between the suburbs (Upper Norwood and Crystal Palace) and the centre of London (St John's Wood, Milton Street and Portman Square) with forays to Swanage in Dorset and the seaside town of Hastings. Kitty, who still hankered after America, grew weary of this nomadic existence: 'The two Aunts have just now, the spring fever for house hunting. We do a great deal of house examination but, as usual, I think it will result in no suitable house at our price being found and the feeling that after all, we had better not do it as a house is a tie, We go through this every year after getting tired of a Winter in lodgings. It would be agreeable to have a house once more and have all our household goods round us again.'[26]

In her letters to Alice Stone Blackwell she gave witty, sometimes poignant, glimpses of life in a Victorian boarding house: 'My big room with its fire is a great comfort. I sew, write and read there, very rarely going into the parlour. Said parlour is hot and stuffy at night with four gas burners going and ten people who *will* have fresh air excluded . . . . At present there is not a boarder I can [admire]. They do nothing except fancy-work and read novels. One lady has been to Switzerland but does not even remember the names of the mountains round Lucerne or Interlaken! I gave her up after that. Do you know deafness is really almost a blessing in a boarding house?'[27]

But even her poor hearing was no defence against one young woman who practised the piano every evening. 'She has a regular routine of pieces and songs and goes through them after the manner of a barrel organ. I should think General Grayson, who has the rooms on the opposite side of the hall, would wish her piano burnt for she sings Scotch songs badly and that must be a trial for a gentleman.'[28]

General Grayson, 'the owner of a very red nose', was a widower. As this made him a potential suitor of Kitty, Elizabeth regarded him as the enemy. Much to Kitty's embarrassment, she made plain her dislike by cutting him 'in the most pointed way' whenever they met on the doorstep. Every Thursday the General held a Bible meeting in his parlour and, as Kitty noted with some amusement, 'of the thirty or forty who attend, all except two of these are young middle aged ladies'.[29]

A big event for Kitty, who yearned for young companionship, was the arrival in May 1875 of Elizabeth's niece Florence Blackwell, Sam and

Nettie's eldest daughter. Although she bore their name, Florence was everything a normal Blackwell was not. Considered flighty, shallow, lazy and without the slightest interest in reform of any kind, she had shocked the American suffragist leader Susan B. Anthony by telling her that she did not believe in women's rights. Florence's main interest in life was the opposite sex. For the intelligent and energetic Kitty, it was hard to adjust to this strange creature who had no urge to do anything but flirt with young men in the boarding-house parlour. Kitty vented her frustration to Alice:

> Floy is very far from strong tho' much better than when she landed. I don't think a young lady of eighteen who regards everything as a 'bore' on her first European visit, can't walk, takes no interest in things, is full of aches, imagines she has some fearful disease if she has a little extra pain somewhere, lounges about on the sofa like a limp rag, can be called strong! She has been brought up without any special interest and, being social, has run like the rest of Somerville girls into flirting. I told her that there was only one thing in which she was really 'grown up' . . . her desire to be admired by men.[30]

Underlying this outburst is the sense that Kitty was simply jealous, and who could blame her? Condemned always to observe other people's romances but never allowed to develop one herself, her natural good nature was tested to its limits. Not only did she have her deafness to contend with (and she was painfully aware of Elizabeth's eugenicist views) but she also accepted that she was *de facto* in bondage to her adoptive mother. Thus, she spoke from the heart when she wrote to Alice: 'No one ever has or ever will fall in love with me and it's fortunate, as I should have to say *no* even if it were to break my heart. I've known that for ten years. It has not been pleasant for naturally one does not like to feel different from other people.'[31]

In order to improve Florence's social awareness, Elizabeth imposed a strict routine that included a daily reckoning of accounts but forbade novel reading before dinner except on very rainy days. Kitty gleefully reported to Alice how Florence had 'received a lecture upon "going naked on the pier" (viz wearing drawers which were no earthly protection) and was informed that she should not leave her room till she had made suitable flannel drawers'.[32]

It was a clash of cultures and no doubt all parties concerned were relieved when George Blackwell, with his new wife Emma Stone (Lucy Stone Blackwell's niece) collected Florence in April 1876, after their European honeymoon, to take her back with them to America. George's marriage was another emotional blow to Kitty. For many years she had fostered a crush on him (a secret shared only with Alice) but, as usual, she put a brave face on the matter: '*Of course*, I rejoice in Uncle George's happiness . . . if only Emma is equally happy . . . I shall consider the whole thing *perfect*.'[33]

A few months before Florence arrived in England, Elizabeth had written to the girl's mother Nettie, outlining her plan to return to Europe with Kitty for an extended stay: 'My life has been such a very one sided affair that I am really woefully ignorant of a vast amount of the most interesting subjects that our earthly life can teach us'. Rather than attempt to set up again in medical practice (an objective for which she had long since lost all enthusiasm) she believed that she had just enough money from her American investments to finance their travels and achieve 'the best kind of education that I can command for myself and Kitty under the physical disadvantages that she has to contend with – and I also'.[34] This was a rare reference to her own health problems caused by her glass eye and recurrent gastric illness.

Kitty was thrilled with the prospect. She adored the stimulus of foreign travel and if Europe was not America, it was undoubtedly a great deal better than England. Furthermore, in the weeks after Florence's departure, Elizabeth's life had reached a low ebb. Not only did the lack of a permanent home make it difficult for her to concentrate on her public life (which apart from some lectures she gave at the London School of Medicine for Women seems to have virtually ground to a halt), but she also suffered another bout of sickness: 'I have been seriously ill for the last month in London . . . I have taken the opinion of four doctors, and got four different views of my case . . . the balance being however in favor of the gall stone theory . . . to which I myself do not agree.'[35]

This latest Continental tour, however, was to yield unexpected results for both women. While Elizabeth emerged from their eighteen months abroad on the brink of a second career as a writer and authority on sexual ethics, Kitty returned to England nursing a broken heart. The catalyst for both conditions was a young man named Alfred Sachs whom they met in a *pensione* on the Italian Riviera late in 1876.

Elizabeth and Kitty had left England on 19 October and, after spending a few weeks with Anna at Wimille, had travelled slowly south until reaching Bordighera where they intended to stay several months. Sachs, clearly lonely, soon made friends with Elizabeth and Kitty, accompanying them on walks and joining them at their table for meals. But in an unfolding of events worthy of E.M. Forster's *A Room with a View*, the other guests in the Villa Novara began to gossip maliciously about the *ménage à trois* in their midst. Chief among the stirrers was the Baroness von Plettenberg, whose husband was an ADC on the staff of the Kaiser. Kitty was furious with her.

> I wish to explode upon the general silliness of women-kind – all Blackwells excepted. I am just now so cross and vexed that I should like to pinch somebody or give a piece of my mind to a person in this house . . . They cannot let a young man of twenty-six go about with a woman of fifty-six and one of twenty-nine without trying to spoil his pleasure and ours by putting false ideas into his head . . . she talked to him on subjects which the other ladies would consider wrong for a woman to know anything of even in the true, wise way Aunt B knows such things <u>but</u> mind you, they don't think it at all wrong to talk of such things in a hinting, hateful way. Mr Sachs is very glad to find someone like Aunty, who can speak to him wisely as a woman, a Doctor and a mother. The other ladies would not care if he drank, smoked and went to the devil – in fact 'men must' they say. Aunt B teaches no such lessons – but really was helping Mr S.[36]

Early in their friendship, Sachs unburdened himself to Elizabeth about his dissolute youth in Vienna where visits to prostitutes had formed a routine part of his existence. As he had been travelling alone for more than a year 'in search of health', it is likely that he was recovering from some form of sexually transmitted disease. As far as Elizabeth was concerned, his arrival in Bordighera was an astonishing piece of luck. Here was a personable young man from a good family (his father was a successful merchant in Vienna) who was not only prepared to talk to her with complete frankness about his sexuality but also to listen responsively to her theories on morality. She had, in effect, been presented with a perfect specimen to put under her moral microscope.

The fact that Sachs was Jewish was almost as intriguing as his sexual history. Marian Lewes's latest novel, *Daniel Deronda*,[37] published only a few months earlier, had done much to raise awareness of Jewish culture. Kitty, who had read the book, must have thought that with the appearance of the 'fresh, young, handsome, boyish' Alfred Sachs, Daniel Deronda himself had walked into their lives: 'I must tell you that he is a Jew . . . .

I never had any prejudice against the Jews, on the contrary, Aunt B has had so many warm friends among Jews that I've rather liked them. His name is Alfred which in Hebrew is Abraham! All people of the name of Cohen belong to the priestly class of Jews this accounts I suppose for Miss Lewes' choice of the name in *Daniel Deronda*.'[38]

Ignoring the hotel tittle-tattle, Elizabeth and Kitty continued to deepen their friendship with Sachs and in letters to America even referred to him as Elizabeth's 'adopted son'. This produced a confused response from the family that unconsciously reflected the Freudian complexity of the situation: 'Uncle Sam in his last says "I was quite disappointed in Mr Sachs' sonship – I hoped it had reference to your adopted daughter." Floy writes "I am afraid you are falling in love with that young merchant. *Don't*! It would break Alice's heart." From Maria [a friend] "Are you *quite* sure Kitty that it is with Dr. Blackwell Mr Sachs is in love? If you should marry a long-haired, lager-drinking meerschaum smoking bespectacled German . . . *Don't*".'[39]

Despite her spirited denials, Kitty had in fact fallen in love with young Sachs as she eventually admitted to Alice: 'I am about to make a confession which will astonish you as coming from your demure old K. If you ever tell a living soul; if you don't burn this letter as soon as read and let me know it's cremated, I'll never forgive you . . . I have developed a decided weakness for our boy . . . . Was there ever anything so ridiculous to have a sentimentality for a boy not yet twenty five, a Jew and a reprobate? Lucky I am nearly thirty and not twenty-two . . . being an aged female I suppose I shall come to my senses.'[40]

It soon became clear that she faced formidable competition: 'I never saw Aunt Elizabeth take to anyone so completely as she has to "our boy"'. The affection seems to have been mutual: 'Floy and Emma may find it hard of belief, but it is undoubtedly the case that Mr Sachs is in love with Aunty B.' Kitty summed up the problem: 'Aunty is very fond of him, I am very fond of him too.'[41] For Kitty, this emotional triangle became increasingly uncomfortable. She found herself forced to walk far ahead or behind Elizabeth and Sachs in order not to disrupt their intense conversations that were considered unsuitable for her ears. She did, however, pick up the odd snippet including Elizabeth's denunciation of the classics for the 'mischief' they did to young boys and Sachs's rejoinder that the Old Testament was just as bad. The wretched Kitty was doubly displaced. It was bad enough that Sachs was monopolised by Aunt B but she also began to feel ousted from Elizabeth's affections: 'I sometimes wish I could vanish from this world and put Herr S in my place. I am very sure that he would more than fill it, if not at once very soon afterwards.'[42]

As a result of her intimate conversations with Sachs, by April 1877 Elizabeth had decided to write a book on the 'true relations of the sexes' which she planned to have translated into French, German and Russian. She wrote to Barbara Bodichon requesting help in the awkward task of gathering statistics to prove the 'injurious effects to the Race of immorality'. Having also decided that the best hope for 'her boy' was early marriage (she told Sachs that she would attend his wedding only if he married for love and not, as his father wished, for money), she added a postscript: 'Make the acquaintance of any good young Jewess that you can. I want one but she must be able to make a healthy wife.'[43]

Kitty found some relief from unrequited love when she and Elizabeth were once more alone after Sachs left them in Venice. From there they travelled to Innsbruck, where Elizabeth had agreed to sit for a portrait commissioned by Marie Zakrzewska. Her old colleague, who had recently visited her in England, was eager that a portrait of Elizabeth should eventually hang in the New York Infirmary.[44] After a couple of sittings Elizabeth began to take an interest in the young American artist, Frank Duveneck, prompting Kitty to remark, 'if we remained long, he would be a second case of adoption . . . she was cut out to be the Mamma of a dozen sons. She gets on with and has such a good influence over young men.'[45] But before Elizabeth could begin to exert her influence over Duveneck, Sachs reappeared. They met at Kitzbuhl on 6 July. Elizabeth interpreted Kitty's obvious distress as a growing dislike for the young man, quite unaware that each night the lovelorn Kitty cried herself to sleep.

They parted from Sachs in Austria, never to meet again. He made one attempt to visit Elizabeth in England but she did not encourage him, claiming that she would be unable to introduce him to any of her friends because of his immoral past. They kept up a correspondence until 1880 when a brief message announcing his engagement brought their curious relationship to a close. Elizabeth's experiences with Sachs clearly led her to believe that she had a special mission to save young men as she tactlessly remarked to Kitty, 'I wonder to what boy you will play duenna next?'[46]

By the summer of 1877, Elizabeth had completed the first draft of her proposed book. Kitty, who had not been allowed to read it, complained bitterly:

I've not seen the sketch of the book. It is not considered proper for such a juvenile as myself! Zoe Underhill[47] being a married woman, tho' only four months older than I am, has seen the sketch. I tell Aunty it is very well to say the book is only for parents to read, but she may be quite sure the children will read it also. Zoe hates the subject but, having a son to educate and Aunty having opened her eyes to the importance of the matter, she takes great interest. This is confirmed by what her physician, Dr Drummond, said . . . He told her above everything to care for Tottie's [Zoe Underhill's son] moral education to give him elevated interest and told her that the child's physical life depended upon her doing so that Tottie was not strong and would die if he led the life of most young men.[48]

In September 1877, Elizabeth gathered more material for the book at the International Congress of the Abolition of Government Regulation of Prostitution in Geneva, attended by all her fellow anti-Contagious Diseases Acts campaigners. Following the conference, she left Kitty in Nice (where Marian was now living) to visit Barbara Bodichon in England who had suffered a stroke. Perceptively assessing her friend's situation, she wrote to Kitty: 'I see I shall have to help B in many ways. Everyone has their plan for her management . . . but no one seems to think it necessary to find out Barbara's own plan and support that. It is what I must do.'[49] Her concern for Barbara did not, however, prevent her from spending a further eight months with Kitty on the Continent, based mainly in Nice.

But by the end of March 1878 Elizabeth was eager to return to England. Once home and having established herself and Kitty in lodgings in the south London suburb of Norwood, she set out to find a publisher for her book. She planned to call it *Counsel to Parents on the Moral Education of their Children in Relation to Sex*. She expected it (with some relish) to cause a stir but also hoped that it would establish her as a major voice on the whole vexed subject of sexual behaviour.

TWENTY-ONE

Birds and Bees

If *Counsel to Parents on the Moral Education of their Children in Relation to Sex* (published in 1879) is not the snappiest of titles, it nevertheless encapsulated a radical new idea – that parents should discuss sex with their children. This novel suggestion was the book's most important achievement. For, despite Elizabeth's belief that the public would be shocked by its contents, it is, as Emily Blackwell remarked, a rather dull little volume that might almost be read aloud in mixed company.[1]

Certainly, the book offers no guidance to parents on how to introduce their offspring to the physiology of sex. Indeed, if children were left to rely on *Counsel to Parents* to answer the eternal question of 'where do babies come from?' they would still be looking under gooseberry bushes. But, as might be expected, Elizabeth did dwell at length on the need for the young to understand that men must be subject to the same moral code as women: 'All rational efforts for the improvement of society must be based upon Nature's true intention, viz: the equality of the sexes in birth and in duration of life, not upon the false condition of inequality produced by our own ignorance.'[2]

Inspired by the confessions of Albert Sachs, the book's chief purpose was to make parents fully aware of the appalling fate awaiting their children (especially their sons) if they failed to educate them to be morally responsible citizens. Kitty, having at last been allowed to read the manuscript, was surprised to see 'how much of the book is the amplifying of conversations which Aunt B has told me about her having with that boy'.[3] Dipping into the Nonconformist imagery that came to her so naturally, Elizabeth depicted the hideous fate awaiting the degenerate young man:

He has tasted the physical delights of sex, separated from its more exquisite spiritual joys. This unnatural divorce degrades whilst it intoxicates him. Having tasted these physical pleasures, he can no more do without them than the drunkard without his dram. He ignorantly tramples under foot his birthright of rich compound infinite human love, enthralled by the simple limited animal passion. His Will is no longer free. He has destroyed that grand endowment of Man – that freedom of the youthful Will, which is the priceless possession of innocence and of virtue, and has subjected himself to the slavery of lust.[4]

The physical afflictions that he could expect to suffer were limitless. 'The brain and spinal marrow and the lungs, are the vital organs most frequently injured by loose life. But whatever be the weak point of the constitution from inherited or acquired morbid tendencies, that will probably be the point through which disease or death will enter.'[5] No reprobate could hope to escape 'either the physical deterioration or the mental degradation which results from the irrational and unhuman [*sic*] exercise of the great endowment of sex'.[6] Elizabeth exercised her *coup de grâce* by asserting with great authority (but no scientific evidence) that immorality (like the colour of eyes) could be inherited. Having digested these apocalyptic warnings, it is little wonder that her friends, such as Zoe Underhill, began to regard their sons' future with increasing alarm.

Another friend, who read *Counsel to Parents* in draft, expressed great admiration but had little doubt that if it were to be published, Elizabeth would become 'the most abused woman in England'.[7] It is hard now, even accepting the standards of the time, to understand what all the fuss was about. In the context of Victorian attitudes to sex, Elizabeth's philosophy was hardly revolutionary, but despite this she had great difficulty in finding a publisher. Kitty reported to Alice: 'Aunty has had her manuscript refused by several of the leading publishers. They *dare* not take it. She will try a few more and then if refused may publish at her own risk. I hope she will not have to do the thing herself – it costs so much.'[8]

It was, in fact, first printed privately but a few months later Hatchards of Piccadilly agreed to take it. The firm soon had reason to regret its decision. Bishop Thomas Hatchard's widow was so outraged by the book that she allegedly threw it on the fire, demanding that it be withdrawn immediately. Lawyers were hurriedly consulted and a compromise only reached when it was agreed to market it as a medical work, thus protecting the general public from its salacious contents.[9]

Despite all the pre-publication angst, *Counsel to Parents* was well received both in England and America, where it was published in 1880.

Church Bells commented: 'What she writes is not altogether easy reading, nor altogether pleasant; but we desire to offer her our most hearty thanks for her wise and earnest works, pleading as they do with all the force of thorough knowledge and long experience, for keeping the body in chastity.' The *New York Sun* was equally complimentary: 'We know of no other work on the same urgent, but awkward topic, which combines so much substantial worth with such purity of form.'[10]

Elizabeth was delighted with the response. Although *Counsel to Parents* marked only the beginning of fifteen years of prolific output, it remained the most widely read of all her publications and in print until 1913. There was, however, at least one reader who was so puzzled by certain matters alluded to in the book that she felt compelled to seek clarification: 'I have not any idea and have in vain tried to settle in my own mind what you mean by self abuse in reference to little boys. You may think it strange that I do not consult my husband . . . he has so intense a horror of all impurity that he does not like to think or talk on such subjects . . . and I cannot consult him as freely as I would wish . . . yet I feel that I must know how to avoid dangerous intercourse for my children.'[11]

She was not the only individual to seek Elizabeth's advice on masturbation. The Reverend R.A. Bullen, her colleague in the Social Purity Alliance, also wrote to her requesting 'a simple prescription for young men that are troubled with temptation to self-abuse. I have one somewhere made of "Bromide of potassium" and "Bicarb: Do." So many young men write to me for such a prescription . . . or rather, they ask for counsel to help them resist temptation.'[12]

Elizabeth agreed with most Victorian commentators on sex in believing masturbation to be an unmitigated evil. In her canon it ranked with fornication as one of the two 'radical vices from which all forms of unnatural vice springs'.[13] She therefore devoted a whole chapter to the subject in her next book, *The Human Element in Sex* (1884), writing in terms that made plain (to even the most innocent mother) that children as well as adults were in mortal danger from the habit: 'Of Self-abuse (called also Masturbation, Onanism etc.) it is necessary to speak fully. This vice may infect the nursery as well as the school; and in innumerable cases it induces precocity of physical sensation and prepares the way for every variety of sexual evil.'[14] She went on: 'This mental suggestion may be produced by the irritation of worms, by some local eruption, by the wickedness of the nurse, occasionally, though very rarely, by malformation or unnatural development of the parts themselves. There is grave reason also for believing that transmitted sensuality may blight the innocent offspring.'[15]

It was not only men who suffered at the hands of this 'cruel foe', as Elizabeth made clear: 'My attention was painfully drawn to the dangers of self-abuse more than forty years ago by an agonised letter received from an intelligent and pious lady, dying from the effects of this inveterate habit. She had been a teacher in a Sunday school, and the delight of a refined and intelligent circle of friends. But this habit, begun in childhood in ignorance of any moral or physical wrong which might result to her nature, had become so rooted, that her brain was giving way under the effects of nervous derangement thus produced, whilst her will had lost the power of self-control.'[16]

Sir James Paget was one of the few cool, calm voices of reason amid the general hysteria surrounding onanism. In his *Clinical Lectures and Essays* he wrote, 'masturbation does neither more nor less harm than sexual intercourse practiced with the same frequency in the same conditions of general health, and circumstances.'[17] Although Elizabeth disagreed with him, she did at least resist some of the more extreme cures prescribed for the practice such as cork cushions, genital cages or straitjackets. Neither did she, as did so many of her contemporaries, question the motives of young women who chose to ride bicycles.

For Elizabeth, 'self-abuse' was a problem (like numerous others) that could best be overcome by deploying the superior ethical sensitivities and ceaseless vigilance of the middle-class mother. It was this mythical creature, keeper of her children's (and servants') morals, to whom it fell to gently steer the child away from disaster by telling it 'that it may make little children ill to do this thing'.[18] As childhood masturbation inevitably led to adult fornication which in turn threatened the whole human race, it was imperative, in Elizabeth's view, that her maternal readers should be left in no doubt of their awesome responsibility. It does not seem to have occurred to her that by placing such a heavy moral burden on mothers in this, as in so much else, she was sustaining the myth that kept women firmly tied to their domestic role – a role from which she herself had so conspicuously escaped forty years earlier.

In one area of sexual behaviour, however, Elizabeth's views were less conventional. Unlike many other Victorians, she believed that women were just as capable of enjoying sex as men. In his book *The Physiology of Marriage*[19] the American William A. Alcott stated, 'Woman, as is well known, in a natural state – unperverted, unseduced, and healthy – seldom, if ever, makes any of those advances, which clearly indicate sexual desire; and for this very plain reason that she does not feel them.' Elizabeth profoundly disagreed.

Using her MD as both shield and sword, she had long been accustomed to entering debates on subjects normally considered unfit for her sex. But, given her unmarried (and presumably chaste) status, her championing of female sexual passion was, even by her standards, a brave initiative. Having once made up her mind to speak out on the matter, however, she did so with her customary confidence: 'The different form which physical sensation necessarily takes in the two sexes and its intimate connection with and development through the mind (love) serve often to blind even thoughtful and painstaking persons, as to the immense power of sexual attraction felt by women.'[20]

And, as she revealed to Kitty in an autobiographical letter written in 1887, when it came to physical desire Elizabeth, despite being single, knew what she was talking about. She frankly admitted that since childhood she had always been 'keenly susceptible to the influence of sex'. At the time she first decided to study medicine, she had been 'experiencing an unusually strong struggle between attraction towards a highly educated man with whom [she] had been intimately thrown and the distinct perception that his views were too narrow and rigid, to allow of any close and ennobling companionship'. She had even preserved a bunch of flowers the young man had given her in a packet labelled 'young love's last dream'. It was so rare for Elizabeth to show any vulnerability in either her public or private utterances that the following confession is curiously touching: 'I look back now with real pity at the inexperience of that enthusiastic young girl who thus hoped to stifle the master passion of human existence.'[21]

In her defence of female sexuality, Elizabeth made the obvious point that terror or pain could easily destroy physical pleasure for either sex but added perceptively: 'a tortured girl, done to death by brutal soldiers, may possess a stronger power of human sexual passion than her destroyers'.[22] Injury from childbirth, she noted, or 'brutal or awkward conjugal approaches, may cause unavoidable shrinking from sexual congress, often wrongly attributed to absence of sexual passion'. 'But', and this was her main point, 'the severe . . . suffering experienced by many widows who were strongly attached to their lost partners is . . . not simply a mental loss . . . but an immense physical deprivation.'[23]

She also referred to specific female needs, 'Although physical sexual pleasure is not attached exclusively, or in woman chiefly, to the act of coition, it is also a well-established fact that in healthy loving women, uninjured by the too frequent lesions which result from childbirth, increasing physical satisfaction attaches to the ultimate physical expression of love.' For someone for whom principle was always more important than individual pain or pleasure, Elizabeth went on to make the surprisingly sympathetic observation that 'repose and general well-being results from this natural occasional intercourse, while the total deprivation of it produces irritability'.[24]

Not all women welcomed her plea for greater understanding of their sexuality. In response to an article entitled 'Cruelty and Lust' that Elizabeth contributed to the American purity magazine *The Philanthropist*,[25] Josephine Shaw Lowell (a prominent reformer in New York) wrote:

> I believe her quite mistaken in thinking it either useful or right to make the statement she does concerning the sexual instincts of women. Whatever may be the effect on a young girl's development and conduct of those instincts, the fact that, unless there is a morbid condition, she is unconscious of their existence, make a tremendous difference between her and a boy of a corresponding age . . . would be a very great mistake should it ever be generally considered and recognised by women themselves that their passions were of equal force with men's. Instead of tending to help virtue in men to say such a thing, I believe it tends to break down virtue in women.[26]

But while Elizabeth supported sexual passion, she also believed in its strict regulation. It was not only possible, she argued, for everyone (especially men) to exercise self-control, it was also essential for the survival of Christendom. And no union, however passionate, should *ever* be abetted by artificial contraception. Contraception was yet another blatant disregard of God's divine law that could only result in physical harm to the man and woman who practised it and to any children they later conceived, resulting in a population (as Francis Newman predicted) of criminals, rogues, dwarfs and degenerates.[27]

Elizabeth did, however, accept the Reverend Thomas Robert Malthus' mathematically based theory that, if left to expand naturally, a population would inevitably outstrip its resources. She therefore also believed that no household should be burdened with more children than it could easily bear, making this point as early as 1870 in a talk delivered to the Working Women's College, entitled 'How to Keep a Household in Health'.[28] Following a confused account of her lecture in the *Pall Mall Gazette* she had, to her acute embarrassment, received a stream of letters (some enclosing money) from 'various classes' of people including members of parliament, army officers and clergymen, begging her to advise them on contraception.[29] Even more disturbing was the reaction of one woman who assumed that Elizabeth was promoting abortion. Eighteen years later, determined to put the record straight, she published *A Medical Address on the Benevolence of Malthus contrasted with the Corruptions of Neo-Malthusianism*.[30]

While Malthus himself had merely recommended late marriage or abstinence as methods of birth control, the neo-Malthusians firmly believed that artificial contraception was not only a more reliable way of limiting the population but also a momentous breakthrough in the achievement of human happiness. Elizabeth, however, maintained that their total disregard for the *moral* law in respect of the population debate merely encouraged sexual degeneracy. 'The benevolent intentions of old Malthus recognised the power of the human being to exercise self-command. This rational view is being replaced by the advocacy of unrestrained lust in Neo-Malthusianism.'[31]

Furthermore, she argued that, far from bestowing a new sexual freedom on women, neo-Malthusianism subjected and degraded them. She quoted from a book (in its sixty-first edition) that asserted contraception devices must always be used by the woman since 'it spoils the passion and impulsiveness of the venereal act, if the man have to think of them'. Elizabeth was swift to point out that, having thus placed all responsibility on the woman for preventing conception, men were absolved of any need to use self-control. Rejecting the possibility that most women might still be thankful for a means of preventing unwanted pregnancies and ignoring the obvious benefits to their health, she rallied all 'right-minded women' to take seriously the threat that these 'shocking and disgusting proceedings' were posing, adding: '. . . his corruption has spread into all classes, and reached all ages, and the poison is infecting our social atmosphere'.[32]

Indeed, for Elizabeth, the sin of contraception was every bit as wicked as that of masturbation – 'Both masturbation and imperfect sexual union, are unnatural conditions'.[33] And she did not hesitate to support her case with 'scientific' observation: 'In fact the physical appearances of the female masturbator's internal organs, are identical with those of the married woman, where precautions have always been taken to prevent conception.'[34]

Interestingly, Elizabeth referred to another sexual sin that at the time received little recognition – marital rape. 'It is gradually becoming clear to this age, that rape may be committed in marriage, as well as without legal sanction. A man who commits rape in marriage is even a meaner criminal than one who exposes himself to the just punishment which is attached to violence outside marriage.'[35] But even she seems to have regarded this crime as a lesser evil than either masturbation or contraception.

Elizabeth's summing up of the birth control issue was unambiguous: 'From the outset of marriage the wife must determine the times of union, this is the only natural method of regulating the size of the family. Through the guidance of sexual intercourse by the law of the female constitution, the increase of the race will be in accordance with reason, and our highest welfare.'[36]

Elizabeth had made her case. If, as she postulated, sex meant as much to women as it did to men, then it followed that they should expect the same fidelity from their husbands that society demanded of them. Furthermore, given their quasi-mystical status as moral guardians and mothers of the race, it was clearly God's intention that women should control the marriage bed. When society was persuaded of these basic truths, *both* sexes would come to understand that female emancipation, far from being an improbable theory, was nothing less than an integral part of God's divine law. And, once equality was established in the bedroom, it could be only a matter of time before it spread to the ballot box and the legislature.

If sex and childbearing were so fundamental to female fulfilment, how then did Elizabeth square her own position as a professional, unmarried and childless woman? Her ability to skew or invent evidence to suit her own theories is nowhere better illustrated than in the following sentence: 'The character of the childless woman does not suffer from the absence of that beneficent discipline and development which come from parentage, as does the character of the man. It is very instructive to observe how unmarried or childless women replace by adoptions or by pets their unexercised natural affections.'[37]

Certainly 'dog-friends' played a vital role in Elizabeth's own emotional life, as the many intimate references to 'Burr' and 'Don' in her diary reveal: 'December 11 1887: Burr's cloak stolen. December 12: Bought homeopathic remedies for Don. December 16: Don's troubles began. December 23: Don himself again.'[38] The latter's death was the cause of deep grief: 'Kitty and I laid our dear old Don in his grave, Sarah putting our first dahlia in his collar. I said a few words of conviction that we shall meet again in spiritual recognition, and then we laid the earth on our dear old friend who has been our loving companion for 9½ years. The house feels desolate. At dinner I thought how I fed him with juicy bits for his last meal, how he lay by me on the sofa with my arm around him awaiting his unknown fate. This sense of loss makes me ill, I so long for the dear old fellow.'[39]

The yearning to own a dog was just one of many reasons why Elizabeth intensified her hunt for a permanent home on her return from Europe in 1878. After much fruitless searching (Kitty complained to Alice that she had packed the trunks eighteen times in five months) she finally took a lease on a small house on top of a hill in the old part of Hastings overlooking the English Channel. In May 1879 they moved into Rock House, which was to remain their home until Elizabeth's death thirty-one years later. In 1883, on Kitty's insistence, Elizabeth bought the freehold: '*We* have bought Rock House . . . The house is *my* choice; tis *my* liking for it which has made Aunt B buy it finally.'[40] Kitty's exultation is understandable. For once Elizabeth had put her adopted child's wishes first, giving her the longed-for proof that she was more daughter than servant.

Not that Elizabeth was unhappy at Rock House. The views of the sea and fishing fleets reminded her of her childhood in New York, and London, where she spent so much of her time, was a convenient train ride away. But she never learned to love Hastings. Writing to Barbara Bodichon in 1885 she complained: 'In Hastings my work has hitherto been discouragingly checked by the coldness of the people – I suppose because I don't go to their hypocritical churches and chapels.'[41] Despite her lack of enthusiasm for its inhabitants and her heavy commitments elsewhere, she was nevertheless drawn into the town's affairs, and became a well-known local figure.

In April 1881 Elizabeth, together with her friend Mrs S. Woolcott Browne, launched yet another society – the Moral Reform Union. Similar in its aims to the Social Purity Alliance, its specific purpose was to open up a new front in the fight against the Contagious Diseases Acts but at the same time to disseminate as widely as possible information across the whole spectrum of sexual ethics. A Hastings branch of the Moral Reform Union was set up by Elizabeth in December 1881, prompting Kitty to write to Alice: 'Aunt B very busy. She has formed a society for looking after the morals of the young of both sexes – it meets every week. She says the good people don't know that they are being formed gradually into a vigilance committee! She reads a paper at Mme. de Noailles' . . . about ninety seven people to be present.'[42]

The Comtesse de Noailles, still hovering on the periphery of Elizabeth's various schemes, owned a house in nearby Eastbourne, where she was famous for her canoeing exploits. She subsidised a series of lectures in Hastings initiated by Elizabeth in 1883 and a few years later became financially involved with her Home Colonisation plans. Water purity was yet another concern she shared with Elizabeth: 'Have you a good dairyman? I hear that all the farms around Hastings are in a fearful state; the cows are given very impure water to drink, and must therefore give impure milk. I hope that your dairyman is an exception.'[43]

The two women's relationship – always an uneasy one – nevertheless endured into their old age. In her last communication with the Comtesse, written in 1905, forty-five years after their first meeting, Elizabeth turned down an invitation to visit her on the French Riviera but added: 'Like you, I always hope and feel that good will triumph in all the many lines that have been my special interests.'[44] The Comtesse died a sad and lonely old woman on the French Riviera in 1906. Even in death she managed to cause financial confusion by leaving two contradictory wills which took lawyers several decades to unravel.

In 1869 legislation had been passed entitling women who were ratepayers to vote in municipal elections. Elizabeth took full advantage of her rights, voting for the first time on 29 November 1870 when Elizabeth Garrett Anderson (having been nominated by a group of working men) successfully stood for election to the London School Board. On that occasion, Elizabeth wrote: 'I walked off in the conscious dignity of a voting citizen, persuaded that the responsibilities of a mighty empire rested upon my shoulders and with stern resolves always to be a rate payer, and never to hide my grandeur behind a husband!'[45]

Her involvement with local affairs in Hastings convinced Elizabeth that municipal politics was one area in which women could exert a benign influence by insisting that only candidates with impeccable moral pedigrees offer themselves for election. Consequently, by the mid-1880s the Hastings branch of the Moral Reform Union had become more politically focused, urging 'every local voter to consider character of more importance than party politics in the choice of Candidates, and thus secure the spread of honesty, purity, and temperance in local representative bodies'.[46] This high-principled but unrealistic stance was yet further illustration of the gulf existing between Elizabeth's idealism and the world in which she lived. Even with the wealth of experience that came with her advancing years, there was to be no compromise in her pursuit of perfection.

After moving to Hastings, she was given several opportunities to become involved in local politics but showed little inclination to hold office. As a young woman she had rebuffed the American feminists, believing their aims too trivial. Thirty-odd years later, she still had little time for the mundane realities of everyday politics and even less for the inadequacies of Hastings councillors: 'I am profoundly sorry for these poor ratepayers who have no one to guide them, and are only used by self-seeking politicians for corrupt party purposes.'[47]

On 25 March 1885 she wrote in her diary: 'Asked to stand for Poor Law Guardian. After serious consideration of engrossing duties involved, I consented as a duty . . . but I refuse to canvass.' Three weeks later she noted: 'Some ladies have been working zealously for me, but I am not elected to my great relief. I drove to the Workhouse to watch the counting of votes. All very civil but what a common lot!'[48]

Elizabeth's consistent belief that her mission in life was superior to that of the ordinary party political activist was one of her deep failings. Preferring to condemn from the moral high ground than to seek change from within, she distanced herself so firmly from the political process that she effectively ruled out any possibility of transforming her social vision into reality. Arguably this was her means of dealing with the painful realisation that the perfect society – like tomorrow – is always a day away.

In any case, by the early 1890s the quest for a perfect world seemed, even to Elizabeth, less urgent than the need to prevent the current one from sliding yet further into the moral abyss. The gathering threat to society from vivisection, compulsory vaccination, and the deeply disturbing claims of the bacteriologists caused her, during the last decade of the century, to switch the main focus of her interests from sexual to medical ethics.

TWENTY-TWO

Last Act

'The only disappointment which comes to me now as I draw towards the close of a life full of joy and gratitude, is the surprise with which I recognize that our women physicians do not all and always see the glorious moral mission which as women physicians they are called on to fulfil.'[1] This lament, published in the American journal *The Philanthropist* in 1889, illustrates Elizabeth's extraordinary ability to support (with equal passion) two opposing ideas. All her professional life, she had fought tooth and nail to ensure that women entered and practised medicine on an equal footing with men. Yet, just as this principle was beginning to gain wider currency, she wanted them to act quite differently from their male colleagues. The reason for this paradoxical behaviour was her belief that, as men had become so enslaved to secular science, it was now up to women doctors to defend the fundamental link between medicine and Christian ethics. 'I am absolutely sure that Women Physicians must show that morality is essential to true medicine, and must organise a movement in that direction,' Elizabeth wrote in her diary on 6 March 1889.[2]

To a doctor like Mary Putnam Jacobi, however, the idea that women medics should work in a moral vacuum uninfluenced by scientific discovery or individual inclination was nothing less than grotesque. And, in a long, blunt letter to Elizabeth written on Christmas Day 1888, she made her views plain. 'My "antagonistic hairs" are only raised in regard to . . . the well known Transcendentalist method of arriving at conclusions by the force of meditative insight and the refusing to submit these to test of verification.' Pulling no punches, she continued: 'You resemble your sister Anna sufficiently to prefer to remain within the sphere of large, half mystical assertion . . . You have no method or system to convince opponents. It is a question of belief or disbelief – never of proof.'

Warming to her theme, she went on to analyse Elizabeth's medical philosophy with devastating accuracy:

Now I have always thought of you that you had a *large* mind but one relatively untrained in technicalities . . . it is your mind that conceived the idea of women physicians in modern life, and on a plane at which few have ever thought of it. I do not know that anyone . . . has ever entered fully into all you saw in this idea; how it claimed a full equality and independence for woman as nothing else ever had or perhaps could; an intellectual, practical and social emancipation . . . But while your dream has become potent enough to really stir the depths of two hemispheres, you have always disliked, ignored and neglected medicine . . . You never really descended from your vision into the sphere of practical life within which that vision, if anywhere must be realised.

On the specific question of women's role in medicine, Mary Putnam Jacobi was equally direct: 'I do not think women physicians should be urged to strike out for independent views until they have demonstrated an equality of achievement in the urgent practical problems – not of sociology but of science.'[3]

But these arrows, however well aimed, merely bounced off their target. In a letter to her niece, Alice Stone Blackwell, Elizabeth wrote: 'Poor Mary Putnam, her life has gone wrong somehow. With all her bright cleverness her judgement can never be relied on for she cannot catch a glimpse of Truth – unhappily . . . It is now my greatest anxiety that women physicians do not instinctively see the difference between knowledge and truth and thus are too much under male error and influence.'[4]

Elizabeth did not just focus her disapproval on Mary Putnam Jacobi. She was equally critical of Elizabeth Garrett Anderson, whom she accused of performing too many unnecessary and unsuccessful operations. Indeed, she believed most gynaecological surgery to be of questionable value:

I consider that the loss of a natural internal organ is a very grave mutilation of the human body, and the permanent effects upon the subjects of such mutilation, have never been carefully and honestly collected. I am convinced that a very different aspect would be given to a very large amount of so-called brilliant surgery if the testimony of the subjects of such surgery could be honestly tabulated. I have tried to bring this necessity of far more carefully statistics before some of our lady surgeons over here, but they are too much under the influence of the surgical mania at present to realise the importance of my suggestion. Indeed I heard one of our cleverest medical women, quite lately, state that special feminine functions were such a nuisance that it would be a blessing if all women could have undergone a certain surgical operation. This shallow way of regarding human nature . . . marks too often the attitude of some women.[5]

Although she had herself wanted to be a surgeon before she lost her eye, Elizabeth now viewed surgery as an aggressive intervention into God's territory and one, therefore, that should only be used sparingly. The prevention of disease – not its cure – must be the highest aim of medicine. On 22 May 1894, she published an attack on Elizabeth Garrett Anderson in the *Hastings Daily Chronicle*:

> The temptations to operate upon women are great and peculiar and it is not to be wondered at that the first note of alarm has been sounded in connection with a hospital for women [the New Hospital]. In the first place there is a great deal of mystery about certain feminine ailments. Secondly, a woman is not likely to question what is being done so much as a man . . . And, lastly, the profession of 'ladies' doctor is known to be very lucrative, thanks to tight lacing and other acts of indiscretion on the part of many women, and to the facility with which a more or less hysterical woman may be induced to believe that her ailments are ten times as serious as they really are.

Having also suggested in this article that much of the surgery performed on women was merely to relieve the tedium of outpatient work, she added a final barbed thrust: 'We shall never have our hospitals thoroughly entitled to public confidence until the older members of the medical profession openly take up arms against the younger members, who are converting houses of charity into butchers' shops.'[6]

Elizabeth Garrett Anderson was furious. But, after a heated exchange of letters the two women called an uneasy truce. In fact, the *Hastings Daily Chronicle* article was not entirely unjustified. Dr Garrett Anderson's success rate as a surgeon was enough in question to prompt the resignation of several members of her staff. However, instead of calling for better surgical training or closer supervision in the operating theatre Elizabeth continued to condemn surgery wholesale, ignoring the words of Dr Putnam Jacobi: 'When you shudder at "mutilations," it seems to me you can never have handled a degenerated ovary or a suppurating Fallopian tube . . . or you would admit that the mutilation had been effected by the ignorance or neglect of a series of physicians, before the surgeon intervened. You always

seem so much more impressed with the personalities . . . sufficiently faulty
. . . of doctors, than with the terrific difficulties of the problems they have
to face . . . There is no such special sanctity about the ovary!'[7]

If Mary Putnam Jacobi and Elizabeth Garrett Anderson were irretrievably
lost to the 'narrow, male intellect'[8] there were others who more closely
shared Elizabeth's view of women doctors' special missionary role in society.
In May 1880, the Association of Registered Medical Women was launched
with Elizabeth presiding. Its modest success in arranging seminars and
lobbying on behalf of its membership delighted Elizabeth, who had long
since recognised the need for women to have their own professional
societies. 'Our meeting at dinner was genuinely cheerful – all the accessories
were charming – a noble room looking out on the broad sweep of the
Thames, a table set with all luxuries of silver, glass and flowers and a
number of intelligent bright earnest young faces gathered round the board.'[9]
Elizabeth rarely let such occasions go by without reminding her younger
colleagues that there must be limits to scientific investigation – knowledge
was not its own justification. It was their sacred duty, she argued, to resist
the evils of vaccination, vivisection, germ theory, excessive surgery and 'mad
delusions' such as Louis Pasteur's cure for rabies.

In 1889 she visited the Pasteur Institute in Paris, where all her worst fears
were realised: 'After inspecting the Hall of rabbits, guinea pigs and pigeons
used in experiments for rabies, anthrax etc., I went to the cages of three
dogs also used for experiments in rabies, who were in various stages of
madness, one dying after its ten days' agony; a second in the full fury of
madness; a third in frantic terror clinging to the bars of his cage, imploring
to be let out.'[10]

Of all the many causes that Elizabeth championed during her long life, none
aroused her passion more strongly than that of antivivisection. Over the next
decade (spurred on by the adoring looks of her own 'dog-friends') she fought
experimentation on animals with every weapon at her disposal. She argued
that animals and humans were too different for vivisection to be of any
practical value. And, as no medical advance had ever been proven to result
from its practice, it was utterly unjustified. 'Cruelty will *never* reveal truth.'[11]

Furthermore, she believed that young impressionable students forced to
watch the torture of animals would be in danger of passing on to their
offspring an instinct for cruelty, citing as proof of this theory the notorious
American case of a butcher's son convicted at the age of fifteen of
murdering two little girls. This was precisely the kind of pseudo-science

that so infuriated Mary Putnam, who quite openly practised vivisection. She also continued to teach at the New York Infirmary Medical College, causing Elizabeth to remark in a letter to her great ally in such matters, Alice Stone Blackwell, 'Our worst enemy I fear is Mary Putnam'.[12]

Elizabeth was determined at all costs to prevent the practice of vivisection at both the London School of Medicine for Women and the New York Infirmary Medical College, where Emily continued to be Dean and where, in the early 1890s, two of their nieces were studying. Suspecting that Emily was not being entirely straight with her, Elizabeth enlisted Alice's sleuthing skills to uncover exactly what was going on in the new laboratory: 'Can you quietly find out if Edith's reference to a course of "operative surgery in the *Laboratory*" really means mutilating living animals, as the phrase would imply . . . you need not fear being in any way implicated. What I want are facts and unless I can gain those facts, I cannot write in so serious a manner to your Aunt Emily as to *compel* an answer from her.'[13]

So incensed was Elizabeth at the idea of vivisection being practised at the New York Infirmary Medical College that she threatened to cross the Atlantic in order to confront the perpetrators personally, claiming that she would 'far rather destroy the school than suffer such infamies to continue'.[14] Much to the relief of her family she never made the journey, preferring instead to concentrate her antivivisectionist efforts in England through such organisations as the Leigh Browne Trust, which she had founded with her wealthy friend Mrs Woolcott Browne in 1884 'with the object of promoting and encouraging original research in Physiology and Biology without experimentation on living animals of a nature to cause pain'.[15]

If, in Elizabeth's opinion, vivisection was the most evil manifestation of modern materialistic science, vaccination was little better. The 1853 legislation (strengthened in 1867) making smallpox vaccination compulsory continued to meet with a good deal of popular resistance. Many people chose to pay a fine or even risk imprisonment rather than subject their children to the procedure. Elizabeth had herself once vaccinated a child whom she believed had died as a result. This devastating experience confirmed her instinctive prejudice against injecting disease into healthy tissue. But while she certainly urged women doctors to resist vaccination, she was not as apocalyptic in her condemnation of it as some of her fellow sanitarians. The Comtesse de Noailles' physician, Dr Garth Wilkinson (whom Elizabeth had first met in Hampstead in 1849), was nothing if not colourful in his attack on the practice:

As forced upon every British Cradle, I see [vaccination] as a Monster instead of a Poisonous Midge; a Devourer of Nations. As a Destroyer of the Honesty and Humanity of Medicine, which is through it a deeply-degraded Profession. As a Tyrant which is the Parent of a brood of Tyrants, and, through Pasteur and his like a Universal Pollution Master. As a Ghoul which sits upon Parliament, and enforces Contamination by Law, and prepares the way for endless violations of personal liberty and sound sense at the bidding of cruel experts. Not denying other forms of Social Wickedness, I now, after careful study, regard Vaccination as one of the greatest and deepest forms, abolishing the last hope and resort of races, the new-born soundness of the Human Body.[16]

A lighter commentary on the subject (preserved by Elizabeth among her papers) was published in the *Shooting Times* in January 1891:

MODERN MEDICINE

First they pumped him full of virus from some
   Mediocre cow,
Lest the small-pox might assail him, and leave pit-marks
   On his brow;
Then one day a bull-dog bit him – he was gunning down
   At Quogue –
And they filled his veins in Paris with an extract of mad
   Dog;
Then he caught tuberculosis, so they took him to Berlin,
And injected half a gallon of bacilli into him:
Well, his friends were all delighted at the quickness of the cure,
Till he caught the typhoid fever, and speedy death was
   Sure;
Then the doctors with some sewage did inoculate a hen,
And injected half its gastric juice into his abdomen;
But as soon as he recovered, as of course he had to do,
There came along a rattlesnake and bit his thumb in two;
Once again his veins were open to receive about a gill
Of some serpentine solution with the venom in it still;
To prepare him for a voyage in an Asiatic sea,
New blood was pumped into him from a lep'rous old Chinee;
Soon his appetite had vanished, and he could not eat at all,

So the virus of dyspepsia was injected in the Fall;
But his blood was so diluted by the remedies he'd taken
That one day he laid him down and died, and never
   Did awaken:
With the Brown-Sequard elixir, though they tried
   Resuscitation,
He never shewed a symptom of reviving animation;
Yet his doctor still could save him (he persistently maintains),
If he could inject a little *Life* into his veins.[17]

As both Elizabeth's professional life and the nineteenth century drew to a close, it was clear that no medical advance – least of all germ theory – would ever modify the fundamental beliefs to which she had held so fast since the outset of her career. Hygiene was, for her, still the panacea, the universal remedy that could 'counteract the evil influence of heredity, get rid of epidemics, improve the stamina of the race, advance in longevity and in the natural enjoyment of our earthly span of life'.[18]

In her unconvincing attempts to reconcile an authoritarian God with science Elizabeth was hardly alone. Many other sanitarians refused to accept the bacteriologists' evidence – compelling though it was. If from a modern perspective their position seems inexplicable, it should be remembered that they still profoundly believed that sickness was rooted in sin. By demonstrating the random cause of so much disease, the germ theorists stripped away much of the moral dimension to health, thus undermining the very basis on which many social reformers had built their case – Elizabeth among them.

Despite her lifelong lip-service to science, therefore, Elizabeth did not hesitate to attack it when she perceived it to be straying from what she regarded as its proper function – a tool for revealing God's divine law. Germ theory, vaccination, vivisection and contraception were all perversions of 'true' scientific practice and therefore must be resolutely opposed. To those medics who, like Mary Putnam Jacobi, preferred the microscope to the mystic, this attitude was plainly Luddite. Yet it is worth reflecting that despite everything medical science has achieved in the century since Elizabeth's death, those issues so close to her heart – vivisection, vaccination and alternative medicine – remain as contentious as ever.

As Elizabeth's theories grew more idiosyncratic with her advancing years, there was, at least, one forum where she could be always sure of a sympathetic hearing – the Christo-Theosophical Society. Founded in 1890 it was, like its parent organisation, the Theosophical Society, committed to the concept of a world community but unlike the latter it maintained a specifically Christian focus. Not only was it exactly the sort of non-denominational organisation guaranteed to appeal to Elizabeth, but it also claimed among its membership a number of earnest young men – a species with whom she had long felt that she had a special affinity.

One of them, a barrister named Rowland Estcourt, became a particular favourite. He filled a void that had existed in Elizabeth's life since the ending of her relationship with Alfred Sachs. 'Young Mr Estcourt and his friend Mr Johnston called yesterday and sat three hours today discussing life's duties and problems . . . I thoroughly like that very fine spirit Estcourt. I will try and help him.'[19] Then again, 'Long confidential talk with RE till late . . . a Christ like spirit . . . saw the young friend off by 5 o'clock train . . . a distinct gain in life has come'.[20]

The attraction was clearly mutual since Estcourt was soon confiding intimate details of his marriage to Elizabeth. Referring to his wife he wrote: 'She is not, and knows she is not, the exact type of beauty which is most fatal to me and hence the physical is the least powerful of her attractions. Probably a good thing for some reasons . . .'[21] Their friendship lasted many years. 'I don't think you realise what a very large part you occupy in my life,'[22] he wrote to Elizabeth in 1895, but eventually foundered when Estcourt (who claimed descent from George IV and might therefore have suffered from porphyria) became mentally unstable.

Elizabeth's intense friendship with Estcourt was not the only liaison of its kind that she formed in later life. On 31 January 1885 she wrote in her diary: 'This month has been a memorable one. I have lived in an exalted state of mental emotion too keen to last. But it has been a revelation of what friendship might be in its highest phase such as I have never enjoyed before, and full of the brightest prophecy for a future life. I shall always be grateful to JR for thus revealing me to myself!'[23] The identity of this persuasive character remains a mystery but, given Elizabeth's record, it seems likely that it was yet another adoring young man. A few days later she recorded: '64 years old today – confirmed in the great discovery that growing old, means growing young'.[24]

Always quick to point out others' failings, Elizabeth nevertheless had a great capacity to form deep and lasting relationships and to draw people of all ages into her orbit. Her truest and most loyal friend, Barbara Bodichon, lived near Hastings, thus enabling the two women to remain in close touch until the latter's death in 1891. It was through Barbara that Elizabeth had first met Marian Lewes, whose marriage in 1880 to John Cross (twenty years her junior) had prompted her to remark, 'I rejoiced at the notice of George Eliot's marriage . . . I profoundly believe that she has . . . done wisely'.[25]

It was Cross's biography of his wife, published in 1885,[26] that triggered Elizabeth's decision to write her own autobiography. 'They have George Elliot's [*sic*] life here,' she wrote to Kitty from Mrs Woolcott Browne's house in London, 'but I am disappointed with the first volume which I've read. Much that is clever but I don't think we shall want to buy it . . . "Oh do write your auto-biography," said Mrs Browne, "it is so much more interesting than George Elliot's!" '[27]

Pioneer Work in Opening the Medical Profession to Women (catchy titles were never Elizabeth's strong point) was published in 1895 – largely based on her carefully edited letters. Many of her more acerbic comments were excised for publication, which makes the book duller than it might otherwise have been. Yet, it is still an absorbing – if at times self-satisfied – account of her life up to her return to England in 1869. Kitty strongly urged her to write a second volume to cover her social reform work, but the project never came to fruition.

Despite polite reviews, sales of *Pioneer Work* were slow, as indeed they were for most of Elizabeth's numerous publications. Undaunted, during the late 1890s she reprinted a number of them at her own expense. Although disappointed that so much of her writing failed to reach a wider public, she did at least have the satisfaction of seeing her most successful book, *Counsel to Parents*, translated into French.[28] This was particularly pleasing since she knew of no country in greater need of moral advice than France – a view shared by many Anglo-Saxon commentators who, as Elizabeth put it, all bore testimony to 'the growing and awful corruption of that poor Paris'.[29]

Although Elizabeth maintained a number of her social reform interests well into the twentieth century, the publication of her autobiography in 1895 marked a watershed in her life both physically and psychologically. Just as her appetite for committee meetings began to fade, the hill to Rock House seemed to grow steeper. She now inspected cemeteries with the same curiosity that she had once shown for houses when searching for somewhere to live. But, despite her growing frailty, old instincts died hard. While her diary entry for 1 January 1897 begins 'During the past year my strength has declined in marked degree particularly since the London visit last November', it concludes 'but the Humane Science lectures, with all the relations with younger men that they have established, interest me profoundly'.[30]

And, only three weeks after writing this, she was back in London lobbying Sir James Paget on hypnotism. 'Found my old Professor at eighty-three quite out of medical connexions but he received me very cordially; considered me "a credit to the Profession" . . . About hypnotism, he did not see any way of restraining it unless an assault were proved, and looked at it in the same way as action against enforcing vaccination, viz that to punish fools for their folly, only increased the number of fools. I wished him a friendly and final farewell, feeling that we lived on a different spiritual plane.'[31] This was certainly true. Ignoring their philosophical differences, it is hard to imagine Elizabeth prescribing anyone – as Paget did Marian Lewes – a pint of champagne a day.

Flashes of the old Elizabeth continued to appear from time to time. In 1901 she became animated over Ebenezer Howard's Garden City movement, sharing her enthusiasm with her old collaborator, Mrs Woolcott Browne:

> Have you seen any notice of . . . the 'Garden City' meeting? That project interests me much and I think that Ebenezer Howard's book 'Tomorrow' would interest you. The advocacy of true principles . . . of living, seems to me more interesting than anything else, in this short earthly life of ours . . . certainly advancement of true noble co-operation is one of the most useful efforts in which we can now engage. The drawing people back to the land under healthy conditions, is a most important work; and it seems to me all the more necessary now as we are killing off so many of our men . . . and our little Island itself seems slowly, but gradually, disappearing in the sea!![32]

Her conscious farewell to Sir James Paget was just one of many such partings during the 1890s as friends and family grew infirm and died. She accepted her own approaching death with equanimity: 'Although the bodily strength and my memory for daily events are failing, yet more and more these things do not seem to belong to my real self. I get clear glimpses of the larger life beyond, to which I look forward with joyful anticipation.'[33]

Throughout her seventies, much of Elizabeth's energy was spent in looking after Anna and Marian, who in 1890 had bought the two halves of a semi-detached house in Hastings in order that the three of them might end their days together. Marian, the professional invalid, finally died in 1897 but Anna lived until 1900 – becoming ever more eccentric and a continual thorn in Elizabeth's side. Indeed little had changed in their relationship since their childhood: 'Anna is a very clever woman, but she is utterly lacking in well balanced common sense which leads to good practical judgement . . . I have long since found that to prevent Anna's toleration of me becoming active dislike, I must carefully refrain from either contradicting her or reasoning with her. She has joined some occult London Society involving an oath of secrecy for which she is daily employed in secret study and writing . . . a vegetable diet is essential. She has conceived also a inveterate hatred of Mr Gladstone.'[34]

Under the circumstances, it is hardly surprising that despite living as close neighbours, the two sisters showed far greater affection for their respective pets in their final years than for each other. Certainly the death of her dog Burr in July 1899 stirred Elizabeth far more deeply than that of her sister six months later. Contrary to the last, Anna demanded in her will to be cremated (at a time when it was still highly unconventional) and that her ashes 'be thrown away in some open lonely place on a hill or common or anywhere convenient'.[35]

Although Elizabeth was never reconciled with Anna, she did attempt to mend fences with her sister-in-law, Lucy Stone Blackwell, whose women's rights activism she had once so publicly despised. Shortly before the latter's death in 1893 from cancer, she wrote to her: 'We have been soldiers in different Army Corps of humanitarian advance but I have always recognized that we are fellow soldiers.'[36] In fact, Elizabeth's views on feminism had changed little over the years but at least in old age she was prepared to acknowledge that 'the way in which active women are taking up all sorts of large interest is very remarkable. There is evidently some good coming out of this hateful militarism, which deprives so many women of their natural family life. For although I heartily believe in the Mother as the highest type of human life; yet I see the effort of unmarried women is beginning to raise higher thought about the method of woman's life.'[37]

Perhaps when she wrote this, she had in mind Miss Ede – a perfect example of the new breed of unmarried woman. Unable to study medicine because her brother's education took priority, Miss Ede set up a printing press with a female friend in order to finance her studies herself. Needing to consult Elizabeth on some medical matter, the spirited young women rode from Essex to Hastings on their tricycle. Kitty described their arrival to Alice with undisguised admiration: 'Just before we left, the two young ladies turned up. They had come down from Loughton, 70 miles or more, on a tricycle and were not the least tired . . . We were asked to come up to the extreme end of the St Leonard's esplanade to see them mounted on the cycle. We got to the spot before the ladies and had the advantage of seeing them come a distance down the road. They looked so pretty, worked well together, and rode it so easily! They were dressed alike in dark blue flannel jackets and the same black soft felt hats with silk twisted round. They looked better than any two people I've ever seen yet on a tricycle.'[38]

In 1901, the year that both Ellen and Sam Blackwell died, Henry urged Elizabeth to make one last journey to America to see her surviving three siblings and to witness for herself 'the amazing growth of this country . . . it is a new earth (I cannot say heaven)'.[39] She finally made the trip with Kitty in 1906 at the age of eighty-five. It was a characteristically brave decision – particularly since she knew that she would suffer appalling seasickness on the voyage.

They spent four months in America celebrating Emily's eightieth birthday in Maine (at the house which she shared with her companion, Dr Elizabeth Cushier) and some weeks on Martha's Vineyard, the summer home of numerous Blackwells both young and old. It is curious that Elizabeth did not visit the New York Infirmary which she had launched so memorably nearly fifty years before, but possibly the family judged this too great an emotional undertaking for such an old lady. The medical college had closed seven years earlier – its function having been made redundant when both Johns Hopkins and Cornell universities began to enrol women medical students on equal terms with men.

One excitement that Elizabeth's family did allow was a ride in a motor car. As she sat in this potent symbol of the new century, it is tempting to imagine her casting her mind back seventy-four years to 1832 and the sailing ship that had taken eight weeks to carry her and her family across the Atlantic. One of her great-nieces, then seven years old, recalled her aunt sitting in the back seat of the (more conventional) family carriage holding her little parasol primly over her head. 'I felt that she must really look like the Queen of England.'[40] Physically exhausting though the visit to America was for Elizabeth, it perfectly achieved its purpose of allowing her to bid what she, and everyone else, knew must be a final farewell to her family.

Henry, who had since his wife's death struggled to keep her feminist magazine, the *Woman's Journal*, in print, died three years later in 1909, shortly after attending the annual women's suffrage convention in Seattle. It is ironic that he should have been so much more committed to the women's rights movement than his 'first woman doctor' sister. Yet, in essence, their aims were not dissimilar and their affection for one another survived their differences – even his atheism.

In the summer of 1899, Elizabeth and Kitty had spent a month in Scotland. The holiday was such a success that in subsequent years it was regularly repeated. But in August 1907, while staying at Kilmun near Glasgow, Elizabeth had a fall from which she never recovered. Kitty took her back to Hastings where, desperately short of money and with little outside help, she devotedly nursed 'her doctor' for the next three years. Elizabeth died on 31 May 1910, six days after suffering a stroke. Within four months Florence Nightingale and Emily Blackwell were also dead.

Elizabeth had lived in Hastings longer than she had anywhere else but, as Emily pointed out in a letter to Alice Stone Blackwell, 'she resided there for health, economy, and convenience to London, and no special liking for, or attachment to the place'.[41] It was decided, therefore, that she should be buried at Kilmun in a romantic graveyard overlooking Holy Loch. Kitty collected newspaper accounts of the funeral that took place on 5 June 1910 – one of which set the scene: ''There was unwonted animation in the quiet township on the Holy Loch. The morning steamers brought numbers of mourners, and throughout the forenoon the ancient burying place, where stands the mausoleum with its domed roof, became a mecca for stranger and townsfolk alike.'[42] Elizabeth had outlived most of her close friends but a number of women's organisations, recognising their debt to her pioneering example, sent representatives to the funeral. A large wreath arrived from England from a number of women doctors bearing the inscription: 'A Pioneer – from some of those who are trying to follow in her footsteps'.[43]

Kitty, having sold Rock House, several years later decided to live in Kilmun – still unable to part from the woman whom she had loved and served so loyally. For more than fifty years she had (as a member of the Blackwell family put it) fitted herself 'into all Elizabeth's angles like an eider-down quilt'.[44] She became a much-cherished figure in the small Scottish community and such a valued supporter of the Argyll and Sutherland Highlanders that after the First World War she was awarded a medal. Eventually, in 1921, half blind and deaf, but having lost none of her optimism, she returned to America to live with Alice Stone Blackwell until her death in 1936. At her own request, her ashes were taken to Scotland and placed in the same grave as Elizabeth.

There were fulsome obituaries of Elizabeth Blackwell in many publications including the *Lancet*[45] and the *British Medical Journal* (which described her as 'the most womanly of women'[46]) on both sides of the Atlantic, as well as various suggestions for a suitable memorial. Kitty wanted to erect a stained-glass window in a Hastings church but this was not an idea that appealed to Elizabeth Garrett Anderson, who wrote brusquely: 'I am never at all keen about memorials and I do not feel disposed to contribute to putting up a church window. It would really be no memorial at all. A scholarship or a prize awarded . . . at our medical school . . . would be a memorial and do good.'[47] One Cecilia Tubbs suggested 'a drinking fountain mainly for dogs, but also to include humans . . . on it an inscription recording her life and work & her love for animals (no allusion to vivisection) and a medallion portrait'.[48] In the event, the Blackwell family erected a handsome Celtic stone cross over the grave inscribed with Elizabeth's concluding sentence from her pamphlet *The Religion of Health*: 'It is only when we have learned to recognize that God's law for the human body is as sacred as, nay, is one with God's law for the human soul, that we shall begin to understand the religion of health.'[49]

But Elizabeth's lasting memorial is the vast number of women practising medicine today. Despite her tenacious belief in her mission, she would have been surprised to know that close to the centenary of her death, it is estimated that there will be more women than men registered as doctors in Great Britain. Her own words written in 1887 to her old colleague Dr Marie Zakrzewska are her epitaph: 'I think we are really happy in this medical movement. We must have acted at the right time, for how seldom it is, that those who are privileged to initiate an important reform see such wonderful results from the effort during their lifetime.'[50]

Notes

In the interests of clarity punctuation in the quotations has been modernised.

ABBREVIATIONS
Institutions

LC   Library of Congress, Washington DC
SL   Schlesinger Library, Radcliffe Institute for Advanced Study, Harvard University, Cambridge, Massachusetts
Col   Columbia University, New York City

Names

A.B.   Anna Blackwell
A.B.B.   Antoinette Brown Blackwell
A.S.B.   Alice Stone Blackwell
B.L.S.B. Barbara Leigh Smith Bodichon
E.B.   Elizabeth Blackwell
F.N.   Florence Nightingale
G.W.B. George Washington Blackwell
K.B.B.   Kitty Barry Blackwell
H.B.B.   Henry Browne Blackwell
L.S.B.   Lucy Stone Blackwell
M.B.   Marian Blackwell
S.C.B.   Samuel Charles Blackwell

Introduction

1. *Punch*, 1849, vol. VI, p. 226
2. Marian Lewes to E.B., 27 February 1859, LC
3. E.B. to Emily Collins, 12 August 1848, *History of Woman Suffrage*, Elizabeth Cady Stanton (ed.), vol. I, pp. 90–1
4. E.B., *Pioneer Work*, p. 145
5. A.S.B. to K.B.B., 11 March 1888, LC
6. E.B. to B.L.S.B., 14 January 1861, Col
7. George Brune Shattuck, *Boston Medical and Surgical Journal*, 110, 1884, pp. 594–5

Chapter One

1. A.B., Reminiscences written for H.B.B., 1880–85, SL and LC. Except when otherwise noted all quotations in Chapter One are taken from this source.
2. *The only Genuine Trial of Henry Lane*, Mitchell Library, Sydney
3. These deaths may have been caused by lead poisoning or possibly a genetic brain developmental disorder.
4. SL
5. Samuel Blackwell, diary, SL
6. E.B., *Pioneer Work in Opening the Medical Profession to Women*, London and New York, J.M. Dent & Sons Ltd and E.P. Dutton & Co., 1914, p. 7
7. H.B.B., autobiographical papers, SL

Chapter Two

1. Samuel Blackwell, *Notes on Two Years Residence in New York, A Guide to the City for Immigrants*, 1835, SL

2. Basil R.N. Hall, *Travels in North America in the Years 1827 and 1828*, 3 vols, Edinburgh (no publisher cited), 1829, vol. 2, p. 43
3. Fanny Trollope, *Domestic Manners of the Americans*, London, Whittaker, Treacher, 1832
4. John Jacob Astor (1763–1848) arrived in America a penniless German immigrant. In 1808 he established the American Fur Company, later becoming New York's biggest landowner and the richest man in America.
5. Walt Whitman, *Specimen Days and Collect*, Glasgow, Wilson & McCormick, 1883, pp. 17–18
6. Samuel Guppy to Samuel Blackwell, 1 November 1832, SL
7. E.B. diary, LC. Except when otherwise noted all quotations in Chapter Two are taken from this source.
8. Samuel Blackwell, *Notes on Two Years Residence in New York*
9. H.B.B., autobiographical papers, LC
10. *Ibid.* and E.B., *Pioneer Work*, pp. 7–8
11. H.B.B., autobiographical papers, LC
12. E.B., 28 January 1836, SL
13. Samuel Blackwell to Kenyon Blackwell, 27 September 1836, SL
14. *Ibid.*
15. Samuel Blackwell to M.C. Howells, 13 January 1838, SL
16. *Ibid.*
17. Samuel Blackwell to Hannah Blackwell, 4 February 1838, SL

Chapter Three

1. E.B., diary, LC. Except when otherwise noted all quotations in Chapter Three are taken from this source
2. T.G. Bradford, *Illustrated Atlas of the United States*, Boston and New York, Wiley & Putnam, 1838, p. 90
3. Harriet Martineau, *Retrospect of Western Travel*, London, Saunder & Otley, 1838, p. 223
4. *Ibid.*
5. Captain Frederick Marryat, *Diary in America*, Jules Zanger (ed.), London, Nicholas Vane, 1960, p. 260
6. *Sarmiento's Travels in the United States in 1847*, translated by M.A. Rockland, Princeton University Press, 1970, p. 299
7. Lyman Beecher, *Autobiography, Correspondence etc. of Lyman Beecher D.D.*, Charles Beecher (ed.), New York, Harper, 1864, 2 vols, vol. 2, p. 167
8. Catharine Beecher, *A Treatise on Domestic Economy for the Use of Young Ladies at Home and at School*, Boston, Marsh, Capen, Lyons & Webb, 1841
9. Catharine Beecher, *Suggestions Respecting Improvement in Education*, Hartford, Connecticut, Packard & Butler, 1829
10. Captain Frederick Marryat, *Diary in America*, pp. 275–9

Chapter Four

1. Fanny Trollope, *Domestic Manners of the Americans*, London, Whittaker, Treacher, 1832
2. Hannah Blackwell to H.B.B., 17 March 1841, LC
3. Ralph Waldo Emerson, *Nature*, London, H.G. Clarke, 1844, first published 1836
4. *Pioneer Work*, p. 11
5. Emmanuel Swedenborg (1688–1772) was a scientist, philosopher, theologian and mystic whose ecumenical approach to Christianity much appealed to E.B. and her reformer circle.
6. E.B. to H.B.B., 18 March 1841, LC
7. *Pioneer Work*, p. 22
8. E.B. to A.B., 20 May 1848, SL

9. E.B. to family, 5 March 1844, LC
10. *Ibid.*
11. *Henderson, A Guide to Audubon's Hometown in Kentucky*, Bacon, Percy & Doggett, 1941, p. 35
12. E.B. to M.B., 4 April 1844, SL
13. *Pioneer Work*, p. 14
14. E.B. to M.B., 4 April 1844, S.L.
15. *Ibid.*
16. E.B. to H.B.B., n.d., LC
17. *Pioneer Work*, p. 20
18. Harriet Beecher Stowe, 'Immediate Emancipation: A Sketch', *New-York Evangelist*, 16, 2 January 1845
19. Harriet Beecher Stowe, *Uncle Tom's Cabin, or, Life among the Lowly*, London, H.G. Bohn, 1852
20. Margaret Fuller, *Woman in the Nineteenth Century*, Greeley & McElrath, New York, 1845
21. *Ibid.*, Larry J. Reynolds (ed.), W.W. Norton & Company, New York, London, 1998, p. 5
22. *Pioneer Work*, p. 22
23. *Ibid.*, p. 26
24. *Ibid.*, p. 23
25. *Ibid.*
26. John Evelyn, *Diary*, 19 January 1686, Oxford, Clarendon Press, 1955
27. The removal of a stone from Samuel Pepys's bladder on 26 March 1656 is one notable instance of a successful operation before science came to dominate medicine.
28. Quoted in Roy Porter, *The Greatest Benefit to Mankind, A Medical History of Humanity from Antiquity to the Present*, London, HarperCollins, 1997, p. 129
29. Fredrika Bremer, *Homes of the New World*, New York, 1853
30. Mary Safford Blake, *Women's Journal*, 23 November 1872, p. 376; quoted in

Mary Roth Walsh, *Doctors Wanted: No Women Need Apply*, New Haven and London, Yale University Press, 1977, p. 34

Chapter Five

1. E.B. to Emily Blackwell, 2 July 1845, SL
2. *Ibid.*
3. *Ibid.*
4. *Ibid.*
5. S.C.B., journal, July 1845, SL
6. E.B. to Emily Blackwell, 2 July 1845, SL
7. *Asheville Citizen Times*, 21 November 1941, Pack Memorial Library, Asheville, North Carolina
8. *Pioneer Work*, pp. 27-28
9. E.B. to M.B., 13 August 1845, LC
10. *Ibid.*
11. E.B. to Hannah Blackwell, 25 July 1845, LC
12. These included *First Lines of Physiology; Designed for the Use of Students of Medicine*, Daniel Oliver, Boston, Marsh, Capen & Lyon, 1835, *A Treatise on Food and Diet*, Jonathan Pereira, New York & Boston, Fowler & Wells, 1843 and *Popular Medicine*, which is unidentified. E.B. to M.B., 13 August 1845, LC
13. E.B. to M.B., 4 December 1845, LC
14. John Stuart Mill to Thomas Carlyle, 25 November 1833, *Letters of John Stuart Mill*, Hugh Elliot (ed.), Longman Green & Co., 1910, vol. I, p. 75
15. E.B. to M.B., 4 December 1845, LC
16. *Annals of Medical History*, Paul B. Hoeber Inc., NY, reprinted from third series, vol. 4 no. 5, pp. 382–9
17. *Ibid.*
18. E.B. to Emily Blackwell, 14 February 1847, SL

19. E.B. to M.B., 22 March 1846, SL
20. E.B. to M.B., 15 May 1846, SL
21. E.B. to M.B., 30 January 1847, SL
22. E.B. to H.B.B., 12 April 1846, SL
23. E.B. to M.B., 8 March 1846, LC
24. E.B. to M.B., 22 June 1847, LC
25. E.B. to M.B., 30 August 1846, LC
26. E.B. to Hannah Blackwell, 28 February, 1847, LC
27. E.B. to Hannah Blackwell, 28 December 1846, LC
28. E.B. to Emily Blackwell, 14 February 1847, SL
29. E.B. to M.B., 15 May 1846, SL

Chapter Six

1. E.B. to M.B., 7 November 1846, LC
2. Dr Joseph Warrington to E.B., quoted by E.B. in a letter to Hannah Blackwell, 28 February 1847, *Pioneer Work*, p. 40
3. The most famous example of a woman disguising herself as a man in order to become a doctor is James Barry MD, 1795–1865. She had a long career in the army, ending up as Inspector General of hospitals in the British army. See Brian Hurwitz, Ruth Richardson, 'Inspector General James Barry MD: putting the woman in her place', *British Medical Journal*, vol. 298, January to June 1989, pp. 229–305
4. *Pioneer Work*, pp. 49–50
5. *Pioneer Work*, p. 49
6. E.B. to M.B., 27 June 1847, LC
7. Susan E. Cayleff, *Wash and be Healed*, Philadelphia, Temple University Press, 1987; quoted in Joan D. Hedrick, *Harriet Beecher Stowe*, Oxford University Press, 1994, p. 173
8. E.B. to M.B., 22 June 1847, LC
9. *Ibid.*
10. *Ibid.*
11. E.B. to M.B., 30 January 1847, SL

12. E.B. to M.B, 22 June 1847
13. *Ibid.*
14. *Ibid.*
15. *Pioneer Work*, p. 52
16. E.B. to Emily Blackwell, 27 October 1847, SL
17. Castleton Medical College in Vermont also accepted Elizabeth Blackwell but she did not receive their letter until after she had begun her studies in Geneva. See: Frederick C. Waite, 'Two Early Letters by Elizabeth Blackwell', *Bulletin of the History of Medicine*, 21, 1947, pp. 110–12
18. *Pioneer Work*, p. 53.
19. Dr Stephen Smith, *In Memory of Dr Elizabeth Blackwell and Dr Emily Blackwell*, Academy of Medicine, New York, 25 January 1911
20. J. Disturnell, *Gazette of the State of New York*, Albany, 1842
21. E.B. to M.B., 9 November 1847, LC
22. *Ibid.*
23. *Pioneer Work*, p. 57
24. E.B. class notes, LC
25. Samuel Craddock to D.E. Craddock, 25 October 1847, Williams and Craddock Family Papers, Cornell University
26. E.B. to M.B., 29 December 1848, LC
27. *Pioneer Work*, p. 58
28. *Ibid.*

Chapter Seven

1. E.B. to M.B., 9 March 1848, SL
2. E.B. to Emily Blackwell, 16 April 1848, SL
3. E.B. to M.B., 9 March 1848, SL
4. E.B. to M.B., 14 March 1848, LC
5. *Pioneer Work*, p. 63
6. John Welsh Croskey MD, *History of Blockley*, Philadelphia, F.A. Davis Company, 1929, p. 131

7. *Pioneer Work*, p. 64
8. E.B. to G.W.B., n.d. but probably 23 June 1848, SL
9. E.B. to Emily Blackwell, 16 April 1848, SL
10. E.B. to H.B.B., 20 August 1848, SL
11. E.B. to Emily Collins, 12 August 1848, in *History of Woman Suffrage*, Elizabeth Cady Stanton (ed.), New York, 1881, vol. 1, pp. 90–1
12. E.B. to M.B., 29 December 1848, LC
13. E.B. to Emily Collins, 12 August 1848, *History of Woman Suffrage*, vol. I, pp. 90–1
14. E.B. to A.B., 20 May 1848, SL
15. *Ibid.*
16. M.B. to Eliza Lane, (letter copied) 14 February 1849, SL
17. E.B. to H.B.B., 20 August 1848, SL
18. *Ibid.*
19. E.B. to Emily Blackwell, 15 October 1848, SL
20. *Ibid.*
21. *Pioneer Work*, p. 66

Chapter Eight

1. E.B., 'Ship Fever, An Inaugural Thesis, submitted for the degree of M.D., at Geneva Medical College', January 1849, *Buffalo Medical Journal and Monthly Review*, Austin Flint MD (ed.), vol. 4, no. 9, February 1849, pp. 523–31
2. *Pioneer Work*, p. 69
3. M.B. to H.B.B., n.d., SL
4. E.B. to H.B.B., 17 December 1848, SL
5. See *Woman's Journal*, Boston, 12 June 1909, p. 95 and A.S.B., 'Because These Women Dared', *The Civic Pilot*, vol. II, no. 7, March 1924
6. *Pioneer Work*, p. 69
7. Margaret Munro De Lancey to her sister-in-law, 23 January 1849, De Lancey papers, Museum of the City of New York, published by Wendell Tripp, *New York History*, April 1962
8. *Geneva Gazette*, 26 January 1849, p. 2
9. Charles Alfred Lee, *Valedictory Address to the Graduating class of Geneva Medical College at the Public Commencement, 23 January 1849, published by Request of the Class*, Buffalo, Jewett Thomas & Co., 1849
10. *Punch*, 1849, vol. VI, p. 226
11. 'Doctress in Medicine', *Boston Medical and Surgical Journal*, vol. 40, I, 7 February 1849, pp. 25–6
12. 'The Late Degree to a Female', *Boston Medical and Surgical Journal*, vol. 40, 3, 21 February 1849, pp. 58–9
13. 'The Late Medical Degree at Geneva', *Boston Medical and Surgical Journal*, vol. 40, 4, 28 February 1849, p. 87
14. *Buffalo Medical Journal*, Austin Flint MD (ed.), vol. 3, 8 January 1848, pp. 494–6
15. Charles Alfred Lee, *Valedictory Address*
16. E.B. to H.B.B., 20 February 1849, SL
17. A copy of the original document is in the Blackwell papers, Library of Congress, on which it is noted that the original was in the possession of Mrs Frank Vanderlip, sometime president of the New York Infirmary for Indigent Women and Children.
18. E.B. to Hannah Blackwell, 25 February 1849, LC
19. *Ibid.*
20. *Ibid.*
21. *Pioneer Work*, p. 76–7
22. *Pioneer Work*, p. 77
23. *Ibid.*

Chapter Nine

1. E.B., circular letter, 2 May 1849, LC
2. *Ibid.*
3. *Ibid.*

4. *Ibid.*
5. *Ibid.*
6. E.B. circular letter, 10 May 1849, LC
7. *Ibid.*
8. *Ibid.*
9. *Ibid.*
10. E.B. circular letter, 17 May 1849, LC
11. *Ibid.*
12. *Ibid.*
13. *Pioneer Work*, p. 85
14. Theodore Parker to R.W. Emerson, 12 August 1844, *Letters of R.W. Emerson*, Ralph R. Rusk (ed.), New York, 1939, vol. III, p. 287
15. *Pioneer Work*, p. 86
16. John Harley Warner, 'American Doctors in London during the Age of Paris Medicine', *Against the Spirit of the System?*, Princeton University Press, 1998, p. 341
17. E. Williams, 'Foreign Correspondence' Vienna, 20 October 1854, *Western Journal of Medicine and Surgery*, ii, 1854, p. 444; quoted in John Harley Warner, 'American Doctors in London during the Age of Paris Medicine', pp. 346–7
18. *Pioneer Work*, p. 89
19. E.B. to A.B., 22 May 1849
20. *Ibid.*
21. Alphonse de Lamartine, quoted in Phillip Mansell, *Paris between Empires*, John Murray, 2001, p. 374
22. E.B. to William Elder, 30 May 1849, LC
23. E.B. to M.B., 5 June 1849, LC
24. *Pioneer Work*, p. 94
25. *Pioneer Work*, p. 98
26. E.B. to Howard Blackwell, *Pioneer Work*, July 1849, LC
27. *Ibid.*
28. *Pioneer Work*, p. 112
29. *Pioneer Work*, p. 107
30. *Pioneer Work*, p. 109
31. E.B. circular letter, n.d., 1849, LC
32. *Pioneer Work*, p. 110
33. *Pioneer Work*, p. 117

Chapter Ten

1. In 1881 the obstetrician Carl Crede (1819–81) introduced a highly effective prophylactic treatment for ophthalmia neonatorum involving the placing of several drops of a 2 per cent solution of silver nitrate in the newborn baby's eyes. This treatment continued to be standard practice until the 1960s.
2. A.B., circular letter, 22 November 1849, LC
3. E.B. to Dr Samuel Dickson, 15 December 1850, LC
4. *Pioneer Work*, p. 126
5. A.B. circular letter, 22 November 1849, LC
6. *Pioneer Work*, p. 122.
7. E.B. circular letter, 7 March 1850, LC
8. A.B. to S.C.B., 13 June 1850, SL
9. E.B. to Charles and Eliza Lane, n.d., 1850, SL
10. Paul Dubois was obstetrician to Empress Josephine and present at the birth of the imperial prince. He performed a successful mastectomy (without anaesthetic) in 1811 on the diarist Fanny Burney, of which she has left a vivid account.
11. A.B to H.B.B., 7 June 1850, LC
12. E.B. circular letter, 7 March 1850, LC
13. *Ibid.*
14. Robert Chambers, *Vestiges of the Natural History of Creation*, James A. Secord (ed.), Chicago, 1994, first published 1844
15. H.B.B. to Emily Blackwell, 23 August 1850, SL
16. E.B. circular letter, 7 March 1850, LC
17. A.B. to Eliza Lane (letter copied) 1 August 1850, SL

18. *Pioneer Work*, p. 133.
19. E.B. to Dr Samuel Dickson, 15 December 1850, LC
20. E.B., diary, 3 July 1850
21. E.B. circular letter, June 1850, LC
22. *Ibid.*
23. E.B., diary, 26 June 1850, LC
24. *Ibid.*
25. *Pioneer Work*, p. 132.
26. E.B. to Emily Blackwell, 5 June 1850, LC
27. E.B. to Dr Samuel Dickson, 15 December 1850, LC
28. *Ibid.*
29. E.B. circular letter, 20 October 1850, LC
30. Stephen Paget (ed.), *Memoirs and Letters of Sir James Paget*, London, New York, Longman, Green & Co, 1903, pp. 168–9
31. Quoted in James A. Haught (ed.), *2000 Years of Disbelief*, Amherst, Prometheus Books, 1996, p. 181
32. E.B. to Dr Samuel Dickson, 15 December 1850, LC
33. E.B. circular letter, 20 October 1850, LC
34. E.B. to Emily Blackwell, 20 November 1850, LC
35. E.B. to M.B., 24 December 1850, LC
36. E.B. to friends, 20 October 1850, LC
37. E.B. to M.B., 24 December 1850, LC
38. *Ibid.*

Chapter Eleven

1. E.B. to Dr Samuel Dickson, 15 December 1850, LC
2. Bessie Rayner Parkes to B.L.S.B., 13 November 1850, Col
3. E.B. to Emily Blackwell, 20 November 1851, LC. Bessie's youthful feminism is all the more noteworthy when it is remembered that her son Hilaire Belloc (1870–1953) became one of the most outspoken critics of female emancipation in his generation.
4. See articles by B.L.S.B, 'Esculapius', in *Hastings and St Leonard News*, 1848
5. *Ibid.*
6. E.B. to M.B., 24 December 1850, LC
7. *Ibid.*
8. *Ibid.*
9. Lady Byron to E.B., 27 May 1851, LC
10. E.B., *Pioneer Work*, p. 147
11. *Pioneer Work*, p. 148
12. *Ibid.*
13. Frances Anne Kemble, *Journal of a Residence on a Georgian Plantation in 1838–39*, John A. Scott (ed.), Athens, University of Georgia Press, 1984, originally published New York, Knopf, 1961
14. Lady Byron to E.B., 27 March 1851, LC
15. *Ibid.*
16. Lady Byron to E.B., 15 April 1851, LC
17. E.B. to Lady Byron, 7 April 1851, LC
18. E.B. to Lady Byron, 4 March 1851, LC
19. E.B. to Lady Byron, 27 April 1851, LC
20. *Pioneer Work*, p. 150
21. *Pioneer Work*, p. 143
22. A.B. to Eliza Lane, 7 July 1851 (letter copied), SL
23. *Pioneer Work*, p. 152
24. Sir James Paget, 'What becomes of Medical Students?', in *St Bartholomew's Hospital Report*, vol. 5, 1869, pp. 238–42; quoted in *The Royal Hospital of Saint Bartholomew 1123–1973*, Medvei and Thornton (eds), London, 1974, p. 69
25. *Pioneer Work*, p. 153

Chapter Twelve

1. E.B. to Emily Blackwell, 9 May 1852
2. *Ibid.*

3. Advertisement in the *New York Sun*, 18 March 1839, quoted in Clifford Browder, *The Wickedest Woman in New York: Madame Restell, the Abortionist*, Hamden, CT, Archdon Books, 1988, p. 9

4. Emily Blackwell to E.B., 27 April 1851, SL

5. Emily Blackwell, diary, 23 November 1851, SL

6. *Ibid.*, 30 October 1851

7. E.B., *The Laws of Life with Special Reference to the Physical Education of Girls*, London, Sampson Low, Son & Co., 1859, p. 140. First published New York, G. Putnam, 1852

8. *The Laws of Life*, p. 78

9. *The Laws of Life*, p. 148

10. E.B. to Mrs Darlington, 27 May 1852, quoted in *History of Woman Suffrage*, vol. 1, p. 831

11. E.B. to LS.B., n.d. (incomplete), SL

12. L.S.B to E.B., 10 June 1854, LC

13. E.B. to H.B.B., 26 December 1852, SL

14. Emily Blackwell, diary, 25 July 1852, SL

15. Emily Blackwell, diary, 2 September 1852

16. Emily Blackwell, diary, 7 November 1852

17. Emily Blackwell, diary, 9 January 1853

18. E.B. to Emily Blackwell, SL

Chapter Thirteen

1. E.B. to H.B.B., 17 September 1853, LC

2. E.B. to Lady Byron, n.d., LC

3. E.B. to A.B., 25 July 1853, LC

4. *Ibid.*

5. E.B. to Lady Byron, 2 March 1852, LC

6. W.B. Carpenter, 'On the Influence of Suggestion in Modifying and Directing Muscular Movement, Independently of Volition', *Proceedings of the Royal Institution of Great Britain*, 1852, 1: pp. 147–53

7. Michael Faraday, *Experimental Investigation of Table Turning*, Atheneum, July 1853, pp. 801–3

8. E.B. to Lady Byron, 2 March 1852, LC

9. E.B. to Lady Byron, 13 November 1851, LC

10. Emily Blackwell to E.B., 25 December 1852, SL

11. Emily Blackwell to E.B., n.d., SL

12. Emily Blackwell, diary, 9 June 1853, SL

13. E.G. Burrows and Mike Wallace, *Gotham, A History of New York City to 1898*, New York and Oxford, Oxford University Press, 1999, p. 747

14. Emily Blackwell, diary, 14 August 1852, SL

15. *Ibid.*, 17 February 1854

16. *Monthly Journal of Medical Science*, 1849, 9, p. 628; quoted in John A. Shepherd, *Simpson and Syme of Edinburgh*, Edinburgh and London, E. & S. Livingstone Ltd, 1969, p. 81

17. Emily Blackwell to E.B., 2 June 1854, SL

18. E.B. to Emily Blackwell, 12 May 1854, LC

19. E.B. to B.L.S.B, 25 September 1855, Col

20. E.B. to Emily Blackwell, 1 October 1854, LC

21. E.B. to The Reform Firm, 5 June 1856, Col

22. E.B. to Emily Blackwell, 1 October 1854, LC

23. Emily Blackwell to E.B., 20 June 1854, SL

24. A.B. to Bessie Rayner Parkes, 26 August 1854, Girton College, Bodichon papers, GC88 Parkes/1a. After Marian Evans began living with George Lewes, she

chose to be known as Mrs Lewes although they never married.

25. A.B. circular letter, 16 December 1853, SL

26. E.B. to Emily Blackwell, 23 January 1855, SL

27. Emily Blackwell to E.B., 2–5 January 1855, SL

28. E.B. to Emily Blackwell, 12 May 1854, LC

29. Henry Blackwell was referring to the knee-length dress worn over Turkish-style trousers promoted by Amelia Bloomer (1818–94) in her feminist magazine *The Lily* in 1853, as a sensible alternative to the restrictive clothing women normally wore. It attracted ridicule from all quarters and quickly lost popularity.

30. H.B.B. to S.C.B., 2 June 1853, LC

31. H.B.B. to L.S.B., 1 September 1854, LC

32. Emily Blackwell to E.B., 29 January 1855, SL

33. The text of the marriage protest was published in the *Liberator*, 4 May 1855

34. E.B. to H.B.B, 22 February 1855, LC

35. I Corinthians, Chapter 14, verse 34

36. Gilson typescript, SL, p.171

37. In the Congregational form of government, a local congregation had full authority to choose and ordain its own minister.

38. S.C.B. diary, 8 November 1853 (copied), LC

39. L.S.B. to A.B.B., 20 January 1856, LC

Chapter Fourteen

1. Emily Blackwell to E.B., 25 February 1855, SL

2. E.B. to Emily Blackwell, n.d., 1855, LC

3. E.B. to H.B.B., 23 December 1855, SL

4. E.B., *Address on the Medical Education of Women*, Baker and Duyckinck, New York, 1856

5. Emily Blackwell to E.B., 8 November 1854, SL

6. E.B. to Emily Blackwell, 13 November 1854, LC

7. F.N. to Emily Blackwell, 12 May 1856, SL

8. Agnes C. Vietor, *A Woman's Quest*, D. Appleton & Co., 1924, p. 189

9. *Ibid.*

10. Charles Dickens, *American Notes*, London, Chapman & Hall, 1850, p. 62

11. *The First Hundred Years*, New York Infirmary Centennial, 1954, SL

12. Marie Zakrzewska to Harriot Hunt, 14 May 1857, Massachusetts Historical Society

13. Agnes C. Vietor, *A Woman's Quest*, p. 218

14. *A Woman's Quest*, pp. 218–19

15. E.B. to G.W.B., 22 June 1857, SL

16. E.B., *Pioneer Work*, p. 170

17. E.B. to G.W.B., 9 June 1858, SL

18. B.L.S.B., *A Brief Summary in Plain Language, of the Most Important Laws Concerning Women*, 1854, London, 1869

19. John Jane Smith Wharton, *An Exposition of the Laws relating to the Women of England, showing their rights, remedies and responsibilities*, London, 1853

20. Quoted in Pam Hirsch, *Barbara Leigh Smith Bodichon*, Chatto & Windus, 1998, p. 87

21. B.L.S.B., *Women and Work*, London 1857, p. 11

22. E.B. to Lady Byron., 27 December 1857, LC

23. E.B. to G.W.B., 9 June 1858, SL

Chapter Fifteen

1. E.B. to Emily Blackwell, Paris, n.d 1858, LC

2. *Ibid.*
3. *Ibid.*
4. E.B. to Emily Blackwell, November 1858, LC
5. *Ibid.*
6. E.B. to Emily, n.d. February 1859, *Pioneer Work*, p. 175 (this letter must have been written in January)
7. Letter from the Comtesse de Noailles to Maria Pasqua, private collection
8. E.B. to B.L.S.B., Paris, 29 January 1859, Col
9. F.N. to E.B., 10 February 1859, LC
10. E.B. to F.N., n.d., probably February 1859, LC
11. F.N. to John Stuart Mill, 12 September 1860, original in the Nursing Archives, Mugar Library, Boston University, box 2 folder 4. Reprinted in *Ever Yours Florence Nightingale, Selected Letters*, Martha Vicinus, Bea Nergaard (eds), Virago, 1989, no. 74, p. 209
12. E.B. to B.L.S.B., 16 March 1859, Col
13. F.N. to Sidney Herbert, 24 May 1859, quoted in C. Woodham Smith, *Florence Nightingale*, London, Constable, 1950, p. 344
14. F.N. to E.B., Great Malvern, 10 February 1859, LC
15. *British Medical Journal*, 9 April 1859, p. 293
16. E.B. to B.L.S.B., 7 May 1859, Col
17. Marian Lewes to E.B., 27 February 1859, LC
18. E.B. to Blackwell family, 25 May 1859, LC
19. This consisted of Emelia Gurney, wife of Russell Gurney MP, Clementia Taylor, wife of the social activist Peter Taylor and the writer and reformer, Anna Goldsmid, daughter of Sir Isaac Lyon Goldsmid Bt.
20. E.B. to B.L.S.B., 21 December 1859, Col
21. E.B. to B.L.S.B., 25 April 1860, Col
22. *A House Divided, America in the Age of Lincoln*, Chicago Historical Society, 1990, p. 63
23. Lincoln's second inaugural address, 4 March 1865
24. E.B. to B.L.S.B., n.d., Col
25. E.B. to B.L.S.B., 5 June 1861, Col
26. *Ibid.*
27. E.B. to B.L.S.B., 2 March 1860, Col
28. E.B. to B.L.S.B., 25 April 1860, Col
29. E.B. to B.L.S.B., 23 June 1860, Col

Chapter Sixteen

1. E.B. to K.B.B., 8 June 1864, LC
2. *Ibid.*
3. E.B., *Pioneer Work*, p. 191
4. E.B. to K.B.B., 8 June 1864, LC
5. See: *Lincoln's Emancipation Proclamation: The End of Slavery in America*, Allen C. Guelzo, New York, Simon and Schuster, 2004
6. E.B. to K.B.B., n.d., probably November 1864, LC
7. Burrows and Wallace, *Gotham*, p. 890
8. Comtesse de Noailles to E.B., n.d., SL
9. E.B. to B.L.S.B., 30 December 1860, Col
10. E.B. to B.L.S.B., 30 December 1861, Col
11. A.B.B. to S.C.B., probably 1859, SL; quoted in Elizabeth Cazden, *Antoinette Brown Blackwell*, New York, The Feminist Press, 1983, p. 125
12. E.B. to B.L.S.B., 7 September 1864, Col
13. E.B. to B.L.S.B., 21 December 1859, Women's Library, Metropolitan University, London
14. E.B. to B.L.S.B., 5 June 1861, Col
15. New York Infirmary for Indigent Women and Children, Annual Reports, LC
16. E.B. to B.L.S.B., 14 January 1861, Col
17. E.B. to B.L.S.B., 18 January 1865, Col

18. E.B., *Address on the Medical Education of Women*, New York, Baptist Taylor, 1864

19. *Ibid.*

20. E.B. to B.L.S.B., n.d., 1861, Col

21. E.B. to B.L.S.B., 7 September 1864, Col

22. E.B. to B.L.S.B., 2 December 1860, Col

23. E.B. to B.L.S.B., 23 June 1860, Col

24. *Ibid.*

25. *Ibid.*

26. E.B. to B.L.S.B., 2 December 1860, Col

27. E.B. to B.L.S.B., 23 May 1865, Col

28. Emily Blackwell, diary, 5 March 1866, SL

29. A.B. to Blackwell family, 20 March 1866, SL

30. E.B. to M.B., 5 October 1866, LC

31. *British Medical Journal*, 27 November 1869, p. 586

32. Mary Putnam Jacobi to Victorine Haven Putnam, 13 January 1870, *Life and Letters of Mary Putnam Jacobi*, Ruth Putnam (ed.), New York & London, G.P. Putnam's Sons, 1925, p. 233

33. *Ibid.*

34. *Life and Letters*, 14 February 1867

35. E.B. to M.B., 5 October 1866, LC

36. E.B. to B.L.S.B., 13 January 1867, Col

37. *Address Delivered at the Opening of the Women's Medical College at the New York Infirmary*, New York, E.O. Jenkins, 1869

38. Sophia Jex-Blake to her mother, 8 November 1868; quoted in Margaret Todd MD, *The Life of Sophia Jex-Blake*, London, Macmillan, 1918, p. 207

39. *The Life of Sophia Jex-Blake*, p. 206

Chapter Seventeen

1. *British Medical Journal*, 18 June 1870, p. 636

2. Margaret Todd, *The Life of Sophia Jex-Blake*, London, Macmillan, 1918, p. 33

3. *Ibid.*, p. 264

4. Life of Sir Robert Christison, Bart, edited by his sons, London and Edinburgh, William Blackwood and Sons, vol. II p.50

5. *British Medical Journal*, 30 April 1870, p. 444

6. Quoted in Shirley Roberts, *The Life of Sophia Jex-Blake*, Routledge, 1993, p. 95

7. Sophia Jex-Blake to E.B., quoted in Margaret Todd, *The Life of Sophia Jex-Blake*, p. 356

8. The lecture was published as: *Medical Women*, Macmillan, 1886

9. Extract from the Judgement of the Lord Ordinary, as reproduced in Jex-Blake's *Medical Women*

10. E.B. to B.L.S.B., 21 December 1859, Women's Library

11. Margaret Todd, *The Life of Sophia Jex-Blake*, p. 423

12. *The Times*, 5 August 1873

13. *The Times*, 23 August 1873

14. General Medical Council minute books, 26 June 1875

15. E.B. to A.B.B., 1 January 1875, SL

16. General Medical Council minute books, 26 June 1875

17. E.B. to K.B.B., n.d., summer 1874, SL

18. Margaret Todd, *The Life of Sophia Jex-Blake*, p. 424

19. E.B. to unknown recipient, n.d., SL

20. E.B. to B.L.S.B., 4 October 1874, Col

21. Margaret Todd, *The Life of Sophia Jex-Blake*, p. 429

22. E.B. to B.L.S.B., 6 August 1875, Col

23. J. Stansfeld, 'Medical Women', in *Nineteenth Century*, July 1877; quoted in Shirley Roberts, *Sophia Jex-Blake*, p. 161

Chapter Eighteen

1. See: J.L. Hammond and Barbara Hammond, *James Stansfeld: A Victorian Champion of Sexual Equality*, London, Longman, Green & Co., 1932, p. 122
2. *James Stansfeld*, quoted p. 165
3. E.B. to M.B., 24 December 1850, quoted in *Pioneer Work*, p. 146
4. The Society was founded by Lord Brougham in 1856.
5. *Daily Bristol Times and Mirror*, 5 October 1869
6. *Pioneer Work*, p. 195
7. *The Lancet*, 9 October 1869, p. 515
8. *Pioneer Work*, p. 197
9. *Ibid.*
10. *Pioneer Work*, p. 196
11. Charles Kingsley to John Stuart Mill, 1870, *Charles Kingsley, Letters and Memories of his Life*, Fanny Kingsley (ed.), London and New York, Macmillan, 1890, p. 305
12. *Ibid.*
13. K.B.B. to A.S.B., 28 January 1875, LC
14. Charles Kingsley to John Stuart Mill, 1870, *Charles Kingsley, Letters and Memories of his Life*, p. 305
15. A.S.G. Butler, *A Portrait of Josephine Butler*, London, Faber and Faber, 1954, p. 82
16. Josephine Butler, *Woman's Work and Woman's Culture*, Macmillan, London, 1869, p. xiii
17. F.N. to E.B., 7 February 1870, LC
18. F.N. to E.B., 13 October 1870, LC
19. *Ibid.*
20. F.N. to E.B., 6 May 1871, SL
21. Marian Lewes to E.B., 18 March 1871, LC
22. *Pall Mall Gazette*, 25 January 1870
23. E.B., 'The Responsibility of Women Physicians in Relation to the Contagious Diseases Acts', address given to a medical meeting in London, 27 April 1897, included in *Essays in Medical Sociology*, revised and reproduced for private circulation, London 1899, p. 125
24. *Ibid.*
25. *Ibid.*
26. E.B., *Wrong and Right Methods of Dealing With Social Evil, as Shown by English Parliamentary Evidence*, New York, A. Brentano, 1883
27. E.B., *Purchase of Women, the Great Economic Blunder*, London, John Kensit 1887, p. 36
28. Social Purity Alliance, *Annual Report from April 30 1887 to April 30 1888* and *Report of Annual General Meeting*, London, Social Purity Alliance, 1888
29. E.B. to Aaron M. and Anna Rice Powell, 26 January 1886, published in the *Philanthropist*, 1, no. 3, March 1886
30. E.B., Rescue *Work in Relation to Prostitution and Disease: An Address Given at the Conference of Rescue Workers Held in London, June 1881*, London, T. Danke, 1881
31. Moral Reform Union, Annual Report 1884–1886, London
32. E.B., 'The Responsibility of Women Physicians in Relation to the CD Acts'
33. E.B. to L.S.B., 12 May 1880, LC
34. Sir James Stansfeld to E.B., 21 April 1880, LC
35. K.B.B. to A.S.B., 15 November 1885, LC
36. E.B., diary, 9 September 1885, LC

Chapter Nineteen

1. E.B. to K.B.B., 23 February, LC
2. *Ibid.*
3. E.B. to K.B.B., 3 June 1870, SL

4. Sir Benjamin Brodie was the eldest son (and as such inherited his father's baronetcy in 1861) of the Sir Benjamin Brodie who had made possible E.B.'s inclusion on the British Medical Register in 1859.
5. E.B. to K.B.B., 1 December 1869, LC
6. *Ibid.*
7. *Ibid.*
8. Millicent Fawcett (1847–1929), a younger sister of Elizabeth Garrett Anderson, married the blind, radical MP Henry Fawcett (1833–4). She became a formidable leader of the women's suffrage movement.
9. Matthew Vassar, a pioneer in women's education, founded Vassar College in upstate New York in 1861. The aim of the College was to offer women a liberal arts education equal to that of the best men's colleges of the day.
10. E.B. to K.B.B., 1 December 1869, LC
11. E.B. to B.L.S.B., 23 August 1869, Col
12. E.B. to S.C.B., 23 May 1870, SL
13. E.B. to K.B.B., 12 October 1869, SL
14. E.B. to K.B.B., 21 November 1869, SL
15. E.B. to K.B.B., 5 May 1870, LC
16. *The Queen*, 11 January 1873
17. Susan Durant to Emma Wallis, October 1866, Royal Archives Windsor, RA VIC/Add X 2/89
18. Queen Victoria to Sir Theodore Martin, 29 May 1870, quoted in Joyce Marlow, *Votes for Women*, Virago 2000. The original letter is in the Royal Archives, Windsor.
19. The bust of Harriet Beecher Stowe is in the Beecher Stowe Centre, Hartford, Connecticut
20. Susan Durant to her father George Durant, 18 May 1866, Royal Archives Windsor, RA VIC/Add X 2/69
21. K.B.B. to A.S.B., 29 February 1873, LC
22. K.B.B. to A.S.B., 9 October 1872, LC

23. K.B.B. to A.S.B., 5 October 1893, LC
24. E.B. to Mary Putnam Jacobi, 31 December 1871, in *Life and Letters of Mary Putnam Jacobi*, Ruth Putnam (ed.), New York, G.P. Putnam's Sons, 1925, p. 308
25. N.H.S. Sixth Annual Report, 1879 (British Library)
26. N.H.S. pamphlets, 1884, Allman and Son, 67 New Oxford Street (British Library)
27. E.B. *On The Religion of Health*, S.W. Partridge and Co. (British Library)
28. E.B. to B.L.S.B., n.d., Col
29. E.B. *How to Keep a Household in Health: An Address Delivered before the Working Women's College*, London, W.W. Head, 1870
30. K.B.B. to A.S.B., 3 October 1872, LC

Chapter Twenty

1. K.B.B. to A.S.B, 1 August 1873, LC
2. E.B. to H.B.B., 7 December 1873, LC
3. E.B., travel diary, 18 November 1873, SL
4. K.B.B. to A.S.B., 23 September 1873, LC
5. E.B. to H.B.B., 15 November 1870, LC
6. E.B. to S.C.B., 7 September 1874, LC
7. E.B. to H.B.B., 20 August 1882, LC
8. *Ibid.*
9. *The Society of Psychical Research: An Outline of Its History*, London, Society of Psychical Research, 1948
10. E.B. to Mrs Annie Leigh Browne, April 1902, LC
11. Alfred Russel Wallace, *Land Nationalisation: Its Necessity and Aims: Being a Comparison of the Landlord and Tenant with That of Occupying Ownership in Their Influence on the People*, Swan Sonnenschein, 1892

12. E.B., 'Christian Socialism', *Essays in Medical Sociology*, London, Ernest Bell, 1902, pp. 155–60, first published in 1882

13. *Pioneer Work*, pp. 201–2

14. E.B., circular letter, 30 April 1875, LC

15. Melusina Fay Peirce, *Co-operative Housekeeping*, Boston, J.R. Osgood and Co., 1884

16. K.B.B. to A.S.B., 14 July 1884, LC

17. E.B. to Emily Blackwell, n.d., LC

18. Alfred R. Wallace to E.B., 27 September 1882, LC

19. William Morris to E.B., 18 November 1884, LC

20. E.B. to B.L.S.B., 5 February 1884, LC

21. Henry George, *Progress and Poverty*, printed privately 1879, New York, Appleton & Co., 1880

22. K.B.B. to A.S.B., 10 January 1884, LC

23. Herbert V. Mills, *Poverty and the State; or, Work for the Unemployed, An Enquiry into the Causes . . . of Enforced Idleness, etc.*, London, Kegan Paul, 1886

24. E.B., diary, 31 December 1898, LC

25. K.B.B. to A.S.B., 1 May 1875, LC

26. K.B.B. to A.S.B., 17 January 1876, LC

27. K.B.B. to A.S.B., 14 February 1876, LC

28. K.B.B. to A.S.B., 24 February 1875, LC

29. *Ibid.*

30. K.B.B. to A.S.B., 5 August 1875, LC

31. K.B.B. to A.S.B., 24 March 1877, LC

32. K.B.B. to A.S.B., 9 November 1875, LC

33. K.B.B. to A.S.B., 9 September, 1875, LC

34. E.B. to A.B.B., 1 January 1875, SL

35. E.B. to B.L.S.B., 21 May 1876, Col

36. K.B.B. to A.S.B., 5 January 1877, LC

37. George Eliot, *Daniel Deronda*, Edinburgh and London, William Blackwood & Sons, 1876

38. K.B.B. to A.S.B., 24 March 1877, LC

39. *Ibid.*

40. *Ibid.*

41. *Ibid.*

42. *Ibid.*

43. E.B. to B.L.S.B., 8 April 1877, Women's Library, London

44. Marie Zakrzewska commissioned the Cincinnati artist Frank Duveneck to paint the portrait, which she intended to bequeath to the New York Infirmary. It reached Boston in the autumn of 1877 in damaged condition but its present whereabouts (if indeed it survived) is unknown. See Nancy Sahli, 'Frank Duveneck Paints Elizabeth Blackwell', *Ohio History*, vol. 85, no. 4, 1976, pp. 319–25

45. K.B.B. to A.S.B., 10 May 1877, LC

46. K.B.B. to A.S.B., 20 September 1877, LC

47. Zoe Dana Underhill was the daughter of the New York publisher Charles A. Dana. He worked at the *New York Herald Tribune* until 1862 and was one of the original trustees of E.B.'s New York Dispensary.

48. K.B.B. to A.S.B., 31 August 1877, LC

49. E.B. to K.B.B., 8 October 1877, SL

Chapter Twenty-one

1. Emily Blackwell to L.S.B., 29 January 1879, LC

2. E.B., *Counsel to Parents on the Moral Education of their Children in Relation to Sex*, London, Hatchards, 1882, p. 25

3. K.B.B. to A.S.B., 13 February 1878, LC

4. *Counsel to Parents*, p. 38

5. *Counsel to Parents*, p. 39

6. *Counsel to Parents*, p. 38

7. K.B.B. to A.S.B, 3 March 1878, LC

8. K.B.B. to A.S.B., 5 June 1878, LC

9. E.B., m.s. notes on publication of *Counsel to Parents*, LC, and K.B.B. to A.S.B., 15 September 1879, LC

10. *Church Bells*, December 1879, and undated review from the *New York Sun*, among a printed compilation of reviews, SL
11. Harriet D. Griffith to E.B., 27 May, 6 June 1883, LC
12. Reverend R.A. Bullen to E.B., 28 January 1881, LC
13. E.B., *The Human Element in Sex*, London, J. & A. Churchill, 1884, p. 32
14. *The Human Element in Sex*, p. 32
15. *The Human Element in Sex*, p. 34
16. *The Human Element in Sex*, p. 40
17. James Paget, *Clinical Lectures and Essays*, H. Marsh (ed.), London, 1875, p. 285
18. *The Human Element in Sex*, p. 38
19. William A. Alcott, *The Physiology of Marriage*, Boston, John P. Jewett & Co., 1856, p. 167
20. *The Human Element in Sex*, op. cit, p. 49
21. E.B. to K.B.B., 2 January 1887, SL
22. *The Human Element in Sex*, pp. 51–2
23. *Ibid.*, pp. 50–1
24. *Ibid.*, p. 51
25. *The Philanthropist*, vol. VI, no. 12, December 1891
26. Josephine Shaw Lowell to Anna Rice Powell, 13 December 1891, LC
27. Francis William Newman, *The Corruption now called Neo Malthusianism*, Moral Reform Union, London 1889, note by E.B., p. 6
28. E.B., *How to Keep a Household in Health*, London, Ladies Sanitary Association, 1870
29. E.B., *Benevolence of Malthus Contrasted with the Corruptions of Neo-Malthusianism*, London, T.W. Danks & Co., 1888, p. 4
30. *Ibid.*
31. *Ibid.*, p. 9
32. *Ibid.*, p. 16
33. *Ibid.*, p. 27
34. *Ibid.*, p. 25
35. *Ibid.*, p. 28
36. *Ibid.*, p. 34
37. *Ibid.*, p. 11
38. E.B., diary, December 1887, LC
39. E.B., description of Don's burial on cash account page in 1896 diary, LC
40. K.B.B. to A.S.B., 14 October 1883, LC
41. E.B. to B.L.S.B., 25 November 1885, Women's Library
42. K.B.B. to A.S.B., 22 January 1882, LC
43. Comtesse de Noailles to E.B., n.d., SL
44. E.B. to Comtesse de Noailles, 1905, SL
45. E.B. to H.B.B., 15 and 18 November 1870, LC
46. Printed announcement, Hastings Municipal Branch of the Moral Reform Union, LC
47. E.B. diary, 28 February 1885, LC
48. E.B. diary, 25 March and 16 April 1885, LC

Chapter Twenty-two

1. E.B. to *The Philanthropist*, February 1889, SL
2. E.B., diary, 6 March 1889, LC
3. Mary Putnam Jacobi to E.B., 25 December 1888, LC
4. E.B. to A.S.B., n.d., LC
5. E.B. to A.S.B., 30 June n.y., LC
6. *Hastings Daily Chronicle*, 22 May 1894, clipping, SL
7. Mary Putnam Jacobi to E.B., 25 December 1888, LC
8. E.B. to A.S.B., n.d., LC
9. E.B. to L.S.B, 12 May 1880, LC
10. *On the Humane Prevention of Rabies*, St Leonards, J.F. Nock (printer), 1891
11. E.B. to A.S.B., 27 May 1993, LC
12. E.B. to A.S.B., n.d., LC
13. E.B. to A.S.B., 10 April 1891, LC
14. E.B. to A.S.B., n.d., LC

15. Leigh Browne Trust flyer, May 1895, SL

16. Clement John Wilkinson, *Garth Wilkinson: A Memoir of his Life, with a Selection of his Letters*, London, Kegan Paul, Trench, Trubner, 1911, p. 265

17. From the *Shooting Times*, 10 January 1891, signed, Frank E. Lintaber in Puck, LC

18. E.B. *Why Hygienic Conferences Fail: Lessons Taught by the International Congress of 1891*, London, George Bell & Sons, 1892

19. E.B., diary, 15 February 1885, LC

20. E.B. diary, 18 May and 20–1 September 1886, LC

21. Rowland Estcourt to E.B., 22 June 1890, LC

22. Rowland Estcourt to E.B., 22 December 1895, LC

23. E.B., diary, 31 January 1885, LC

24. E.B., diary, 3 February 1885, LC

25. E.B. to B.L.S.B., n.d., Col

26. J.W. Cross, *George Eliot's Life as Related in her Letters and Journal*, 3 vols, Edinburgh and London, 1885, reprinted with additions, 1886

27. E.B. to K.B.B., 9 February 1886, SL

28. *Conseils aux parents sur l'education morale de leurs enfants au point de vue des facultés sexuelles*, Paris, G. Baillière, 1881

29. E.B. to B.L.S.B., n.d., Women's Library

30. E.B., diary, 1 January 1896, LC

31. E.B., diary, 20 January 1896, LC

32. E.B. to Mrs Woolcott Browne, 14 December 1901, LC

33. E.B., diary, 31 December 1898, LC

34. E.B. to A.S.B., n.d., LC

35. A.B.'s will, 7 February 1898, SL

36. E.B. to L.S.B., n.d., LC

37. E.B. to Emma Blackwell, n.d., SL

38. K.B.B. to A.S.B., 4 November 1883, LC

39. H.B.B. to E.B., 14 November 1901, SL

40. Ethel Blackwell Jones Whidden to Rachel Baker, 20 May 1943, New York Academy of Medicine Library

41. Emily Blackwell to A.S.B., 19 August 1910 (typed copy), LC

42. Unsourced obituary, SL

43. Unsourced obituary, SL

44. *Pioneer Work*, p. 213

45. *The Lancet*, 11 June 1910, pp. 1657–8

46. *British Medical Journal*, 18 June 1910, p. 1523

47. Elizabeth Garrett Anderson to Miss Sheppard, 13 August 1910, SL

48. F. Cecilia Tubbs to K.B.B., 1 August 1910, SL

49. E.B., *The Religion of Health*, Edinburgh and Glasgow, John Menzies & Co., 1878

50. E.B. to Marie Zakrzewska, 4 February 1887, Sophia Smith Collection

Select Bibliography

Manuscript Collections

Columbia University, New York City: Elizabeth Blackwell–Barbara Bodichon Correspondence, Elizabeth Blackwell Papers, Rare Book and Manuscript Library

Cornell University, Ithaca, New York: Williams and Craddock Family Papers, Division of Rare and Manuscript Collections, Kroch Library

Florence Nightingale Museum, London

Geneva Historical Society, Geneva, New York

Girton College, Cambridge: Parkes Papers, Archive and Special Collections

General Medical Council, London

Harriet Beecher Stowe Centre, Hartford, Connecticut

Library of Congress, Washington DC, Blackwell Family Papers, Manuscript Division

Massachusetts Historical Society, Boston

Metropolitan Archives, London

Museum of the City of New York, De Lancey papers

New York Academy of Medicine, Malloch Rare Book and History Room

Pack Memorial Library, Asheville, North Carolina

Royal Archives, Windsor Castle, Berkshire

Schlesinger Library, Radcliffe Institute for Advanced Study, Harvard University: The Blackwell Family Papers are catalogued in three separate collections: A77, A145 and MC 411

Smith College, Northampton, Massachusetts: New England Hospital for Women and Children Records, Sophia Smith Collection.

South Carolina Historical Society, Charleston

Wellcome Library, London, Rare Books and Autograph Section

Women's Library, London Metropolitan University, Autograph Letter Collection

Works by Elizabeth Blackwell

'Lyndhurst', in *The Columbian Lady's and Gentleman's Magazine*, V, no. 4, June 1846, pp. 274–8

The Position of Women, in *The Philadelphia Press*, 25 August 1847

'Ship Fever: An Inaugural Thesis', submitted for the degree of M.D., at Geneva Medical College, January 1849, *Buffalo Medical Journal and Monthly Review*, IV, no. 9, February 1849, pp. 523–31

The Laws of Life with Special Reference to the Physical Education of Girls, New York, George P. Putnam, 1852

Address on the Medical Education of Women, New York, Baker & Duyckinck, 1856

Letter to Young Ladies Desirous of Studying Medicine, in *The English Woman's Journal*, IV, no. 23, January 1860, pp. 329–32

Medicine as a Profession for Women, New York, printed for the Trustees of the New York Infirmary for Women and Children, 1860 (with Emily Blackwell)

Address on the Medical Education of Women, New York, Baptist & Taylor, 1864 (with Emily Blackwell)

How to Keep a Household in Health: An Address Delivered Before the Working Woman's College, London, W.W. Head, 1870

How to Keep a Household in Health, London, Ladies Sanitary Association, 1870

Lectures on the Laws of Life with Special Reference to Girls, London, Sampson Low & Company, 1871

Counsel to Parents on the Moral Education of their Children, Hirst Smyth & Son, London 1878

The Religion of Health, Edinburgh and Glasgow, John Menzies & Co., 1878

The Human Element in Sex: Being a Consideration of the Facts in Relation to the Physical and Mental Organisation of Men and Women; Addressed to Students of Medicine, London, McGowan's Steam Printing Co. Ltd, 1880

'Medicine and Morality', in the *Modern Review*, II, no. 3, October 1881, pp. 750–61

Medicine and Morality, London, Speight & Sons, Printers, 1881

Conseils aux parents sur l'éducation morale de leurs enfants au point de vue des facultés sexuelles, Paris, G. Ballière, 1881

Rescue Work in Relation to Prostitution and Disease: An Address Given at the Conference of Rescue Workers Held in London, June 1881, London, T. Danks, 1881

Rescue Work in Relation to Prostitution and Disease, New York, Fowler & Wells, 1882

Christian Socialism, Thoughts Suggested by the Easter Season, Hastings, D. Williams, 1882

Wrong and Right Methods of Dealing with Social Evil, as Shown by Lately-Published Parliamentary Evidence, London, E. Williams, 1883

Wrong and Right Methods of Dealing with Social Evil, As Shown by English Parliamentary Evidence, New York, A. Brentano, 1883

The Human Element in Sex, London, J. & A. Churchill, 1884, 1894

Purchase of Women: The Great Economic Blunder, London, John Kensit, 1887

A Medical Address on the Benevolence of Malthus, Contrasted with the Corruptions of Neo-Malthusianism, London, T.W. Danks, 1888

The Influence of Women in the Profession of Medicine: Address Given at the Opening of the Winter Session of the London School of Medicine for Women, London, G. Bell & Sons, 1889

A Serious Protest Sent to the Alumnae Association of the Women's Medical College of the New York Infirmary, privately printed, 1890

Christianity in Medicine: An Address Delivered Before the Christo-Theosophical Society, December 18th 1890, privately printed, 1890

'Cruelty and Lust' – Appeal to Women, in *The Philanthropist*, VI, no. 12, December 1891, pp. 1–3

Erroneous Method in Medical Education, London, Women's Printing Society, 1891

On the Human Prevention of Rabies, St Leonards, J.F. Nock, 1891

Christian Duty in Regard to Vice: A Letter Addressed to the Brussels International Congress Against State Regulation of Vice, London, Moral Reform Union, 1891

Criticism of Gronlund's Co-operative Commonwealth, St Leonards, J.F. Nock, 1992

Why Hygienic Conferences Fail: Lessons Taught by the International Congress of 1891, London, George Bell & Sons, 1892

'Legal Enactments in Relation to Vice', in *The Philanthropist*, IX, no. 9, September 1893, pp. 1–3

'A Reminiscence of Forty Years Ago', in *St Bartholomew's Hospital Journal*, 1 12, September 1894, pp. 191–2

Pioneer Work in Opening the Medical Profession to Women, London, Longman, Green & Co., 1895

Pioneer Work in Opening the Medical Profession to Women, London and New York, J.M. Dent & Sons, and E.P. Dutton, 1914

'English Experience and Purity Work', in *The Philanthropist*, XI, no. 6, June 1896, pp. 2–4

The Responsibility of Women Physicians in Relation to the Contagious Diseases Acts: Address Given to a Medical Meeting in London, April 27th 1897, privately printed, 1897

Scientific Method in Biology, London, Elliot Stock, 1898

Essays in Medical Sociology, London, privately printed, 1899

Essays in Medical Sociology, 2 vols., London, Ernest Bell, 1902

Works about Elizabeth Blackwell

Baker, Rachel Minninberg, *The First Woman Doctor: The Story of Elizabeth Blackwell*, M.D., London, G.G. Harrap, 1946

Chambers, Peggy, *A Doctor Alone: A Biography of Elizabeth Blackwell*, London, Bodley Head, 1956

Fancourt, Mary St John, *They Dared to be Doctors: Elizabeth Blackwell and Elizabeth Garrett Anderson*, London, Longman, 1965

Forster, Margaret, *Significant Sisters: The Grassroots of Active Feminism 1839–1939*, London, Secker & Warburg, 1984

Gillie, Annis, 'Elizabeth Blackwell and the Medical Register from 1858', in *British Medical Journal*, 22 November 1958, pp. 1253–7

Johnston, Malcolm Sanders, *Elizabeth Blackwell and her Alma Mater*, Geneva, New York, W.F. Humphrey Press, 1947

McNutt, Sarah J., *Dr. Elizabeth Blackwell: Her Character and Personality*, reprinted from *The Medical Record*, 19 November 1921, New York, William Wood, 1921

Ross, Ishbel, *Child of Destiny: The Life Story of the First Woman Doctor*, London, Gollancz, 1950

Sahli, Nancy Ann, 'Elizabeth Blackwell, M.D.: A Biography', Ph.D thesis, University of Pennsylvania, 1974

Sanes, Samuel, 'Elizabeth Blackwell: Her First Medical Publication', in *Bulletin of the History of Medicine*, vol. XVI, no. 1, June 1944, pp. 83–8

Tabor, Margaret E., *Pioneer Women: Elizabeth Fry, Elizabeth Blackwell, Florence Nightingale, Mary Slessor*, London, Sheldon Press, New York, Macmillan, 1925

Waite, Frederick C., 'Two Early Letters by Elizabeth Blackwell', in *Bulletin of the History of Medicine*, vol. XXI, no. 1, January–February, 1947, pp. 110–12

Wilson, Dorothy Clarke, *Lone Woman: The Story of Elizabeth Blackwell, the First Woman Doctor*, London, Hodder & Stoughton, 1970

Wright, Mary, *Elizabeth Blackwell of Bristol: The First Woman Doctor*, Bristol, Bristol Branch of the Historical Association, 1995

Other Works

Anderson, Louisa Garrett, *Elizabeth Garrett Anderson 1836–1917*, London, Faber and Faber, 1939

Bell, Enid Moberly, *Storming the Citadel: The Rise of the Woman Doctor*, Constable, 1953

Belloc, Bessie Rayner Parkes, *Essays on Woman's Work*, London, A. Strahan, 1865

Blackwell, Alice Stone, *Lucy Stone: Pioneer of Woman's Rights*, Boston, Little, Brown 1930

Bonner, Thomas Neville, *To The Ends of the Earth: Women's Search for Education in Medicine*, Cambridge Massachusetts and London, Harvard University Press, 1992

Bodichon, Barbara Leigh Smith, *An American Diary, 1857–8*, Joseph W. Reed, Jr, London, Routledge & Kegan Paul, 1972

Bodichon, Barbara Leigh Smith, *Women and Work*, London, Bosworth and Harrison, 1857

Brisbane, Redelia, *Albert Brisbane: A Mental Biography with a Character Study*, Boston, Arena, 1893

Burton, Katherine, *Paradise Planters: The Story of Brook Farm*, New York, London and Toronto, Longman, Green, 1939

Bynum, W.E. and Porter, Roy, *Medical Fringe and Medical Orthodoxy 1750–1850*, London, Sydney, Wolfeboro, New Hampshire, Croom Helm, 1987

Cartwright, E.F., *A Social History of Medicine*, London and New York, Longman, 1977

Cazden, Elizabeth, *Antoinette Brown Blackwell*, Old Westbury, New York, The Feminist Press, 1983

Christman, Henry M. (ed.), *Walt Whitman's New York: From Manhattan to Montauk*, Lanham, New York, Oxford, New Amsterdam, 1963

Clark, Edward H., *Sex in Education; or, A Fair Chance for Girls*, Boston, James R. Osgood, 1874

Clendening, Logan, *Source Book of Medical History*, New York, Dover Publications, 1960

Coates, Tim (ed.), *Florence Nightingale and the Crimea, 1854–55*, London, Stationery Office, 2000, first published 1855, 1856

Cook, Sir Edward, *The Life of Florence Nightingale*, London, Macmillan, 1914

Cope, Zachary, *Florence Nightingale and the Doctors*, Philadelphia, J.B. Lippincott Company, 1958

Crawford, Elizabeth, *Enterprising Women: The Garretts and their Circle*, London, Francis Boutle, 2002

Croskey, John Welsh, *History of Blockley: A History of the Philadelphia General Hospital from its Inception, 1731–1928*, Philadelphia, F.A. Davis Company, 1929

Emerson, Ralph Waldo, *Essays*, London, Macmillan, 1901

Francis, Richard, *Transcendental Utopias*, Ithaca and London, Cornell University Press, 1997

Frothingham, Octavius Brooks, *Memoir of William Henry Channing*, London, Swan Sonnenschein, Lowrey & Co., 1887

Fuller, Margaret, *Woman in the Nineteenth Century*, Larry J. Reynolds (ed.), New York, London, W.W. Norton, 1998, first published 1845

Georgii, Augustus, *A few words on kinesipathy, or Swedish medical gymnastics: the application of active and passive movements to the cure of diseases, according to the method of P.H. Ling; and on the importance of introducing mechanical agency into the practice of medicine*, London, Ballière, 1850

Goffin, Magdalen, *Maria Pasqua*, Oxford, London, New York, Oxford University Press, 1979

Goldsmith, Barbara, *Other Powers: The Age of Suffrage, Spiritualism, and the Scandalous Victoria Woodhull*, New York, Alfred A. Knopf, 1998

Griffith, Elizabeth, *In Her Own Right: The Life of Elizabeth Cady Stanton*, Oxford and New York, Oxford University Press, 1984

Haller, John S., Jr and Haller, Robin M., *The Physician and Sexuality in Victorian America*, Carbondale and Edwardsville, Southern Illinois University Press, 1995, originally published 1974

Hammond, J.L. and Hammond, Barbara, *James Stansfeld: A Victorian Champion of Sex Equality*, London, Longman, Green, 1932

Hedrick, Joan D., *Harriet Beecher Stowe*, New York, Oxford, Oxford University Press, 1994

Heffer, Simon, *Moral Desperado: A Life of Thomas Carlyle*, London, Weidenfeld and Nicolson, 1995

Hellerstein, Erna Olafson, Hume, Leslie Parker and Offen, Karen M. (eds), *Victorian Women: A Documentary Account of Women's Lives in Nineteenth-century England, France and the United States*, Stanford, Stanford University Press, 1981

Herndl, Diane Price, *Invalid Women: Figuring Feminine Illness in American Fiction and Culture 1840–1940*, Chapel Hill and London, University of North Carolina Press, 1993

Hibbert, Christopher, *Queen Victoria*, London, HarperCollins, 2000

Hirsch, Pam, *Barbara Leigh Smith Bodichon*, London, Chatto & Windus, 1998

Hughes, Kathryn, *George Eliot*, London, Fourth Estate, 1998

Hunt, Harriot Kesia, *Glances and Glimpses: or, Fifty Years Social, Including Twenty Years Professional Life*, Boston, Jewett, 1856

Hunter, Lynette and Hutton, Sarah, *Women, Science and Medicine, 1500–1700*, Stroud, Sutton Publishing, 1997

Hurd-Mead, Kate Campbell, *Medical Women of America*, New York, Froben Press, 1933

Jacobi, Mary Putnam, *Mary Putnam Jacobi, M.D.: A Pathfinder in Medicine: With Selections from her Writings and a Complete Bibliography*, edited by the Women's Medical Association of New York City, G.P. Putnam's Sons, New York, 1925

James, Henry, *The Bostonians*, Penguin Classics, 2000

Jex-Blake, Sophia, *Medical Women: Two Essays: 1. Medicine as a Profession for Women. II. Medical Education of Women*, Edinburgh, Oliphant, 1872

Keetley, Dawn and Pettegrew, John (eds), *Public Women, Public Words: A Documentary History of American Feminism*, Madison, Madison House Publishers, 1997

Kerber, Linda, *Toward an Intellectual History of Women*, Chapel Hill and London, University of North Carolina Press, 1997

Kerr, Andrea Moore, *Lucy Stone*, New Brunswick, New Jersey, Rutgers University Press, 1992

Kingsley, Fanny (ed.), *Charles Kingsley: His Letters and Memories of His Life*, London and New York, Macmillan, 1890

Kleinberg, S.J., *Women in the United States 1830–1945*, London, Macmillan, 1999

Kolchin, Peter, *American Slavery*, London, Penguin, 1995, first published in Canada by HarperCollins, 1993

Lacey, Candida (ed.) *Barbara Leigh Smith Bodichon and the Langham Place Group*, New York and London, Routledge & Kegan Paul, 1987

MacCarthy, Fiona, *Byron*, London, John Murray, 2002

Mansel, Philip, *Paris between Empires 1814–1852*, London, John Murray, 2001

Manton, Jo, *Elizabeth Garrett Anderson*, London, Methuen, 1965

Mare, Eric de, *London 1851: The Year of the Great Exhibition*, London, Folio Society, 1972

Martineau, Harriet, *Society in America*, edited and abridged by Simon Martin Lipset, New Brunswick, USA, and London, Transaction Publishers, 1981

Medvei, Victor Cornelius and Thornton, John L. (eds), *The Royal Hospital of Saint Bartholomew 1123–1973*, London, 1974

Mellow, James R., *Nathaniel Hawthorne in his Times*, Baltimore and London, Johns Hopkins University Press, 1980

Morantz-Sanchez, Regina, *Sympathy and Science: Women Physicians in American Medicine*, New York, Oxford University Press, 1985

Morantz-Sanchez, Regina Markell, *Conduct Unbecoming a Woman: Medicine on Trial in Turn-of-the-Century Brooklyn*, New York, Oxford, Oxford University Press, 1999

New York Infirmary, *The New York Infirmary: A Century of Devoted Service*, New York Infirmary, 1954

Nightingale, Florence, *Notes on Nursing: What It Is, and What It Is Not*, London, 1860

Nightingale, Florence, *Suggestions for Thought*, Michael D. Calabria and Janet A. Macrae (eds), Philadelphia, University of Pennsylvania Press, 1994

Nutton, Vivian and Porter, Roy (eds), *The History of Medical Education in Britain*, Amsterdam, Atlanta, 1995

Osborne, Charles C., *Anna Maria Helena Comtesse de Noailles*, The Noailles Trust, Church Education Corporation, 1928

Paget, Stephen (ed.), *Memoirs and Letters of Sir James Paget*, London, Longman, Green, 1902

Pichanick, Valerie Kossew, *Harriet Martineau: The Woman and her Work, 1802–76*, Ann Arbor, University of Michigan Press, 1980

Pierson, Joan, *The Real Lady Byron*, London, Robert Hale, 1992

Putnam, Ruth (ed.), *Life and Letters of Mary Putnam Jacobi*, New York, G.P. Putnam's Sons, 1925

Ransom, Teresa, *Fanny Trollope*, Stroud, Sutton, 1995

Reid, Michaela, *Ask Sir James: The Life of Sir James Reid, Personal Physician to Queen Victoria*, Hodder & Stoughton, 1987

Rice Hays, Elinor, *Morning Star: A Biography of Lucy Stone, 1818–1893*, New York, Harcourt, Brace & World, 1961

Rice Hays, Elinor, *Those Extraordinary Blackwells*, New York, Harcourt, Brace & World, 1967

Richardson, Robert D. Jr, *Emerson*, Berkeley, Los Angeles, London, University of California Press, 1995

Roberts, Shirley, *Sophia Jex-Blake*, London and New York, Routledge, 1993

Rothstein, William G., *American Physicians in the 19th Century*, Baltimore and London, Johns Hopkins University Press, 1985

Schultz, Jane E., *Women at the Front: Hospital Workers in Civil War America*, Chapel Hill and London, University of North Carolina Press, 2004

Sears, John van der Zee, *My Friends at Brook Farm, New York*, Desmond FitzGerald, 1912

Shepherd, John A., *Simpson and Syme of Edinburgh*, Edinburgh and London, E. & S. Livingstone, 1969

Shyrock, Richard Harrison, *Medicine and Society in America 1660–1860*, New York, New York University Press, 1960

Sims, Marion J., *The Story of My Life*, edited by H. Marion-Sims, New York, D. Appleton, 1884

Small, Hugh, *Florence Nightingale: Avenging Angel*, London, Constable, 1998

Stanton, Elizabeth Cady, Anthony, Susan B. and Gage, Mathilda Joslyn, *History of Woman Suffrage*, Rochester, Charles Mann, 1889

Stanton, Elizabeth Cady, *Eighty Years and More 1815–1897*, Boston, Northeastern University Press, 1993, first published in 1898

Starr, Paul, *The Social Transformation of American Medicine*, New York, Basic Books, 1982

Stille, Charles J., *History of the United States Sanitary Commission*, New York, Hurd and Houghton, 1866, 1868

Stowe, Harriet Beecher, *Uncle Tom's Cabin; or Negro Life in the Slave States of America*, London, Clarke, 1852

Stowe, Harriet Beecher, *Lady Byron Vindicated: A History of the Byron Controversy*, Boston, Fields, Osgood, 1870

Thomas, Susan, *The Bristol Riots*, issued by the Bristol Branch of the Historical Association, the University, Bristol, 1974

Todd, Margaret, *The Life of Sophia Jex-Blake*, London, Macmillan, 1918

Trollope, Fanny, *Domestic Manners of the Americans*, London, the Folio Society, 1974, first published 1832

Vietor, Agnes, C. (ed.), *A Woman's Quest, The Life of Marie E. Zakrzewska* M.D., *Told by Herself*, New York and London, D. Appleton, 1924

Walsh, Mary Roth, *Doctors Wanted No Women Need Apply*, New Haven and London, Yale University Press, 1977

Wilkinson, Clement John, *James John Garth Wilkinson: A Memoir of his Life, with a Selection of his Letters*, London, Kegan Paul, Trench, Trubner, 1911

Wilson, A.N., *The Victorians*, London, Hutchinson, 2002

Woodham Smith, Cecil, *Florence Nightingale 1820–1910*, London, Constable, 1950

Articles

Blake, John B., 'Women and Medicine in Ante-Bellum America', *Bulletin of the History of Medicine* vol. xxix, March–April 1965, no. 1

Daniel, Annie Sturgis, 'A Cautious Experiment: The History of the New York Infirmary for Women and Children and the Women's Medical College of the New York Infirmary: Also Its Pioneer Founders 1853–1899', in *Medical Woman's Journal* 46, 5, May 1938, pp. 125–31

Flint, Austin (published anonymously), 'Female Physicians', in *Buffalo Medical Journal* 3, 1848, pp. 494–6

'Lectures by a Lady Doctor', in *Chamber's Journal*, no. 276, 16 April 1859, pp. 255–6

'Medical Education of Women at Edinburgh', in *Medical Times and Gazette*, London, 1872, pp. 45, 106, 142, 180, 383

'Medical Women and the University of London', in the *Lancet*, London, 1877, p. 656

Roth, Nathan, 'The Personalities of Two Pioneer Medical Women: Elizabeth Blackwell and Elizabeth Garrett Anderson', *Bulletin of the New York Academy of Medicine*, 47, 1, January 1971, pp. 67–79

Russell, M.P., 'James Barry – 1792 (?)–1865: Inspector General of Army Hospitals', *Edinburgh Medical Journal* 50, 1943, pp. 558–67

Sahli, Nancy, 'A Stick to Break our Heads with: Elizabeth Blackwell and Philadelphia Medicine', *Pennsylvania History*, vol. 44, no. 4, 1977, pp. 335–47

Zakrzewska, Maria Elizabeth, 'Fifty Years Ago: A Retrospect', in *Women's Medical Journal* (Toledo) 1, 1893, pp. 193–5

Index